Praise for *Broadway Anecdotes*

"Peter Hay has collected some truly exciting stories of the Great White Way. *Broadway Anecdotes* is this girl's best friend!"

Carol Channing

"Delightful...a feast for Broadway insiders and outsiders alike, for theatre buffs and theatre people, for gossip fans and drama students. It's bright, breezy, and informative—and what more can one ask?"

Judith Crist

"A juicy new book by Peter Hay...that manages to entertain and educate, rile and soothe with hundreds of stories about the theatre, each one of which could easily be staged."

The New York Post

"Contains a multitude of entertaining stage stories."

Playbill

"*Broadway Anecdotes* is a mine of splendid stories about the theatrical heartland of New York."

Peter Grosvenor, *The Daily Express* (London)

Peter Hay was born in Budapest and educated at Oxford. Working for a dozen years in Canadian theatre and publishing, he moved to California where he has taught drama at USC and UCLA. He is founding artistic director and dramaturge at First Stage in Los Angeles, where he works with writers, directors, and actors to develop new plays and screenplays. He is the author of half a dozen anecdote books, including *Theatrical Anecdotes* and his most recent *Movie Anecdotes*.

Cover illustration by Victor Juhász

Broadway Anecdotes

Peter Hay

BROADWAY
ANECDOTES

Oxford University Press

NEW YORK   OXFORD

Oxford University Press

Oxford   New York   Toronto
Delhi   Bombay   Calcutta   Madras   Karachi
Petaling Jaya   Singapore   Hong Kong   Tokyo
Nairobi   Dar es Salaam   Cape Town
Melbourne   Auckland

and associated companies in
Berlin   Ibadan

First published in 1989 by Oxford University Press, Inc.,
200 Madison Avenue, New York, New York 10016

First issued as an Oxford University Press paperback, 1990

Oxford is a registered trademark of Oxford University Press

Library of Congress Cataloging-in-Publication Data
Hay, Peter (1944-   ).
Broadway anecdotes / Peter Hay.
p.   cm.   Bibliography: p.
Includes index.
1. Theater—Anecdotes.   2. Entertainers—Great Britain—Anecdotes.
3. Entertainers—United States—Anecdotes.   I. Title.
PN2095.H387   1989
192'.02'9—dc19   88-36444   CIP

ISBN 0-19-504621-8
ISBN 0-19-504620-X (PBK.)

2   4   6   8   10   9   7   5   3   1
Printed in the United States of America

*for Leonora and David Hays
with warmest appreciation for
our friendship
and with profound admiration for
what you have created both on and off Broadway
and most especially for that miraculous company
The National Theatre of the Deaf*

Preface

"Broadway means so many different things to so many different people," the journalist Richard Harding Davis remarked in 1891: "in this it differs from almost every other great thoroughfare in the world." Known as the Great White Way for its bright lights, called the Street of the Midnight Sun by "Diamond Jim" Brady, immortalized by Walter Winchell and Damon Runyon as the Hardened Artery or Main Stem inhabited by Guys and Dolls, Broadway embodies the history of live entertainment in America in all its dazzling diversity.

There was the old variety show, and there is still *Variety*, the show-biz paper with its own language. People are still singing in the rain, understudies stand by with eager dreams of becoming overnight stars, and everybody stays up for the overnight reviews at Sardi's. Broadway is the only place where a show can close before it opens, and where a single critic might be held responsible for its failure.

Broadway is a certain kind of musical or play, and even more a certain way of making theatre and music. It is old buildings with ghosts, historic hangouts, and sleazy streets teeming with showmen and hoofers, exotics and eccentrics, have-beens and would-bes. It is a fantastic succession of circus acts, where Eugene O'Neill co-existed with burlesque, and where Helen Hayes trod the boards with Mae West. It is hard realism and sloppy sentiment; all heart and all business; all show and no business. Broadway is a genuine American subculture that transcends an aesthetic or geography: like Hollywood, it is a concept, a milieu, a dream.

Broadway, however, has outlived its cynics and has retained an old-fashioned naïveté and innocence. The not-so-fabulous invalid is still the mecca for every artist working in the theatre, an image fed by such musicals as *42nd Street*, *Chorus Line*, or *All That Jazz*. And even if the rise of regional and non-commercial companies has shifted the searchlights on new American drama elsewhere, Broadway provides the reference points: "out of town" and "on the road," "off" and "off-off" Broadway; because Broadway in New York City remains the ultimate validation of theatrical success.

In this second book of theatrical anecdotes I have collected verbal snapshots of this vibrant world and arranged them for the reader's kaleidoscope. Whereas my first volume gave a taste of the great tradition of theatrical art and craft as it had been preserved in many countries throughout long centuries, most of these *Broadway Anecdotes* are drawn from one city and from within living memory. As I write this, Irving Berlin is still with us: he began singing in a show called *Up and Down Broadway* in 1910. Some stories here go back further, because they are alive with personalities and dialogue, with advice and humor, with names still upon Broadway theatres. We constantly revive the classics, too, because some of those dead, fictional characters that never existed are more real to us than the neighbors next door.

Occasionally I am asked: why so much history and so few anecdotes from last season? One reason is that people tend to remember and tell stories from their youth. Even the young feel more comfortable with recounting stories they had heard from older actors. The pleasing pebbles in the riverbed were rolled over a few times before they became so smooth. So many current stories are old anecdotes in disguise: the same were told about John Barrymore sixty years ago, and about Junius Brutus a century before him. One way of keeping alive these great performers of an evanescent art is to repeat the stories that can be safely attributed to them.

This is never very safe, since anecdotes, even when they originate from a published source, quickly become common property. As hearsay, they would not stand up well in court. There is no agreement even with something as recent and straightforward as how Circle in the Square got its name. As told during an interview taped for this book, Emily Stevens christened the well-known off-Broadway theatre on Sheridan Square. She and the two other founders—Ted Mann and José Quintero—were standing in their new office, when the phone rang for the first time.

"Oh, let me . . . let me answer it," said Quintero, whose first language isn't English and who couldn't quite remember the name. In his excitement, he picked up the receiver and said:

"Chicken in the Basket . . . ?"

José Quintero, in his autobiography *If You Don't Dance They Beat You*, has a quite different recollection. He claims to have come up with the name Circle in the Square himself, after cracking a deliberate joke about Chicken in the Basket. There is nothing unexpected about people (in theatre or out of it) liking to take credit, or in a famous director's wanting to be thought of as an inventive wit rather than a foreigner fumbling with the language. But the actor in the taped interview asserted that he was a friend of José Quintero, which suggested that the ultimate source for his anecdote was Quintero himself. In this instance, there was a living person and a printed source to cast doubt; in most cases there may be neither.

Sometimes there is deliberate mischief. Take a well-known witticism which has been attributed to both Groucho Marx and to George S. Kaufman. After a Broadway opening (as columnist Earl Wilson tells it in his 1949 book *Let 'em Eat Cheesecake*), Walter Winchell asked Groucho Marx what he thought of the show.

"You heard what George Kaufman said about this play, didn't you?" asked Groucho. Winchell shook his head. "Well, Kaufman told me," Marx quoted, " 'I didn't like it, but then I saw it under adverse conditions—the curtain was up.' "

Winchell printed the clever but wounding one-liner with Marx's attribution, with the result that the producer didn't speak to Kaufman for five years, when Groucho finally owned up to the wisecrack himself.

In my chapter *Caught in the Act* I draw a connection between plagiarism and night club acts where the problem has always been chronic. Walter Winchell dubbed Milton Berle the Thief of Bad Gags; the anecdote business is more like the tale of forty thieves. Many of the stories in this book are found so often with so many variations that it seemed futile to cite a particular source in each case. I simply joined the procession of rewrite men. On the other hand, when an anecdote came from the horse's mouth, or is told particularly well, I give the source in a brief introduction, though sometimes the reader may have to consult the bibliography. We do not have footnotes in the theatre, so I tried to avoid too much annotation. The stylistic idiosyncracies of the original extracts have been preserved, except for minor cuts and spelling changes (e.g. *theatre* instead of *theater*). The organization of the material, as with my earlier book, is topical, though much more directed towards personalities than the subject matter. The order within each chapter is arranged through a personal association of ideas, rather than by chronology or any other logic.

The most subjective element of the book lies with the selection itself. No two people will agree completely on what is amusing, witty, or worth preserving. Even the definitions of what makes an anecdote vary. For some it is a joke which must have a funny punchline; for others it is something illustrative or instructive. Politicians, clergymen, and toastmasters use anecdotes, often from collections that are handily organized to serve public speakers. In our statistical age, it is fashionable to attach the qualifier "merely anecdotal" to human stories that cannot be generalized.

For me anecdotes are a distinct literary genre. It may be a minor genre now, but with a respectable pedigree going back to the Greeks and Romans. Anecdote collections, treating a variety of serious subjects ranging from biography and natural history to economics and the law, enjoyed great popularity from the seventeenth to the nineteenth century, especially in France and England. Doctor Johnson's circle, Horace Walpole's inexhaustible gossip, the table-talk of Coleridge, Hazlitt, Southey, Charles Lamb, Samuel Rogers, and Sydney Smith, the antiquarian researches of John Nichols and Isaac D'Israeli, periodicals such as the *Gentleman's Magazine* or *Notes and Queries*, helped to create a "century of anecdote" (the title of one English collection by John Timbs), when nothing was too trivial or too big to capture in this form. The tradition has been revived and continued in several cultures, including my own, rooted in the cafe society of Central Europe.

The theatre, with its born story tellers and rich green-room traditions, has produced many collections of anecdotes since the 1770s, though none, as far as I know, purely devoted to Broadway or American show business. In some ways the portrait I have painted resembles my earlier *Theatrical Anecdotes* in the manner of an artist who keeps returning to the same model. In fact, less than one percent of the material from the earlier book is repeated, and then in a different form. The reader will not find descriptions again of the Astor Place Riot or of the Lincoln assassination though neither event is ignored. And again, I have made no deliberate attempt at completeness, which would be futile with such a book as this.

I am painfully aware of the omissions which could easily fill another volume: stories I never got to or that got away, stories promised but never told, stories discovered a week too late to be included. "Of making many books there is no end," said the Preacher, and this may be true particularly of anecdote books. I stop adding stories only because the publisher cries "hold, enough!" as he wrests the manuscript from my hand; on that dreaded day I see more clearly than ever how much better this book might be if I could just start all over again. My sole comfort is that my ending is the beginning for you the reader.

Los Angeles   P. H.
15 February 1989

Acknowledgments

A book of anecdotes, like a production, is collaborative by definition. A great many (and many great) people have helped me with this book by giving me stories, contacts, or feedback on my previous volume of *Theatrical Anecdotes*. Among the last, I wish to include some of the reviewers and critics, whom I regard as a necessary good.

I am appreciative of my warm relationship with Oxford University Press in New York, and especially grateful for the wisdom and guidance of Sheldon Meyer, Leona Capeless, Stephanie Sakson-Ford, Joellyn Ausanka, Laura Brown, Jeffrey Seroy, Vera Plummer, and others on a very fine professional team. I am grateful to my friend Cora Muirhead for reading the proofs.

This book is inestimably richer for the interviews conducted by my dear friend Leonora Hays, who has been my ears in New York. I want to thank all her friends and all my friends for giving so generously from their store of stories, even though I have not been able to fit all of them in: Robert Anderson, David Berry, Virginia Kaye Bloomgarden, Beverley Bozeman Fuller, Alan Brock, David Brooks, Bryan Clark, Didi Conn, David Craig, Paul D'Andrea, Gautam Dasgupta, Martin Esslin, Peter Feller, Walter Flannigan, Joyce Flynn, Hermine Furst Garcia, Tony Giordano, Murray Gitlan, Milton Goldman, Michael Gordon, Morton Gottlieb, Jacqueline Green, Klára Györgyey, Peter Harvey, David Hays, Richard Herd, Mary Hunter, Paul Jarrico, Jon Jory, Gerard Kahan, Richard Kahlenberg, Joshua Karton, Pat Kearney, Gene Lasko, Colin Lee, Juliet and Lester Lewis, Dorothy Mc-Guire, Alan Mandell, Bonnie Marranca, William Marshall, Elisabeth Marton, Betty Miller, Hilda Mortimer, Oliver Muirhead, Jo Nichols, Edith Oliver, Zsuzsanna Ozsvát, William Partlan, Ethan (John) Phillips, Sasha and David Pressman, Lee Remick, Barbara and Lloyd Richards, Jason Robards, Don Rubin, John Sarantos, Dennis Scott, Rozanne and Arthur Seelen, David Shire, Max Showalter, Carol Sorgenfrei, John Springer, Helen Stenborg, Loren Stephens, Richard Stoddard, Dan Sullivan, Eve Siegel Tettemer, Gwenn Victor, Martin Vidnovic, Fred Voelpel, Nancy Walker, Norman Welsh, George White, Max Wilk, Ralph Williams.

I am fortunate in having a friend in Michael Donaldson, theatrical lawyer and whose grandmother happened to be Frances Starr; how David Belasco made her into a star is found on pages 133–35. I must express my appreciation to my colleagues and former students at the University of California at Los Angeles and the University of Southern California; to the many librarians (especially Anthony Anderson) who helped, and to those who work in the permissions departments of publishing houses and agencies acknowledged elsewhere. My theatre friends are too numerous to list; I feel, however, particularly enriched by my association over the years with First Stage, the Sundance Institute, and the Eugene O'Neill Theater Center.

Finally, I am delighted to thank my mother Eva Hay, and my wife Dorthea Atwater, who both know firsthand what goes into the making of theatre and of books, and yet have encouraged, supported, and often suffered my activities in both fields.

Contents

Broadway Anecdotes

CHAPTER 1

In the Land
of the Puritans

Fallen Angel

In the second half of the nineteenth century, the Reverend Henry Ward Beecher was one of the most influential Americans. His weekly sermons at the Plymouth Congregational Church in Brooklyn were attended by overflow crowds of two to three thousand, while the rest of the country eagerly awaited the printed text in pamphlet form. In the 1870s the Reverend (whose sister wrote *Uncle Tom's Cabin*) was involved in a rather unpleasant adultery scandal, which would have made him feel right at home in our America of the 1980s. In other words, Beecher was a typical if lusty Puritan, who considered theatre among the deadlier sins. One day, in the deathly hush just before his sermon, the clergyman astonished his congregation with the following confession:

"Yes, I have been to the theatre. Mr. Beecher has been to the theatre. Now if you will all wait until you are past seventy years of age and will then go and see Joseph Jefferson in *Rip Van Winkle*, I venture the risk that it will not affect your eligibility for heaven, if you do nothing worse."

Contraband Theatre

The people who disembarked at Plymouth Rock, after which the Reverend Beecher's church was named, were known as Puritans. Their agitations against entertainment or pleasure of any kind closed the doors of English theatres in the middle of the seventeenth century. In Cromwell's Commonwealth plays were illicit; actors were hunted down as common criminals, and their costumes confiscated if they were released from jail. With the Restoration of Charles II, theatre made a fast comeback in England, but faced much greater difficulties in New England, as may be seen from a letter of protest from Samuel Sewall, Chief Justice of Massachusetts.

To the honorable Isaac Addington Esqr. Secretary. To be communicated to his Excellency the Governour, and to the honorable Council.

Boston of the Massachusetts; March 2, 1713–14

There is a rumor, as if some design'd to have a play acted in the Council chamber next Monday, which much surprises me—and as much as in me lies, I do forbid it. The Romans were very fond of their plays, but I never heard they were so far set upon them, as to their Senate-House into a Play-House. Our Town-House was built at great cost and charge, for the sake of very serious and important business: the three chambers above and the Exchange below—business of the Province, County and Town. Let it not be abused with dances or other scenical divertisements. It cannot be a honor to the Queen to have the laws of honesty and sobriety broken in upon. Ovid himself offers invincible argument against public plays:

> *Ut tamen hoc fatear: ludi quoque semina praebent*
> *Nequitiae—*

Let not Christian Boston go beyond heathen Rome in the practice of shameful vanities.

This is the voice of your most humble and obedient Servant,

Samuel Sewall

Getting Away With It

Prohibition usually acts as an incentive, and in 1750 three young men were found busy staging Thomas Otway's tragedy The Orphan. The General Court of Massachusetts, using disturbances that took place at one of the performances as a pretext, enacted a law—

that no person or persons whatsoever may, for his or their gain, or for any price or valuable consideration, let, or suffer to be used or improved, any house, room, or place whatsoever, for acting or carrying on any stage-plays, interludes, or other theatrical entertainments, on pain of forfeiting and paying for each and every day, or time, such house, room, or place, shall let, used, or improved, contrary to this act, twenty pounds. And if, at any time or times whatsoever, from and after the publication of this act, any person or persons shall be present as an actor in or spectator of any stage-play, &c. in any house, &c. where a greater number of persons than twenty shall be assembled together, every such person shall forfeit for each time five pounds. One-half to his majesty, and one-half to the informer.

Museum Theatre

Almost a hundred years later E. H. Sothern, who joined the Boston Museum company in 1879, found the place embalming and full of proper Bostonians.

The "Boston Museum," whither I was bound, was one of the last remnants of Puritan prejudice against the theatre as a place of amusement. It was a "museum," not a "theatre." The word "theatre" was not permitted in any advertisement or playbill. For many years its doors were closed from Saturday afternoon until Monday morning—there being no Saturday evening performance. In the front of the building, on the floors over the box-office, was an exhibition of stuffed animals, wax-figures, mummies, mineral specimens, and other odds and ends, which enabled the tender of conscience to persuade themselves that this was an institution of learning, a school of instruction, and by no means a place of amusement. True, on the first floor was a theatre where plays were given just as in any other theatre, but the intolerable and unholy atmosphere of the playhouse was mitigated by the presence of several decayed Egyptians whose enlightened and tolerant ghosts must have laughed in scorn at such self-deception, while the groups of intelligent animals and the distinguished company of waxworks must, in the "stilly night," have held weird conferences as to what virtue resided in their mouldy forms which could change the abode of Satan into a house for the godly. Certain it is that persons who would have considered their souls damned had they entered the theatre, frequented the Boston Museum without a qualm, although every kind of play was produced there from farce to burlesque. Pretty dancers were not taboo, and the broadest kind of comedy was tolerated.

Says Mr. Clapp, a local historian: "The Museum made an eloquent appeal to the patronage of sober persons affected with scruples against the godless 'theatre.' To this day, there are citizens of Boston who patronize no other place of theatrical amusement than its 'Museum.'" Many of the

most distinguished actors have played here supported by the stock company and before people who would not enter another playhouse to see
them. Writes Mr. Clapp: "The appeal to the prejudiced was as successful
as it was shrewd."

Columbus

The first time that actors got into trouble in the American colonies dates
back to 1665, when three young men were dragged into court in Accomac
County, Virginia. They were accused of putting on a play called Ye Beare
and ye Cubbe, *which one of them had written. They were acquitted.*

Virginia, settled by the Cavaliers, offered a more hospitable climate for
Thespians and it was here that the first professional theatre company
landed and took root, starting in 1752. The venture was conceived by a
couple of well-known English actors in financial difficulties, the brothers
William and Lewis Hallam, and its story was handed down by some of
the pioneer actors of the day. The following account is abridged from
Charles Durang's The Philadelphia Stage from the Year 1749 to the Year
1855. *Charles's father, John Durang (1768–1822), was the first American-*
born dancer and actor to establish a reputation on his country's stage, and
he had appeared frequently with Lewis Hallam, Jr.

The idea of planting the drama in the new world was a bold and an original thought at that early time, and could only have been conceived by an
ardent and vigorous mind. A writer has well said that, "What I admire in
Columbus is not his having discovered a world, but his having gone to
search for it on the faith of an opinion." Hallam's scheme, at the time, was
thought to be perfectly Utopian, and was the subject of green-room jest
and *jeu d'esprit* while he was organizing the details at London. The asylum
which he opened subsequently proved a very desirable refuge for the un-
fortunates of the English stage, at any rate. There were four brothers of the
Hallam family; one was the well-known Admiral Hallam, and the fourth
brother received a wound in his eye from the celebrated Charles Macklin,
in the green-room, which shortly afterward caused his death. Macklin was
very violent in his temper, and, during an altercation with this Mr. Hallam, he thrust his cane into his eye, which perforated the brain. Macklin
was tried for the crime at the Old Bailey, but acquitted, because the act
did not proceed from *malice prepense*. The other brothers were William,
the founder of the American stage, and Lewis, who led the pioneers to the
western world. Under their guidance the drama was first successfully planted

on our soil, and established in the principal cities and towns of the colonies, and flourished long afterward.

Voyage of Discovery

William Hallam, the brain and principal shareholder in the theatrical venture, is generally called "the Father of the American Stage." But he did not sail for the New World himself, appointing his much younger brother Lewis "sole manager and principal low comedian" in charge of the stock company about to set sail in May of 1752. During the voyage of 42 days to Yorktown, the small band of actors kept working on their repertoire, which consisted of no fewer than 24 plays, ranging from Shakespeare to The Committee, a piece intended to satirize the Puritans. Charles Durang preserved a vignette about the voyagers.

During the calmest portions of this pleasant voyage, the occasions were seized upon for rehearsals on the quarter-deck of the vessel; and a majority of the plays were thus perfected in words and stage business. A funny incident occurred, which is worth mentioning, during one of these scenes, toward the latter end of the voyage. The play in rehearsal was *The Merchant of Venice.* They had fixed upon it as the piece to open with in America. The first Thespian altar erected in the new world could not have had a more appropriate offering to handsel and to sanctify its end, than the Muse of Shakespeare, or this pleasing and fanciful offspring of his genius. In this rehearsal, just at the moment where Shylock exclaims, in the trial scene, "The pound of flesh is mine; 'tis dearly bought, and I will have it!" the steward of the *Charming Sally* passed down the companionway, between the Jew and Portia, with a large plate of pork for the dinner of the *dramatis personae*, and, starting at the wild and energetic manner with which Malone (who was rehearsing the part) spoke the line, he relaxed his hold of the dish of pork and beans, which fell at the Jew's feet! The point was too luscious to be lost on the merry Thespians; fits of laughter dismissed the rehearsal.

Give Me Death—Not Plays

The company was well received in Williamsburg, where they first performed on September, 15, 1752, "by permission of the Honorable Robert Dinwiddie, Esq.; His Majesty's Lieutenant-Governor and Commander in Chief of the Colony and Dominion of Virginia." After eleven months

in Virginia, the governor even gave the Hallams' company a letter of rec-
ommendation to New York where, despite his testimony to their good
character, the actors had to cool their heels for several months before ob-
taining a license to perform. After this first season in New York, they went
to Philadelphia, where they had to overcome powerful Quaker opposition.
Then Lewis Hallam died, and his widow married the actor David Doug-
lass, who in 1766 founded the American Company, with Lewis Hallam,
Jr., and John Henry.

The revolutionary atmosphere disrupted the growing theatrical activity
in the colonies. Following the Stamp Act of 1765, a riot led by the Sons of
Liberty broke up a performance in the Beekman Street Theatre in New
York. In 1774, the first Continental Congress, meeting in Philadelphia,
passed a resolution.

We will, in our several stations, encourage frugality, economy, and industry, and promote agriculture, arts and the manufactures of this country, especially that of wool; and will discountenance and discourage every species
of extravagance and dissipation, especially all horse-racing, and all kinds of
gaming, cock-fighting, exhibitions of shews, plays, and other expensive di-
versions and entertainments.

The American Company disbanded, and the professional players did not
return until 1782. Amateurs filled the gap, including a company under the
command of the British general John Burgoyne, who, according to Wil-
liam Dunlap, used theatre as part of his arsenal against the rebels.

The military Thespians began their transatlantic histrionic career, as well
as their less brilliant career of arms, in Boston. As no theatre had been
built in the town, some place admitting of the change must have been
fitted up as such. The accomplished Burgoyne, who commenced dramatic
author in 1775, by *The Maid of the Oaks,* now produced his second drama
in that stronghold of puritanism and unconquerable liberty; and *The Heir-*
ess was preceded by a farce called *The Blockade of Boston,* doubtless intended to ridicule the Yankees, who then held the soldiers of Britain
cooped up on that narrow neck of land, protected by their ships, soon after
expelled them with disgrace, and subsequently received the surrendered
sword of the unfortunate poet on the meadow of Saratoga, as dear to us as
Runnimede to our English forefathers.

It is remembered that, while the officers were performing Burgoyne's
farce, an alarm was given that the rebels had assaulted the lines, and when
a sergeant entered and announced the fact, the audience supposing that his

words, "The rebels have attacked the lines on the Neck," belonged to the farce, applauded the very natural acting of the man, and were not disturbed until successive *encores* convinced them that it was not to the play that the words, however apropos, belonged, and that the prompter of the speaker was not behind the scenes, but behind the trenches.

First Fan

One Virginian, who began his career in Governor Dinwiddie's employ, nurtured a lifelong love of the theatre. It is likely that George Washington had witnessed the Hallams perform *The Merchant of Venice* in 1752. A year earlier he mentions in his journal that he saw the *Tragedy of George Barnwell* in Bridgetown, Barbados, where he had accompanied his consumptive brother Lawrence. During the 1760s and 1770s he frequently records performances in Williamsburg, Alexandria, and Annapolis. Clearly more than a casual fan, Washington would sometimes go to the playhouse three or four nights in a row.

Even after the Continental Congress was trying to discourage plays, George and Martha Washington were watching American soldiers perform, seemingly without irony, some of the classics of the English stage. Colonel William Bradford wrote to his sister Rachel from Valley Forge in May of 1778:

"Last Monday *Cato* [by Addison] was performed before a very numerous & splendid audience. His Excellency & Lady [the Washingtons], Lord Sterling, the Countess and Lady Kitty, and Mrs. Green were part of the assembly. The scenery was in taste, and the performance admirable. Col. George did his part to admiration—he made an excellent die (as they say)—pray heaven he don't die in earnest—for yesterday he was seized with a pleurisy and lies extremely ill. If the enemy does not retire from Philadelphia soon, our theatrical amusement will continue. *The Fair Penitent* with *The Padlock* will soon be acted. *The Recruiting Officer* is also on foot."

During the first year of his presidency Washington had a box at the John Street Theatre. "On the appearance of the president," the papers reported, "the audience rose, and received him with the warmest acclamations—the genuine effusions of the hearts of Freemen."

When Philadelphia became the capital, Washington usually occupied the stage box at the Chestnut Street Theatre, decorated with the seal of the United States. He was accompanied by a military guard and was formally received at the box-door by the manager, Thomas Wignell, who "in a full dress of black, with his hair elaborately powdered in the fashion of the time, and holding two wax candles in silver candlesticks, was accustomed to conduct Washington and his party to their seats."

Fun City

Despite, or perhaps because of its Dutch and Puritan origins, New York has been a fun place ever since it became a big city. The following is a typical description of the days just after the Civil War, from a pseudonymous book titled The Secrets of the Great City: A Work Descriptive of the Virtues and Vices, the Mysteries, Miseries and Crimes of New York City. *It was written by one of those moralists who simply had to see first-hand all the vicious dives he claimed to find so repelling.*

There are seventy-five concert saloons in New York, which employ seven hundred and forty-seven waiter girls. The brothels usually termed dancehalls are included in this estimate, but, as we design referring especially to them in another chapter, we shall pass them by, for the present, and devote this chapter to the concert saloons proper.

Eight years ago, a Philadelphia manager opened a concert hall which he called the "Melodeon" at the old Chinese Assembly Rooms on Broadway. This was the first institution of the kind ever seen in New York, and imitations of it soon became common.

We find the following faithful description of one of these saloons in one of the popular prints of the day.

"On Broadway, near —— street, we notice, just above the entrance to a cellar, a flaming transparency, with the inscription, 'Madame X——'s Arcade.' Going down a few steps, we find our view of the interior obstructed by a large screen, painted white, with the almost nude figure of a dancing Venus coarsely painted thereon. The screen is placed across the entrance, a few feet from the door, obliging us to flank it, à la Sherman, and enter the hall by going around it. We find the floor handsomely covered with matting and oil cloth. On the right-hand side, nearest the door, is the bar, over which presides a genius of the male sex, whose chief attractions consist of a decided red head, and an immense paste breastpin, stuck into the bosom of a ruffled shirt. The bar is well furnished, and any drink called for, from beer to champagne, can be instantly obtained. A significant feature, and one that easily arrests the attention, is a formidable Colt's revolver, a foot in length, suspended immediately over the sideboard. This weapon, it may be observed, is not placed there as an ornament; it is in itself a *monitor*, warning those inclined to be disorderly of the danger of carrying their boisterousness or ruffianism too far. On the walls are black engravings of the French school, fit ornaments for the place. But, while we are taking this casual survey, one of the attendant nymphs, with great scantiness of clothing, affording display for bare shoulders and not un-handsome ankles, appears, and in a voice of affected sweetness wholly at variance with her brazen countenance and impertinent air, requests us to be seated, and asks what we'll have. We modestly ask for 'Two ales,' which are soon placed before us, and paid for."

The Wickedest Man in New York—and Proud of It

Among the men who ran such a place of amusement was the notorious John Allen, the youngest of eight brothers, three of whom were clergymen and three professional burglars. Theodore, the seventh, after whom John had modeled himself, operated a number of dance halls, including the American Mabille at Broadway and Bleecker Street, before killing a fellow gambler and fleeing to South America. John Allen was eager to emulate him, according to Herbert Asbury, a wry chronicler of Old New York:

In Allen's dance-house, as part of the permanent staff, were twenty girls, very chic and handsome in scarlet skirts, low-cut black waists, and red stockings. Each girl also wore red-topped black boots, with circlets of sleigh-bells affixed to the ankles. As a sort of overseer, or major-domo, Al-len installed a bruiser and gang-fighter named George Leese, also called Snatchem, who was described by contemporary journalists as "a beastly and obscene ruffian, with bulging, bulbous, watery-blue eyes, bloated face, and coarse, swaggering gait." This unwholesome thug kept the peace at Allen's house, strutting about with a knife sticking in his boot-top, two re-volvers in his belt, and a bludgeon clutched in his huge fist, for in those degenerate days it was not against the law to carry weapons, concealed or otherwise. What time he was not working at Allen's Snatchem found em-ployment as blood-sucker at the bare-knuckle fights.

Vice and depravity of almost every variety were always to be found at John Allen's house, which in all likelihood was the most vicious resort ever operated in New York. The things that were to be seen there upon pay-ment of a few dollars defy description; moreover, even an attempt to de-scribe them would fracture half the obscenity laws of the state and na-tion.* It is perhaps sufficient to say that even along the waterfront they were considered pretty bad, although of course it was generally admitted that they were the sort of thing everybody ought to see once. It was after a

* Sixty years ago.

slumming trip through the Water Street area that an industrious journalist named Oliver Dyer wrote the article describing Allen as "The Wickedest Man in New York," which was no misnomer. Allen was enormously proud of the title, and not only pasted copies of the article in his window and upon his bar mirror, but had business cards printed bearing this legend:

JOHN ALLEN'S DANCE-HOUSE
304 Water street.
WICKEDEST MAN IN NEW YORK:
Proprietor.

Dyer also dwelt largely, and with much regret, upon the fact that three of Allen's brothers were respectable clergymen, and upon the further fact that Allen himself had for a brief period received theological training. The article aroused much interest, and, always a keen showman, Allen determined to take advantage of his ecclesiastical connections and experiences. He began insisting that he was at heart a devoutly religious man, and announced that he proposed to surround his unholy business with a holy atmosphere, his ultimate object being the spiritual regeneration of the entire waterfront. He began to hold religious singsongs two or three times a week, at which he led his girls and the amazed habitués of the place in song and prayer, and himself expounded a passage from the Gospels. In every room of the house he placed a Bible and various pieces of religious literature, and every Saturday night he gave away New Testaments as souvenirs. He subscribed to the *New York Observer*, *The Independent*, and other religious publications, and on every bench and table was a copy of a popular hymn-book called *The Little Wanderer's Friend*.

The newspapers, especially the *World* and the *Times*, were very skeptical about Allen's professed ambitions to bring religion to the waterfront, but most of the city's evangelical clergymen were profoundly impressed, particularly the Reverend A. C. Arnold of the Howard Mission and Home for Little Wanderers, at No. 40 New Bowery. The Reverend Mr. Arnold attended several of Allen's meetings and urged him to permit an ordained minister to conduct them. At length, on the evening of May 25, 1868, the Reverend Mr. Arnold visited the dance-house in company with six other clergymen and as many laymen. Finding Allen drunk, they proceeded to hold a prayer-meeting, and continued to hold it until four o'clock in the morning, by which time most of their audience were drunk. Newspaper accounts of this meeting and of Allen's curious methods of operating a dive attracted large crowds of curiosity-seekers, and Allen's profits were enormous, as he promptly doubled the price of everything he had to sell.

He now staged his exhibitions merely, so he said, as horrible examples of what formerly went on publicly in his house.

Lucy in the Pie With Diamonds

By the end of the century, variously described as the Gilded Age and the Era of Plush, excess became the rule. In his Incredible New York, *social historian Lloyd Morris describes some famous incidents that reverberated through succeeding decades.*

Herbert Barnum Seeley, a nephew of the late Phineas T. Barnum, was a man of means who led a muted existence on the outer fringes of the social citadel. He craved recognition; he coveted the accolade; he aspired to the fame of a man about town. The approaching marriage of his brother gave him an opportunity to move toward his goal. He determined to give a bachelor dinner at Sherry's in honor of the prospective bridegroom. Inviting some fifty gentlemen of established social position, he hinted that they would be diverted with original entertainment. Originality as conceived by a descendant of the great showman was scarcely to be ignored, and his invitations were accepted with alacrity. Unfortunately Seeley had inherited none of his uncle's astuteness in dealing with theatrical agents. He made a contract with one, then canceled it in favor of another who promised to supply superior talent at a lower price. His frugality proved to be misguided. The aggrieved agent whose contract Seeley revoked decided to have his revenge. On the night of the banquet, accompanined by several professional colleagues, he presented himself to Captain Chapman at the Tenderloin police station. Obscene, disorderly, unlawful doings were taking place at Sherry's, Captain Chapman was told. Before a drunken, lustful crowd of the idle rich, women were dancing "in the altogether." One tearful complainant, afterward identified as a vaudeville agent, asserted that his "daughter" was undoubtedly being forced, against her will, to divest herself of the ultimate safeguards of chastity. The horrified Czar of the Tenderloin listened no longer. With six detectives he raced to Sherry's, broke into that sacred resort of patriarchs and matriarchs, appeared before Seeley and his appalled guests. Alas, not a single specimen of nude femininity was to be found. After pronouncing a stern warning, Captain Chapman and his detectives withdrew.

But the scandalous story broke in the yellow press. Seeley and his unfortunate guests—some of them married men—became nationally notorious. It developed that the performer whom Captain Chapman sought to apprehend was none other than Little Egypt, a buxom cultural missionary who, at the Columbian Exposition in Chicago, had titillated unsophisticated Americans by introducing the stomach dance, or "hoochy-koochy." Had she—as the yellow press alleged—exhibited this exotic depravity to Seeley and his guests, clad in nothing at all, and elevated on a Sherry banquet table? The whole nation wondered. In the end, Little Egypt issued a public statement. She had not danced "in the altogether," although it had been her intention to do so, merely to satisfy her esthetic impulses. After Captain Chapman's unmannerly intrusion, she had danced, but clad in a Zouave jacket and a pair of lace drawers. An encore was demanded, and she was preparing to "throw everything overboard" when, unnerved by Chapman's warning, she abandoned that pleasant project and merely repeated her first dance. Art had suffered; Seeley and his guests had been deprived of a unique experience; but the puritanical morals of the police had triumphed. The scandal of the Seeley banquet rang through the press during many weeks. Americans discounted the testimony of "the sinuous Oriental dancing woman." And Herbert Barnum Seeley, no longer even on the periphery of society, but no longer obscure, was credited with achieving "the gayest, raciest dinner ever given in New York."

Vanities

It was about this time that the young promoter Florenz Ziegfeld first heard Anna Held sing, and began to blaze a trail to fame, fortune, and publicity. He surrounded the French singer, who later became his first wife, with various legends. One involved a wager at a party by a self-styled gentleman that he could kiss Miss Held two hundred times. He gave up after a mere 152, because apparently the pleasure proved too intense. The most celebrated myth, which became forever associated with Anna Held, was that she had to take a daily beauty bath—in milk. When Prohibition came, one of Ziegfeld's imitators, Earl Carroll, who produced an annual revue called Vanities, *got into trouble for another kind of bathing episode. This became one of the celebrated scandals of the 1920s and, according to Stanley Walker's account in* Mrs. Astor's Horse, *also recalled the pie incident of the 1890s.*

Countess Vera Cathcart, who had been detained by immigration authorities because of the charges of "moral turpitude" involving her trip to South Africa with the Earl of Craven, finally was permitted to land. Carroll had announced that he would have her play the lead in her play, *Ashes of Love*, which she had written around her own experiences. A big party was staged at the theatre, at which the Countess and Edrington were the principal guests. At the height of the merriment a bathtub was drawn to the center of the stage. Joyce Hawley, a chorus girl looking for a job, was led out, clad only in a chemise and shoes, which she discarded while Carroll held a cloak in front of her. She got into the tub which, according to some accounts, was filled with wine. According to the stories, Carroll dipped out a glassful and called out, "Gentlemen, the line forms to the right."

The next day the tabloids came out with descriptions of the party. It was said that it had surpassed Henry Barnum Seeley's famous party in 1896, when a naked girl rose from a great pie. Carroll then began telling every one that the party had been perfectly respectable. He said:

"I gave an anniversary party, including the cast of the *Vanities* and the stage hands of the theatre. There were about 200 guests. The party was as orderly and decorous as any affair ever given anywhere. It might have been held in a church for all the revelry there was among the guests. It was a party which any man, even a minister, might have attended with his wife."

At first there was a tendency among officials to let the matter drop, but the agitation continued, and Carroll finally was called before the Federal Grand Jury, which was interested principally in whether real wine had been in the tub. Carroll, who swore that no girl had got into the bathtub and that no intoxicating liquor had been served with his knowledge, was indicted for perjury.

The Party Line

Broadway columnist Walter Winchell was present at the famous Earl Carroll party. Summoned to testify in court, he was asked:

"Was this a regular Broadway party?"

"Well, no," Winchell replied sincerely, "there were too many Senators present."

The columnist was quickly recalled from the stand and was never questioned about the party again.

A Martyr to Art

Earl Carroll was fined $2000 and sentenced to a year and a day. After exhausting his appeals, he spent less than half that time in the federal penitentiary in Atlanta, where he claimed to have "undergone an irreparable loss of self-respect." This was not, however, the first occasion that Carroll had run into the law.

The young producer, who always had a real talent for costuming and lighting effects, was hailed as a dangerous rival to Florenz Ziegfeld and George White. With the production of his second *Vanities* he encountered trouble. He used the radio twice a day to issue a call for young and inexperienced girls to apply for jobs. He stipulated that they must have "good figures, pretty faces and neat ankles" and that they must exhibit themselves before him in bathing suits. If accepted, they would be paid $40 a week. Hundreds of girls answered the call every day. To mothers who complained and asked him if he could not find enough girls on Broadway for his chorus, he replied:

"I am looking for fresh ones. They get old in a few weeks."

He listed the qualifications in the order of their importance as follows:

"First, figure, because we can't change the figure if it isn't acceptable. Second, face, because we can improve on the face. Lastly, merit, because merit doesn't count."

The mothers insisted on sending their protest against his use of the radio to Herbert Hoover, at that time Secretary of Commerce. All this merely added to the publicity. One of the features of this edition of the *Vanities* was the "Pendulum Number" in which Kathryn Ray served as a human pendulum, entirely naked except for a slender sequin band. There was much criticism from the conservatives. Carroll was finally arrested on a charge of exhibiting indecent posters in the lobby of his theater. He insisted that they were "art pure and simple." He was held for trial in Special Sessions. He declined to put up $300 bail pending trial and insisted upon being locked up in the Tombs as a martyr to his art. He said he wanted to "focus attention on self-appointed censors."

Bad Tidings

In 1922 the Theatre Guild invited from Paris Jacques Copeau's Théâtre du Vieux-Colombier. Theodore Komisarjevsky was to direct *The Tidings Brought to Mary*, an adaptation of Paul Claudel's poetic drama. The Russian director brought with him his long-time mistress, whom he intended to cast as the Virgin, and the two had rented an apartment together. Komisarjevsky had made some enemies on a previous visit to New York, and one of these now complained to the Guild that he would have these unholy sinners deported for moral turpitude, unless they moved apart.

It fell on frail Theresa Helburn, then secretary of the newly founded Theatre Guild, to confront the Russian bear on this issue. "Looking up at his great height, I felt like an impertinent Pekinese barking at a bewildered Great Dane," she recalled in her memoirs. She explained the complaint to the foreigner who seemed genuinely baffled.

"You mean to tell me," he growled, "that no one can live together in America, if they are not married?"

"Only Americans," said Miss Helburn, not daring to look at him.

The Queen of Sex

It was during this same period that Mae West was constantly in trouble with the law. Mayor Jimmy Walker—a great lover of Broadway and of actresses, in particular—happened to be out of town in 1927 when the acting mayor, one Joseph V. McKee, conducted raids on *Sex*, written by and starring Miss West. She was convicted of obscenity and served ten days on Welfare Island, where she wrote a poem about the fuzzy prison underwear and dedicated it to the warden.

Raids were bad for business, at least in the legitimate theatre as distinct from burlesque. After closing down her production of *Sex*, Mae West immediately set to work on *Diamond Lil* and *Pleasure Man*. The latter dealt with homosexuality, in a campy way that was more than forty years ahead of its time. *Variety*'s Jack Conway went to see the tryout at the Bronx Opera House and wrote that "it's the queerest show you've ever seen. All of the Queens are in it. . . . The party scene is the payoff. If you see those hussies [actors playing homosexuals] being introduced to do their specialties, you'd pass out. . . . The host sang a couple of parodies, one going, 'When I go out I look for the moon.' Now I ask you. Another guest very appropriately sang, 'Banquets, Parties, and Balls,' and I ask you again. . . ."

Conway advised people to "go early, for some of the lines can't last," but no doubt he also had the vice squad in mind. The show was raided on its opening night on Broadway on October 1, 1928, and closed after three performances.

(*Pleasure Man* was not the first play to deal with homosexuality, and just two years before, a jury acquitted Gilbert Miller for his production of *The Captive*, which had a lesbian angle. But that play dealt with the subject rather obliquely, using "violets as a symbol of the third sex," which, as a writer for *Variety* observed, "kayoed the violet business at florists.")

Siren

In 1944 Mae West returned to Broadway after an absence of fifteen years, during which she moved from Diamond Lil to Catherine the Great. Louis

Kronenberger's review—under the headline MAE WEST SLIPS ON THE STEPPES!—began: "This morning the Siren of Sex lies self-slain by her own pen." George Jean Natl.an called *Catherine Was Great* "a dirty-minded little girl's essay on the Russian Empress, played like a chatelaine of an old time *maison de joie*." The critic went on to say about the 52-year-old sex kitten: "After Mae had rolled her hips for the two hundredth time and nasally droned her glandular intentions in respect to most of the males in the troupe, even the staunchest West disciple felt faintly surfeited and would have settled, with loud cheers, for Cornelia Otis Skinner in Bible readings."

Curiously, Mae West believed she had written a serious historical play. Mike Todd, who bought it because he thought Mae West playing a nymphomaniac with a sense of humor could not miss, began to change his mind when he saw her playing the role straight. After one preview, Todd even sent a telegram to one of his angels, Izzy Rappaport, to refund his investment which he felt he had extracted under false representation. Of course, with Mae West on stage, there was plenty to laugh about. On opening night, the actor playing Lieutenant Bunin, one of her innumerable lovers, tried to embrace her but got entangled with his protruding scabbard.

"Lieutenant," Mae West ad-libbed with her trademark leer, "is that your sword, or are you just glad to see me?"

Incidentally, it was during the successful run of this play that the actress made the nightly curtain speech: "Catherine had three hundred lovers. I did the best I could do in a couple of hours."

My Life as a Belt

Not long after World War II, when the Royal Air Force had dubbed their bulbous life belts "Mae Wests," nightclub columnist Earl Wilson asked Miss West whether she thought she had a large one. She replied that indeed she did.

"They stick right out, you see," she showed Wilson and then, because she knew that he had a thing about bosoms, she confided to the reporter: "You know, my grandmother was built funny. She had three breasts. But I guess I shouldn't give that to you, but to Ripley."

The origin of this mythic anatomical aberration may have been an observation by Broadway columnist John Chapman. Commenting on the enormous publicity that accompanied Mae West's appearance in her own play

Catherine Was Great, he wrote: "I'm afraid it will be a bust, and will give Miss West one more than she needs."

We Did Her Wrong

In contrast with the public persona that Mae West marketed so skillfully throughout her very long career, she claimed to be a hardworking woman who never took a holiday. She was also a devout Catholic who went to church most mornings and kept a vigil light on in her apartment. In 1931, when she was on Broadway in The Constant Sinner, *Mae West complained in a letter to the New York* Times *that she was misunderstood.*

Because my plays have dealt with sex and the dregs of humanity, some persons see fit to assume that I write vividly about such subjects because I know them by experience. . . . Nobody ever saw me in the dives I am supposed to know so intimately. . . . The reason is I never was in one. Nobody ever sees me in nightclubs or cabarets anywhere. Even if I cared for night life, which I don't, I wouldn't have time to indulge myself in it. People who know their Broadway will bear me out that there is no star on the stage today who is less of an exhibitionist, or who shows herself less in public places than myself. I am, in fact, retiring by nature, in my private life to the point of shyness. I even do all my shopping by telephone, because I cannot stand the attention other shoppers give me in a store. I am not upstage or conceited, or anything like that, as anyone who knows me will agree, but it is averse to my nature to feel myself being pointed out in public as a celebrity. . . . I do not drink. I do not smoke. I have my books, my writings, my friends—that is my private life.

A Life of Quiet Desperation

Lillian Russell, who had been born in Canton, Ohio, and educated by nuns in Chicago, sometimes protested against the naughty notoriety which accompanied her during the height of her career. In the spring of 1890 she complained to a journalist:

"The world seems to think that my life is one round of joy and wild gaiety, full of diamonds and champagne and supper parties. Why, it is on the contrary, extremely monotonous and more quiet than that of most women who look after their own houses and go to the theatre once a week."

Gypsy

During the early part of her career, Gypsy Rose Lee belonged to a wandering troupe of chorus girls, who were advertised by the manager as follows: "Fifty beautiful girls—forty-five gorgeous costumes." It was Gypsy's job to persuade them that she was the extra five girls.

Gypsy used to explain her attraction this way: "I know men aren't attracted to me by my mind. They're attracted by what I don't mind."

She had important parts of her body insured. When one of her expensive costumes disappeared during her London engagement, she cabled her insurance company: "Gown lifted in Hotel Imperial." The company cabled back: "Your policy does not cover that."

Navel Gazing

Mike Todd hired Gypsy Rose Lee as star for the *Streets of Paris*, one of the many attractions he devised for the New York World's Fair of 1939. He promoted her as "The Best Undressed Woman in America, Who Proved That the G-String Is More Than Part of a Banjo." The public servants overseeing the Fair were understandably nervous and prescribed in precise terms how far Gypsy could go. "Miss Lee is abiding by the rules of the art as laid down by the Fair authorities," Burns Mantle commented in the *Daily News*. "She is very careful not to take off more than she has on."

Mantle was also correct about one of Mike Todd's stunts, designed to add a little spice. As Gypsy reached to unlatch the last fastening for the last stitch on her body, two professional spinsters let out some screeches and gasps of horror. "I suspect Mr. Todd knows the names of the ladies," Mantle observed, "and it would not surprise me to see and hear them when I go back next time."

And indeed, Mike Todd had hired those audience plants for the whole summer. He never stinted on details.

Sex Goes Legit

When the New York production of Oh, Calcutta! *opened in 1969, reviews were so bad, it was thought that they would close the play rather than the organized forces of morality. The title of the show, conceived by the critic and dramaturg Kenneth Tynan and produced by Hillard Elkins, came from a painting by Clovis Trouille, about whom Kathleen Tynan was then writing an article in Paris. She did not know that the phrase was an ob-*

scene French pun on O quel cul t'as! *In her recent biography of her husband, Mrs. Tynan narrates the opening of the show that has made sex finally legitimate—and commercially viable.*

New York was ready for *Oh, Calcutta!* Norman Mailer was running for Mayor, the magazine stalls were full of explicit images of the body's most hidden regions. The cast, now apparently liberated beyond recall, told stories of the dramatic changes in their private lives. Therapeutic sex clinics were burgeoning. Everybody was exploring sexuality, while I had not yet abandoned my bra. It seemed ironic that my sex-peddler husband was far too concerned about his future career in London, and his reputation in New York, to leave much time for sex.

When Ken returned ten days later, Jacques Levy and his cast were improvising techniques for the closing number. By now *Calcutta* was very much a show within a show, the group numbers encompassing the sketches. The evening opened with a chorus line which strips. After the intermission, the nude cast appeared in a choreographed group grope, with short filmed biographies of each performer projected on the backcloth. At the end, the cast again stepped forward, each as himself or herself, and voiced what the audience might be thinking: "I mean what is the point, I mean what does it prove? . . . Nudity is passé. . . . She really is a natural blonde. . . . That's my daughter up there. . . . If they're having fun, why don't they have erections?"

In rehearsal Jacques had said, "Don't everybody keep shooting for the laugh. We don't want uptown values around here. Don't let yourself be seduced by the audience. Try to make whatever you want to happen happen." "You know," said Ken, sitting up in the balcony, "the actors in this show, and the production staff, behave not like craftsmen but like people in a movie about a Broadway production." No theatre historian since has pointed out that *Oh, Calcutta!* was the precursor of *A Chorus Line.*

Ken went back to London on June 5 and returned five days later. By the twelfth he was preparing to take his name off the show. He wrote to Elkins:

Kathleen and I have been doing some checking. *Everybody* is (ludicrously) under the impression that *Calcutta* is my show. . . . In fact, of course, it is Jacques's show with your backing. . . . What we now have is not an *erotic* show—eroticism means sex plus psychological content—but a *flesh* show. There are ways of concealing this failure—by means of running order and the restoration of items like "You and I" [by David Mercer]. . . . Unless my feelings about "my" show are respected by Tuesday night's performance, I shall have to wield the club Jacques mentioned last night and pull out, not with a whimper but a resounding bang.

During the next few days matters were resolved. Ken resigned himself to the opening night, while agreeing without enthusiasm to give interviews to the press and the major television talk hosts.

The New York *Times* published an interview between Ken and an "intelligent puritan" of his own invention. Was there not enough sex already in the theatre? "There may be quite enough heavy breathing, grimly perspiring, earnestly symbolic sex on the New York stage," Ken replied, tacitly referring to *Che!* and the Performance Group's *Dionysus in '69*, "but what about sex as play, nocturnal diversion, civilized pastime?"

Ken's own sexual preferences, he confided in another journal, were as follows: "The slow revelation of the body, not immediate nudity . . . certain voices and the combination and use of words . . . Mirrors . . . bathrooms. . . . I don't like group sex, and, as a matter of fact, I haven't tried any. . . . For me the most unerotic garments ever invented are body stockings and tights."

Although *Oh, Calcutta!* hardly resembled Ken's ideal, it had an exuberant and undeniable life of its own, and he recognized this. The New York Police Department vice squad, meanwhile, having visited the show on several occasions and objected to genital contact, agreed not to prosecute. As the police commissioner put it, "The pillars of the guidelines are shaking every day."

The Only Dance There Is

When *Oh, Calcutta!* went into rehearsals, director Jacques Levy stressed the aesthetic rather than erotic qualities he sought. Even though Michael Bennett quit before rehearsals, there were sensitivity exercises and wholly choreographed pieces like the *Pas de Deux* which Rudolf Nureyev and Jerome Robbins admired. One famous dancer and actor was more ambivalent. Asked to comment on the show, Sir Robert Helpmann said: "The trouble with nude dancing is that not everything stops when the music stops."

Hairy Filth

The British production of the American musical *Hair* (1967) followed hard upon the abolition of the Lord Chamberlain's office. "Angry" playwright John Osborne told *Time* magazine: "There will be a quick rash of hairy American filth, but it shouldn't threaten the existence of cheerful, decent, serious British filth."

Onward and Upward With the Arts

In the mid-1960s Harold Clurman served on a committee overseeing the building of the Kennedy Center for the Performing Arts in the nation's capital. He attended several discussions about the appointment of a director. Jacqueline Kennedy favored Leonard Bernstein, who was not ready to relinquish the New York Philharmonic. Several other candidates might have qualified artistically, but the committee was informed that Congress would not approve the appointment of a known homosexual. At one point Justice Abe Fortas was brought in to give advice, and Clurman asked him whether the embargo would include two candidates who were notorious womanizers. "Oh, no," said the Associate Justice of the Supreme Court, "Congress won't mind that."

(A few years later Abe Fortas was forced to resign or face impeachment for embezzlement.)

Praised Be the Lord

Though he was from Massachusetts and Puritan stock, Justice Oliver Wendell Holmes enjoyed burlesque. According to Ruth Gordon, who shared the same background and vitality with the great jurist, he was coming out of the Old Howard burlesque show and said: "Thank God, my tastes are low."

CHAPTER 2

Landmarks
and Hangouts

The First Mile

The theatrical district known as Broadway has shifted several times during the past century and a half, before settling down in the blocks surrounding Times Square. Although sometimes described as the longest street in the world (all the way from Manhattan to Albany), it was the first mile that provided the glitter and entertainment to New Yorkers. Toward the end of his long career, Edward B. Marks, a musical agent on Tin Pan Alley, recalled Broadway as it was in the Gilded Age.

The busiest mile at one time (1880–90) on old Broadway started at No. 1 and ran up to the junction of that thoroughfare and Park Row. The roar of passing traffic was tremendous. Bright yellow buses with landscape pictures rumbled over the paving stones as ironshod hoofs beat their tattoo on them, as a noisy contrast to our smooth macadam and rubber tires.

Every driver was for himself and the devil take the hindmost, as there were no traffic rules. Often the collision of the buses brought a row between drivers over the splintering wood, and the big lane was sometimes bedlam between the curses of drivers and the screams of the narrowly escaping passengers. The stages added to the din. These traveled to the then-distant Greenwich Village, and even 10 miles up into the country to faraway Harlem. The private coaches of the wealthy, the barouches and victorias, added to the jam as the horses threaded in and out.

It was worth your life to cross Fulton Street at Broadway. Then the wise Aldermen created the 6-foot Broadway Squad to escort the ladies at intervals when they stopped the roaring stream of traffic. And did these gallant escorts enjoy it, when pretty women, raising their skirts enough to show their ankles and pantalettes, stood waiting to be escorted to the pavement opposite? Well, I'll say so.

Finally a bridge about 15 feet high was built over Broadway at Fulton Street from curb to curb for people to cross on. It was just about in front of St. Paul's. But even this overpass raised a storm of disapproval. The prevailing highly moral citizens claimed it corrupted youth, as youngsters with advanced ideas got under the bridge to watch the hoop-skirted, petti-coated, white-stockinged, tassel-booted ladies as they unwittingly exposed their hidden charms to the eyes of the wicked on their way over the bridge.

It was a zone of gaiety and windows blazed by night all along its length. Buses, stages, carriages jammed the street. A merry throng of theatregoers, spenders and gilded youth.

In winter, sleighs on steel-bound runners largely supplanted wheels and roisters, and warmed by straw, buffalo robes and good spirits within and without, they sang catchy songs and made the welkin ring.

To old New Yorkers, it was a fascinating, enchanting region and the high-class theatres, minstrel halls, open-air gardens and semi-respectable resorts were all well attended.

There was always plenty to see and hear of the gay side of New York for visitors from other cities or from abroad.

The Main Stem

Broadway has been called as much an invention as a street. Along with Damon Runyon and, to a lesser extent, Mark Hellinger, Walter Winchell is credited with creating through columns and short stories the idea of Broadway. In the late 1920s, Winchell tried to put into words what that mystique was.

Broadway has been described in many manners. It exists as a physical fact, as a symbol of a certain sort of national yearning for expression, as a standard of comparison in morals, and as a way of thinking.

As a physical fact, it is a crooked and somewhat narrow street trailing from the lowest tip of Manhattan Island to the city limits of Yonkers and beyond; and so it is, with the disputed exception of Halsted Street, Chicago, the longest metropolitan thoroughfare in the world. . . .

Like any other "community," Broadway for most of its denizens is a place to make a living and to get ahead in life by the methods best suited to the talents God gave them. To the lonely and aspiring hoofer, the fannie-falling comedian, the ukelele player with the special technique and the singer with something peculiar about his voice, trouping the one-night stands in the southern swamps and western prairies, Broadway is the Big Apple, the Main Stem, the goal of all ambition, the pot of gold at the end of a drab and somewhat colorless rainbow. To those who have fought and struggled their way to Broadway and have played for a brief while before its glittering lights and to Broadway's applause—and have lost, or slipped out of, popular favor—it is a tragedy of hopes.

It is a place where actresses and chorus girls, good actors and ham actors, talented people and untalented people are out of work for long stretches at a time, where poverty stalks in tarnished tinsel, and where competition is perhaps crueller and more cut-throat in its methods than in any other place in the world.

It is a hard and destructive community even for those who "click" or make good on it; for those who play on Broadway are neurotic, restless and easily bored. They want novelty and they are quickly fed up with repetition. And that goes for the buyer for a village general store who gets on to New York once or twice a year for a combined business trip and unholy spree, as well as for night-club promoters, gamblers, gunmen, bootleggers, rich spendthrifts, and other regular patrons of New York's night-life.

What you accomplished last season doesn't matter. "What have you got now?" is the incessant query. Yesterday's favorites, so far as Broadway cares a whoop, are tomorrow's also-rans. There is nothing so dead on Broadway as a waning star. As far as Broadway is concerned, a star that is no longer in the ascendant is already extinct.

This recorder has observed Broadway for fourteen years. He has no ax to grind. Broadway's been pretty good to him, too. But the sentiments to which he subscribes are best summed up in the banal song with the refrain:

> "A painted smile, a hard luck tale,
> A helping hand . . .
>   They're all for sale
> On Broadway!"

Animal Farm

Early during the Prohibition, Damon Runyon, the hardbitten and yet sentimental journalist whose stories of Broadway characters were made into Guys and Dolls, reflected on a passage by Charles Dickens the century before, in which the great novelist described pigs on Broadway.

Since Mr. Dickens's time the pigs of Broadway have changed only in form, having taken on the semblance of humans. You can see them today in the streetcars and subway trains, pushing and grunting their way to seats while women stand clinging to the straps. You can see them wandering along Broadway, old hogs familiar with every sty in the city, and young porkers just learning the ways of swine, their little eyes eagerly watching every passing skirt.

Of an evening they gather in cabarets, wallowing in illicit liquor and shouting through a conversational garbage made up of oaths and filthy stories and scandal.

A pig is a pig even when it wears evening clothes . . .

The Original Flock

In 1874 a group of actors formed a supper club modeled after the Lambs, an English club, which had been established in memory of Charles and Mary Lamb. The American Lambs first met at Delmonico's restaurant, and after a couple of locations, moved in 1905 into the heart of Broadway at 44th Street. The famous club facilities, hotel and theatre, designed by Stanford White, were sold in 1974. Under an elected shepherd, the Lambs organized entertainments for charity known as Lambs' Gambols. Membership was open to theatre professionals (even women, after the first half-century) except critics and agents, "to avoid potential friction." The actor Otis Skinner recalls the early days of Lambs and some of the original flock.

Not the least factor in the theatrical life of the 'eighties was the swirl that drew some of us off the stream of Broadway down Twenty-sixth Street to the old Lambs' Club. Its inception had come from Wallack's leading man, handsome Harry Montague, and it became a cherished meeting-place for the English theatre folk engaged in New York. In time its popularity spread among our native actors. It was not the splendidly prosperous club that to-day preserves the name of the Lambs, but a coterie of a few men of the stage and men about town who affected the theatre. Its furnishings were not sumptuous; we were a poor club, but I cannot bring to mind a membership that included Charles Coghlan, Maurice Barrymore, Osmund Tearle, John Drew, Ned and Joe Holland, Robert Mantell, Kyrle Bellew, Digby Bell, DeWolf Hopper, Richard Mansfield, Tom Whiffen, William H. Crane, Nat Goodwin, Henry Dixey, Marshall Wilder, Clay Greene, Augustus Thomas, Steele Mackaye, without the glow of good company stealing about my heart.

Lester Wallack was a sort of perpetual shepherd, being continually reelected to office. Monthly dinners were served with as good food as our resources could command, and in the long list of guests appeared the names of Irving, Wilson Barrett, W. H. Kendall, Chauncey Depew, General Horace Porter, General Sherman, E. S. Willard, William Winter, Edgar Saltus, Buffalo Bill, and many more in honor of whom the fonts of wit and eloquence were tapped.

An afternoon at the Lambs would sometimes find Steele Mackaye, tall, spare, emotional and eloquent, looking like a more stalwart Edgar Allan Poe, holding forth to a knot of listeners on some theory destined never to be realized, some dream never to become articulate. He was always magnetic and compelling.

And one would be pretty sure to find Joe somewhere about—Joe, the well-beloved—the youngest of the sons of that Holland whose funeral service made the fame of "The Little Church around the Corner."

There was a shout from adoring Lambs whenever Maurice Barrymore entered. This founder of the house of Barrymore was English-born, Herbert Blythe—preeminently a man's man, and beyond question a woman's man, of a wit so telling and yet so good-hearted that even the objects of his keen satire joined in laughter at their own expense. On the stage he was always a picture—in private, an Apollo in a slop suit. Amateur champion middle-weight boxer, narrator of a thousand stories, quick in resentment of an insult, generous to a foe, burner of candles at both ends, Bedouin of Broadway, this was the Barrymore that I knew.

A Good Address

In its heyday the Lambs' Club had an array of lock boxes and a fully staffed General Delivery desk, like a small-town post office; doormen could tell with one glance at a large board which members had checked in or out. Actors would rest at the Lambs between making their wearying rounds in the theatre district during the day, and some appeared at night, to sit out an act with full makeup. Then, after the show, there would be noisy company as the players ate late supper at the grill.

The Lambs provided an oasis for the restless nomads of the profession, and a fixed address in an unstable world. Wilton Lackaye (1862–1932), a comic star with a sour personality, was invited by a Little Theatre as a guest speaker. He listened for almost an hour while the chairman made a long-winded and unctuous introduction which he wound down with, "And now the brilliant speaker of the evening will give you his address." Lackaye rose, advanced to the rostrum and said:

"My address is the Lambs' Club."

And he sat down.

Bywords

The Lambs was one of Ring Lardner's favorite hangouts. He rarely spoke, but when he did, his witticisms became bywords. Once, a member whose recently deceased brother had written a poem asked Lardner whether he would recite it for him. Lardner quietly scanned it and then asked: "Did your brother write this before or after he died?"

On another occasion, Lardner bumped into a classical actor with long wild hair and asked: "How do you look when I am sober?"

The Reliquary

The other venerable club for actors that still exists is The Players, founded a hundred years ago by Edwin Booth. Stanford White transformed the house Booth bought at 16 Gramercy Park into a luxurious clubhouse. Objects with historical associations have always been very important to theatre folk, who tend to be both superstitious and sentimental: Edmund Kean went to enormous trouble to repatriate from America a toe of George Frederick Cooke, who drank himself to death in 1812, only to have Mrs. Kean thoughtlessly throw it out. The Players was conceived from its infancy as a treasury of relics sacred to the profession. Brander Matthews describes the club only five years after its founding on the last night of 1888.

In the ample hall is a large marble mantelpiece, and on the bricks of the fireplace beneath it is inscribed this quotation, written by the founder of the club:

> Good frende for friendship's sake forbeare
> To utter what is gossipt heare
> In social chatt, lest, unawares,
> Thy tonge offende thy fellowe plaiers.

Opening out of this hall is an inviting reading-room, with an upper alcove for writing-desks. It is from the steps of this alcove that one can get the best view of the portrait of Mr. Booth, framed over the fireplace of the reading-room. This picture was presented to The Players by Mr. E. C. Benedict. It was painted by Mr. John S. Sargent, and it is one of the most brilliant, vigorous, and vivid portraits of the nineteenth century. It is a full-length, and it represents Mr. Booth standing negligently before the yule-log of the hall, much as he stood on the night when he gave the house to the club. His attitude is easy, and the countenance is lighted by the kindly smile so often seen upon the face of the tragedian. What most endears this picture to The Players is that it is a portrait, not of the actor merely, but rather of Mr. Booth himself, as he is known to his fellow-members.

Between the hall and the dining-room are huge safes to hold the relics and the stray curiosities which are beginning to accumulate. The treasures stored up do not as yet rival those in the Green Vaults of Dresden. Though one may seek here in vain for a wheel of the chariot of Thespis, for the mask of Aristophanes, for the holograph manuscript of a missing comedy by Menander, for the buskin worn by Roscius, and for a return check to the theatre at Herculaneum, still there are not a few curiosities almost as curious as these. There is the sword Frédérick Lemaître drew in the last act of *Ruy Blas*. There is the crooked staff whereon Charlotte Cushman leaned as Meg Merrilies, when she foretold the fate of Guy Mannering. There is the blond wig which Fechter chose to wear as Hamlet, perhaps the most chattered about of all theatrical wigs; that it is, in reality, red and not at all blond is not surprising to those who have mused on the unrealities of life, as Hamlet himself was wont to do. There is a ring that once belonged to David Garrick, and a lock of hair that once belonged to Edmund Kean. There is a spring dagger, formerly the property of Edwin Forrest, the blade of which kindly retired within the hilt when the owner went through the motions of stabbing himself. There is a crucifix used by Signora Ristori in the character of Sor Teresa. Here also are the second, third, and fourth folios of Shakespeare's works, the first folio of Beaumont and Fletcher's, the first folio of Ben Jonson, and the first of Sir William Davenant with an autograph poem. Here are many autographs of high theatrical interest. Here, finally, are certain stately pieces of silver, among them a salver and pitcher presented in 1828 to Junius Brutus Booth, and the loving-cup presented to William Warren a few years before he died.

Here and there throughout the house are to be seen Shakespearean mottoes, even in the most unexpected places. That which adorns one of the mantelpieces in the grill-room is, "Mouth it, as many of our Players do."

Vive la Différence!

In their heyday there used to be a friendly rivalry among the Lambs, the Players, and the Friars, the last still known for its roasts and unprintable jokes. An old aphorism tried to sum up the distinctions between these famous show-business clubs:

The Players are all gentlemen who wish they were actors.

The Lambs are all actors who wish they were gentlemen.

The Friars wish they were both.

I Never Promised You a Roof Garden

In the summer of 1896 the indefatigable Oscar Hammerstein opened a Roof Garden atop the Olympia, which he had built the previous year on the east side of Broadway between 44th and 45th streets. He lavished two million dollars on the lots and buildings, and it marked the beginnings of Times Square. He built the Roof Garden to compete with one atop the Casino, but his had to be more lavish, according to his treasurer, George Blumenthal.

Hammerstein added a new feature of having the whole garden glassed in as a protection from the weather. The opening took place on a very hot night. The garden was sweltering. Then Hammerstein realized that glass attracts and reflects the heat. The next day he started having pipes, which would contain running water, laid across the roof so that water would flow out over the glass. In ten days the problem was solved and the new Roof Garden was a tremendous success.

Oscar tried to create a rustic effect with palms, bridges, a waterfall, and even a miniature lake with ducks floating in it. He even told me to buy two monkeys, which I did, and put them in the palms near the waterfall alongside the stage.

Two or three nights after the opening, the monkeys began acting in a very hilarious way. We finally discovered that the patrons were giving them beer and whiskey. Sure enough, one night one of them was so drunk that it fell into the miniature lake and was drowned. The next day Mr. Hammerstein sent me down to Ruhe's Animal Shop on Grand Street to get another to take its place, as the first was pining mournfully for its mate. To avoid further trouble he put up a sign reading:

> ANYONE GIVING THESE MONKEYS
> INTOXICATING LIQUOR
> WILL BE PROSECUTED

The Roof Garden was such a success that Hammerstein, after he lost the Olympia, opened another one atop his new Victoria which he called Paradise Roof Gardens. That year (1900) he also opened next to it the Republic, *which was run by his son Willie, who soon laid out a miniature farm on top, complete with ducks, swans, a cow with dairy maid, and other domestic animals.*

Many stories about this strange project found their way into the press from Willie's fertile mind. For instance, in the manner of 1906 it was reported that "when a wagon load of hay was passing in front of the *Republic*, a goat jumped off the roof to get at it and died." And the next year the press had another goat story. An innkeeper whom Oscar was supposed to have met in the Swiss Alps "had sent the animal to him and he had given it to Willie for the roof. Willie carelessly turned it loose on the day of its delivery. A few hours later it was found that the goat had eaten all of the geraniums, most of the artificial shrubbery and part of the proscenium arch which was made of papier-mâché."

Rescue Mission

The landmarks and hangouts of Broadway were continually disappearing. Around the first decade of the century, some of Broadway's finest got together to save a favorite place, as Dayton Stoddart chronicled it in Lord Broadway, *the story of* Variety's *founder, Sime Silverman.*

Sime walked into John the Barber's for a shave. It was a Broadway hangout, a modern coffee house, as it were, with George Cohan, Al Woods, Sam Scribner (executive spark-plug of burlesque), and Sam Harris the more prominent members of a crowd, some of whom could have drunk even Sir Richard Steele under the table.

"Morning, John!"

He slipped into the chair, easy in this atmosphere of bay rum, tonics, lotions, laughs. But there were no laughs today, and John, returning with Sime's shaving mug from the shelf, was of dismal mien indeed.

"What's the matter, John? Your wife come back?"

"No sucha bad luck. Worser."

"Hey! Watch the razor. If you wanna cut a throat, take yours, not mine."

John the Barber's hand, usually deft, was unsteady. Why? He told the story. Freeman Bernstein, a customer and picturesque sharpshooter, was also husband of May Ward, burlesque and musical comedy actress. Using the bait of looka-how-rich-Georgie-Cohan-and-Sam-Harris-are-getting, he had hooked John the Barber for $15,000. Not only all the savings, but a mortgage on the shop. Now the shop was gone!

Sime had heard rumors of the gamble. But Bernstein, wise fellow, had pledged John to secrecy. ("Then, ol' boy, think how you'll surprise 'em. You can quit in the middle of a shave and say: 'I'm a big producer, too, so I'm givin' up my business.'")

John was giving it up, all right—by request. News of the flop of *The Cash Girl* had come through from Boston; and the turkey would flap its wings for the last time this Saturday. George M. Cohan made a jaunty entrance, the Yankee Doodle Dandy in person, Broadway tops. Sime li.ed him, indeed had violated his rule of not covering the legit by going to one Cohan show (using the excuse that Cohan doings were vaudeville news), and his review of *Fifty Miles from Boston* was marked chiefly by the comment: "Edna Wallace Hopper played the postmistress with her own hair or some hair hanging down her back."

Cohan heard John's hard-luck story. So did the rest. Cohan, Scribner, Sime, Harris, and Woods kicked in $1500 for a new shop for John the Barber. Outright gift? Not altogether. Just for the laugh, they said they'd take it out in trade. And some of them solemnly gave John half tips thereafter, to make him feel he was repaying.

Broadway in the days of regular fellows.

The Girl from Rector's

Cohan helped to save another institution. George Rector blamed the ruin of his popular establishment at Broadway and Fifth Avenue on Paul Potter, a playwright who had adapted a French farce for producer A. H. Woods. He was walking toward Rector's, his mind preoccupied with what to call his show.

"A slight drizzle set in, and as he reached our restaurant a hansom cab drove up and a very pretty girl stepped out. Her skirts were raised a trifle

higher than schoolgirls wore them and a trifle lower than grandmothers
wear them now [1927]. *She made a beautiful picture, and in a flash the*
observant Potter had his title for his farce. It was The Girl from Rector's."

The show became a hit in 1909, and Rector's prospered enough that
father and son had built a hotel with the same name. But the publicity
also killed them. Because The Girl from Rector's *represented everything*
naughty and Parisian, a traveling businessman was courting marital dis-
cord or disaster if he associated himself in any manner with her. So the
out-of-towners stayed out of the Hotel Rector. George Rector, Jr., remem-
bered to his dying day how George M. Cohan helped him out.

For three months there wasn't one guest in the 250-room hotel, our restaurant trade was nil, and our bar registered zero. We were losing $1,000
a day. George came into the grill one evening after a tour, looked around
at the empty tables and said, "Good-evening, George. Where is the crowd?"

"Good-evening, George," I replied. "There is not, has not and may not
be a crowd."

Now there could not be anything more dull than a conversation between
two men named George unless one of the men happened to be George M.
Cohan. I told him about the effect of Paul Potter's play on the Hotel
Rector. He put his arm around my shoulder and invited me to have dinner
with him.

After dinner we smoked cigars and he said: "George, I don't like to see
this. Rector's has always been a great little place, you're a great little guy,
and I always liked you both. I'm going to show you that I'm a great little
guy. I'm going to live in your hotel and so are my friends. I'm going to
eat in your restaurant again and so are all my pals. Get me a suite of
rooms on the second floor, facing on Broadway. I'm going to live here by
the year. You're a great little guy."

And he went out saying, "You're a great little guy," meanwhile shaking
his head in the affirmative. He stopped at the door to say, "Your hotel is
going to be filled to-morrow. You're a great little guy. So am I."

He kept his word and took a five-room suite in Rector's, even though
he already had an apartment in the Hotel Knickerbocker leased by the
year. Our hotel was completely filled inside of a week. George moved in
bag, baggage, and piano. He would bang that piano at all hours of the
night and on it he composed "Mary Is a Grand Old Name," "Yankee
Doodle Dandy," "Give My Regards to Broadway," and a hundred other
tunes which swept the country. He was a warm friend and his greatest
tribute to anybody was, "You're a great little guy."

A Family Affair

It started as a speakeasy cellar on 52nd Street in 1928, moved to larger premises next to Jack & Charlie's "21," and it was closed by bankruptcy in 1953 as the nightclub era faded from 52nd Street. In between, Leon & Eddie's was one of the most famous "in" places on Swing Street. Leon Enken was the businessman, Eddie Davis—known also as the Saloon Caruso—was the entertainer. "Four times a night," wrote Arnold Shaw in *The Street That Never Slept*, "he went on for 40 to 60 minutes. Boasting a repertoire of more than a thousand songs, he reportedly never repeated a number during an evening."

The late shows at Leon & Eddie's attracted performers from other clubs and Broadway shows. There was also the weekly celebrity night on Monday, both for present and future stars. Young comedians such as Alan King, Jerry Lewis, and Dean Martin all tried out their acts here. In a story that was widely circulated but denied by Eddie Davis, the young Marlon Brando, who lived on the same block, was barred once for wearing the trademark T-shirt from his roles in *A Streetcar Named Desire* and *On the Waterfront*. The nightclub had a roof that could be opened for ventilation, and Brando was supposed to have collected a bucketful of horse droppings from Central Park's bridle path, which he emptied through the roof, echoing a Socony advertisement of the day: "Watch out for the Flying Red Horse."

Leon & Eddie's was a strange combination of family dining and strip joint. Sherry Britton, who worked as a stripper there throughout the 1940s, said that nobody complained about her act. She also recalls how Leon and Eddie made all their customers feel at home: "They never forgot the name of anybody who came in more than once. They remembered birthdays and anniversaries. . . . They maintained an enormous mailing list of more than twenty thousand active names. It was so precious to them that once when a customer dropped dead in the club, Leon turned to his partner after the initial shock had worn off and said absentmindedly: 'Let's not forget to take his name off the mailing list.' "

Be My Guest

Some friends took George S. Kaufman one evening to Leon & Eddie's nightclub. A drunk on the way to the men's room staggered up to their table, hovered, and then finally said:

"I must leave you now. Will you excuse me?"

"Certainly," said Kaufman, "the alternative is too dreadful to contemplate."

Insulting the Customer

Toots Shor, who ran one of the favorite celebrity restaurants in New York of the thirties and forties, may have introduced the now widely copied tradition of being rude to famous customers and charging them extra for it. Toots respected only athletes and sportswriters. "When I have twenty bucks to spend for dinner, and feel like I could stand being called various uncomplimentary names," Earl Wilson wrote in his column, "I go unhesitatingly to Toots's." His favorite name for customers was "crum bums," and if anyone complained about waiting for a table, the gracious host would say: "Get out—go on—who needs ya."

One night Charlie Chaplin, perhaps the most famous face on the planet at the time, was waiting in line. Any other restaurateur would have set up a special table, but Toots Shor went up to the star and said:

"It'll be twenty minutes, Charlie. Be funny for the people."

Louis B. Mayer, when he visited from Hollywood, was an occasional patron. Once the diminutive mogul patronized the 250-pound former speakeasy bouncer too far.

"A nice big room you've got here," said Mayer. "I hope the food is good."

"I've seen some of your pictures," Toots Shor replied.

Toots Shor was also pals with the young Frank Sinatra, when The Voice was still skinny and frail-looking. "Don't tell anybody you eat here, ya bum," Toots told him. "You're no ad for the joint." Despite such treatment, the restaurant at 51 West 51st Street had a fiercely loyal following, which Toots Shor did nothing to discourage. Regulars were actually forbidden to visit any of the rival establishments, and had to have solid alibis, if they were reported back to Shor as having eaten elsewhere. The comedian Joe E. Lewis was working at Hollywood's elite nightclub, Ciro's, when he said: "I'd rather be standing outside Toots's starving than sitting inside Ciro's belching." And the famous journalist Quentin Reynolds declared on his return from an assignment during World War II: "I was homesick for my wife, my father, and Toots."

It was during the war that Toots got in trouble with the Office of Price Administration, exceeding his rationed allowance by 23 thousand pounds of meat. Hundreds of his regular customers rallied around and ate for three months the monotonous meatless menu. Jimmy Walker, the former mayor who was removed for corruption, told all his friends, "Now, we gotta eat at Toots's twice a day instead of once." And another loyalist, when he heard the bad news, wired Shor: "I don't love meat. I love you."

Class

One of Toots Shor's competitors and personal enemies was Sherman Bill-ingsley, who owned the exclusive Stork Club where Walter Winchell held court. A sportswriter friend of Shor, who was even permitted by him to visit the Stork Club, was once asked by the elegant and snobby Billingsley:

"What's Shor got that I haven't got?"

Without hesitation the writer offered:

"Class. Toots is a champion."

Reservation

In the days before desegregation, comedian George Jessel once took Lena Horne to the Stork Club, where he was a regular and he knew the pro-prietor, Sherman Billingsley, to be bigoted. The headwaiter was furiously paging through the reservation book, pretending that there were no free tables. Finally he asked:

"Mr. Jessel, who made the reservation?"

"Abraham Lincoln," replied Jessel.

He and his guest were seated.

Pay Now, Drink Later

Frank Brower, one of the favorite black minstrels of nineteenth-century America, walked into the bar-room of the Metropolitan one day, dusty and unkempt from a long journey, and asked for a glass of brandy. The saloon-keeper handed out the brandy, and then, suspicious of the man's appear-ance, said:

"Just pay for that before you drink it, will you?" Brower, who was about as well known in New York as any man about town, looked up astonished, and stammered:

"W—w-what?"

"Just pay for the brandy before you drink it," the bartender repeated. The minstrel leaned across the counter:

"Why," he asked confidentially, "is it so im-m-mediately f-f-fatal in its effect?"

Chopped Liver and Song

Damon Runyon's favorite hangout was Lindy's, heavily disguised as Mindy's in his stories. His portrait dominated the place even after his death. Comics would gather at Lindy's and practice heckling each other. Irving Berlin also loved Lindy's, so did columnist Earl Wilson. Funny man Joey Adams captured the atmosphere in his 1946 book, From Gags to Riches.

Leo Lindy is as famous as any of the stars who frequent his "store," as he calls it. Only in New York can you see a man-eating shark at the museum and a man eating herring at Lindy's. Lindy has been host to the big of the entertainment world for more years than he can remember. He gives them advice and sends them hot soup and chicken between shows. He sends his cheese cake and marinated herring to the Broadway mob all over the world.

Though the famous restaurateur has no publicity man, he garners more publicity than any other restaurant or night club in the country. All the columnists drop in to talk to the stars, and to find out "what's new?" Lindy divides the "dope" with all the fourth-estaters.

Earl Wilson, the sturgeon general of Lindy's, dropped in at two one morning to inquire about the latest happenings. He fought his way through a large crowd and finally reached Leo Lindy. "Who is in your store tonight?" asked the saloon editor. "Nobody especially famous tonight," answered Leo—"just plain people with money."

The "ickies"* follow the mob. Wherever showpeople gather, the "squares" are sure to follow. That's why restaurant owners look for the "actortainers'" patronage. You can't "buy" a guy in show business. He either likes you and your "joint" or he doesn't. Everybody loves Lindy, and they know they are welcome.

The civilians come to Lindy's to have their cheese cake and see Damon Runyon sitting in the corner with his lovely wife and her strange hats. They love to watch Danny Kaye having laughs with Jack Benny over a plate of borsht. Or watch Bing Crosby eating sour cream, and Bob Hope hanging on to a cream cheese and lox sandwich on bagel.

I was sitting at one of the front tables with Lindy, Danny Kaye, and Bing Crosby one night, when a typical "ickie," who looked as if he comes out once a year, approached "the groaner." "Remember me?" It was the

---

* *Ickies* or *squares*, as they are often called in show-business vernacular, are people who are not "hep" or "in the know" on Broadway. Just plain, nice people who pay to see what's going on.

same question that has haunted entertainers ever since the beginning of time. "You look familiar" was "der Bingle's" answer, the same dodge all actors use.

"Remember when you worked for my organization, The Knights of Pythias, about eighteen years ago," the stranger continued, "and after the show we all had something to eat together? Remember you told us that some day you would be a big star on the radio, the stage, and the screen?"

"Yes, I do recall," said Crosby, trying to be polite.

"So tell me, Bing," pressed the square, "what happened?"

At Sardi's

"Meet Me at Sardi's" is part of the language on Broadway. Eugenia and Vincent Sardi began their famous restaurant just after the First World War. It was moved along to its present location on 44th Street when the Shuberts built the St. James Theatre. The Irish playwright Brendan Behan, visiting New York in connection with the production of The Hostage *(1961), was introduced to the tradition of waiting for reviews at Sardi's.*

There are many very famous restaurants on Broadway and I have chewed many excellent theatrical steaks at Jim Downey's Steak House which, like "Vincent Sardi's," is packed with actors, some of them doing very well, otherwise neither Mr. Sardi nor Mr. Downey would be able to use the kind of automobiles they do, while other actors, as the saying has it, are resting.

A Broadway author—I am proud to call myself one—always waits, on the first night of his play, either in "Sardi's" or "Downey's," and his press agent goes out to get the six newspapers, which are called "the Six Butchers of Broadway."

Now if you get six out of six good reviews, you could ask the President of the United States to sell you the White House, though I don't think this has ever happened. If you get five good reviews, you are doing fairly well and you have to start worrying about 480 Lexington Avenue, which is the home of the income tax. It is not a bad kind of worry though in its own way, if you have got to have worries, and I suppose everyone has to have them. If you have four, you can afford to give a party, or at least you can afford to attend the party which is usually given for you.

If you get three good reviews, it's time like to go home to bed, but if you only get two, you stay there the whole of the following day and don't go out until after dark. If you get one good review, you just make an air reservation very quickly to get back to where you came from, but if you get six bad reviews, you take a sleeping pill. You might even take an overdose!

However, I think I got five or six good reviews. Enough to keep me in business anyway. I know Walter Kerr of the New York *Herald-Tribune* and Howard Taubman of the New York *Times* were both enthusiastic over *The Hostage* and they are the really important reviewers. No, I forget. They are all important. I will be writing another play!

Actually, I got pretty good reviews and when I went into "Sardi's" that night, the crowd stood up and clapped.

Say Cheese

In his book, simply called Sardi's, *Vincent Sardi recalls one of the groups that used to meet at his restaurant in the mid-1930s.*

Winchell was a member of a group that began meeting regularly every day at lunchtime. This group called itself the Cheese Club, and consisted of reporters, free-lance writers, press agents, critics, advertising men, a photographer or two, and occasionally actors and agents. The most faithful members were Irving Hoffman, who was then working as a cartoonist; Kelcey Allen, of *Women's Wear Daily*; Louis Sobol, who was just getting started as a columnist; Sidney Skolsky, who has since become a Hollywood reporter; Mark Hellinger, then a newspaperman and later a movie producer; Richard Maney, Nat Dorfman, Marc Lachman, and several other press agents; Julius Colby, of *Variety*; Whitney Bolton, Bide Dudley, and Heywood Broun, representing the press; Jules Ziegler, an agent; Larry Wiener, an advertising man; Julius Tannen, the comic; Leonard Gallagher, stage manager and producer; and every now and then, when they were in town, George Jessel and Georgie Price. Some days there would be five or six Cheese Club members at their regular round table; other days twenty would show up. The only requirement for membership was to attend a "meeting" every now and then.

The principal function of the Cheese Club members was to provide laughs for each other, but every now and again they set to work on some constructive project. For example, there was an actress, a very attractive girl, who needed work. The club members decided that they would make her famous. Items began appearing in columns all over town, testifying to the charm and talent of the girl. The boys dropped her name everywhere. Before long an agent sold her to a producer for a big part. The girl was well on her way to stardom when, unfortunately, some of the members began getting a bit too attentive—or so some of the other members thought. The cooperative effort dissolved at once, and the girl never did become a star.

Another Cheese Club venture of this kind turned out to be a real break for the subject. Leslie Howard was looking for an actor to appear with him in *The Petrified Forest*. The Cheese Club members heard about this and suggested a young fellow named William Gargan, who was in our place nearly every day.

"He's not well enough known," Howard said.

That was all the boys needed. They immediately began giving Gargan the same treatment the girl had received. His name appeared in all the columns. Favorable reports of his ability turned up everywhere. Lewis Milestone, the movie director, was reported to be very much interested in him as a possibility for pictures. Young Bill was famous overnight and got the part.

I was reminded of this story by Jules Ziegler, the agent, who at that time was working in the office of "Doctor" Louis Shurr, one of the most successful agents of all time. The Doctor came into the place every now and again, too, and sat with the Cheese Club. One day word came to us that he had been arrested the night before. The details of the story gave everyone a great laugh. Shurr was the man who, for years, owned a fur coat which he would allow girl friends to wear while they were out with him. At the end of the date he would take the coat back home with him, so as to allow the next evening's girl to wear it. Girl after girl schemed, planned, and connived to make Shurr hand over the coat as a present, but nobody had ever managed to get it. Well, one night he had an engagement with a girl who lived around the corner from his apartment. When he took her home, he dismissed his chauffeur. He bade the girl good night, took the coat, tossed it over his arm, and started to walk around the corner to his own place. Before he knew what was happening, a prowl-car policeman stopped him and took him to headquarters, booking him on suspicion of stealing a coat. The Doctor took a terrible kidding from Cheese Club members for weeks after that.

Life Imitates Life

During a hot evening in the theatre, the dresser of Mrs. Siddons had sent out to a nearby tavern for a pint of beer. A young lad brought the frothing pitcher and, looking for the person who had ordered the beer, asked, "Where is Mrs. Siddons?" A scene-shifter pointed to the stage where the great Sarah was in the middle of doing Lady Macbeth's sleepwalking scene, and said, "There she is." The boy, who obviously had never been in the theatre, went up to the actress and without any self-consciousness tried to give her the pitcher. She tried to wave him off in the grand manner, but to no avail. At last the people behind the scenes succeeded in getting him off with the beer, amid gales of laughter from the audience.

In an unrehearsed imitation of this theatrical tale, Sandy Dennis was once performing on Broadway, and before the performance had ordered a steak dinner from Frankie and Johnnie's, the famous theatrical eatery on 45th Street. The delivery boy got lost on the way to the dressing room, but spied the actress out on stage having a conversation. With great relief he went up to her in the middle of her scene and said,

"Here's your steak, Miss Dennis."

East Side, West Side

Robert Sylvester, a Broadway columnist in the forties and fifties, recalls in his book No Cover Charge *one of the jazz spots on Swing Street.*

Jimmy Ryan's, the last true jazz spot to survive in Swing Street, opened in September of 1940 and on premiere night lost little time in furnishing an incident which established its proper character. Ryan, who refers to himself as the last of the male chorus boys, had a show business following and pointed for the chorus girl and chorus boy trade. Like Colt before him, he wanted a hangout for his friends and business acquaintances primarily. Things were rough in show business and Ryan scaled his prices accordingly. He featured a twenty-five-cent martini and had a big sign out on the sidewalk advertising the drink.

A violent windstorm swept the block opening night and the twenty-five-cent martini sign was blown halfway down the block. It lodged in the iron grillwork outside the ultra exclusive, determinedly expensive restaurant called "21." It gave the "21" owners a bad turn when they opened for lunch the next day.

To the west of Ryan's, in those days, was Tony's West Side, an intimate, rendezvous-type cafe catering to the smarter set from Broadway, the East Side contingent, and a sprinkling of world travelers. Not long after Ryan's opened, the Metropolitan Opera followed suit for the season. After the opera a man in tails and a girl in mink and jewels climbed out of a cab and entered Ryan's. Ryan is convinced that they were headed for Tony's and made the wrong door. Ryan's jazz band was bellowing, drunks were arguing at the bar, and the smoke was so thick nobody could see the bandstand. The opera couple came in and took a table.

"I told you the West Side would be dreadful," the girl told her escort.

Broadway Playwright

Eugene O'Neill was perhaps the only Broadway playwright in the literal sense: he was born in Times Square. The event took place on October 16, 1888, at the Barrett House (which later became the Cadillac Hotel) at 43rd Street and Broadway. Much of O'Neill's early life was spent in hotels, while his father was touring. Later, on his own, the playwright liked to work in anonymous secondary hotels in New York, where nobody would think of looking for him. He did not like to be disturbed while writing. While working at Provincetown he had a sign tacked on his door: "Go to hell."

Other O'Neill hangouts included Jimmy Priest's saloon, the waterfront dive that he used in Anna Christie, and a Greenwich Village restaurant called Hell's Hole. He also frequented the Old Garden Hotel, on the northeast corner of Madison Avenue and 27th Street, where he met a lot of people from the sporting world.

One gets an idea of how much Eugene O'Neill was a part of the New York City landscape from his friend, the critic George Jean Nathan, who testified in the plagiarism suit brought against Strange Interlude *(1928).*

In the course of examination by the attorney for the plaintiff, one Cohalan, I testified that O'Neill some years before he wrote the play had outlined to me its theme, plot, and general treatment. "Where did this take place?" Cohalan asked me. I replied that O'Neill was living at the time in the old Lafayette Hotel in University Place, that he had started the outline there, and had expanded on it during the walk to an oyster house on Sixth Avenue in the neighborhood of Sixteenth Street, where we had a dinner engagement with a mutual friend.

"There was a bar in that restaurant, wasn't there?" observed the interrogator. I answered that there was. "And you and O'Neill, with your friend, did some drinking there?" he continued. I allowed that he was correct in his surmise. "What did you drink?" he questioned. "Three Old-Fashioned cocktails apiece," I apprised him. "What else?" he asked. "Nothing else at the bar," I replied, "but at dinner we engaged two bottles of Orvieto and rounded off with a couple of Rémy Martin brandies each." "Did you then return once again to the bar?" he pursued. I said, yes, we had. "And what did you drink?" he went on. "Three Old Oscar Pepper highballs apiece," I volunteered. A look of triumph crossed Cohalan's features. "And still," he shouted in my face, "after all those drinks, enough to make any man drunk, you say that your memory was so good that you remember exactly the conversation you allege O'Neill had with you on a walk immediately previous!"

"If," I replied, "I can recall exactly the number and character of the drinks, which you assert were enough to intoxicate anyone, why should I not be able to recall exactly a conversation before I had so much as even one?"

Palace Coup

In her autobiography Sophie Tucker chronicles how the Depression and cheap entertainment provided by the talkies administered the coup de grâce to vaudeville. Back from a triumphant tour in Europe, she performed at the Palace, and the last of the Red-Hot Mamas was determined that they go out together in a blaze of glory.

I was back home at the Palace—the only theatre left in New York that wasn't playing pictures. The demonstration by the audience at my opening performance gladdened my heart. It made me feel that the New York public still wanted real vaudeville. After months playing picture houses, it was like old times. . . . Backstage, the talk flew round that the Palace would soon go into a grind policy—four shows a day with pictures. The gloom was so thick you could cut it with a knife. We all had the feeling that now that E. F. Albee, the czar of vaudeville, was dead, even the Palace wouldn't hold out much longer against pictures. You know how people used to try to help a horse pull a load up a hill by sitting forward on the seat and working with him? That was the way every actor on the bill worked that week at the Palace. As though he could keep New York's only vaudeville theatre by his efforts. I worked that way myself.

On Wednesday night I was standing center stage singing my fool head off when I happened to glance off at the side entrance. Bill, the stage manager, was beckoning to me. I paid no attention. I went right on with my act. A crowd gathered at the entrance. They were all beckoning to me to get off the stage. Then they pointed overhead for me to look up. I looked and saw a tongue of flame shoot out in the flies. Fire! I thought: I can't leave the stage now. I've got to tell the audience to leave quietly so there won't be a panic. The house was packed.

"Take it easy, folks. Don't run. Give everybody a chance to get out."

The front and side doors of the theatre were open and the draft spread the flames above me. I was dressed in a gown covered with bronze sequins. If a spark fell on it, it would go up in a blaze—and me with it. I stood there singing and praying no spark would drop. Then I was yanked off the stage by the property boy and the steel curtain came down.

That was the famous fire at the Palace. Most of the damage was up in the flies and in the orchestra pit. Very little damage out front; only a few mink coats singed. The newspapers ran headlines:

RED-HOT MAMA BURNS UP PALACE THEATRE!

and

SOPHIE'S SONGS SO HOT,
THEATRE BURNS UNDER THEM!

No Escape from New York

Not long after the founding of the Group Theatre in 1931, the visionary architect Frank Lloyd Wright offered to design a theatre building that would inspire and match the young company's vast ambition. He invited the Group's three founding directors—Harold Clurman, Cheryl Crawford, and Lee Strasberg—to show them the model for a magnificent, spacious dream of a building. The young theatre pioneers were struck dumb by Wright's passionate presentation. Finally, Clurman managed to speak.

"But Mr. Wright," he stammered, "where can we find a place for such a theatre in New York City?"

"Oh," the architect replied with withering scorn, "if you wish to remain in the rubbish, noise, and filth of New York, then you are not as advanced as I thought you were."

(Just before he died in 1959, Frank Lloyd Wright managed to build the Dallas Theatre Centre for Paul Baker.)

Rock of Ages

Helen Hayes, often called the First Lady of the American stage, had a second theatre named after her in 1983, after the first one was demolished amidst frantic and futile efforts to save it. Informed of the new honor, Miss Hayes said: "Oh, it's great to be a theatre again!"

CHAPTER 3

Do You Speak
Broadway?

A Lingo of One's Own

Given all the ropes and rigging backstage, it is not that surprising that many early American stagehands were ex-seamen, and they brought some of their slang into the theatre. They continued to call themselves "grips" or "deck hands." They called a tangled rope "foul" and hushed people "to pipe down." H. L. Mencken, in his monumental work on The American Language, *noted the differences in language within the theatrical profession.*

The stage-hands and box-office men have lingoes of their own, and there is a considerable difference between the vocabulary of a high-toned Broadway actor and that of a hoofer (dancer) who grinds, bumps, and strips (i.e. rotates her hips, follows with a sharp, sensuous upheaval of her backside, and then sheds all her clothes save a G-string) in burlesque.

From a lifetime spent in the world of theatre and music, Edward Marks gathered some of the obsolete slang and quaint lore associated with Broadway in the early part of the century.

    Cocktail aisle seat   Augustin Daly always seated his friends down front on the aisle, so they could get more easily to the bar at inter-mission.

Histe the rag   Gallery urchin's cry to raise the curtain.

Candy butchers   Hawkers in burlesque houses, who plugged their wares in raucous, murderous English.

Fluffy ruffles   A summery female character, wearing white ruffled shirtwaist and short skirt in a Frohman production.

Musical mokes   Black-face musical minstrel act, playing various in-struments.

An onion ballad   A tear jerker.

Sidewalk conversation   Pair of wisecracking comedians doing a street scene.

Afterpiece   Short sketch that followed the olio in the old variety the-atres.

An Oscar Hammerstein   Applied to a minstrel high hat on parade.

She's no Fanny Essler   Poor dancer.

Hoofer   Minstrel dancer.

Grecian bend   An old stylish walk, wearing a bustle extending far be-hind, and carrying a parasol in front, giving the figure an exaggerated bend.

Wall Street angels   Theatrical promoters or backers.

Fall guy   Easy mark.

Bedroom songs   Suggestive lyric.

Revelry rags   Dressed to kill.

Bladder   Dissipated female trouper.

Ten per, and cakes   A "ham" actor's salary.

Blood and thunder   Old Bowery dramas.

The nut   Overhead expenses for a show.

Wildcatting a show   Sizing up the town, then booking it.

Snipe the town   Billing the town (with posters).

Turkey   A barnstorming theatrical troupe hastily organized around Thanksgiving.

Milkmen's matinee   Variety shows in early Western mining camps which ran until four in the morning.

First-part ladies   Early variety theatres opened shows with female minstrel first part. After sitting in the ensemble, first-part ladies sold drinks on commission to patrons in the boxes.

The Reds   Choice seats near stage of a tent show.

A short life and a merry one   Reference to short-lived actors.

He's gone with Barnum   He has passed on.

In the Vineyard of the Lord

Just as the Inuit of the far North have two dozen words for snow, theatre folk have scores of expressions for being drunk. Edward Marks, claiming that there are fifty others he lacks the space for, selected the following.

I was—pickled, pie-eyed, cock-eyed, bleary-eyed, glassy-eyed, ossified, spiffed, spifflocated, canned, inebriated, intoxicated, potted, plastered, oiled, boiled, half seas over, on a bender, on a toot, on a bat, on a tear, on a binge, tight, full, high, blotto, stewed, lit, embalmed, ginnied, soused, tanked, shicker, gesoffen happy, fried, passed out, out cold, boozy, besotted, loaded, edge on, bun on, liquored, three sheets to the wind, stiff, under the influence, worshipped at the feet of Bacchus, in my cups, I had a tide aboard.

Fighting Words

Bernard Sobel, longtime publicist for Florenz Ziegfeld and author of several books, saw a connection between the aggressive terms of theatrical argot and the competitive, precarious nature of the profession. In an article called "The Language of the Theatre" (in The Bookman, *April 1929) Sobel wrote the following.*

The stage is perhaps the most highly personalized of all professions. An actor must look to his rights as a lioness guards her cubs. His intelligence, as well as his physical assets, from the color of his hair to the sound of his voice, must be exploited, developed, and embellished to ensure and maintain his success. Thus, every theatrical performance is, in a sense, a matter of internecine warfare, a warfare waged under the very eyes of the audience and in the restricted areas of dialogue, action, and scene. Simply expressed, this means that each player, all the while that he is working for the general success of the play and co-operating with his fellow-players, must, by the very nature of conditions, work paradoxically against them, in order to bring himself forward as prominently as possible. He must personally stand out as an emergent figure in something of which he is only a part, often a small part, this being his only way of winning fame, position, and salary.

The ruthlessness of the struggle is nowhere better indicated than in the general use of the term "kill it," which the stage seems to have appropriated for itself. One electrician takes pride in having coined the expression and getting laughs on "kill yourself" which means merely "black out" and "work on your own."

The actor's devices for curbing, obscuring, and "killing" his fellow players are many, most of them definitely indicated in stage argot. The actor, for instance, who backs up continually while playing, in order to keep his own face to the audience, while pushing his associate in the background, is often told to "come into America," that is, stand still and keep within bounds.

An actor who distracts the attention of the audience by fumbling with his clothes, while someone else is trying to get a laugh is "catching flies." "Cue-biting" means snapping off the lines of the preceding speech in order to destroy their efficacy. A star can avail himself of this device to "step on" his laughs. The actor who maneuvers for the center of the stage is a "stage hog" or "spot-light hunter." "To dry a man up" is to give him the wrong cue; to crab the lines, "laying the skids." Forgetting the lines entirely is "to balloon" or "make an ascension" and thus "stick" or "corpse" the other player. "Milking the audience" is to over-play for applause. A sweetheart in the flies who keeps shouting, "Take another bow, dearie," is called a "bow-teller."

A "plant" is a person stationed in the audience who works with the actor on stage. "Ad-libbing" is improvising. "When Jones got lost back stage I had to ad-lib all over the place until he came on."

Some years ago when Duffy and Sweeney, two vaudeville comedians, were about to start on a long tour, E. F. Albee strove to induce them to take out a membership in the National Vaudeville Association Club. "You have all the privileges of the club," Mr. Albee insisted, "and likewise, in case of death, you have the advantages of a paid up insurance policy for $1000."

The actors were finally induced to take out the policy and signed up and started on their tour. Less than a week after, they sent this telegram to Mr. Albee: "Send out the $1000 quick. We died last night in New Orleans."

Eternal Optimist

In the fall of 1930, one year after the Wall Street crash, columnist Ward Morehouse interviewed A. H. Woods (1870–1951), the Hungarian-born ex-garment worker from the Lower East Side, who became one of the biggest Broadway producers. Like some of his Hollywood counterparts, Woods was noted for his picturesque turn of phrase, which Morehouse captured.

He'd summoned me to the Eltinge Theatre and I found him in his swivel chair, his feet upon his desk. He blew smoke at me from his cigar as he gazed into the cool depths of his great jade ring.

"Sweetheart," he said, "show business is lousy. I've had two hits this year, but where are they now? You call *Grand Hotel* a hit, don't you? And maybe you call *Once in a Lifetime* a hit. I had 'em both but I ain't got them. They were both right here on this desk and I let 'em go. Somebody else makes the million. *Grand Hotel* was mine for eighteen months. Paid $1,500 advance and then I let it slip away . . . Who is that fellow Herman Shumlin, anyway? [He produced *Grand Hotel*, the one that got away.] Did he play for me in *The Great Express Robbery*, or was he in *The Yellow Ticket*? . . . Things are bound to get better, sucker. If they don't I'm going to revive *The Littlest Rebel* with Mary Miles Minter, or put out an all-star cast in *Ladies Night in a Turkish Bath*."

Cigar smoke now hung in a blue haze about his head but his voice came through clearly:

"Watch for that new one of mine, sucker. It's called A *Farewell to Arms* and it's going to be all right."

A. H. Woods' theatrical empire fell apart not long thereafter.

In Translation

On January 30, 1930, the Manchester *Guardian* reprinted the following headline for *Variety*:

> Pash Flaps M.C.
> Fan Clubs Rated
> Worthless to Theatres
> As B.O. Gag

The newspaper then translated for its British readers the intention of this code "to convey the assurance that impassioned young women (flaps, flappers), organized into clubs because of their admiration for the master of ceremonies (usually the leader of the orchestra), have been found useless as a device for increasing box office receipts."

Word Gourmet

In an obituary of Sime Silverman ran by his newspaper on September 16,
1933, Epes W. Sargent wrote that in the beginning Variety *was written in*
the English language, but that it never really caught on until Sime changed
the style "and wrote as a majority of the actors of that day spoke. . . . It
was not that he could not write English, but that most Variety *actors of*
that day did not speak it." Even before his death, Silverman's original con-
tributions to the language were taken seriously. In the fairly upscale literary
magazine The Bookman (*December 1930*), *Hiram Motherwell wrote what*
almost amounts to a fan letter.

Of all these American languages, surely none is richer or more responsive
than that of Lobster Alley—which is to say the theatrical section of New
York—as it has grown under the patronage and guidance of the weekly
newspaper, *Variety*, and of its inspired editor, Sime Silverman.

Variety is one of the truly great newspapers of America. None can sur-
pass it in the abundance, accuracy, and timeliness of news carried, and,
above all, in editorial honesty and courage. Here, however, I am writing of
Variety not as a purveyor of news but as a creator of language—yes, of literature. For by all accepted standards some of the best writing in *Variety*
is literature. To those belonging to its group it conveys its message swiftly
and concisely in living words which evoke clear images and quick emotional response.

For the sake of brevity and directness, *Variety* is always willing to coin
a word. Its readiness to innovate new verbs used to panic me but now I
ecstasize over it. And its novel nouns invariably have color or flavor. Which
expression (provided you know the language) do you prefer: "a great deal
of money," or "heavy sugar"; "jokes in questionable taste," or "blue gags?"
Are you not saddened by the fact that Times Square hotel biz is on the
terrific fritz?

The concise expressions in which *Variety* abounds (whether picked up
from the Rialto or injected into Broadway's speech) are a delight to the
gourmet of words. Instead of stating that a certain play is a financial failure
it reports laconically, "show looks floppo." Handsome guides hired by dude
ranches to provide a touch of romance for rich eastern women as "S.A.
[Sex Appeal] cowboys." "Dirt in shorts" is action or dialogue in one-reel
films which might offend the audience's sensibilities. The difficulty in de-
fining such dirt derives from the fact that "what the acute town's self-
appointed dick might sense as dirt, after it has passed through years on the

stage with nothing but laughs greeting it, is something the producers cannot anticipate."

Functional Literacy

After an interval of forty-one years Ruth Gordon ran into Marcel Pagnol
at Arthur Rubinstein's house.

"Do you speak English now?" She remembered talking to him all those
years ago.

"No, but I can read it," replied the French playwright. "I read Shakespeare very well. *Variety* I still cannot read."

Whoopee

Like Sime Silverman and his writers on *Variety*, Walter Winchell made a
palpable impact on the American language. But because *Variety* is still
very much alive, the newspaper has had a more enduring and ever-changing
influence on showbiz lingo than the dead columnist. In 1933, the year of
Sime Silverman's death, Winchell was ranked by publisher and lexicogra-
pher W. J. Funk among the most fecund originators of slang—the others
included Johnny O'Connor and Jack Conway (also on the staff of *Variety*), Tad Dorgan, the cartoonist; Damon Runyon, George Ade, Ring
Lardner, Arthur (Bugs) Baer, Rube Goldberg, Johnny Stanley and Johnny
Lyman, Wilson Mizner and Milt Gross.

But most of the famous Winchellisms—*Chicagorilla* or *intelligentlemen*,
for example—passed with the age, even before he did. Winchell christened
Broadway the Hardened Artery, and wrote about America's Squeakeheart
and Hard-Times Square; he said Joosh for Jewish; moom-pitcher for motion picture; Park Rowgue for a newspaperman. One of his favorite expressions was "making whoopee." When some learned scholars showed that
whoopee was an old word going back to the fifteenth century and used by
Mark Twain and Kipling, the columnist replied:

"They contend *whoopee* is older than Shakespeare. Well, all right. I
never claimed it, anyhow. But let 'em take *makin' whoopee* from me, and
look out!"

But time seems to have taken care of that, too: nobody is makin' whoopee
much any more.

Nose to Nose

One of the more famous stories told about Jimmy Durante has John Barrymore coming backstage at the Club Durant, expressing admiration for his acting.

"You know, Jimmy," said The Face to The Nose, "some day you ought to play Hamlet."

"Ta hell with 'em small towns," came back Jimmy with total sincerity, "Noo Yawk's the only place for me."

Another exchange supposed to have taken place aboard the *Conte di Savoie:* Durante ran into the Queen of Spain. After they were introduced, the comedian was on his best behavior:

"Queen, it's a plesha, I tella ya, it's a plesha."

"You're very amusing," said her majesty graciously.

"Likewise, Queen, likewise."

Expert Linguist

Clifton Fadiman recalls the time when Jimmy Durante was one of the guest experts on his radio program, Information Please.

Hoping for some typically Durantean entanglement with the English language, I asked the experts, "Can you touch your scapula with your patella?" Jimmy's comment was unexpected:

"I hope your program ain't getting off-color."

Separated by a Common Language

It was Oscar Wilde who had observed that "the English have really everything in common with the Americans, except of course language." And it was that other Oscar—Levant—who accused Vernon Duke, the Russian-born composer with a British accent: "You speak with a monocle in your throat."

Plays transferred across the Atlantic often face a problem of translation or the lack of it. George Ade protested in vain when in 1908 the London producers of *The College Widow*, his popular play about American college football, insisted on distributing a glossary with the program, so that audiences could decipher the text scene by scene. "Put up a holler," became "indignantly protested," "a web-footed Rube," was turned into "an uncouth countryman," "the tall grass," into "the country, the far west," the "campus" into the "college lawn," the "rush line" into "the forwards in football," while "bucking the line," it was explained as "football slang, meaning breaking through the line."

Since the play was set in Ade's native Indiana, there was a booklet with pictures which explained about Hoosier "types" and took pains to point out that Mr. Ade was merely humorous, not anatomical, when he described one of the characters as a "prominent" waitress.

Balls to You

Until 1968 all plays, homegrown and foreign, performed on an English stage were required to be submitted to the Lord Chamberlain for licensing. Readers working in this government office, a relic from Tudor times, readily censored obscenities, blasphemies, and anything that might offend the monarch. They also liked to be helpful with creative suggestions about replacing their own deletions. Uta Hagen recalls six or seven pages of changes when she went to London with *Who's Afraid of Virginia Woolf?* "Out of a number of 'Jesus Christs' we were allowed three. I thought it wonderful that we were allowed some and not others." When her entrance line, "Jesus H. Christ!" was censored, Edward Albee changed it to "Mary H. Magdalen," which the Lord Chamberlain was gracious enough to accept. But Hagen, having played it one way for a year, was too nervous on opening night about the changes in London and she blew it: "Jesus H. Magdalen!" she swore.

The Lord Chamberlain allowed "hump the hostess," because "hump" occurred in Shakespeare, though undoubtedly without the hostess. But scrotum—a perfectly clean, clinical word—failed the Shakespearean test. Arthur Hill, playing George, was required to say that he had had a little operation "on the underside of his privacies." He tried, but after one night, when he struggled with the quaint expression, he turned pale and afterward told Uta Hagen: "I'm never going to say that again, that's just awful."

On one issue, the American side scored a clear victory. His Lordship felt particular about the phrase "She was his right ball." After various British suggestions to substitute testicle or nut, Edward Albee remembered the old Southern expression of having a "right bawl," or a good cry. He simply changed the spelling, and it passed.

CHAPTER 4

Characters

In the Sauce

Actors have more drinking stories than any other profession except perhaps journalists. Some of the famous ones are attached to Junius Brutus Booth. One archetypal anecdote has the father of John Wilkes and Edwin stumbling about backstage, trying to find his way, when he encountered the anxious manager of the theatre. "Where's the stage," the actor asked not very reassuringly, "and what's the play?"

During a performance of his Othello, the elder Booth was taking longer than usual over his death scene. Just when the audience thought he had finally given up the ghost, they were startled to see the actor staggering to his feet and peering out into the auditorium: "How did you like that?" he wanted to know.

Booth's celebrated aquiline profile was destroyed by a brawl during which his nose was broken. When a female admirer once remarked that she could not get over his nose, Booth is said to have replied: "No wonder, madam, for the bridge is gone."

Sobering Up

The elder Booth was not the first or last among actors to be famous for his drinking. At one point he was playing King Henry IV at the Old Bowery Theatre, and rather deep in the sauce, he began to stumble in his very first scene. After a few minutes, the star was not too drunk to pick up a few hisses coming from the gallery. He suddenly stopped, and advanced to the footlights:

"Ladies and gentlemen," he said to the well-behaved front rows of the orchestra, "you see that I am not in good condition to play tonight. But if you will only wait five minutes, while I go behind the scenes to cool my head in a pail of water, I'll come out and show you the damnedest King Henry you ever saw in your life!"

Suckered

It was not often that P. T. Barnum failed to please his public, but he describes one occasion when he collected an impressionist.

An actor, named La Rue, presented himself as an imitator of celebrated histrionic personages, including Macready, Forrest, Kemble, the elder Booth, Kean, Hamblin, and others. Taking him into the green-room for a private rehearsal, and finding his imitations excellent, I engaged him. For three nights he gave great satisfaction, but early in the fourth evening he staggered into the Museum so drunk that he could hardly stand, and in half an hour he must be on the stage! Calling an assistant, we took La Rue between us, and marched him up Broadway as far as Chambers Street, and back to the lower end of the Park, hoping to sober him. At this point we put his head under a pump, and gave him a good ducking, with visible beneficial effect,—then a walk around the Park, and another ducking,— when he assured me that he should be able to give his imitations "to a charm."

"You drunken brute," said I, "if you fail, and disappoint my audience, I will throw you out of the window."

He declared that he was "all right," and I led him behind the scenes, where I waited with considerable trepidation to watch his movements on the stage. He began by saying:

"Ladies and gentlemen: I will now give you an imitation of Mr. Booth, the eminent tragedian."

His tongue was thick, his language somewhat incoherent, and I had great misgivings as he proceeded; but as no token of disapprobation came from the audience, I began to hope he would go through with his parts without exciting suspicion of his condition. But before he had half finished his representation of Booth, in the soliloquy in the opening act of Richard III., the house discovered that he was very drunk, and began to hiss. This only seemed to stimulate him to make an effort to appear sober, which, as is usual in such cases, only made matters worse, and the hissing increased. I lost all patience, and going on the stage and taking the drunken fellow by the collar, I apologized to the audience, assuring them that he should not appear before them again. I was about to march him off, when he stepped to the front, and said:

"Ladies and gentlemen: Mr. Booth often appeared on the stage in a state of inebriety, and I was simply giving you a truthful representation of him on such occasions. I beg to be permitted to proceed with my imitations."

The audience at once supposed it was all right, and cried out, "go on, go on"; which he did, and at every imitation of Booth, whether as Richard, Shylock, or Sir Giles Overreach, he received a hearty round of applause. I was quite delighted with his success; but when he came to imitate Forrest and Hamblin, necessarily representing them as drunk also, the audience could be no longer deluded; the hissing was almost deafening, and I was forced to lead the actor off. It was his last appearance on my stage.

Falling Off

Tallulah Bankhead's contribution to the Allied war effort included going on the wagon. She stayed on it for four years. Then, just before V-day, she had her first drink in several years. Reminded by a friend that the war was still going on, she replied: "I know, darling, but I've already conceded the victory!"

Sobering Fact

For the last fifteen years of his life Will McConnell was a strict teetotaler. In his early days, according to one euphemist, "a too excessive geniality interfered with his prosperity." In exact terms, McConnell had lost control of three theatres that he had partly owned.

"I should think you would find it hard not to drink, thrown with the people you meet," one of his friends remarked.

"It's no trouble at all to stop drinking," said the ex-manager ruefully, "after you've drunk up three theatres."

A Jack of All Trades

John S. Potter (1809–69) was famous in the nineteenth century as a sort of Johnny Appleseed, who built a vast array of theatre buildings all over the United States. While performing in California in the earliest gold-rush days, the veteran actor Walter Leman came across "the ubiquitous, the ever-persuasive, the always-promising John S. Potter."

Mr. Potter was a most remarkable character; he was gifted with the organ of hope so largely that he could see a silver lining to the darkest cloud in the managerial horizon, and, like Micawber, was always certain of something "turning up." But the main difficulty with him was his inability to inspire his actors and actresses with the same buoyant feeling.

He had opened I don't know how many theatres in the West and in the Mississippi Valley before he reached California, and during his California career he had opened as many more; he was always in management; he had the reputation in the West of being able to keep his forces together without any treasure-chest or commissariat, simply by his persuasive tongue.

A friend once found him complaining that but for the *ambition* of his company his season would have been prosperous, and being asked what their ambition had to do with their failure, he replied that if they hadn't been so ambitious for their salary he could have made money and kept them all together. Another time, to a poor histrion who begged in vain for a dollar or two of his unpaid salary, he replied: "What, ask for salary when blackberries are ripe!"

He would any time play any part in the drama at ten minutes' notice, in a black cloak and wig, and would get the curtain up and down again, shift all the scenes, attend to the properties during the performance, and within five minutes or less after the fall of the curtain would have the receipts from the box office in his pocket, and be out of sight of his "ambitious" actors, who waited around in vain for "salary."

The Joker

Toward the end of his life, Joseph Jefferson recalled one of those fellow Thespians who, in Oscar Wilde's words, put more of his talent into his life than into his art.

Among the well-remembered characters of my dramatic life was an actor named Salisbury. The only influence that he exerted upon the stage during his career was, I regret to say, anything but a good one. "Guying" was formerly a slang term, but it has of late years become a technical one for trifling with a part upon the stage. The art of guying was Mr. Salisbury's forte, and it was the only thing that he did well. Life was one huge joke to him: he treated nothing seriously. He was the delight of actors and the bane of managers. It is related of him that he once sent a telegram to Mr. Rice of the Chicago Theater applying for an engagement. The manager sent back this answer: "I would not engage you if you would come for nothing"; to which Salisbury replied: "Terms accepted. Will be with you to-morrow."

This man's memory was so wonderful that it was almost impossible to ask him a question without getting a Shakespearean quotation in reply. If he was imperfect in his part, which was generally the case with him, he would interpolate speeches from other characters, talking the most absurd nonsense, and turning a serious scene into ridicule. Sometimes the audience, detecting this impertinence, would hiss. This rebuke was the only thing that would check him, for any slight put upon himself was keenly felt; but the next night the chastisement would be forgotten, and he would repeat his indiscretion. It was said of him that he was generous to a fault; and I think he must have been, for he never paid his washerwoman. One morning the poor old laundress was dunning him for her hard earnings. He was standing at the stage door, surrounded by a circle of admirers, and turning furiously upon the old woman, he paraphrased Macbeth's speech to the ghost of Banquo in the following words: "Avaunt, and quit my sight! Thy tubs are marrowless; there is no starch in my fine shirts that thou didst glare withal! Approach thou like the Russian manager, the Hyrcan critic, or the 'Old Rye whisky-us'; or, be alive again, and make it salary day. If, trembling then, I do inhibit thee, confess me but a babe of a Salisbury." The laundress fled in despair, only too glad to escape unpaid from the supposed lunatic.

The Uncrushable Tragedian

The younger Sothern (E. H.) recalls how his father (E. A.), casting about for a quaint character, managed to catch one of the great eccentrics of New York.

One night during the summer of 1875, in company with my father and his manager, Horace Wall, I attended the walking contest at the old Madison Square Garden. Edward Payson Weston was the attraction, and a great crowd cheered him on. My father was shortly to produce Henry J. Byron's comedy, *The Prompter's Box*, which he had rechristened, *The Crushed*

Tragedian. The type of old actor he wished to portray he was well acquainted with, for he had encountered many such a quaint genius during his early experiences in England. He had not, however, determined on the exact make-up for his part, and his mind was busy trying to reduce the features and the peculiarities of his various models to a single type—a sort of composite picture. Suddenly, on this evening, he stopped short in his talk with Horace Wall and said: "Look, there is the crushed tragedian."

"Where?" said Wall.

My father pointed to a man twenty feet away. "It is Fitzaltamont himself," said he.

"That is the Count Johannes," replied Wall, and he proceeded to explain that Johannes, who was truly no count but one plain unvarnished Jones, had of late exploited himself in Shakespeare's tragedies to the vast delight of persons given to the hurling of missiles, and that it was the custom of the "count" to perform behind a huge net which was stretched between himself and his admirers so that their hysterical tributes of eggs, potatoes, and other edibles might be received (if in discussing the conflict between genius and enthusiasm one may employ the language of the ring) without Hamlet's melancholy being enhanced by a black eye, Othello's revenge impeded by the tapping of his claret, or Macbeth's apostrophe to the bloody dagger interrupted by a blow on the bread-basket.

Then and there my father decided that here was the very type for which he had been seeking. We followed Count Johannes about the Garden for an hour, my father noting his manner, his gesture, his poses. So well did he absorb the man-of-title's peculiar graces that, when a few months later *The Crushed Tragedian* had won the favor of the town, that nobleman became so incensed at the portraiture that, to my father's great delight and the mirth of the community, he instituted an action for libel.

Dressed to Kill

The legal firm of William Howe and Abraham Hummel was notorious in New York during the Gilded Age for handling the most difficult cases for Broadway's low life, which of course included the theatrical world. Howe, the older and larger of this Laurel and Hardy duo, was known for his extravagant costumes and courtroom histrionics, portrayed by Richard H. Rovere in a 1946 New Yorker profile.

"Old Bill" Howe was a stocky man weighing nearly three hundred pounds, with closely cropped white hair and moustache—pompous, gruff, and with immense assurance. But apart from his versatility in the tricks of the legal trade, his face was not so much his fortune as his costume. He wore it, I suppose, in part to advertise himself and in part because it was his idea of elegance. Did not Mark Twain habitually wear a white Panama suit even in London?

Howe's personal application of the famous maxim of Polonius resulted in an appearance like nothing else on earth—a cross between Coney Island barker and costermonger. In imitation, it was said of Commodore Perry, he always wore a blue yachting cap, sometimes a navigator's blue coat and white trousers, but more often a loudly checked brown suit, with low-cut vest, displaying the starched bosom of a bright pink shirt, and a pink collar innocent of tie, in place of which he sported a gigantic diamond stud, with others of equal size adorning his chest. These he changed on occasion to pearls in the afternoon. Diamonds glittered upon his fingers; on his feet were either yachting shoes or dinky patent leathers with cloth uppers; in his lapel a rose or carnation; in his breast pocket a huge silk handkerchief into which he shed, with enormous effect, showers of crocodile tears while defending his clients.

Blackmail for Fun and Profit

Abe Hummel, the younger of these criminal lawyers (in both senses of that phrase), became the first entertainment lawyer on Broadway. He was more respected than feared as a civic figure (he is credited with dubbing the midtown section the Tenderloin); his disbarment and flight to Europe where he lived off his fortune until the mid-1920s just added to the legend, as Richard Rovere explains.

Hummel's methods as a divorce lawyer and his work as a blackmailer were an open secret through all the years he carried on. They were the subject of jokes in the newspapers and on the stage. "What's that?" a straight man would ask a vaudeville comic when a noise like thunder sounded from the wings. "Why, that's Howe & Hummel filing an affidavit," the comic said. The gag was not obscure, at least to the kind of people who could afford musical comedies. Howe & Hummel affidavits were as much a hazard of philandering as the house detective. Generally, they charged seduction under the promise of marriage, and they were redeemable by the alleged seducers at sums varying between five and ten thousand dollars, cash, half of which went to the disappointed young ladies and half to Howe & Hummel. Lawyers still alive [in 1946] who represented the victims of this blackmail estimate that the number of men shaken down by Hummel between 1885 and 1905 must have been well up in the hundreds. It is a curious fact, though, that while everyone knew what Hummel was up to and everyone knew of a victim or two, the total number of Hummel's victims and the identity of all but a handful has never been known or recorded.

Hummel was the most systematic of blackmailers. He did not sit idly by waiting for soiled doves to fly in his office window. He was constantly beating the bushes for fresh affidavit copy. He assigned two of his employees, Lewis Allan and Abraham Kaffenburgh, who was his nephew, to go out along Broadway and the Bowery in search of unexploited seductions. Allan and Kaffenburgh became as familiar figures backstage as scene shifters and wardrobe mistresses. They would make the acquaintance of young actresses and chorus girls and explain to them how, by friendly co-operation with Howe & Hummel, last year's infatuations could be converted into next year's fur coats. They had the girls rummaging around in their memories for old seductions the way antique dealers get home owners tearing up their attics in search of old glassware and ladderback chairs. When a girl came across with a likely story, she was escorted downtown to Hummel, who got the details from her and set them down in affidavit form. The existence of the affidavit would then be made known to the man named in it, and he was given his choice of breach-of-promise suit with wide publicity and with no details spared or a quick settlement. It was often charged that these affidavits were faked from start to finish and that Hummel was also the manager of a kind of badger game, in which his young women accomplices would contrive compromising situations in which they and their admirers might be advertently discovered. The most reliable authorities hold that this was never the case. The seductions described in the affidavits may not have been genuine seductions, the element of beguiled innocence being absent in most cases, nor is it likely that many real promises were breached; but it is doubtful if any of Hummel's victims ever paid for an adventure he had not had. In fact, George Gordon Battle, another lawyer who occasionally represented a victim of the racket, maintains that in many cases there was a kind of rough justice in the penalties Hummel imposed. "It was an exceedingly low business," Battle said recently, "but I'll have to say this about Abe: I never heard of his framing anyone, and I never heard of a case where the girl didn't get her half. Also, I don't think there were many cases in which there wasn't something to be said for the girl's side of the story. What Abe got was pure blackmail money, but it didn't seem to me too unjust that the girls should get what they did out of it."

Hummel's victims sometimes became his clients. This happened in the case of Stanford White, who, after twice being forced to pony up, decided that it would be sound economy to pay Howe & Hummel a regular retainer to keep down his expenses. Hummel tried to blackmail young John Barrymore, but Barrymore was blackmail-proof. He would put no price at all on virtue. He got to like Hummel, though, and the two became friends. Hummel became his lawyer, drawing up his contracts with managers and counseling him in his first divorce.

When the Saints Come Marching In

David Belasco adopted the clerical collar, which became his trademark, as a tribute to a childhood idol, Father McGuire. "It was hero-worship that first led him to imitate the Father in the manner of dress," gossip columnist Sidney Skolsky wrote. "Later he probably realized that a saint in the theatrical profession would be a novelty."

On the other hand, Texas Guinan, the famous nightclub owner during Prohibition, was raised by nuns at Loretta Convent in Waco, Texas. Mary Louise Guinan, as she was known then, had six uncles who served as Catholic priests. She did have one thing in common with the clerical producer. Belasco was once grazed by a bullet on his forehead, when he was allegedly trying to defend a woman's honor. Texas Guinan had also been shot once—by herself. It was a stage accident while she was on the road in *The Gay Musician*. She was rushed to a hospital in a locomotive engine and she had a steel tube in her side for over a year. Afterwards, Texas was only comfortable when sitting on two chairs.

Frank Fay, for all his failings, or perhaps because of them, was a devout Catholic. During the run of *Harvey*, a member of the cast wanted to ingratiate himself with the star of the show by accompanying him to Mass every morning. After the play finally ended, so did this man's devotions. Running into him a while later at the Lambs' Club bar, Fay pointed him out: "Look at that bastard: a run-of-the-play Catholic."

The Fabulous Mizner

Even in the Broadway world of larger-than-life characters, Wilson Mizner stood out. Born in California in 1876, he was successively (and sometimes simultaneously) a gold-rush prospector and gambler, boxing promoter, actor, collaborator, art dealer, Florida real estate developer, and screenwriter in Hollywood where he also owned at one time the Brown Derby. "He was fundamentally a confidence man," wrote one of his biographers Alva Johnson, "whom circumstances occasionally induced to go straight." Above all,

Mizner was known as the dean of wits in the generation before the Algon-
quin Round Table. "Although he wrote practically nothing," according to
Johnson, "he is probably quoted more than any other American of this
century." In The Fabulous Wilson Mizner (1935), *Edward Dean Sullivan*
gives us a snapshot of his grand entrance on the White Way.

Early in 1905 Wilson Mizner arrived in New York and made his first contact with Broadway. It was less of a meeting than a head-on collision, for
Broadway was just what this veteran of the wilds required—and a new and
most amusing giant of the Arctic brotherhood got attention with his first
burst of laughter.

All his natural contacts, through his California antecedents, would direct
his steps to Fifth Avenue, but his Klondike and Nevada credentials led
him straight to theatrical, newspaper and gambling welcomers. And he had
not reached the end of his first week of this fortuitous invasion of the Big
Town when Broadway began to look up and pay homage to a genuinely ab-
sorbing personality.

At the moment poems and stories of the Klondike cluttered the magazines and newspapers and in Mizner, those who ever seek the inside detail
of the news of the hour found the perfect Arctic witness and a masterful
raconteur. Regarding the distant source of that golden substance which
had its great scattering ground in the Broadway of that day, Mizner told
all that was to be revealed, in song and story.

Those whose business it is to record matters of interest for the newspapers began to quote a genial wit and those who want to hear nothing unless it is new, odd or interesting sought out Mizner's table and made pro-
visions for getting him near a piano wherever possible. Two contacts had
a special value in making of Wilson Mizner the talk of the town by 1907—
Paul Armstrong, playwright, and Frank Ward O'Malley, New York's greatest reporter.

The sardonic Armstrong, seeing immediate dramatic opportunity in the
store of underworld lore known to Mizner, taunted him into work that was
congenial and brought prompt prestige on Broadway. O'Malley, delighted
with this brilliant newcomer, sent his name spinning into the presses
when at work and took him everywhere during his hours of ease.

Ever anxious to avoid work in any of its *nuances*, Mizner was largely an
oral dramatist. Six talks with Paul Armstrong provided the punch lines
which put over *Alias Jimmy Valentine*, one of the smash hits of the day,
and promptly Mizner was besieged by other playwrights, seeking his collaboration. With George Bronson Howard he wrote *The Only Law* and as
soon as he was free he was lured by Paul Armstrong into further collabora-

tion to produce *The Deep Purple*, a sensational exposé of the badger game which marked a new high for frankness in the American theatre.

Never disturbed about either his reputation or associations, the utter frankness of Mizner regarding matters usually cloaked in Victorian obscurity early distinguished him. Always regarding himself as a drifter and ne'er-do-well, Mizner had the sympathy and patience which attracted all sorts of unconventional people, and from such contacts came some of his keenest and most applauded mots.

Although Mizner coined the warning: "Never give a sucker an even break" he was known as the easiest touch on Broadway. "I never worry about money," he once explained, "unless a rich man comes anywhere near me. Then I can't sleep until I find a way to get in on the take."

It was Phineas Barnum who declared that "there's a sucker born every minute." To this Mizner added—"and two to take him." As far back as his Barbary Coast Days in San Francisco, Mizner had used the greeting, "Hello Sucker" which, during the prohibition era in New York, was the greeting of Texas Guinan in Manhattan's costliest *covert* joints.

"In fact," Mizner said, "everyone in the world is a fall guy or sucker for nearly anything outside of his own racket. I've bitten off more than I could chew, or sign the check for, a thousand times and therefore anything I do is in self-defense. The first dawn of smartness is to stop trying things you don't know anything about—especially if they run to anything over a dollar."

House Rules

At the height of his theatrical career, Wilson Mizner took over management of the Strand Hotel, where he provided temporary shelter to fifty homeless characters of the Broadway area. Anarchy reigned, and after a while Mizner was forced to post some rules in each room and throughout the hotel. One read: "NO OPIUM SMOKING IN THE ELEVATORS!" And another: "CARRY OUT YOUR OWN DEAD!"

Playing Himself

Wilson Mizner was such an obvious character that he was often stolen by hard-up scribes toiling on Broadway and in Hollywood. Anita Loos made use of him in the 1936 film *San Francisco;* and several Miznerisms (including the smash line "I may vomit,") turn up in *The Man Who Came to Dinner* (1939), which Moss Hart and George S. Kaufman wrote around several well-known theatrical figures. In that play everybody knew and was delighted by the Falstaffian character of Sheridan Whiteside, based on Alexander Woollcott, the eccentric critic of the *New York Times* under whom Kaufman began his journalistic career.

Woollcott had urged, bullied, and cajoled Moss Hart for a couple of years to immortalize him, and was so pleased when Hart read him the script that he began to consider the possibility of playing Whiteside, who spends the play in a wheelchair.

"I'm perfect for the part," he declared to a doubting Kaufman, "I'm the only man you know who can strut sitting down."

In the end, Monty Woolley quit his job at the Yale Drama School to create the role on Broadway. When the play became the hit of the season, a Boston lawyer sued that the character of Sheridan Whiteside had been plagiarized from a play *Sticks and Stones*.

"It will probably turn out, Aleck," wrote Kaufman to Woollcott, "that you got it from there too."

Woollcott did end up playing in the third road company of *The Man Who Came to Dinner* and was enormously popular until he had to leave the tour because of a heart attack. An overweight man of uncertain sexuality, Woollcott the critic alternated between vitriol and treacle; Woollcott the man was described as between Nero and St. Francis of Assisi. He was more professional as a personality; as an actor he remained an enthusiastic amateur. Woollcott had already played himself almost a decade earlier in S. N. Behrman's *Brief Moment* (1931), in which the biggest laugh came when an actress railed at him:

"If you were a woman what a bitch you would have made."

Diamonds Are Forever

One of the immortal—and literally larger than life—characters forever associated with Broadway during the "age of plush" was the colorful Diamond Jim Brady. Apart from his appreciation of jewelry, which was his business, and theatre and women, he was one of the great eaters of all time. It took a grateful beneficiary of his amazing appetite, restaurant owner George Rector, to appraise this gourmand.

He was an odd character, and the first of the successful salesmen who utilized the bright lights of Broadway to promote the sale of his commodities. His name was derived from his jewelry, and when Diamond Jim had all his illumination in place, he looked like an excursion steamer at twilight. He had powerful diamonds in his shirt front that cast beams strong enough to sunburn an unwary pedestrian. He had diamonds in his cuffs and actually wore diamond suspender buttons, fore and aft. The fore may have been good taste, but the aft were parvenu. He wore diamonds on his fingers and there was a rumor that he had diamond bridge work. His vest buttons also were precious stones, and I think that when remonstrated with for his excessive display of gems, Mr. Brady remarked, "Them as has 'em wears 'em."

Although his business life led him among the bright lights, Diamond Jim never smoked or drank. But how he ate! He loved to be surrounded by handsome men and beautiful women at the table, and it was no unusual thing for us to lay covers for eight or ten guests of Mr. Brady. If they all kept their appointments, fine! If but two or three were able to be present, fine! And if nobody showed up but Diamond Jim, fine! Mr. Brady proceeded gravely to eat the ten dinners himself.

It is possible to obtain some idea of his terrific capacity by his average menu under normal conditions. When I say he never drank, I mean intoxicating beverages. His favorite drink was orange juice. I knew just what he wanted, and before he appeared at the table I always commandeered the most enormous carafe in the house. This was filled to the brim with orange juice and cracked ice. He tossed that off without quivering a chin. It was immediately replaced with a duplicate carafe, to be followed by a third, and possibly a fourth before the dinner was over and the last waiter had fainted in the arms of an exhausted chef.

The next item was oysters. Mr. Brady was very fond of seafood. He would eat two or three dozen Lynnhaven oysters, each measuring six inches from tip to tail, if an oyster has either. Wilson Mizner, observing Diamond Jim eating oysters, remarked, "Jim likes his oysters sprinkled with clams." Observing the same diner from a nearby listening post, Mr. Mizner also continued his observations with "Jim likes his sirloin steaks smothered in veal cutlets."

After Diamond Jim had nibbled daintily on three dozen papa oysters, it would be an even bet that he would order another dozen or so just to relieve the monotony. Then would follow a dozen hard-shell crabs, claws and all. There was no soup, which discounts Mizner's statement that Jim fanned the soup with his hat.

After the crabs, then would come the deluge of lobsters. Lobsters were Rector's specialty and I took special pride in serving none but the finest. Six or seven giants would suffice. Diamond Jim ate them like an expert and cracked their claws like a man. There was no waste except the actual bony structure, which was dropped gracefully aside. A bus boy removed the debris as rapidly as it accumulated, otherwise Diamond Jim would have been in the same fix as the American gunboat in China.

Anyway, we removed all the victims of Jim's dinner as fast as we could bring up the ambulances. Then he would order a steak and toy with it until it vanished. But steaks and chops were not his hobby. He loved seafood. Coffee, cakes, and pastry would follow. He selected his cakes carefully—in handfuls. When he pointed at a platter of French pastry he didn't mean any special piece of pastry. He meant the platter.

Then he would order a two-pound box of bonbons from the candy girl and pass them around among his guests. If any guest took a piece of the candy Diamond Jim would then order another two-pound box for himself. In fact, so great was his love of sweets that he bought a controlling interest in the biggest of candy factories of that time.

I almost forgot to add that when Diamond Jim had dinner in Rector's it was the usual prelude to an evening at the theatre. On the way to the show he would stop his cab at a store and purchase another two-pound box of candy manufactured by the company he controlled. That would be finished before the curtain rose, and it was nothing unusual for him to buy another box between acts. After the show he would return to Rector's for a midnight snack.

A Frank Exchange of Views

In the 1920s, when it was fashionable to break the law, knowing some of the big-time criminals amounted almost to chic. Walter Winchell was well aware of this and he tried to cultivate some of the better-known hoodlums. It was all in the line of being a reporter; besides, the columnist enjoyed the reputation that he had high sources in the underworld and could predict major showdowns and shootouts. His hour of glory came in September 1939, when Louis (Lepke) Buchalter, on the FBI's "most wanted list" for racketeering and murder, decided to surrender himself (holding a mezzuzah) through Winchell, who then phoned J. Edgar Hoover.

On an earlier occasion, the gossip columnist was walking down Broadway in the company of a well-known gangster, when he stopped to admire a roadster in a showroom window. The hood immediately offered to buy the automobile for him, but Winchell declined, citing that it might be interpreted as being in return for favors he had done for the outlaw.

"Favors?" the gangster laughed. "What favors could a little punk like you do a big guy like me?"

The Godfather

When Frank Costello was jailed for racketeering, he continued to live as lavishly in jail as he had done on the outside. As an example of his undiminished power, journalist Gay Talese tells the story of Costello's attorney, Edward Williams, visiting him and complaining that he had promised to take his parents that evening to *My Fair Lady* on their wedding anniversary, but his ticket agent failed to come through with the promised seats.

"Mr. Williams, you shoulda told me," said Costello in the great tradition, "maybe I coulda helped."

The lawyer could not figure out how his jailed client could get him the hottest tickets on Broadway with less than three hours to spare. Back at his hotel, Williams heard a rap on the door, and opening it, "a broad-shouldered man under a slouch hat grunted something, handed over an envelope containing four tickets to that evening's performance of *My Fair Lady*, then quickly disappeared down the hall."

In Medias Res

Alexander Incze emigrated from Hungary and for a while edited *Stage Magazine* in New York. He had loved the theatre all his life, but could not often afford prices on Broadway. He developed a notorious habit of turning up during one of the intermissions, and then slipping into the theatre unnoticed to watch the rest of the show. His critical judgment was valued by producers, and once in the 1940s Gilbert Miller sent him a script he was thinking of producing.

"I like the latter part," Incze told him, "but I don't think much of the first act."

"What do you know about first acts?" Miller retorted. "You've never seen one in your life."

How the Rich Get Richer

In the early days of television, Lester Lewis was producing a show called Hollywood Screentest, *which featured a guest star and also introduced good, but unknown stage actors to a wider audience. In the days before unions, Juliet Lewis, the producer's wife, did the costumes and makeup for the show.*

I had arranged to meet Edward Everett Horton at Brooks Costume early in the morning. Rehearsal did not start until 11, so I asked whether he would like to have breakfast with me.

"That would be delightful," he said. I picked up the tab, and we went to rehearse. Lester had ordered lunch to be brought in. By the end of the day, we were madly in love with this darling man, and Lester asked Horton:

"How would you like to have dinner with us?"

And he said he would be delighted. Off we went to Sardi's, where during dinner Eddie regaled us with wonderful stories. Afterward, we got a cab and dropped him off at his apartment on West 55th Street. When he got out of the cab, Eddie said:

"This has been the best day in my life."

Lester and I chuckled, but could not quite believe it literally, so one of us asked:

"Why do you say that?"

"I left my apartment this morning," said Eddie Horton, "with five dollars in my pocket, and after a wonderful day, I'm coming home with five dollars."

This was the man who owned the whole of Encino, California.

From then on the Lewises became fast friends with the star. One day, Lester walked into Sardi's and noticed that Edward Horton was having lunch with Dorothy and Richard Rodgers, whom Lewis also knew quite well. He accepted an invitation to join them for lunch. When the bill came, nobody reached for it, so Lester Lewis picked up the tab with a flourish:

"It's an honor," he said, "to pick up the check for two of the wealthiest men I know."

Legacy

The Actors' Fund of America to help needy theatre professionals was established in 1882, with Lester Wallack as its first president. Over the years, this charity has raised funds through benefits. There have been bequests, too, large and small, but none stranger perhaps than the legacy of Conrad Cantzen, who died seemingly penniless. Alan Brock, Hungarian-born actor and agent, told the following story originally in Playbill *(1965).*

Conrad Cantzen was in his seventies when he used to visit me in my office in the Palace Theatre building in New York. To most people he was just another broken-down actor looking for work, but to me he was a gentleman-actor in the finest Victorian tradition. I liked his neatness, his elaborate manners, his starched high collars and flowing ties.

That Cantzen was poor could be deduced from his clothes. They betrayed years of service. He usually wore brown corduroy trousers and jacket, and, in cold weather, an old-fashioned overcoat with shiny velvet collar. But he was particular—especially about his high-top shoes. They were always faultlessly polished, even to the hooks and laces. He'd wink when he'd tell me how far he could stretch a can of shoeblacking.

About shoes Cantzen was emphatic.

"It's an actor's business to see that he is always dressed in his best, and most important are shoes. They must always have a high polish and never be run-down at the heels. An actor can't hold his head up if his heels are run-down."

There was nothing really remarkable about all this—surely nothing to foretell that the old man would leave a legacy that would affect the lives of thousands of future actors and actresses.

Each time that Conrad Cantzen called, he made it a personal visit, not just the dull routine of making the rounds looking for work. His unending flow of anecdotes fascinated me. He had acted with many of the great of his day: Robert Mantell in *The Face in the Moonlight*, Effie Ellsler in *When Knighthood Was in Flower*, Charles Coburn in a long tour of classic repertory, Rudolf Schildkraut in *Gallery Gods*, Laurette Taylor in *Bird of Paradise*, Florence Reed in *The Shanghai Gesture*. His anecdotes were quiet and well-timed—no rushing a point or exaggerating the part that he himself had played. He seemed thoroughly content with having been a minor figure in the profession; to him it was the privilege of having been there, with *them*, that mattered.

One day Cantzen did get a job. He was selected by Walter Hampden, the distinguished actor-manager, to play a supporting role in Ibsen's *An Enemy of the People*. The play opened on February 15, 1937, to excellent notices and had a long run on Broadway. Then he went on the road with it, I went to Hollywood, and somehow our paths never crossed again.

The next time I heard of Conrad Cantzen was on June 29, 1945, when I read of his death in a New York newspaper. Mention was made of his career in the 1890s, that there had been later, intermittent engagements with many great stars of the American stage. His last weeks had been spent at St. Luke's Hospital. He died alone at the age of 78, with $11.85 in his pockets. But discovered among his papers in his room in Union City, N.J., was a bequest that amounted to $266,890.

Because I had always thought of Cantzen as an elderly actor down on his luck, my curiosity was aroused. I went to the offices of the Actors' Fund. There I learned the story. In his will Conrad Cantzen had made certain that his fellow actors would never again be obliged to look for work in run-down shoes.

"Many times I have been on my uppers," the will stated, "and the thinner the soles of my shoes were, the less courage I had to face the manager in looking for a job."

The bequest stipulated that any unemployed actor, by simple application to the Actors' Fund, could, twice yearly, be given a certificate exchangeable for footwear at an established shoe store in Manhattan. "There was no hint," according to the Actors' Fund biography of this unusual benefactor, "as to how he had acquired this money—the 18 savings accounts with balances amounting to close to $100,000, the $127,000 worth of corporate stocks. It was simply there, the sum total of all the meals he had not eaten, the drinks he had denied himself, the rooms he had not occupied on the road, preferring to spend the night in railroad stations, bus terminals or even parks."

Jazzman

One of the brash jazzmen in the thirties and forties, Eddie Condon arrived one day at a Broadway theatre to play guitar with the stage band. He was fired on the spot for wearing a brown shoe on one foot and a black one on the other. "What's the difference?" Eddie protested, "I keep one foot under the chair." Later, when he had his own band, Eddie Condon had just two rules: "Everybody must wear shoes. And anybody who falls off the bandstand must get back without help."

Condon had little patience for high-brow critics who wrote learned analyses of jazz. He said of French critic Hugues Panassie, who was usually very complimentary about Eddie's playing:

"Why should that bum come over here and tell us how to play jazz? I've never gone over to France and told them how to jump on a grape, have I?"

Sweetness and Light

Dorothy Parker was bored listening to an actress who had not been on the stage for twenty years but was gushing forth sentiments like, "I just simply loathe the idea of leaving the theatre, I'm so wedded to it." Miss Parker stopped her dead by asking: "Why don't you sue, then, for non-support?"

Dorothy Parker poured acid not only on the stage and the actors on it. When she got a chance to insult an audience member, she grabbed it.

"Say, aren't you Dorothy Parker?" the woman asked from the next seat.
"Yes, do you mind?" the writer returned to her notes.

Even Cheaper Second-hand

Stella Adler would have sympathized with Queen Victoria, who told
William Gladstone to refrain from addressing her as if she were at a public meeting. At a dinner party given by Max Reinhardt during the late
1930s, the conversation was being monopolized by the German writer
Franz Werfel, who held forth on a variety of subjects that shut out others
at the table.

"Please Mr. Werfel," Stella Adler interrupted him in that voice that
hundreds of her acting students would come to dread: "I am a woman
sitting next to you. If you cannot speak to me in recognition of that fact
and will continue as you have been doing, I must tell you—I can go out
to a bookstore and buy *all* your ideas for five dollars!"

Sure of Himself

Louis Shurr was the archetypal New York agent in the 1930s. Overweight
and overdressed, Shurr was not easily impressed. One of his actors came to
the office one day, took off his hat and displayed some daisies and aspara-
gus growing seemingly from his skull.

"I think I've got something for Ripley's *Believe It or Not*," the actor
announced."

"Why?" asked Shurr.

The most famous story told of Shurr (as well as of others) concerns a
vaudevillian who explained to him a new act, ending his spiel with this:

"And then I'll dive off a gallery box onto the stage, committing suicide
right in front of the audience. It will certainly wow them."

"Maybe," Shurr replied coolly, "but what will you do for an encore?"

Agents' Brains

*Milton Goldman, perhaps the most prominent actors' agent in New York
for the past thirty years, enjoys telling the following joke against his profession.*

A cannibal chief goes to the meat market and wants to buy some brains.
The butcher shows him a variety of merchandise:

"We've got lawyers' brains: that's $25 a pound. And here we have doctors' brains—$50 a pound, and over there are agents' brains—$100 per pound."

The cannibal is puzzled about the great range in prices:

"Why do agents' brains cost so much more?" he wanted to know.

"Do you have any idea," the vendor asked, "how many agents it takes to produce a single pound of brains?"

Bottoms Up

In the early part of her career, Katharine Hepburn was constantly dogged by the press about her unconventional personal life. During one of the waves of rumors that she was secretly married, Hepburn lost her temper and shouted back at a pack of reporters:

"Yes, of course I'm married, and I have six children—three of whom are colored."

Earl Wilson once visited to interview Hepburn in the 1930s at her father's house in Hartford. The whole town was abuzz with what the famous actress wore while tearing around town on a bicycle.

"I wear some old white shorts," she explained to Wilson. "They get a little dirty, and they look almost flesh color. I've got an English racing bike and I get my hands way down on the bars and my bottom way up on the seat. Then I go like mad. People see my bottom in those flesh-colored shorts way up there on the seat, and from where they're looking I guess they rally (rilly) (relly) thought I had absolutely nothing on. They thought they were seeing my bare bottom. Well, now, rally! It was enough to make them say, 'What the hell is that?' Then they'd see it was me, and they'd try to pretend I was respectable. But I suppose it's hard for anybody to look refined and respectable when your head is lower than your bottom."

CHAPTER 5

*When Giants
Walked the Earth*

"Old" Jefferson

The first Joseph Jefferson came to America in 1795, having been born appropriately enough in Plymouth on the English coast. His contemporary, William Dunlap described him as "of a small, light figure, well-formed, with a singular physiognomy, a nose perfectly Grecian, and blue eyes full of laughter. He had the faculty of exciting mirth to as great a degree by power of feature, although, handsome, as any ugly-featured, low comedian ever seen."

Joseph the First was so perfect a character actor, playing old men, that his colleagues dubbed him "Old Jefferson" as a tribute to his art. The story went that a sympathetic lady, watching him bent over and tottering on the stage, decided to raise a subscription to enable the veteran to spend his last days in retirement. She went to the theatre the next morning to consult with the management about her charitable plan; she even carried with her a list of well-known names with her own at the top. Jefferson, lively and young, happened to be passing by the office at the critical moment. He was stopped and introduced to his would-be benefactress, who was exceedingly surprised and, becoming confused, beat a hasty retreat.

Exit Laughing

Joseph Jefferson's mother, simply known as Miss May, was universally admired for her sunny disposition; Tate Wilkinson, a contemporary, also describes her "as one of the most elegant women I ever beheld." Her father hated actors and consented to her marriage only when Thomas Jefferson agreed to forfeit her dowry if she ever became an actress. (He agreed, and she became an actress all the same.) Mrs. Jefferson died on July 18, 1776, it was said, "of excessive laughter."

The disposition stayed with the family, and Joseph Jefferson III used to laugh so heartily that "he always felt a sharp twinge of pain at the base of his brain." The great Jefferson was born in Philadelphia in 1829 and went on the stage at the age of three as Cora's child in Sheridan's Pizarro. *A year later he was carried on in a paper bag by Thomas Rice, the first blackface minstrel and famous inventor of the popular Jim Crow character. Jefferson tinkered for years with the idea of doing Rip Van Winkle but it did not seem to click until one day in England, in a famous incident captured in his* Autobiography.

On Sunday evening, being alone in my lodgings, I got out for my own admiration my new wig and beard—the pride of my heart—which I was to use in the last act. I could not resist trying them on for the twentieth time, I think; so I got in front of the glass and adjusted them to my perfect satisfaction. I soon became enthused, and began acting and posing in front of the mirror. In about twenty minutes there came a knock at the door.

"Who's there?" said I.

"It's me, if you please," said the gentle but agitated voice of the chambermaid. "May I come in?"

"Certainly not," I replied; for I had no desire to be seen in my present make-up.

"Is there anything wrong in the room, sir?" said she.

"Nothing at all. Go away," I replied.

"Well, sir," she continued, "there's a policeman at the door, and he says as 'ow there 's a crazy old man in your room, a-flingin' of his 'arnds and a-goin' on hawful, and there 's a crowd of people across the street a-blockin' up the way."

I turned towards the window, and to my horror I found that I had forgotten to put down the curtain, and, as it seemed to me, the entire population of London was taking in my first night. I had been unconsciously acting with the lights full up, to an astonished audience who had not paid for their admission. As I tore off my wig and beard a shout went up.

Quickly pulling down the curtain, I threw myself in a chair, overcome with mortification at the occurrence. In a few minutes the comical side of the picture presented itself, and I must have laughed for half an hour. I had been suffering from an attack of nervous dyspepsia, consequent upon the excitement of the past week, and I firmly believe that this continuous fit of laughter cured me.

On Monday, September 5, I made my first appearance before a London audience, and was received with a cordial welcome. The play of *Rip Van Winkle* was entirely new to the English public, and its success secured for it a run of one hundred and seventy nights.

Booth by Booth

Edwin Booth, the great actor of his generation, tells about his father, who was the great one in his.

Whatever the part he had to personate, he was from the time of its rehearsal until he slept at night imbued with its very essence. If *Othello* was billed for the evening he would, perhaps, wear a crescent pin on his breast that day; or, disregarding the fact that Shakespeare's Moor was a Christian, he would mumble maxims of the Koran. Once, when he was about to perform *Othello* in Baltimore, a band of Arabs visited that city to exhibit their acrobatic feats and jugglery. To my mother's great disgust, but to the infinite delight of her children, my father entertained the unsavory sons of "Araby the blest" in the parlor. As a linguist he was proficient, and among his many tongues he had acquired some use of Arabic, in which he conversed with his guests, or rather with their spokesman, Budh, whose name suggested consanguinity; "for," said he, "Booth and Budh are from the same root." If Shylock was to be his part at night, he was a Jew all day; and if in Baltimore at the time, he would pass hours with a learned Israelite, who lived near by, discussing Hebrew history in the vernacular and insisting that, although he was of Welsh descent, that nation is of Hebraic origin; a belief for which there is some foundation. As the pirate, Bertram, he once reproved me for scolding a negro messenger-boy who unwittingly crossed the stage in view of the audience, by saying—"Let him alone, sir! Let him alone! He is one of my gang." My last experience of his vagaries, was at our final parting on the ship that bore him forever from me. He asked a sailor on deck to take his luggage to his cabin. The fellow replied—"I'm no flunky." "What are you, sir?" demanded my father. "I'm a thief," responded the brute. Instantly the actor assumed his favorite part of Bertram at this "cue," and said—"Your hand, comrade, I'm a pirate!"

the sailor laughed and rejoined, "All right, my covey; where's your traps?" and carried the trunk to the stateroom. His influence on the lowest minds was as great as it was strong over the highest intellects with which he came in contact.

He disliked to assume those characters (especially historical ones) to which his size was not adapted. Being requested by his old friend and manager, Wemyss, to study Richelieu for the latter's benefit, my father replied—"No, sir! No. The Cardinal was tall and gaunt; I cannot look him. Nonsense! Announce me as Jerry Sneak or John Lump—not Richelieu." (The comic characters named, were the only two that my father retained in his repertory; and 'twas pity that he did so.) Wemyss coaxed and finally prevailed. An old red gown was found in the very limited wardrobe of the theatre, my father having no appropriate costume for the part, and thus shabbily attired, His Eminence with Father Joseph appeared before an expectant audience. The dialogue hitched and halted for a while, until losing self-control, Richelieu seized his companion by the arms and waltzed him about the stage, to the amazement of the spectators and the dismay of Wemyss, who quickly lowered the curtain and frantically tore the hair of his wig, as the star coolly inquired—"Well, my boy, how d'ye like my Richelieu?" He disappeared for several days after this freak, to return with welcome to the scene of his mad exploit.

Bully

Edwin Forrest was the first great tragedian born in America. His rivalry spoiled his friendship with William Macready, the "Eminent Tragedian" from England and led in May 1849 to the Astor Place Riot, the ugliest incident in theatrical history, in which twenty-two innocent bystanders were killed and three dozen seriously injured. Forrest, though he had many good qualities and was the first to nurture American drama, was not pleasant to work with, according to his first biographer, James Rees.

Mr. Forrest was once playing in Richmond, Virginia, when one of the minor actors annoyed him terribly by persisting in reading his few lines in *Richelieu* incorrectly. Forrest showed him several times how to do it, but to no purpose, and then commenced abusing him. "Look here, Mr. Forrest," finally said the poor fellow, in sheer despair, "if I could read it in that way I wouldn't be getting six dollars a week here." Forrest said only: "You are right; I ought not to expect much for that sum," and left him alone, but on the conclusion of the engagement sent him a check for forty dollars, with a recommendation to act up to the worth of that.

To use a slang word, he was extremely apt to "bully" all in the theatre, from the manager down. But he once met his match. It was when he was playing at the old Broadway Theatre, near Pearl Street. His pieces were followed by an exhibition of lions by their tamer, a certain Herr Driesbach. Forrest was one day saying that he had never been afraid in all his life— could not imagine the emotion. Driesbach made no remark at the time, but in the evening, when the curtain had fallen, invited Forrest home with him. Forrest assented, and the two, entering a house, walked a long distance, through many devious passages, all dark, until finally Driesbach, opening a door, said: "This way, Mr. Forrest." Forrest entered, and immediately heard the door slammed and locked behind him. He had not time to express any surprise at this, for at the same moment he felt something soft rubbing against his leg, and, putting out his hand, touched what felt like a cat's back. A rasping growl saluted the motion, and he saw two fiery, glaring eyeballs looking up at him. "Are you afraid, Mr. Forrest?" asked Driesbach, invisible in the darkness. "Not a bit." Driesbach said something; the growl deepened and became hoarser, the back began to arch and the eyes to shine more fiercely. Forrest held out for two or three minutes; but the symptoms became so terrifying that he owned up in so many words that he was afraid. "Now let me out, you infernal scoundrel," he said to the lion-tamer; "and I'll break every bone in your body." He was imprudent there, for Driesbach kept him, not daring to move a finger, with the lion rubbing against his leg all the time, until Forrest promised not only immunity, but a champagne supper into the bargain.

Renaissance Man

The last titan of the old school of acting was Richard Mansfield. The year the actor died, in 1907, Clayton Hamilton worked with him on Peer Gynt. *He later remembered the actor's astonishing versatility on- and offstage.*

Mansfield's mother, Erminia Rudersdorff, was a celebrated opera singer; and from his very infancy he was carefully taught to breathe, to speak, to sing, to walk, to gesticulate, to dance. He was essentially an artist, and he was brought up with a realization that all the arts are branches on one tree. Consequently, when he arrived at his maturity, there was almost nothing that he could not do. He was an excellent painter, and he could sculpt with ease. He wrote poems for the *Atlantic Monthly*, and many essays which demonstrated an equal eloquence in English prose. He was an able linguist and spoke both French and German beautifully. He wrote several plays. He composed both words and music of a lovely book of songs.

He could play several musical instruments, and was especially adept at improvising on the piano. But to me the greatest of his technical accomplishments was the amazing development of his voice. The average person talks from the adenoids out, and few even of our current actors can produce a voice from lower than the larynx; but Mansfield had been taught from early childhood to pump every syllable from his diaphragm, with the full power of his lungs behind it.

With Mansfield, the art of speaking was based on breath control, as was the art of singing with Caruso. When he played Brutus in the quarrel scene of *Julius Caesar*, he sat inconspicuously in a darkened corner of the tent, while Joseph Haworth, cast as Cassius, was allowed to take the stage, with the limelight full upon him, and pour out his lines in a tremendous torrent. Mansfield remained quiescent—till a single, sudden phrase. But when he roared out, "Away, slight man!" the walls of the theatre shook as with an earthquake. It was as if Cassius had been blown bodily out of the tent and off the stage.

Even at this late date, it may strike many middle-aged theatregoers as a startling revelation when I state the actual fact that Mansfield was only five feet six inches tall; for when they saw him as Beau Brummell or as Henry V, they were easily convinced that he was of towering height. Once, when I asked him by what means he created this illusion, he answered proudly, "They see what I make them imagine that they see."

Rear View

One of Minnie Maddern Fiske's greatest roles was Hedda Gabler. Charles Hanson Towne recalled her performance at the Harlem Opera House in the beginning of the century.

It was the time when Mrs. Fiske had gone in for great naturalism, speaking sometimes indistinctly, as people will in real life (though I confess that I never had the slightest difficulty in catching every one of her lines). She made it a point to turn her back to her listeners, too, again as anyone might do in a drawing-room. I had been raving about her art to a certain young lady who had never seen her; and so, during the Christmas holidays, we trudged to Harlem, and I was certain that Mrs. Fiske would captivate my charming companion as she had always captivated me.

There came the big scene when Hedda burns the manuscript in the grate. True to her method, Mrs. Fiske knelt down, her face only half visible to us out in front, and poked her head very close to the flames, murmuring tensely, "I'm burning our child, Eilert Lovborg, I'm burning our child!" Whereupon my friend turned to me, as the curtain fell, and whispered, "Well, *you* may know what she said, and Santa Claus up the chimney may know; but I'm blest if *I* know!" Now, it must be said that cold type can give no indication of the pace Mrs. Fiske used in speaking, the terrific force of her utterance, the sharp, precise attack she made on certain words. And I suppose there was some justification for my friend's criticism; but happily, long before she left the stage forever, she abandoned her rapid diction, and was as audible as the most remote spectator could desire.

It was at this earlier period that Mrs. Fiske was rehearsing her company one day, and, so determined was she that each member of the cast should follow her example in a certain moment of the play, that she turned to her young cousin, Emily Stevens, and cried out (I had the story on Miss Stevens' word of honor)—"Now, Emily! in this great emotional scene, I wish your face to depict every emotion that a woman can feel—love, hope, joy, pain (each word shout out like the lash of a whip)—and be *sure* that you turn your back to the audience!"

George Arliss, who played Judge Brack opposite her Hedda Gabler, recalled a more generous motive than mere naturalism.

She was so interested in getting the best out of everybody else that she always seemed to regard herself as a negligible quantity in the play. I remember saying to her, "Are you going to speak all that with your back to the audience?"

"Yes," she said, "I want them to see your face."

"But," I remonstrated, "it's a very long speech for you to deliver in that position."

"Yes, I know," she sighed. "It's such a long speech, I want to get through with it as quickly as I can."

Giving More Than His Regards

George M. Cohan was a well-known philanthropist in the literal meaning of the word: he always gave to individuals, not to organizations. Although he tried to keep his charity work a secret, it was rumored that Cohan had given away more than a million dollars during his career. He once sent a friend, George Golden, to Colorado to recover his health. He handed Golden $10,000 in cash and told him to write if he needed more.

Beyond mere money, the greater part of Cohan's generosity consisted of helping struggling performers, by giving them songs and acts. He wrote more than a thousand songs, and was the first to charge royalties for vaudeville skits. Cohan also wrote many plays which he gave away, without his name on them. His touch was considered so magical that at one point all sorts of people he hardly knew would send their manuscripts to him to be "Cohanized."

One of Cohan's more celebrated exploits came when he was staying at the Savoy in London, and decided to take all the waiters and bus boys out on a night on the town. The next morning there was no service in the hotel, but George M. Cohan had no complaints about service on any of his return visits.

His generosity went beyond his intentions. Cohan's famous *Forty-five Minutes from Broadway* was credited with a real estate boom in New Rochelle; the town spread so quickly that it ended up being only thirty minutes from Broadway.

Ever More, Barrymore

Anecdotes are handed down the ages attached to different famous people. Several archetypal stories of the theatre feature the Barrymores, the royal family of the American theatre, and in particular Jack, its black sheep.

The following has been told of Ethel Barrymore, but an earlier version, long current at the Lambs, attributes it to her father. Maurice was appearing in a flop, and was being ragged about it by Wilton Lackaye. Barrymore was trying to explain that the theatre, which was originally designed for opera, drowned out his co-star, Madame Beere, a lady known for her off-color humor. "In that house," argued Barry, "one can be obscene, not heard."

When he was doing Hamlet, John Barrymore was careful to explain to the girls who were carrying on the dead Ophelia in the burial scene that they were supposed to be virgins. "My dear Mr. Barrymore," one of them replied, "we are extras, not character actresses."

After his success in *Hamlet*, Barrymore gave some college lectures on Shakespeare and his plays. In the question and answer period that followed the talk, a student asked whether Romeo and Juliet, young as they were, could have enjoyed a full physical relationship. "They certainly did in the Chicago company," Barrymore recalled.

Turkish Bath

Sweeney and Duffy were a famous vaudeville team, except when James Duffy forgot to turn up for the show. One afternoon, Fred Sweeney was on stage and Duffy was nowhere to be found. The stage manager found him at the actor's favorite Turkish bath.

"For God's sake, Duffy, what are you doing here?" he yelled. "You are on now!"

"I am?" the unperturbed vaudevillian came back, without missing a beat: "How am I doing?"

Proud Moment

Duffy and Sweeney were doing their act down in Memphis, Tennessee. All their sure-fire jokes, one after the other, fell flat. Finally, Duffy could stand the silence no more. He went downstage, peered over the footlights and addressed the audience:

"Citizens of Memphis! This is one of the happiest and proudest moments of our lives. Your reception has been overwhelming. And now, please remain in your seats a few minutes longer, while my partner, Mr. Sweeney, will pass down the aisle with a baseball bat and beat the be-Jesus out of you."

The management quickly closed the act.

Funny Man

Helen Hayes was five years old, attending Miss Minnie Hawks's dancing school. The school gave a public recital, which took place in the same Washington, D.C., theatre where Lew Fields happened to be performing. (He was one-half of the famous Fields and Weber vaudeville team, that gave us—among other things—the joke about "Dat vas no lady, dat vas my vife.") Fields had come in to pick up his mail and watched for a few moments little Helen do an imitation of a "Gibson Girl," popularized by Annabelle Whitford in The Ziegfeld Follies. *It was enough for him to leave a message: "Tell that little girl's mother that if she ever wants the child to go on the stage she should see me." Four years later, Helen Hayes was appearing with Lew Fields on Broadway in* Old Dutch. *In a 1937 article for* Stage *magazine, she recalled that important association.*

He taught me a great deal. Anything I have now in the way of precision or accuracy in the timing of comedy I learned from Lew Fields. He was an indefatigable worker. He played every performance as though it were a first night.

In those days musical-comedy people were a hardy lot. The language was somewhat colorful. Somebody was always challenging somebody else to go "out into the alley and fight it out." One day an actor grew a little profane on the stage. Lew Fields stood up and announced that there was to be no more bad language, and that all quarrels were to be settled in the dressing rooms. "There's to be no profanity before the child," he said.

Lew Fields was eternally good-natured and gentle. The only thing he couldn't bear was a ham actor or an insincere one. There was one like that in the company for a time and Fields made his life miserable, I think. . . . He was childlike in his attitude toward [John] Bunny, and with the cruelty of a child he could not resist teasing him. Besides, he suspected that Bunny was a bit of a stuffed shirt. He also suspected, and with some justice, that Bunny was sneaking away to the Vitagraph Studios during the day. Making pictures was a slightly disreputable occupation in those days. Bunny used to arrive at the theatre thoroughly exhausted and too tired to give a good performance. He had a way of falling fast asleep between his scenes, and Lew Fields was not above inserting a match in the toe of his shoe and lighting it, or dashing up to Bunny in a great flutter to announce that the Governor or the President or the Mayor or Flo Ziegfeld was in the audience that night. In one scene Fields was called upon to slap a glued sticker over Bunny's mouth. Every now and then he applied a redolent libation of limburger cheese over the glue. It all kept Bunny, who was half dead, in an excruciating state of jitters. I wonder he didn't end the season a thin man.

I saw Lew Fields angry only once, when a director, after keeping the chorus girls working all night, lost patience with one and pushed her roughly across the stage. Fields climbed over the footlights, walked calmly to the director and said, "You can get out!" It was just before an opening and the director was an important one. But he knew Fields meant it. Without a word, and thoroughly dazed, he put on his coat and left the theatre.

But Lew Fields usually gained his ends by a gentler reminder or a joke. During the run of *The Summer Widowers* the roof over the stage developed a leak. He complained to the theatre owners but nothing was done. So one evening he played the whole show with an umbrella over his head, letting the audience in on the joke. It was a very funny performance. The roof was fixed the next day.

Vignettes of a Jazz Singer

Showman Billy Rose remembered to his dying day seeing Al Jolson one night in *Bombo* (1921). Halfway through the second act, he stepped to the footlights and asked, "Do you want the rest of this plot, or would you rather have me sing a few songs?" The cast went home and Jolson took off his coat. He jammed until one o'clock and literally had to beg the audience to leave.

Al Jolson never took singing lessons until he was thirty-five. He stopped after the sixth lesson because he thought they were hurting his voice.

No matter how famous and loved he was as a performer, Jolson never could get rid of stage fright, which grew worse and worse with the years. Once he was due to perform at the Winter Garden. At eight o'clock he was found wandering bareheaded in the rain. He had to be gently coaxed to return to the theatre.

Jolson hated cold weather. On a cold night in Chicago, after a performance of *Bombo*, Jolson returned to his hotel when he noticed a sign flashing across from his suite: "It's June in Miami. It's June in Miami." The following morning he left for Miami, without telling anyone and leaving his show behind.

One of the Jolson myths, perpetuated in the movies, is that his father was a cantor. In fact, he was a "schochet," the man who kills chicken in the approved kosher manner. When Ruby Keeler opened in *Whoopee* in Pittsburgh, Jolson sent a telegram to Eddie Cantor: "Remember, this is the first time a Cantor was ever billed over a Jolson."

Plain Folks

In accepting the gold medal for drama from the National Institute of Arts and Letters, Tennessee Williams told the following story about his attitude to people.

One time Maureen Stapleton recived a phone call from a friend who said that so-and-so was getting married, and the caller said, "Why is she marrying that man, you know he is a homosexual," and Maureen said, "Well, what about the bride?" And the caller said, "Well, of course we know she's a lesbian. And you know they're not even being married by a real

minister, but by one who's been defrocked!" And Maureen said, "Will
you do me one favor? Will you please invite Tennessee Williams? Because
he'll say, "Oh, they're just plain folks!"

The Difference

When Alfred Lunt got his big break in legitimate theatre, he set about
preparing himself to play George Tewkesbury Reynolds III, a man about
town in Booth Tarkington's play *The Country Cousin* (1917). He went
at once on a special trip to Chicago, ordered four new suits from Marshall
Field, had engraved calling cards made for his character, and finally bought
an expensive gold cigarette case for the one moment in the play when he
had to light up. His friend Ray Weaver, who accompanied him on the
trip, was shocked.

"You could have bought a tin cigarette case in a five-and-dime store,
Alfred," he gasped. "Who'd know the difference?"

"I would," Alfred Lunt replied.

CHAPTER 6

Entrances

Come to Your Senses

Every major figure or teacher in the theatre has been at one time or another approached by a supplicant for help about getting into the profession. The usual, and perhaps only defensible advice is to discourage, which is what Edwin Booth did, with unusual vehemence, in this letter to a young man who had written that he was prepared to give up his regular job and family life to pursue Thespis.

Boothden, Newport, July 27th, 1884

My dear Mr. de Zayas:

I was indeed "startled," and I must confess, pained by your letter announcing your determination to abandon your profession for that of the stage, and in sincere frankness I beg you to reconsider the matter, for I really have no hope for a satisfactory result from such a change.

The feelings which prompt you to take this step—I mean your "love, enthusiasm, and natural inclination"—do not imply an ability for the art. There are hundreds of disappointed lives wasting on the stage where they felt, as you do, that a brilliant destiny awaited them.

You may be able to recite in private with perfect ease and propriety, even with excellence, and yet have no other qualification for the highest form of dramatic expression. It is a life of wearisome drudgery; and requires years of toil, and bitter disappointment, to achieve a position worth having.

I have known many who, like you, gave up home, friends, and respected positions for the glitter of the actor's callings and who now are fixed for life in subordinate positions, unworthy of their breeding, education, and natural refinement. I beg you, as your friend and sincere well-wisher, to abandon the mistaken resolve, and enjoy the drama as a spectator, which pleasure, as an actor, you would never know, and retain family, friends, and happy home that now are yours. Had nature fitted me for any other calling I should never have chosen the stage; were I able to employ my thoughts and labor in any other field I would gladly turn my back on the theatre forever. An art whose possessors and followers should be of the very highest culture, is the mere make-shift of every speculator and bore that can hire a theatre or get hold of some sensational rubbish to gull the public. I am not very much in love with my calling as it is now (and, I fear, will ever be), therefore you see how loath I am to encourage anyone to adopt it.

I think you will take my advice as it is meant—in sincere friendship and believe that my only wish is to spare you sorrow that must follow the course you would pursue.

With cordial regards for yourself and family,

I am truly yours,
Edwin Booth

A Modest Proposal

Clyde Fitch (1865–1909), one of the most successful American playwrights at the turn of the century, received quite a bit of fan mail. And then there was also the following letter:

Dear Mr. Clyde Fitch:

For eight years, ever since I was a girl of twenty-five, I have been a hopeless invalid, confined to my couch by day and by night. During this time my only consolation has been making lace, and I have now completed a wedding veil of very beautiful design, and large enough to cover me from head to foot. I am naturally desirous of making use of same, and have thought how nice it would be if you would write me a play, the chief scene of which is a wedding, in which I might wear it.

Before I was sick I once played in private theatricals, and friends said I was very beautiful, though they may have been prejudiced. I know that I am not an actress like Bernhardt or Mrs. Leslie Carter; but your plays do not generally call for acting, and even if you did rise to greater heights, the chief scene, you know, would find me beneath the wedding veil, which would conceal everything.

May say that I am a little better now, and nothing would pull me together, the doctor says, like having a real interest in life. It seems to me that this is a great opportunity for you to shine in your art and do a good deed, too.

Admiringly yours,

Dressing Down

Otis Skinner (1858–1942) was a beginner when Lawrence Barrett, the great tragedian, administered him a lesson.

During the second season I had the chance to play Antony in Boston—within two miles of my birthplace in Cambridge. The audience at the Park Theatre included many personal friends and friends of my family. Call after call came after Marc Antony's two strong scenes, until finally my conscience smote me. Louis James came out of his dressing-room and stood generously smiling as the curtain went up and down. In nervous fear that I was appropriating a reward never meant for me, I seized him by the hand and led him out with me. While the subsequent "tent scene" of Brutus and Cassius was proceeding, Mr. Barrett's dresser came to my room and said that the chief wanted to see me. He was sitting bolt upright in his Roman armor.

"Sit down, sir," he said.

I sat.

"Mr. Skinner, I wish first to congratulate you on your success to-night."

"Thank you, Mr. Barrett."

"Now let me tell you something, young man. You have done one of the most unprofessional things to-night I've ever encountered. You have patronized my leading man. Patronized, sir! Led him before the audience! If you arrogate to yourself that privilege, where am I?"

In vain I tried to tell him that my action had been prompted not by effrontery, but by confusion.

"Pooh, sir!" he answered. "If you had had fifty calls, they would all have been for Antony. That's what Antony is for, sir, to get calls."

I felt myself growing smaller and smaller.

"Look at me! Who cares for Cassius! My only reward is the artist's reward. They never call for Cassius."

Just then the dresser rushed in hastily. The tent scene was over. "They're calling for you, Mr. Barrett!" he cried.

The offended tragedian forgot his rage. He fairly ran out to take his call. He was human after all.

Advice

The young Ethel Barrymore was playing in *Cousin Kate* (1903) at the Majestic Theatre in Boston. Next door, on his last American tour, Sir Henry Irving was packing them into the Colonial. After one matinee, the grand old man of the English stage ran into the bright new hope of the American theatre in the alley between the two houses.

"Ethel, my dear, how is your play?" asked Sir Henry.

"The Boston critics roasted us."

"But *Cousin Kate* is a good play, and did very well in London."

"It wasn't the play so much, but I got it."

"And what did they say?"

"That I traded on my mannerisms," said the actress.

"Make sure, my dear," said Irving, patting her on the head, "they never say anything else."

The Final Note

Ruth Gordon was making her Broadway debut. She was very young and very nervous. As she told Charles Champlin, arts editor of the Los Angeles *Times*, she sought out the director and told him that she couldn't possibly go on. The director did everything in his power to reassure her, by telling her how good she was and what great future lay ahead of her.

"Don't you have some final notes, some last-minute advice for me?" asked the desperate actress.

The director pondered and shrugged.

"Oh, there's one small thing I might say."

"Yes, yes?"

"Watch those mannerisms."

Selling Out

Helen Hayes made her first dramatic impact on New York in J. M. Barrie's *Dear Brutus*, under actor-manager William Gillette. Then she got an offer to tour with George Tyler, a rival manager. Gillette went to Helen's mother:

"What did Tyler do for your daughter that I did not?" he wanted to know.

"He offered a large increase in salary and we will have our own drawing room on every train."

"So you've sold Helen," said Gillette icily, "for a couple of Pullmann tickets."

Unwilling Dispension of Disbelief

In 1916, the young Alfred Lunt was engaged by Lillie Langtry to play the Orpheum vaudeville circuit with her. Once the mistress of Edward VII and the greatest beauty of the age, the Jersey Lily had by then faded somewhat, but after four shows she would still be dancing half the night and required her leading man—as was the custom—to keep her happy the other half.

In a sketch called *Ashes*, young Lunt was supposed to play the blackmailer of a married woman, by revealing to her husband love letters she had written during their affair many years before. He was 24, Miss Langtry 63, and the absurdity proved too much for one critic who complained: "When did she give him those letters—in the cradle?"

Boy Meets Girl

Alfred Lunt was stagestruck very early on, and as a boy kept a scrapbook filled with photographs and stories of the great performers. The star who struck him most was Ellen Terry, the great English actress in the late nineteenth century. Years later he was to meet Lynn Fontanne, who became his wife and lifelong acting partner. Miss Fontanne began her career under Ellen Terry's tutelage in England, and she bore an uncanny resemblance to the older actress.

Lunt actually met Fontanne at the New Amsterdam Theatre in 1919, during auditions for *Clarence*, a play Booth Tarkington wrote specifically with Alfred in mind. Lynn, some five years older than him, asked for the introduction. As the young man stepped off the backstage staircase to shake her hand, he lost his footing and fell flat on his face in front of her. Hearing about this auspicious meeting, George S. Kaufman later remarked: "Well, he certainly fell for her."

On a Clear Day

Fanny Brice was originally called Fannie Borach; she borrowed her stage name from a next-door neighbor called John Brice. She told him that some day he'd see his name in lights. John Brice later did indeed become a watchman on the Ninth Avenue elevated train, and if his eyes were any good, he might well have seen the prophecy come true.

Learning the Ropes

When Will Rogers began in vaudeville, opening and closing shows on the Klaw & Erlanger circuit, his was strictly a "dumb" act. His properties consisted of a lariat, a white horse with a rider. As the orchestra played "Cheyenne," Rogers shuffled down center stage with a rope in each hand. The horse and rider would come galloping out of the wings across the stage, and Rogers would throw the rope in his right hand around the horse and the one in his left hand around the rider. The trick was executed so swiftly that the spectators could not see or appreciate what actually happened. A fellow actor suggested to Will that if he stopped the music and explained what he intended to do, the stunt would have greater appeal.

At the next show Rogers walked out and held up his hand. "Stop that noise," he said. The audience roared with delight. "Folks," the cowboy continued, "you can see I got one of these ropes in each hand. When the hoss and rider come out, I'm going to try to throw one of 'em over the hoss and the other over the rider."

Again the audience laughed. Rogers was upset.

"They laughed at me," he complained backstage to the other players who assured him that had made a hit:

"Sure they laughed. You were funny."

"Funny? Say, I can speak English as good as those folks out there. No, no, I'll never open my mouth again."

For another five years "Will Rogers and Company" toured the vaudeville circuit. Bick McKee, the horseman who with Teddy, the white horse, constituted "the company," later recalled:

"Sometimes Bill used to make wisecracks at me as I stood in the wings, and often they were heard by those in the first two or three rows of the orchestra. They always laughed and I tried to get Bill to talk louder, but he was bashful. One day a theatre manager, wondering what was going on, stood beside me and he got a lot of laughs, too. 'Why don't you put that out to the audience?' he asked. Rogers, thinking he meant the roping loop he was spinning out over the audience, explained it was the longest rope he had but he'd try it sometime."

It took years for Will Rogers to discover that his greatest talent lay in his wit and wisecracks with which he amused stagehands and fellow players. One of his earliest quips was remembered for years afterwards. He was twirling his rope in a vaudeville act when during a lull he remarked carelessly to the audience: "Swingin' a rope is all right—if your neck ain't in it."

The audience, taken by surprise, roared at the quip. Rogers, as usual, was surprised at the response.

Sorry, I Didn't Mean To Be Funny

Anne Nichols, author of the smash-hit *Abie's Irish Rose*, got into writing through necessity and accident. She and her husband, Henry Duffy, were in vaudeville and were too poor to buy sketches for their act. She wrote a sentimental melodrama which she had hoped would move the audience to tears. Instead they laughed, and the confused actress-author fled from the stage in confusion. She only discovered her new talent when the delighted manager came to her dressing room with a contract.

Over the Top

Fred Astaire started out dancing with his sister Adele who was a year older. They were then still called the Austerlitz kids and their earliest experiments at school in Highwood, New Jersey, got off to a rocky start, when Adele suddenly sprouted so fast that she made Fred look ludicrously small to dance with her. They spent nine years perfecting their song and dance acts in vaudeville, before making it to Broadway in *Over the Top* (1917) when Fred was all of eighteen years old.

The siblings were complete opposites in temperament. Whereas Adele loved the attentions of rich young men, Fred was entirely caught up in his work. She would breeze in a few minutes before curtain time, her brother having spent two hours fussing about the props and limbering up. Although Fred grew up in his sister's shadow (people referred to him as "that talented Austerlitz girl's little brother"), he was protective of her. Adele was singing once on radio with Rudy Vallee's orchestra, when a Broadway columnist criticized her voice. Even though Fred had nothing to do with the performance, the next time the critic came to interview him backstage, he told him: "Please, if you ever take an aim at us, direct

it at me, not at Adele, will you?" Adele, who claimed that her love of
theatre was not inbred but "an acquired taste—like olives," finally married
an English lord in 1932 and retired from the stage, just as Fred was blos-
soming forth as a comic actor. They last appeared together in *The Band
Wagon*, in which Fred had to play a huge variety of character roles, because it was the Depression and the producers were trying to save money.
After its opening, Fred Astaire walked into the Lambs' Club, where one
of his colleagues greeted him jubilantly: "Boy, I hear you're an actor!" It
was news to him, even though he was 32 years old then and had been
performing for almost quarter of a century.

There Goes an Actor

*Jack Benny always remembered the pride he felt when he left vaudeville
and became an actor in a legitimate show. The year was 1926 and Lee
Shubert had offered him a role in* Great Temptations *at the Winter Garden.*

This was what I had always wanted—to get on Broadway, to be an actor.
Jack Benny . . . *actor!* Actor! Boy, that was music! I wanted people on
the street to point to me and exclaim: "*There* goes an actor!" And with
the flashy Broadway outfit I bought—I'll bet I turned heads two blocks
away. I must have looked like a sunset with buttons.

Then one night as I was leaving the theatre, I overheard a stagehand
mumble, "There goes that guy Benny. He always looks like an actor."

For a moment I floated along engulfed in the cloud of my own conceit.

"Yep, Benny always looks like an actor," came another voice, "except
when he's on stage."

Child's Play

Eddie Cantor, George Jessel and Walter Winchell all started together in
vaudeville, with one of Gus Edwards's well-known kid acts.

"We had a great cast," Eddie Cantor once reminisced to Jack Benny:
"Walter Winchell, Georgie Jessel, me, and twelve girls. Winchell was ambitious. Even then he always had a typewriter in his room. I was ambitious,
too. I always had schoolbooks in my dressing room."

"And what about Jessel?" Jack Benny asked.

"He was the most ambitious," Cantor mused. "He had the twelve girls
in his room."

At one point Jessel and Winchell were singing to the accompaniment of
slides in a nickelodeon, when Winchell got the sack. A new sign went up

which said: "It's worth five cents alone to hear little Georgie Jessel sing." Recalling the episode thirty years later, when the three had risen to be among the highest paid people in America, Winchell commented: "And it still goes."

Discovery

In late 1934 director Arthur Hopkins was having trouble trying to find an actor to play Duke Mantee, the desperate outlaw in Robert Sherwood's The Petrified Forest.

One day I stopped in at the Golden Theatre, where a quick failure was just expiring. Between the ticket door and the stage at the Golden there is a curtain that shuts off the stage. While still behind the curtain I heard a dry, tired voice. Instantly I knew that it was the voice of Duke Mantee.

When I saw the actor I was somewhat taken aback, for he was one I had never much admired. He was an antiquated juvenile who had spent most of his stage life in white pants, swinging a tennis racket. He seemed as far from the cold-blooded killer as one could get, but the voice persisted, and the voice was Mantee's. So I engaged him, and thus started the catapulting career of Humphrey Bogart.

Bogie's Baby

Lauren Bacall, whom everybody calls Betty, tried to be in all the right places where an aspiring actress might get a break. She ushered at the Morosco Theatre and she worked as hostess at the Stage Door Canteen, which was filled nightly with all the most prominent Broadway producers. She was also selling *Cue* magazine outside Sardi's restaurant and that is where it finally happened, just as it was supposed to in a scene out of the movies. Max Gordon, the producer, noticed her and asked:

"What's a beautiful girl like you doing selling magazines? You should be on the stage."

"Nobody will give me a job," said Miss Bacall.

"Be at my office tomorrow morning," and Gordon handed her his card.

The producer introduced her to George S. Kaufman, who was directing for him a play called *Franklin Street* (1942) by Ruth Goetz. Lauren Bacall was cast in a bit part of an aspiring actress. The play opened in Wilmington and closed in Washington, D.C., and in later years Humphrey Bogart used to tease her as "that well-known actress from Wilmington."

Ushers

One-time-honored path for stagestruck youngsters to get into the theatre
has been ushering. Bette Davis got her start in a Cape Cod summer thea-
tre; Tennessee Williams at the Strand, Earl Carroll was a balcony guide in
Pittsburgh; and publicist Dick Maney at Moore's in Seattle. Morton
Gottlieb remembers starting the first off-Broadway theatre, New Stages in
Greenwich Village, in 1947, as a completely union shop except for ushers.
He and Peter Zeissler were rounding up young hopefuls like Maureen
Stapleton and producer Arthur Cantor.

Two ushers who got sidetracked: writer and editor E. B. White (at the
Met), and Harry Truman, who worked the Orpheum in Kansas City.

It was the parsimonious Shuberts who, soon after they got into business,
figured out that hiring female ushers might save them money. Later during the Depression, the Shuberts used the position for their welfare program
of saving hundreds of actors from starvation. Many chorines worked as
ushers, despite the complaint made by a critic in St. Louis, who wrote:
"We admire Mr. Shubert's loyalty, but we do wish he would pension his
overage chorus girls to some other cause than the St. Louis Municipal
Light Opera Company."

Natural Talent

Ethel Zimmerman was discovered when she was a stenographer in Astoria,
Long Island. She had been singing at weddings and doing one-night stands
at clubs when agent Lou Irwin found her and booked her into the Brooklyn Paramount. At eighteen, she dropped the Zim from her name, to make
it easier to fit on a marquee.

In 1930, producer Vinton Freedley was looking for a rhythm singer for
a new George Gershwin musical, *Girl Crazy*, starring Ginger Rogers and
Willie Howard. He heard her sing in Brooklyn, and took her at once to
Gershwin's penthouse on Riverside Drive. Unimpressed and completely
self-assured, the young singer belted out a couple of tunes. Gershwin asked
about her voice teachers. Ethel told him she had been singing since the
age of five, but she had never taken a lesson from a music teacher in her
life.

"And don't you go near them," Gershwin advised her. "You have a
wonderful natural voice; they'll only get you self-conscious about your
breathing and accent, and you'd get all tensed up."

Then Gershwin played the two songs he had written for the character.

Ethel was thinking about how she might phrase them, but the composer mistook it for a lack of enthusiasm.

"Miss Merman, if there's anything you don't like about these songs," said Broadway's hottest composer, "I'd be happy to make changes for you."

"I think these will do very nicely," she replied.

Debut

Maurice Zolotow chronicled what happened next.

On Wednesday evening, October 15, 1930, this unknown girl from Long Island swaggered out on the stage of the Alvin Theatre, and as they say around Broadway, murdered a hard-boiled, sophisticated audience, as she opened her mouth and informed them that she had rhythm, she had music, she had her man and who could ask for anything more. She just swayed there in a shimmering red blouse and a tight black satin slashed skirt, and gave out more and more choruses of "I Got Rhythm" as the applause cascaded around her. By the time the reviews came out, a new star was born and Ginger Rogers was playing second soprano to Ethel Merman.

Probably the only person who hadn't read the reviews of *Girl Crazy* the next morning was Ethel Merman. After the opening, she had gone to a party at the Central Park Casino. She had a lunch date with Gershwin in New York and she was late. She apologized for being late. He said it was all right. He was excited.

"Well, what do you think of these reviews?"

"I didn't see them," she said casually, cutting into a thick slab of roast prime ribs of beef *au jus naturel*.

"You didn't—what?" he cried.

"No, I didn't have time," she said. "I was rushing to meet you."

"Whew," he said, weakly.

"The meat is good," she said, cheerfully.

"Ethel," he said, "look." He pulled the reviews out of his pocket. He spread them on the table. "They're all raves—sensational notices—you're in with both feet."

She looked up at him, swallowed what she was chewing, and grinned. "It figured," she said calmly.

Lou Irwin, who represented her during the next decade, said of her: "That gal sweats icewater, I'm telling you. She's the only actress I know that on opening night will put on a performance as relaxed as if the show has been running a year."

Overnight Star

After ten years of struggle and obscurity, Mary Martin suddenly became the talk of the town after her Broadway debut in Cole Porter's Leave It to Me *(1938). "She was a hick from Texas," one producer remembered her. "She didn't know much about how to dress and she had a lot to learn about makeup and fixing hair. She wasn't especially good-looking." And Mary Martin herself told journalist Joe McCarthy the story of how she was discovered.*

"Everybody told me to remodel my nose, which was too big," Mary told me. "I managed to support myself, not too well, by singing in nightclubs. Now let me tell you an interesting story about myself and Bing Crosby. At least, I think it's interesting. One night Bing heard me singing 'Shoe-Shine Boy' at a small place called The Casanova. He kept me at the piano, singing that same song over and over again, until three o'clock in the morning. He said he loved my singing and he promised to help me get a job in the movies. But weeks and weeks went by and I never heard from him."

While she was waiting to hear from Crosby, Mary had her first big lucky break. At a Sunday-night "opportunity show" in the old Trocadero nightclub, she performed before an audience of important show-business people an old classic aria, "Il Bacio" ("The Kiss"). First she sang the song conventionally straight. The audience seemed bored. Then she did the song again with a hot swinging rhythm. When she finished her number, everybody in the room stood up and cheered. The next day she received telephone calls from several movie studios and an invitation from Laurence Schwab to appear in a New York musical, which she accepted. Schwab's project never materialized but he arranged for her to get the "My Heart Belongs to Daddy" role in *Leave It to Me*.

"Now comes the rest of the Bing Crosby story," Mary said. "After the run of *Leave It to Me*, I landed a nice movie contract at Paramount. There I met Dick Halliday, a story editor at the studio who became my second and last husband and the father of my second and last child, our daughter Heller. Her name is really Mary, but ever since she was a baby we've called her Heller because she's always been a heller. I had to pass up a chance to play in *Holiday Inn* with Bing Crosby and Fred Astaire while I was at Paramount because I was in the hospital at that time, getting Heller born. I worked with Bing on a few other pictures, but I never mentioned to him that night at The Casanova when he kept me at the piano singing 'Shoe-Shine Boy' until three in the morning. Finally, one day on the set when we were together, I walked over to a piano and started to tap out 'Shoe-Shine Boy.' Bing said to me, 'Don't play that song, Mary. It hurts me. One night I sat up until all hours listening to a girl sing that number. The next day I went to a lot of trouble arranging a screen test for her. Then I went back to the joint where she was working to tell her the big news. She was gone and nobody there could tell me how to get in touch with her. I often wonder what happened to her.' I said to Bing, 'You're looking at her right now.' Isn't that something?"

Billy Rose recalled auditioning Mary Martin in Fort Worth in 1936. After listening to her warbling a song called "Gloomy Sunday," Rose advised her to get married and tend to dishes and diapers. "A few years later," Rose wrote in his memoirs, "a lovely in a Mainbocher gown came up to my table at the Stork Club and kissed me on the top of my head."

How They Met

Life magazine writer Lincoln Barnett, in his profile of Richard Rodgers, writes how the composer first met both his famous collaborators.

When Rodgers was fifteen he wrote his first complete score—for an amateur show put on by a boys' athletic club in behalf of the New York *Sun's* cigarette fund for American soldiers in France. The show was presented in the grand ballroom of the Hotel Plaza before a large and dressy audience; Rodgers conducted the orchestra, and the sight of the rows of white shirt fronts and glittering frocks and the sound of applause acclaiming his music gave him a taste of dramatic triumph which he never forgot. The following year he met two young men who were to be closely associated with him in the future. One was Herbert Fields, son of the great comedian Lew Fields; the other was Lorenz Hart. Fields was five years older than Rodgers; Hart, seven years older, had already graduated from Columbia with the class of '16. The latter was a strange and tragic personality. The younger son of an indulgent mother (whom he once described as a "sweet, menacing old lady"), he was gnomish in appearance, barely five feet in height, with a head that seemed too large for his frail body to sustain. Brilliant, intellectual, a German scholar, and a superlatively agile versifier with a talent for inventive rhyming approached by no one else since W. S. Gilbert, he was also bitter, sardonic, and unstable, given to alternating moods of noisy gaiety and black despair. His tragedy was that this instability increased rather than lessened with the unfolding of his talent and fame.

Rodgers and Hart shook hands for the first time with a single idea in mind. Rodgers needed a lyric writer; Hart needed a composer. Their collaboration began immediately, and a few months later one of their songs was purchased and used in a now forgotten musical called *A Lonely Romeo*. The song itself, "Any Old Place with You," is memorable today chiefly because it is probably the only song ever written by a sixteen-year-old boy to land in a professional Broadway show. A few months later Rodgers entered Columbia with the class of '23 and promptly submitted a complete score in the annual Varsity Show competition. Although no freshman had ever before won this contest, Rodgers's score was selected for production. One of the judges happened to be a member of the class of '16 named Oscar Hammerstein II, who had only recently abandoned law school for the stage. Hart wrote the lyrics to Rodgers's music in accordance with a Varsity Show tradition permitting alumni to participate; Fields devised the dances. The product of their collaboration, *Fly with Me*, not only overshadowed all previous Varsity Shows but received serious notices in the New York newspapers. "From that moment on," a mutual friend recalls, "Larry simply waited for Dick to grow up and graduate from college."

Each One Teach One

After his parents divorced, Stephen Sondheim lived on his mother's farm in Bucks County, Pennsylvania. At fifteen he collaborated on a musical with a couple of schoolmates and he wanted to show it to one of the neighbors, to get an objective opinion on it. The neighbor happened to be Oscar Hammerstein II, and young Sondheim asked him to give his professional opinion of the work, as if they didn't know each other.

"I went home with delusions of grandeur in my head," Sondheim is fond of recalling; he imagined that Oscar and Dick Rodgers would drop whatever they were doing and produce the new work by the "first fifteen-year-old ever to have a musical done on Broadway." The next morning Hammerstein called and young Stephen went over to hear the verdict:

"You want my opinion as though I didn't really know you? Well, it's the worst thing I've ever read." Then the world-famous lyricist spent most of the day with his future successor going through the whole book, line by line, song by song. "That afternoon," Sondheim acknowledges, "I learned more about songwriting and the musical theatre than most people learn in a lifetime."

Not Like Little Girls

Stephen Sondheim never got to work professionally with Oscar Hammerstein, and his collaboration with Richard Rodgers on *Do I Hear a Waltz*
(1965) was decidedly an unhappy one. Just before the show opened,
Rodgers told a New York *Times* reporter that he had first met Steve
Sondheim in 1942 while working with Hammerstein on *Oklahoma!*. "I
watched him grow from an attractive little boy to a monster."

But Sondheim got in the last lick. In a 1973 cover story for *Newsweek*
he defined Oscar Hammerstein as a man of limited talent with infinite
soul, and Richard Rodgers as a man of infinite talent and a limited soul.

Small World

One of Kim Stanley's earliest jobs in New York was modeling dresses for
Herbert Sondheim, the father of Stephen.

Eugene O'Neill's mother, who became a fine pianist, attended the same
convent school with the critic George Jean Nathan's mother.

Henry Fonda's mother was a close friend of Dorothy Brando, Marlon's
mother. They belonged to the same Christian Science Church in Omaha.
Mrs. Brando—called DoDo or Do by her friends—was a leading light at
the Omaha Community Playhouse. One day, young Henry Fonda, who
was visiting home from college, received a desperate call from Mrs. Brando.
The Playhouse was rehearsing Philip Barry's *You and I* and had just lost
the leading man.

"You'd be perfect, Hank," Do Brando pleaded.

"Good God," said Fonda, "I don't know how to act." He stayed with
the Omaha Community Playhouse for three years, and played opposite
Mrs. Brando in O'Neill's *Beyond the Horizon*. "She was a goddam good
actress," Fonda recalled in later life. "She could have made it on Broadway
but didn't have the ambition to tackle it."

The Bald Facts

It was the costume designer Irene Sharaff who probably gave the greatest
impetus to Yul Brynner's career. When the practically unknown actor was
cast for *The King and I* (1951) he was almost bald, but with a black fringe
around the back and a few strands on top. After discussing the costumes,
he asked what he should do about his hair.

"Shave it!" said Miss Sharaff impulsively.

"Oh no! I can't do that." Brynner protested. He was worried about a dip on the top of his head. After the designer reassured him that she could always get him a wig if the operation proved unsuccessful, Yul Brynner shaved his head, rubbed his pate with oil, which became his personal trademark and for a while at least made baldness sexy in America.

Let Me Out

At the start of her career, Joan Rivers was performing in a garage off-off Broadway with the Noel Gayle Players. Anyone who has seen Neil Simon's The Goodbye Girl, *where Richard Dreyfuss acts out a gay interpretation of Richard III, can picture the situation. In her book of memoirs,* Enter Talking, *Miss Rivers paints the experience of most struggling New York actors.*

The first weekend, *See the Jaguar* went well. As usual, it was an invited audience and responsive—though the applause came at odd and unpredictable times. Barefoot in a red calico sun dress, I was the daughter of a man who lived to hunt animals and whose dream was to have a caged jaguar at his roadside gas station. My lover was defying my father and wanted to take me away and I remember there was a cage and, instead of a jaguar, a bare-chested boy was locked inside it—the role played on Broadway by Jimmy Dean.

My moments onstage seemed to go very well, so this time I called in every single favor, contacted every person I had ever visited on my rounds, saying, "Please come and see me as Janna." It was my third production and by then I had worn them to a frazzle, so they all came on the *same* Friday night. On that night, before the performance, I peeked out from behind the sheet strung up to create a dressing room and I saw, lined up on the folding chairs, every agent and secretary I had ever romanced for an entire year. The room seemed totally filled by them, every person I thought could help me—the secretary from the Martin Goodman office, the casting girl from the Theatre Guild, the secretary from Kermit Bloomgarden's office— every off Broadway producer I had ever met. Even Strasberg's secretary from The Actors Studio.

Their presence threw me totally. They were now going to find out that I really did not have talent, that I was not good enough, that everything had been a mistake. Now they would *know.* So I did what I still do when there is somebody famous in the audience, somebody who will judge me:

I became almost disabled with tension, like a violin whose strings are too tight.

During the show everything that could go wrong, went wrong. Nobody was connecting at all onstage. Doors stuck, props were not in place, lights went on and off at the wrong times. Down in the garage, in addition to the usual racket of tires and motors, somebody's car seemed to have been stolen because there were police sirens and a lot of English and Spanish voices screaming "Fuck you!" A truck must have blown up because fumes filled the theatre like a fog. And during a particularly tense though understated moment of drama, a stream of fire engines, sirens wailing, passed beneath the windows . . . and passed . . . and passed—it must have been the Chicago Fire—drowning out every sound onstage. We froze and waited . . . and waited . . . and waited . . . as though we had switched from a play to a tableau.

The whole performance was like a film whose happy scenes suddenly turn evil and you realize it is a horror movie. Everything that had seemed glamorous and fun and camp turned grotesque, exposing a sorry lot of painted-up amateurs, foolishly deluding ourselves. I realized that I had no acting technique at all and was working only on emotion. When the emotion was not there, I had nothing—except my tension, which made me speed up and stutter, saying, "I'll be a tree that goes to w-w-w-w-wood: no f-f-f-f-flower and no f-f-f-f-fruit!" I despised myself utterly.

The roomful of secretaries and agents was not rapt. I could glimpse people fanning themselves with the program, could hear them shifting in the folding chairs and opening their purses to look for subway money and riffling through the program to see if this interminable play was two or three acts.

In the third act the boy in the cage must have really felt his lines—"Let me out"—because the broomstick bars suddenly came apart in his hands. Now the poor schlep had to hold the cage together and after my big speech about how this boy's spirit must go free and his body with it and I'm going to let him go now, the boy just handed me the bars and slunk away.

At the end, with no curtain, there was a blackout and the cast appeared together for the curtain call. Then my philosophy class at Barnard finally paid off. I understood the proposition of one hand clapping.

Acting Without a Microwave

David Pressman was teaching at Boston University, and one of his students was Olympia Dukakis.

Quite early in her studies, she was doing a scene from Shakespeare in a class and had trouble relating to the world of Lady Macbeth.

"How can I play her," she asked, "if I don't believe in ghosts?" Peter Cass was teaching that class, and he said patiently:

"This is theatre, Olympia. It's not you—it's the character who believes in ghosts."

But she was genuinely confused, and persisted:

"But isn't it important for the role that I personally believe?"

"Who cares, if you believe or not? Who cares?" Peter said somewhat more exasperated.

I had forgotten whether I had said anything, but recently when she had won the Academy Award for *Moonstruck*, I called Olympia to congratulate her on what a splendid actress she had become.

"You know, David," she said, "when I came to Boston U. I was very discouraged and unhappy in the program during the first month. I was sitting in a corner all by myself during one of your classes, and you came up to me and said something I have never forgotten: "It's alright, Olympia, it takes at least twenty years to become an actress.""

Under Every Good Man

Kathryn Harkin, who was later married to Zero Mostel, remembers that when she started out as a dancer, there used to be a saying in the business: "Do a good show every night because Ziegfeld may be out front." This was long after Ziegfeld's death.

She heard another piece of advice that used to be given to chorus girls: "Get under a good man, and work up."

CHAPTER 7

Star Turns

Stars Are Different from You and Me

For those who do not believe that stars are special people, there is this testimony from Walter Matthau, quoted by columnist Radie Harris.

I only saw Vivien Leigh once in my life in person. That was at the Ritz-Carlton Hotel in Boston. I got into the elevator and she was there. And I got goose pimples. I got off on the third floor, like a fool. The goose pimples remained for ten minutes, which I am told, is a medical phenomenon.

Star-struck

When David Merrick was first introduced to Arthur Miller, who had been an idol to him, the playwright was accompanied by Marilyn Monroe, then at the height of her glamorous fame. It says something about the stature of both men that the producer forever remembered the impact of this meeting: "I just couldn't stop staring at Arthur Miller."

Memory

Jesse Block, an old vaudevillian, looked up Fanny Brice in Hollywood, and reminded her that they had been on the same bill at the Oriental Theatre in Chicago.

"I never played the Oriental," Miss Brice said.

"We did," Block went on, "and after the show we went to the College Inn."

"I never went to the College Inn with you."

"And I pointed out Al Capone to you—surely you remember that?"

"Who's Al Capone?" she persisted with a straight face.

"Fanny," then Block said, "that was the week that you got $7500 at the Oriental."

"I did not," Miss Brice said, "I got $8000."

Breaking Out

Joseph Jefferson made his reputation working under the management of the formidable Laura Keene, in hits such as Our American Cousin. *By 1859 he was chafing to make it on his own, something that did not fit in with her plans.*

Miss Keene was highly incensed at my proposed departure. She considered that, having been the first to bring me to New York, to her my loyalty was due, and in common gratitude I was bound not to desert the theatre for the purpose, as she supposed, of joining the opposition forces. I replied that, so far as my ingratitude was concerned, I failed to see in what way she had placed me under obligations; that I presumed when she engaged me for her theatre it was from a motive of professional interest, and I could scarcely think it was from any affection for me, as we had never met until the engagement was made. This kind of logic had anything but a conciliating effect. So I concluded by saying that I had no idea of casting my lot with the opposition, but that it was my intention to star. "Star! Oh, dear! Bless me! Indeed!" She did not say this, but she certainly looked it; and as she turned her eyes heavenward there was a slight elevation in the tip of her beautiful nose that gave me no encouragement of an offer from her under these circumstances. With a slight tinge of contempt she asked me with what I intended to star. I answered that, with her permission, I purposed to act *Our American Cousin.* "Which I decline to give. The play is my property, and you shall not act it outside of this theatre." And she swept from the greenroom with anything but the air of a *comédienne*.

The houses were still overflowing, and there was every prospect that *Our American Cousin* would run through the season; but Miss Keene was tired of acting her part in the comedy, and was determined to take the play off and produce *A Midsummer Night's Dream*, which had been in preparation for some time, and in fact was now in readiness. The management was anxious that Mr. Blake, who had been idle for some four months, should be in the cast, so that the play might contain the full strength of its expensive company.

The Duchess, being in high dudgeon with me, deputed her business manager, Mr. Lutz, to approach me on the subject of the cast, proposing that I should resign the part of Bottom to Mr. Blake, and at the same time requesting me to play Puck. This I positively refused to do. I told him plainly that Miss Keene had taken an antagonistic stand towards me, and that I felt that she would not appreciate a favor even if I might feel disposed to grant it, and would treat any concession that I should make as weakness. He said that Miss Keene had begged him to urge the matter, as she did not know how else to get Mr. Blake and myself into the cast. "Very well," said I; "if that is all, tell her I will play Bottom, and let Mr. Blake play Puck." And so we parted. Of course I did not suppose that he would carry this absurd message, as Mr. Blake would have turned the scale at two hundred and fifty pounds, and looked about as much like Puck as he resembled a fairy queen. But, not being familiar with Shakespeare, and having no idea what the characters were like, he gave her my suggestion word for word. This put the fair lady in a high temper, and she did not speak to me for a week. But I stood on my rights, and was cast for Bottom, Miss Keene essaying the part of Puck herself. After three or four rehearsals I discovered I should fail in the part of Bottom, and therefore deemed it wise to make "discretion the better part of valor," and resign the character, which I did upon the condition that I might take the play of *Our American Cousin* upon a starring tour, and give the management one-half of the profits for the use of the play.

Mutual Admiration

Herman Vezin, a nineteenth-century actor, recalled in his old age how as a youth he had overheard an actor compliment Edwin Forrest on the way he played Lear.

"Play Lear!" Forrest exclaimed. "I play Hamlet, Othello, Macbeth; but by heavens, sir, I am Lear!"

Vezin remembered a similar modesty in Dion Boucicault, the prolific dramatist, who had been caught in the act of praising a fellow playwright. Fortunately, it was Shakespeare, and Boucicault quickly excused himself: "Surely," he explained, "great men may admire each other."

The Perfectionist

William Lyon Phelps, the essayist and lifelong Yale professor, recalled in his Autobiography *the star quality in Richard Mansfield.*

On 2 May of that year [1905] Richard Mansfield produced *The Merchant of Venice* in New Haven. The house was sold out and we waited expectantly for some twenty minutes, wondering why the curtain did not rise. Finally the local manager appeared and read a statement dictated by Mr. Mansfield that ran something like this: "Owing to my incredible and unpardonable stupidity and negligence, the lights have not been properly arranged for the performance. Mr. Mansfield has finally consented to play, under protest, but he wishes the audience to understand that the bad lighting is my fault and not his." The audience would have noticed nothing amiss if this statement had not been read. Between the acts I found out that Mr. Mansfield had insisted that no performance be given and that the money be refunded to the spectators. His own acting was of course very fine; I think his death some years later the greatest loss the American stage ever suffered. After the performance that evening, a few of us met him at dinner at the Graduates' Club and talked until three in the morning. I asked him if it were true that he had refused to play. "Of course it is true, and I ought not to have played." "But, Mr. Mansfield, people had come from all over the state to see you; they would have been bitterly disappointed if there had been no performance." "I can't help that," he said, "no true artist should appear unless the conditions are right." He spoke bitterly about Joseph Jefferson, saying Jefferson had refused to help him at a critical moment in his career. Mansfield was difficult to get along with, but he was a great actor. When he played Shaw for the first time in America, the Irishman wrote him how a certain passage should be spoken to bring out the love interest, and Mansfield cabled him, "Love interest be damned." And Shaw cabled, "The same to you." Mr. Shaw told me in 1935, that when Mansfield was playing *The Devil's Disciple* in New York, a lady said to the playwright in London, "Mansfield ought to get down on his knees and thank God for such a play," to which Mr. Shaw replied, "Yes, but he wishes to God someone else had written it."

Co-star

During the Broadway run of John Barrymore's *Hamlet,* Jane Cowl came to a matinee performance. She was a star, and her mere presence proved a great distraction for the audience. She made matters worse by a running commentary she shared volubly with members of her entourage. Barrymore, who was known for interrupting his performances to lecture unruly spectators, did not seem to notice the star until his curtain call, when he bowed deeply towards Jane Cowl's box and said: "I'd like to take this opportunity to thank Miss Cowl for the privilege of co-starring with her this afternoon."

Nausea

Edna Ferber was a complete stranger to theatre when one of her novels was adapted for the stage. Ethel Barrymore starred in the title role of Our Mrs. Chesney, *and she gave Miss Ferber a quick education, which she acknowledged in* A Peculiar Treasure, *a book of memoirs published in 1939.*

From Ethel Barrymore I learned how a star may conduct herself in the theatre. I say may because I never have encountered anyone like her since. Certainly many a lesser lady of the stage has brought the potential murderess in me to the fore. I learned a good deal about her. A fine musician, she had wanted to be a concert pianist. On the road tryout she would play Sibelius to us on a smeary hotel piano, she had the pianist's strong almost masculine hands with blunt fingers. She carried a large flat scarlet box of Pall Mall cigarettes wherever she went; she was a very beautiful and exhilarating person indeed with that amazingly fine poreless skin, the enormous blue eyes, the classic Barrymore nose, the biting Barrymore wit.

We opened in Atlantic City for a tryout. The Apollo Theatre on the boardwalk was a favorite tryout house. The opening day was an eye opener for the young lady from Wisconsin. We were stopping at the old Shelburne, a rather ramshackle frame affair in that day and famous for its excellent food. Late in the morning I went round to Miss Barrymore's apartment to see how she was getting on. She had asked not to be left alone. She was nervous and frightened on opening days, even in a tryout town. There were one or two others in her sitting room. Miss Barrymore was just dressing, she stuck her head out of the bathroom door to greet us. She had rehearsed very late the night before, her face was dripping with water, she had a towel clutched in her hand, her hair was all about her shoulders, she was a triumph of sheer beauty over adversity. I put that impression thriftily away in my memory. Twenty years later, when I tried to describe the fresh girlish beauty of Lotta Bostrom in the novel *Come and Get It* as she was washing up in a train compartment after a night's journey I remembered Ethel Barrymore's face like a morning glory with the dew on it. And I just described that.

Miss Barrymore spent the rest of that day buying hats and vomiting.

She couldn't sit still. She couldn't digest anything. We went up and down the Atlantic City boardwalk, that dreary stretch of wood and sand and false-front shacks, and she bought hats and hats and hats, none of which she ever wore afterward. One, I recall, had a vast bird on it, and another was a fuzzy white knitted thing of the pussy-cat type such as young girls wear in Currier & Ives prints when shown skating on the old millpond.

We opened in New York at the Lyceum Theatre October 19, 1915. I went round to see Miss Barrymore in her dressing room. She was terribly nauseated. Between seizures she went on carefully making up. The call boy made his rounds. Half-hour, Miss Barrymore! . . . Mr. Frank, the house manager, came round to report on the Names in the house. . . . Fifteen minutes, Miss Barrymore! . . . She looked like one waiting for the tumbrel to take her to the guillotine. . . . Overture, Miss Barrymore! (I used this later in the play called *The Royal Family*.) . . . First-act curtain, Miss Barrymore.

She stood up, gave herself that last searching look in the brilliantly lighted make-up mirror, made a last futile dab with the rabbit's foot and powder puff, stood in the wings a moment, set herself, threw over her shoulder at us that gay desperate self-amused look and walked on with the string of traveling men who were registering at the small-town hotel of the first scene, her little drummer's suitcase in her hand.

Manners

A story told of both Ethel Barrymore and Beatrice Lillie involved a young actress who managed to obtain a dinner invitation to the house of one of these *grandes dames*. Inexplicably, the actress did not show and, inexcusably, she never called to apologize. Some time later, the two women ran into each other at a gallery opening.

"I believe I was invited to your house last week for dinner," the young actress began to explain.

"And did you come?" inquired Miss Barrymore.

Inverse Snob

Beatrice Lillie, though married to an English aristocrat, was anything but
a snob. During a reception for Josephine Baker on one of the latter's visits to
New York she waited patiently to be introduced to the guest of honor.
When they finally met, Miss Baker, who liked to put on airs, held out her
hand and said in her affected French accent:

"Eet is a great plaisir, Lady Peel."

Bea Lillie looked at the hand and said:

"Ah likes you too, honey."

Having a Scene

During rehearsals of Philip Barry's *Foolish Notion* (1945) in Wilmington,
Delaware, where it was to have its tryout, Tallulah Bankhead was extremely irritated by a young actress in a bit part. She complained each
rehearsal about her and mounted a campaign to get rid of her. Finally, on
the eve of the dress rehearsal, the star summoned the director, John C.
Wilson, and the producers, Theresa Helburn and Lawrence Langner of the
Theatre Guild, to her suite at the DuPont Hotel. There she launched into
her familiar tirade against the shortcomings of this unfortunate actress.

Finally the director managed to get a word in:

"But Tallulah," Wilson said in his most conciliating manner, "we have
already fired the girl. She's on the train back to New York."

"I know that, Jack," Tallulah turned on him, "but for heaven's sake, let
me have my scene."

Bore Wars

Tallulah Bankhead came from an intensely political family. Her father,
William B. Bankhead, was Speaker of the House, her grandfather and an
uncle both United States Senators. She herself, as an ardent Democrat,
campaigned for FDR and espoused many liberal causes. She was remark-
ably clearsighted in seeing no difference between Hitler and Stalin. Following the pact between the two dictators, when Stalin invaded Finland,
Tallulah Bankhead became very active in the Stage and Artists' Committee
for Finnish Relief.

She was acting in Lillian Hellman's hit play *The Little Foxes*, and, not
content with donating three months' worth of her salary (a considerable
thousand dollars a week at the time), she was also trying to persuade the
author and her producer Herman Shumlin to stage a benefit performance

to help the Finns. They both refused, having managed to persuade themselves that tiny Finland was somehow the aggressor against the mighty Soviet Union. During a lengthy and very public debate in the newspapers, Tallulah Bankhead and Lillian Hellman went at each other with claws and fangs.

"I think she's a dreary bore," the actress said of the playwright. "She writes like an angel, but she's a dreary bore as spinach is a dreary bore. I say she's spinach and the hellman with her."

Lillian Hellman, who had once called Tallulah "one of the great actresses of our time," responded:

"Hate from Miss Bankhead is a small badge of honor, and praise undesirable. Miss Bankhead will never again act in a play of mine because I can only stand a certain amount of boredom."

"She can't use that word against me," Tallulah protested. "I called her a bore first."

Running

A long run, somebody once said, is when you pay back your investors. But for actors, playing the same role night after night, eight times a week, sometimes for years, poses many problems. Keeping things fresh is the most obvious one. Remembering lines, too long taken for granted, is another. According to Alfred Drake, during the run of Oklahoma! *Howard Da Silva tried for the sake of variety to play the part of Jud as John Barrymore would have played it in imitation of his brother Lionel.*

Florence Williams remembers playing Judith Anderson's daughter in The Old Maid *(1935).*

We had a small funny scene together. One night, though, she suddenly changed her reading of the lines, and it took me about three days to readjust so that I was getting my laughs. As soon as the laughs were back she changed again, and I had to scramble after her. This went on for two months. When I got the laughs, she'd change her readings. The stage manager kept scolding me for having lost the laughs; he didn't dare talk to her. Finally, I couldn't stand it any more, and I said, "Judith, I'm miserable when you change readings. I'm just not experienced enough to keep up." And she said, "Oh, I'm so sorry, my dear. I thought it would amuse you, too! I get so *bored*." She never did it again.

There's Nothing Like a Dame

Judith Anderson was born an Australian, which is why she could be knighted. Asked if being made a Dame had made any difference in her life, she once replied:

"I find myself wearing gloves more often."

Not long ago, the Los Angeles Drama Critics Circle honored Dame Judith Anderson with a Lifetime Achievement award. Dan Sullivan, drama critic of the Los Angeles *Times*, called Dame Judith to invite her to the dinner, but in the end he had to go out of town and missed the occasion. On his return, Sullivan called the actress at her home in Santa Barbara, to find out how things went.

"Oh, it was agony," she said, in that voice that Robinson Jeffers once described as "liquid fire." I didn't get home until four in the morning, it was just awful."

"Next year, when we give you another award," the critic suggested in a conciliatory tone, "we will try to do it right."

"Next time—you mail it!" thundered Dame Judith.

Posthumous Acting

In 1946 the struggle to establish Israel as an independent state was moving toward its climax and the Jewish community in America was deeply involved. Palestine was still governed by a pro-Arab British Mandate which went to extraordinary lengths to bar the surviving remnant of the Nazi Holocaust from entering. As the United Nations debated the partitioning of Palestine, the normally hard-bitten journalist and playwright Ben Hecht was one of the people who joined the fray, and he galvanized an extraordinary group of artists to create a pageant drama to raise money for the American League for a Free Palestine. A Flag Is Born was directed by Luther Adler, Kurt Weill wrote the music, and it starred Celia Adler and Paul Muni as a refugee couple who died on stage before reaching the promised land. It was also Marlon Brando's fourth role on Broadway. In the final scene, it fell to him to cover the dead Paul Muni's body, including the face, with a flag, and then deliver a rousing speech to a crescendo of music that closed the show. Muni suggested one day that it might be more dramatic to leave his face uncovered during that speech. Brando recalled the following.

I agreed with him, but in the next performance I forgot all about his suggestion and covered him completely, face and all. I began my big speech, and when I looked down I saw the flag crawl down his forehead, slip away from his eyes along the bridge of his nose, slowly exposing his face inch by inch. It was like magic.

I saw Muni's upstage hand, the one hidden from the audience, pulling down the flag by gathering folds in his fist. The old hambone couldn't stand not having his face in the final scene. I was afraid I'd break up, so I stopped in the middle of the speech, kneeled, pulled the flag away from his face and tucked it tenderly under his chin. His expression was beatific. Imagine! He was supposed to be dead, but he was still acting. If the curtain hadn't come down, he'd have acted out all the stages of *rigor mortis* setting in.

It's Not Over Until It's Over

Maurice Schwartz (1890–1960), a legendary actor-manager of the Yiddish theatre, was famous for his ability to conduct business with his lawyers in the wings and then rush on stage to act out the final scene of a tragedy. After he had expired as the Hassidic rabbi towards the end of his dramatization of I. J. Singer's *Yoshe Kalb*, Schwartz switched to his role as a director and continued to exhort his fellow actors from under the shroud:

"Louder!" he would whisper, "louder!"

One of Sanford Meisner's favorite stories in teaching about stage control concerned the great Sarah Adler—wife of Jacob and mother of Stella. She was doing one of her tear-jerking goodbye scenes, just before final curtain. The theatre was electric with emotion, tears were rolling down Sarah's face, and the audience began to build the applause. But there was still one more beat to be wrung from that scene, so she turned to her adoring audience, raised a little finger and said sharply, "Not yet!" and then went back into character to finish the scene as she thought it ought to be finished.

How to Upstage Yourself

Miriam Hopkins and Victor Jory were starring in *The Perfect Marriage* (1944), written by Samuel Raphaelson, one of Ernst Lubitsch's screenwriters. The opening scene is a wedding anniversary celebration, where the couple is trying to recapture some of the romance that had gone out of their lives. On opening night, as soon as Victor Jory grabbed her, Miriam Hopkins passed out—she was given to fainting fits. Jory carried her to the bed and had to ad-lib through the rest of the scene until she came to.

It was not until later that Jory found out that Miriam Hopkins had cabled her apologies to various columnists, citing her fits as the cause. Strangely enough, she sent these telegrams before she fainted. "It was a little too much," Jory later recalled. "I have worked with actors who have upstaged their co-workers so far that they upstaged themselves. Miriam was one of those."

No Dummy

Ethel Merman was even-tempered and compliant with changes that were brought into rehearsal. But there came a point, one or two weeks before official opening, when she could not absorb any new material. In vain did Stephen Sondheim write an extra verse for her in *Gypsy* (1959), and when he tried to complain to the Dramatists Guild, he was told about the time La Merman was waiting for Irving Berlin to finish the song for "Hostess with the Mostes' on the Ball" in *Call Me Madam*. She sang a dummy lyric during the pre-Broadway tour, and when the show got to New York, Berlin came to her dressing room one day in triumph:

"Here it is! I've finally perfected the lyric."

"Call me Miss Birds Eye," said the star. "The show is frozen." And for the next three years she sang only the dummy lyric.

Their Names in Lights

As soon as Ethel Merman and Jimmy Durante were signed by producers Russel Crouse and Howard Lindsay to star in a musical called *Red Hot and Blue*, a fight broke out over who should get first billing. When Merman's agent tried to use the argument that "the lady's name always goes first," Durante came back:

"Oh, yeah? How about Mister and Missis?"

In the end a compromise was reached by crossing the names:

Billing

During plans for a television version of Ben Jonson's *Volpone*, starring Orson Welles and Jackie Gleason, there were heated discussions about which of them would get top billing. Recalling how he told Welles that he could put his name first, the Great One added: "Now I know how Fargo felt."

Where Credit Is Due

Until he wrote the book and lyrics for *Oklahoma!* and *Carmen Jones*, Oscar Hammerstein II was not given as much credit for his talent as his musical collaborators. The lyricist took this in good humor and in that year of his greatest success (1943) he paid for an advertisement in the annual issue of *Variety*, which traditionally contains thinly veiled messages of self-congratulation by members of the show business community. Hammerstein instead took this opportunity to remind his colleagues of five of his most notorious flops, ending with the celebrated line: "I've done it before—and I can do it again!"

Hammerstein's wife, Dorothy, was much more sensitive to slights to her husband, and once when she heard somebody refer to Jerome Kern's *Ol' Man River*, she immediately hit back:

"Oscar Hammerstein wrote *Ol' Man River*. Jerome Kern wrote 'Ta-ta dumdum, ta ta-ta dumdum.' "

Unheard of

Stephen Sondheim got one of his big breaks when Leonard Bernstein called to ask him to co-write the lyrics for *West Side Story* (1957). Sondheim wanted to prove himself as a composer but, despite advice by his mentor, Oscar Hammerstein II, tried to excuse himself from the assignment by saying he didn't know any poor people, let alone Puerto Ricans.

After another two years, when the show finally opened to favorable reviews, Bernstein saw Sondheim moping around the theatre and realized that the young man felt he had not received enough credit for his contribution to the hit show, which the older and more famous man knew to be considerable. So Bernstein called up his agent and his music publisher and insisted that the score be reprinted and his name be taken off as co-lyricist, so that Sondheim could get sole credit. "I think, quite frankly," Sondheim's longtime agent Flora Roberts marveled, "what Lenny did is fairly unheard of in the theatre. Too many people get credit for things they don't do, much less remove their names."

The Scarecrow and the Ingenue

Beverley Bozeman was a young dancer and choreographer in 1949 when the producers of Where's Charley? *needed a replacement for the part of Amy. The show was George Abbott and Frank Loesser's musical version of* Charley's Aunt, *choreographed by George Balanchine and starring Ray Bolger in his greatest stage success. Bozeman auditioned and got the part of the ingenue.*

I am twenty-two years old, it's my first Broadway lead, and it's with the Scarecrow from *The Wizard of Oz*. What could be bad? I had been warned that Ray Bolger, who had been in the show for a year and had some split-second changes from Charley into drag, had a tendency, when something went wrong, to take it out on the first person he encountered. I had been in the show for two weeks and I had seen nothing to worry about. Then I got a newly designed gown, which David Ffolks, the costume designer, said I had to have, even though I liked the old one. He decided I needed a real ingenue cupcake dress in pale yellow, with tulle sleeves, ruffles, bows, bouffants, everything one could possibly want. Anyway, something happened just before the final big waltz, the Red Rose Cotillion. I come on, the chorus is all lined up and Ray staggers on, having just changed back from Aunt to Charley in tails. I saw at once that something was wrong: he's got steam coming out of his ears. He takes one look at me, and I am in an unfamiliar dress. We start waltzing, but as he turns me out, I see him sticking out his foot and trip me. I land on my buns stage center of the St. James Theatre. When you slip you go down so fast you don't know what's happening. But he had tripped me on purpose, I saw it, and went down slowly, thinking: "O-h-h-h, the Scarecrow of Oz is screwing me up."

I was sitting there in these mounds of yellow, looking like a nosegay. But I knew that if I let him get away with this, I'd be a patsy forever. The orchestra is marking by now, and so I thought, "Okay, I'm gonna make arms. I did a port de bras overhead to the right, a little port de bras to the left. Ray is dancing around, saying, "Get up!" "Hm-mm, hm-mm," I said and I'm making arms. "Get up!" he ordered me more urgently now. "When you give me your hand," I said. He got that one. The kids in the chorus are all in a semi-circle going "ooh-hoo, ooh-hoo," and the orchestra is going "um-cha-cha, um-cha-cha," and I just sat there. Finally, Ray came over, and the only way he could give me his hand was to bend over as though he was bowing. I took my time before I gave him my hand, and somehow we picked up the tempo and got back into the waltz. When he looked at

me I said: "Don't you ever do that again to me, you sonofabitch." He
didn't even blink. From then on we were fine. I saw him do his number
on other people, but I'm still proud that at twenty-two I was smart enough
to give as good as I got. At the time, when we finished the number, I was
in tears, of course, because my idol, the Scarecrow of Oz, had tripped me
up deliberately.

Star to the Rescue

*Jerry Herman was so young when David Merrick hired him to write the
book for* Hello, Dolly! *(1964) that he fudged about his age. He recalls
making a breakthrough during the tryout in Detroit.*

Originally I had written a song, "Penny in My Pocket," to close act one
about Horace Vandergelder (played by David Burns) becoming half-a-
millionaire. After just a few nights I realized it was wrong. Audiences were
falling in love with Dolly as Carol Channing played her, and wanted to
know more about her character. After a performance I told Gower Champion, the director: "I have an idea what's wrong with the end of act one."
He agreed with my analysis. So I went back to my hotel room and wrote
"Before the Parade Passes By." It took only about thirty minutes because I
was so excited.

It was late at night but I had to show off my new child to someone. So
even though I knew it was improper, I called Carol, who was unaware of
my discussion with Gower. Her voice sounded quite asleep, and I said,
"Please forgive me for calling so late, but I have just written a new song
for you, to end the first act, and I'll explode if I can't play it right now."

Carol immediately put on a bathrobe and took the elevator down to my
floor. And there in my hotel room I played and sang "Before the Parade
Passes By," for the very first time. On hearing it, Carol, too, became so excited that she learned the song in the next ten minutes. And then we called
and woke up Gower Champion who did the same thing: he put on his
bathrobe and came down to my room. And there Carol Channing brought
to life the song which became the heart of the show, because it embodies
Dolly's character and her decision to rejoin the human race. Since the change
involved ordering new scenery, costumes and a whole new staging, it was
important that Gower be thoroughly convinced. Nothing could have done
that more clearly than Carol's commitment—singing there in the middle
of the night, on top of her strenuous performance earlier that evening. I

can't think of too many stars who would be so supportive of their composer-lyricist at three o'clock in the morning.

How to Deal with Producers

Katharine Hepburn, now among the most admired stage and film actors alive, did not achieve her eminence by being obliging and nice. She faced many setbacks during her career. Dorothy Parker's withering comment on her performance in *The Lake* ("Miss Hepburn played the whole gamut from A to B") might have scored a knockout with a less determined actor.

Soon after her graduation from Bryn Mawr, Hepburn got an acting job touring in *Death Takes a Holiday*. Before long, she recalled, the producers told her that they'd grant her the privilege of resigning from the cast.

"Well," Miss Hepburn replied, "I'm not taking that privilege, so if you want to fire me go ahead, but get out of here because you'll be lucky if I don't kill you."

How to Deal with a Director

Katharine Hepburn returned to Broadway, after a long absence, in *Coco* (1969). She made a grand staircase entrance as Coco Chanel in the musical based on the French designer's life. It was a triumphant entry, yet Hepburn played it crying, because in the scene that followed Coco had to tell her staff that she was closing down her business. Director Michael Benthall found her entrance sad and tried to get her to change it:

"It creates a downbeat mood."

"I don't agree with you," said La Hepburn, "and we won't discuss it again."

And they never did.

How to Deal with the Text

Katharine Hepburn's first word in the second act of *Coco* was the word "SHIT!," which always brought the house down, because it was so completely out of character for the actress, and yet summed up the feelings of the character she was playing. The word had been suggested by Hepburn herself, and when librettist Alan Jay Lerner tried to soften its shock by substituting the French word *merde*, she vetoed it. "Not everyone speaks French," she told him.

How to Deal with an Audience

During the tour of *Coco* in Cleveland, suddenly a flashbulb went off near
the stage. Katharine Hepburn stopped in the middle of her scene and
peered out into the audience:

"Who the hell did that?" she wanted to know.

A young girl nervously confessed.

"If you had any guts, you would leave," Miss Hepburn raged, then
added: "If we don't have regard for each other, it will be the end of us."

Then she apologized to the audience and went back to the scene.

Ego

*Sidney Poitier was already an established movie star when he joined the
company of* A Raisin in the Sun *(1959),* Lorraine Hansberry's ground-
breaking drama that was produced by Philip Rose and directed on Broadway by Lloyd Richards. Poitier recounts in his memoirs,* This Life, *the
special problems of a star.*

We had to go into Chicago for some weeks before a theatre loosened up
in New York, and opening night in Chicago turned out to be phenomenal
for everyone, but especially for Claudia McNeil, who played the mother.
In Chicago I was not on speaking terms with Lorraine, who was understandably happy because her play was doing so well and couldn't grasp
why I was dissatisfied. The reason was complicated. I believed from the
first day I went into researsal that the play should not unfold from the
mother's point of view. I still believe that. I think that for maximum effect,
A Raisin in the Sun should unfold from the point of view of the son,
Walter Lee Younger. (Yes, I played Walter Lee.) Because Claudia registered so powerfully in the play and because the audience responded so wonderfully to her *and* the play, the producer, director, and author were all
satisfied. And yet I kept insisting that the mother shouldn't be the focus
of the play.

They accused me of "star" behavior. Of wanting to be the top dog on
stage. . . . My feelings were real and strong, but I had no idea where they
sprang from. Were they a reflection of my parents? My self? Were they
political? Yes? No? Maybe? With no adequate response at my fingertips
that would dispel their confusion, or arrest their suspicions, they went on
to accuse me of (among other things) being unreasonably sensitive to this
issue for unattractive and selfish personal reasons. But I still saw it that
way, and I had an ally—the talented, highly intelligent Ruby Dee. We

decided on an approach, and conspired to keep the strength in the character of Walter Lee Younger, which meant my playing *against* Claudia
McNeil, who is a tower of strength as a stage personality. I had to change
my whole performance to prevent the mother character from so dominat-
ing the stage that it would cast a negative focus on the black male. But
the excellent reviews in Chicago hardened management's resolve to "put
it to bed." After all, what strange kind of nut must I be to keep quarreling
with success? By the end of the run in Chicago, management's position
was: All Poitier is thinking of is that he's the star of the play and Claudia
McNeil is getting all the audience's response.

But how could that have been? Wasn't I more secure than that? Didn't
I receive marvelous reviews everywhere we went? Didn't I get terrific
responses from the audiences too? Indeed I did! Then their stinging accu-
sations were obviously not true—unless, God forbid, I was miles and miles
off base, completely out of touch with my ego and therefore blinded to
the merit of their argument. Heavenly Father! Could I be that far out of
touch? You're damn right I could. I wasn't exactly what you could call a
Rock of Gibraltar at that time in my life, and besides, they were very
bright people, Lorraine, Phil, and Lloyd. Yes, they might be right—even
then I recognized that there could be honest differences of opinion and
judgment. But however much I leaned in the direction of objectivity, trying to give them the benefit of every doubt, I still was aware of the whiff
of gold in the air. That intoxicating element was quietly orchestrating
management's sharp responses to my specific challenge, as if I were an
unholy threat to a bonanza whose aroma was already creeping over the
horizon. And to management's not unreasonable desire to keep the play
running forever had to be added the fact that I was committed to remain
in the play no more than six months. Claudia McNeil had a "run of the
play" contract, and they had seen by Chicago that she was going to be a
big part of the future commerciality of the play, whereas I was leaving in
six months to fulfill motion picture commitments.

Anyway, the play opened in New York with me playing it the way I
wanted to play it, and it was an enormous success.

The Barrymore Theatre was a place of magic that opening night. As
the curtain fell at the end of the third act, the audience came to its feet
in a standing ovation that brought tears to the eyes of our cast. That audience, many of them with tears streaming down their faces, stomped,
howled, and screamed with joy. Finally, the thunderous applause took on
a rhythmic clapping and they began shouting. "Author, author, author."
Lorraine Hansberry was standing in the audience with members of her
family, and Ruby Dee told me to go and get her. I jumped from the stage

into the audience, took her by the hand, and led her up onto the stage, where the audience and her actors continued to pay her the tribute she so very much deserved. . . .

The breach between me and the management continued unrelieved for a number of reasons, not the least of which were my complaints about unprofessional behavior on stage during performances of one actor who, for reasons that remained a mystery, would make subtle changes in performance style that would weaken the effectiveness of others' performances. Management, still suspecting that ego was the root cause of my earlier complaint, concluded that the new charges probably had no basis beyond my ego's addiction to the occasional stroking.

To Be—And Not to Be

In 1969 Nicol Williamson was appearing as Hamlet in Boston, prior to a limited run on Broadway. On opening night, the British actor suddenly announced, in the middle of a scene, that he was giving up his acting career and walked offstage. After he calmed down somewhat, he returned to his performance amidst general applause.

Bad Girl

In 1970 Joan Fontaine was touring various summer theatres in Alan Ayckbourn's comedy, *Relatively Speaking*. Remembering what it felt like to listen to the star's endless stream of demands, whims, and complaints, one of the producers said: "It got to be so bad that back in the hotel room I would watch a late night rerun of *Rebecca* and found myself rooting for Mrs. Danvers."

Age Cannot Wither

Rosemary Harris was once on a talkshow hosted by Dick Cavett, and a fellow guest was Lynn Fontanne. In her mid-eighties, the frail, tiny actress was laboriously guided on to the set. Then the stage manager started the countdown to airtime: "Six . . . five . . . four . . . three . . . two . . . one." During those few seconds Lynn Fontanne managed to shed at least thirty years.

Rear View

At an after-performance party, Laurette Taylor (1884–1946) was having a pleasant conversation with a man, who eventually excused himself and joined another group. As she watched him leave, Miss Taylor's face suddenly darkened and she turned on her hostess:

"How dare he come here! I saw that man walk out on the show this evening!"

"How could you be sure?" asked the hostess.

"I may sometimes forget a face," replied the star, "but I never forget a back!"

CHAPTER 8

Showmen

The Yellow Brick Road

The name of P. T. Barnum (1810–91) is synonymous with the razzle-dazzle of American showmanship. In his detailed and readable autobiography, he was neither secretive nor modest about his techniques. Once he was a victim of his own success.

In 1865, the space occupied for my Museum purposes was more than double what it was in 1842. The Lecture Room, originally narrow, ill-contrived and inconvenient, was so enlarged and improved that it became one of the most commodious and beautiful amusement halls in the City of New York. At first, my attractions and inducements were merely the collection of curiosities by day, and an evening entertainment, consisting of such variety performances as were current in ordinary shows. Then Saturday afternoons, and, soon afterwards, Wednesday afternoons were devoted to entertainments and the popularity of the Museum grew so rapidly that I presently found it expedient and profitable to open the great Lecture Room every afternoon, as well as every evening, on every weekday in the year. The first experiments in this direction more than justified my expectations, for the day exhibitions were always more thronged than those of the evening. Of course I made the most of the holidays, advertising extensively and presenting extra inducements; nor did attractions elsewhere seem to keep the crowd from coming to the Museum. On great holidays, I gave as many as twelve performances to as many different audiences.

By degrees the character of the stage performances was changed. The transient attractions of the Museum were constantly diversified, and educated dogs, industrious fleas, automatons, jugglers, ventriloquists, living statuary, tableaux, gipsies, Albinoes, fat boys, giants, dwarfs, rope-dancers, live "Yankees," pantomime, instrumental music, singing and dancing in great variety dioramas, panoramas, models of Niagara, Dublin, Paris, and Jerusalem; Hannington's dioramas of the Creation, the Deluge, Fairy Grotto, Storm at Sea; the first English Punch and Judy in this country, Italian Fantoccini, mechanical figures, fancy glass-blowing, knitting machines and other triumphs in the mechanical arts; dissolving views, American Indians, who enacted their warlike and religious ceremonies on the stage,—these, among others, were all exceedingly successful.

I thoroughly understood the art of advertising, not merely by means of printer's ink, which I have always used freely, and to which I confess myself so much indebted for my success, but by turning every possible circumstance to my account. It was my monomania to make the Museum the town wonder and town talk. I often seized upon an opportunity by instinct, even before I had a very definite conception as to how it should be used, and it seemed, somehow, to mature itself and serve my purpose. As an illustration, one morning a stout, hearty-looking man, came into my ticket-office and begged some money. I asked him why he did not work and earn his living? He replied that he could get nothing to do and that he would be glad of any job at a dollar a day. I handed him a quarter of a dollar, told him to go and get his breakfast and return, and I would employ him at light labor at a dollar and a half a day. When he returned I gave him five common bricks.

"Now," said I, "go and lay a brick on the sidewalk at the corner of Broadway and Ann Street; another close by the Museum; a third diagonally across the way at the corner of Broadway and Vesey Street, by the Astor House; put down the fourth on the sidewalk in front of St. Paul's Church, opposite; then, with the fifth brick in hand, take up a rapid march from one point to the other, making the circuit, exchanging your brick at every point, and say nothing to any one."

"What is the object of this?" inquired the man.

"No matter," I replied; "all you need to know is that it brings you fifteen cents wages per hour. It is a bit of my fun, and to assist me properly you must seem to be as deaf as a post; wear a serious countenance; answer no questions; pay no attention to any one; but attend faithfully to the work and at the end of every hour by St. Paul's clock show this ticket at the Museum door; enter, walking solemnly through every hall in the building; pass out, and resume your work."

With the remark that it was "all one to him, so long as he could earn his living," the man placed his bricks and began his round. Half an hour afterwards, at least five hundred people were watching his mysterious movements. He had assumed a military step and bearing, and looking as sober as a judge, he made no response whatever to the constant inquiries as to the object of his singular conduct. At the end of the first hour, the sidewalks in the vicinity were packed with people all anxious to solve the mystery. The man, as directed, then went into the Museum, devoting fifteen minutes to a solemn survey of the halls, and afterwards returning to his round. This was repeated every hour till sundown and whenever the man went into the Museum a dozen or more persons would buy tickets and follow him, hoping to gratify their curiosity in regard to the purpose of his movements. This was continued for several days—the curious people who followed the man into the Museum considerably more than paying his wages—till finally the policeman, to whom I had imparted my object, complained that the obstruction of the sidewalk by crowds had become so serious that I must call in my "brick man." This trivial incident excited considerable talk and amusement; it advertised me; and it materially advanced my purpose of making a lively corner near the Museum.

Another Sucker Born

In the 1840s, the young Chauncey M. Depew became part of the continuous supply of suckers that P. T. Barnum needed for his attractions.

My first contact with Mr. Barnum occurred when I was a boy up in Peekskill. At that time he had a museum and a show in a building at the corner of Ann Street and Broadway, opposite the old Astor House. By skilful advertising he kept people all over the country expecting something new and wonderful and anxious to visit his show.

There had been an Indian massacre on the Western plains. The particulars filled the newspapers and led to action by the government in retaliation. Barnum advertised that he had succeeded in securing the Sioux warriors whom the government had captured, and who would re-enact every day the bloody battle in which they were victorious.

It was one of the hottest afternoons in August when I appeared there from the country. The Indians were on the top floor, under the roof. The performance was sufficiently blood-curdling to satisfy the most exacting reader of a penny-dreadful. After the performance, when the audience left, I was too fascinated to go, and remained in the rear of the hall, gazing at these dreadful savages. One of them took off his head-gear, dropped his tomahawk and scalping-knife, and said in the broadest Irish to his neighbor: "Moike, if this weather don't cool off, I will be nothing but a grease spot." This was among the many illusions which have been dissipated for me in a long life. Nothwithstanding that, I still have faith, and dearly love to be fooled, but not to have the fraud exposed.

Posthumous Invitation

P. T. Barnum instituted the habit of sending complimentary tickets to local clergymen when his traveling show hit town, in the hope of getting publicity and moral endorsement from the pulpit. The tradition was carried on by the circus bearing his name, even after Barnum was dead. One time, the Reverend Walker who had succeeded the deceased Reverend Hawks to his pastorate in Hartford, Connecticut, received tickets for the circus, with the compliments of the famous showman. Doctor Walker studied the invitation that was addressed to his predecessor, and then remarked:

"Doctor Hawks is dead and Mr. Barnum is dead; evidently they haven't met."

In the Palmy Days

William Mitchell (1798–1856) popularized the musical burlesque in America. His famous management of the Olympic Theatre (1839–50), chronicled by the theatre historian Laurence Hutton in his Plays and Players, *illustrates how much the reputation of a particular company owes to the personality of its leader.*

Personally as a manager he was popular, his bearing was manly and courteous to all with whom, in a business and social way, he came in contact; he was straightforward in his dealings with men, was possessed of tact and a seeming innate knowledge of everything that was promising of success in a player or a play.

As an actor himself, Mr. Mitchell was in his line almost inimitable, at all events so say old playgoers who remember him and his representations of such parts as Jem Baggs and Crummles; he could "make up" the most irresistibly funny faces ever seen on the New York or any other stage, and he was the only manager who ever dared to make his entire audience members, so to speak, of his stock company. To the pit he was never known to appeal without meeting with its entire approbation; were his auditors there uproarious he would chide; did they appreciate a "point" he would make manifest his own appreciation of their applause. He would stop suddenly in the midst of a scene from *Macbeth*, and marching down to the footlights would say, with the utmost seriousness, that "If any boy in the pit thought he could do that any better he might come on to the stage and try!" The effect upon the boys in the pit can be imagined. Not only the pit but the whole house "came down" at this, although no boy was ever known to go on the stage to try.

There seemed to be a perfect sympathy between Mitchell and his audiences, and the habitual visitor to the Olympic cannot remember an occasion when the desire to please on the part of the performer did not meet with the ready and cordial approval of the house, or when any shortcoming or disability was not as cordially and as readily overlooked or forbearingly borne. To this sympathy and fellow feeling may be ascribed much of Mitchell's success, for prosper at that time he and the Olympic did, and to the eight or nine years of his management do the old playgoers refer when they speak of "the palmy days of the Olympic."

What Shall We Do for Something New?

John Brougham managed the Broadway Lyceum in the mid-nineteenth century. "If ever America has had an Aristophanes," wrote Laurence Hutton a generation later, "John Brougham was his name." Mainly known for social satire and literary burlesques, Brougham is a largely unrecognized experimenter, who anticipated some of the technical and formal innovations we may associate with Pirandello and Brecht. For example in a piece called What Shall We Do for Something New? *which was ostensibly a travesty of the opera* La Sonnambula, *"the sex of the whole dramatis personae was reversed," and in an age of elaborate sets, none were used. "The flat that was to represent the town," Laurence Hutton explained, "was simply a blank, lead-colored surface, with the announcement in straggling black letters printed conspicuously upon it, 'This is a Village.' Scenery, other than this, there was none; a labeled substitute informing the audience what each wing, property or flat was supposed to be, as 'This is a Tree,' or 'This is a Pump,' being the only attempt at scenic display."*

Following this piece, in 1851, John Brougham produced A Row at the

Lyceum, or Green-Room Secrets, *called by Laurence Hutton "the most Broughamesque of Broughamisms . . . the most remarkable of all of his remarkable productions, and one of the most original plays ever put upon any stage." He also describes how the audience received it.*

The curtain rose to a crowded house on a scene at rehearsal, after the manner of Sheridan's *Critic*, the actors and actresses in their ordinary street dresses, looking in every respect like the not more than ordinary men and women they really were, when paint and tinsel, sock and buskin, were discarded, dropping in casually like other ordinary mortals on business bent, to read and discuss Carlyle's new and wonderful production.

It was the green-room proper of a theatre, with all the green-room accessories and surroundings, the scenes and incidents, concords and discords of a green-room gathering; and was as heartily enjoyed by the Lyceum audience as would one of Wallack's famous Saturday night "houses" of the present, enjoy being invited to visit *en masse* that unknown and mysterious land contained "behind the scenes," and to assist at Mr. Boucicault's reading of *The Shaughran* to the assembled company for the first time.

The audience was thoroughly interested and amused at the *realism* of the performance, when, "Enter Mrs. B.," the scene changes, and the "Row at the Lyceum" begins. While she greets her friends, looks over her part, objects to her "business," and lays her claims to something "more in her line," a stout, middle-aged gentleman, seated in the middle of the pit, clothed in a Quakerish garb, who had hitherto quietly listened and laughed with the rest, rises suddenly in his place, with umbrella clasped firmly in both hands, and held up on a line with his nose, to the astonishment of the house, calmly and sedately addresses the stage and the house, in words to this effect: "That woman looks for all the world like Clementina! Her voice is very like—the form the same." And then, with emphasis: "It is! it is! my wife!" at the same time leaving his seat in great excitement, he rushes toward the footlights, and cries wildly and loudly, "Come off that stage, thou miserable woman!"

The utmost confusion quickly reigned in the theatre. The audience, at first amused at the interruption, seeing that the Quaker gentleman was in earnest, soon took sides for or against him, and saluted him with all sorts of encouraging and discouraging cries as he fought his way toward the orchestra. "Who is he?" "Who is she?" "Shame! shame!" "Put him out!" "Go it, Broadbrim!" "Sit down!" "Police!" Hootings, hissings, cat-calls, making the scene as tumultuous as can be well imagined.

At this stage of the proceedings, the dramatic performances of *Green-*

Room Secrets were entirely stopped. The artists were utterly unable to proceed on account of the uproar in front. The ladies were frightened; the gentlemen, addressing the house, and striving vainly to restore order, were quite powerless to proceed; while Mrs. B——, the innocent cause of all the trouble, evidently preparing for flight, was agitated and very nervous. All this time the irate husband was struggling to reach his wife, and fighting his way toward her. He finally climbed over the orchestra, the red-shirted defender of the young woman close behind him, when both were collared by a policeman or two, dragged upon the stage, made to face the house, the regulation stage semicircle was formed before the footlights, and the epilogue was spoken,—the audience beginning to recognize in the efficient policemen, the supes of the establishment; in the fire-laddie of the soap-locks and tilted tile, Mr. W. J. Florence, a member of the company; in the indignant husband, Mr. Brougham himself; in the recovered wife, Mrs. Brougham; and to realize that the *Row at the Lyceum* was a premeditated and magnificent "sell."

The deception was very cleverly managed, only those in the secret having any idea that all of this uproarious disturbance in the auditorium was part of the play, and the *dénouement* was received with shouts of laughter and applause. The piece ran for some time, amused the town, and brought profit and fame to the manager. The original victims to the hoax, eager to see the effects upon other unsuspecting people, went again and again; took their friends to be sold; these friends in their turn taking their friends; everybody who had "bitten" having that anxiety to see somebody else "bite,"— that desire to relieve themselves at the expense of others, that is natural to "poor humanity," and filling the house as long as anybody was left to "nibble," when more novelty was demanded, and the *Row at the Lyceum* was withdrawn.

The Wood That Could Not See Forrest

One of the most powerful theatrical managers in Philadelphia was William Wood (1779–1861), a caustic man who very rarely praised anybody. One day, he was in the green-room reminiscing in front of the whole company that the finest debut he had ever witnessed was that of a young man from Philadelphia, playing Norval in the tragedy of *Douglas*. Edwin Forrest was present, so he rose and bowing with comic gravity, said:

"Mr. Wood, I was that young gentleman."

The other actors were delighted to see that Wood had betrayed himself into making an unintentional compliment, until the manager replied:

"Well, sir, you have never done so well since."

The Bully

One of the dominant personalities in the management of theatres and
stars was the Boston-based impresario John Stetson (1836–96). Starting off
as a professional athlete, Stetson was known as a big, blustering bully
(though the Western hats were manufactured by another Stetson). In
some ways he was the theatrical ancestor of Sam Goldwyn: both were
shrewd businessmen with pretensions, and unwittingly provided entertain-
ment within show business circles with their ignorance and malapropisms.
As these passed from mouth to mouth, people began to invent apocryphal
stories. Some of the authentic ones were collected by Robert Grau in his
Forty Years Observation of Music and the Drama *(1909).*

When Stetson was managing the Globe Theatre in Boston, one of his annual visiting stars was Mrs. D. P. Bowers and just before her appearance in
each city, her managers caused large posters to be placed everywhere with
only her three initials (of very large size) on them: D. P. B. On the opening night of her engagement in the Hub the theatre was not as crowded as
the great Boston manager would desire, so that he was in a rather poor humor. In the lobby a stranger pointed to one of the big posters across the
way and inquired of Stetson:
"What do those three big letters over there stand for?" To which Stetson gruffly replied:
"Damn poor business!"
On another occasion Stetson had as the feature at the "Globe," Lillian
Olcott in Sardou's *Theodora*. The lithographs were most attractive and
one, a big three-sheet, had a portrait of Theodora entering the cage wherein
were three man-eating lions. Stetson was standing in the foyer of the the-
atre when he was thus accosted:
"Is this a good play, Theodora?"
"Yes," said Stetson.
"Are those real lions?" asked the man.
"Yes," murmured the manager.
"Is it true that Theodora goes in the cage with the lions?"
Stetson, not pleased with the business the play was doing, replied roughly,
"No, but I wish to God she would."

Stetson was sitting in the front row of the orchestra on an important night
of a comic opera's first production. This was most unusual for him as he
always made it a rule to watch these first nights from the wings. However,
on this night he was listening to the overture and his attention was at-

tracted by the cornet player who was idle, although all of the other instruments were heard. Stetson said nothing until the cornetist had been silent for nearly a moment. Turning to him, Stetson demanded to know why he was not playing his instrument. The cornetist, greatly disturbed by this sudden approach, answered in a trembling voice: "I have sixteen bars rest."

"Rest! did you say?" asked Stetson.

"Yes," said the musician.

"I don't pay to rest. I pay you to play and if you don't blow your horn and keep blowing it you can go to the box office and get your money and rest as long as you like," was the excited retort.

John Stetson was manager of James O'Neill for many years, and the star who was so long identified with *The Count of Monte Cristo* prospered greatly under the Bostonian's guidance. Once the representative of Stetson wired him that his presence was needed in Chicago, where the company was appearing at McVicker's Theatre. The treasurer of this establishment was at the time a Mr. Sharp, who, after the death of J. H. McVicker, became manager. It happened that Stetson arrived in Chicago about noon on a Saturday, which was, of course, a matinee day, and it is quite evident that he did not relish being called upon to make the long journey. At all events, as he proceeded along Madison Street the matinee crowds were pouring into the theatre. Stetson's attention was attracted by a huge sign which read:

MATINEE TO-DAY AT 2 SHARP.

Of course this meant that the performance would start promptly at the hour advertised, but Stetson's ire was aroused at what he thought a presumption on the part of the house treasurer. Approaching the box-office, before he had a chance to exchange greetings with any of his friends or representatives, he shook his finger in the face of the "knight" of the box-office, saying: "See here! Take that sign in and have it changed. I am running this house, and I want the sign to read:

MATINEE AT 2. STETSON.

Passion Play

Around 1880 an earnest man by the name of Salmi Morse created a sensation by producing a modern version of the New Testament. He brought the show from San Francisco to New York, and his remaining ambition was to win over the hard-nosed John Stetson in Boston to his cause. His success resulted in perhaps the most famous of the Stetson stories.

Stetson was not difficult to approach, none of the old-time managers were, and it was possible to reach his heart too, even if he was brusque and supposedly illiterate. He was a brilliant man, with a dignified air that stood out strongly despite the fact that he in no way sought to appear as an imposing figure. He was inclined to try the Passion Play in Boston. He informed Morse that the production would have to be on a spectacular basis, even if only a single performance could be given, and the two began to figure on the cast and numbers required for an appropriate rendition.

Morse became enthusiastic, as was his natural demeanor, and began to dwell on the strength of the scene where the Savior takes leave of his beloved disciples and breaks bread with them, saying that he would reproduce this scene faithfully.

"I will have the twelve apostles costumed by Mr. Eaves, in a manner that will be decidedly effective," said Morse.

To which Stetson responded in that voice and with that vigor for which he was noted:

"There you go again, trying to economize. Twelve Apostles? I thought you were going to be spectacular. We will have forty apostles at least."

Starmaker

The young David Belasco was a stage manager of the spectacular Passion Play, *and he called James O'Neill's performance as Christ "the greatest performance of a generation." Belasco himself grew into the dominant producer, director and even writer of his time. He was the complete showman, with a particular flair for creating and molding stars. One of the brightest was Frances Starr, and in his still readable book,* The Theatre Through Its Stage Door, *Belasco describes his method.*

It was the wealth of imagination I detected in Frances Starr's acting the first time I saw her that convinced me at once of the possibilities in store for her, if she were properly directed. When I made up my mind to invite her into my company, I felt sure I could place her among the stars if only she would prove strong enough, physically, for the struggle. I understood much better than she what effort it would cost, what trying experiences were ahead of her. She was a frail girl, with a highly strung, nervous temperament, and I decided that what she needed most at the outset was to be built up in health. As a result of my first interview with her after her contract had been signed, I instructed her to consult a physician and engage a trained nurse. When I told her I must insist upon prescribing her diet and regulating her physical exercise, she was inclined at first to resent interference in her personal affairs. Quite naturally, she had supposed that my only requirement of her would be to act. But when I explained the long rehearsals that are preliminary to my productions and showed her the need of a sound physical foundation for the nervous energy I would require her to exert, she began to appreciate better the wisdom of my suggestions. For many weeks all I asked her to do was to eat nutritious food, drink milk, take daily exercise in the open air, and go to bed early. This was actually the beginning of the making of Miss Starr into the splendid actress she has since become.

When, after a time in David Warfield's company, she appeared in the romantic character of the Spanish girl in *The Rose of the Rancho*, she so completely fulfilled all my expectations that I was certain she would give a brilliant account of herself in roles demanding intense emotionalism, if only I could contrive somehow to stir her imagination to an even higher pitch.

The opportunity came when Eugene Walter wrote *The Easiest Way* for me. In it he had drawn, in the character of Laura Murdock, one of those unfortunate women who wish to live in luxury on nothing a week—a pitifully weak, unmoral, constitutionally mendacious creature who drifts to perdition along the path of least resistance. Mr. Walter had created this vivid and truthful, though thoroughly unsympathetic, character with a view to having Charlotte Walker impersonate it, and he was quite insistent that the part be given to her. But as I studied it, the peculiar qualities which I felt sure Frances Starr could impart to it were always before my eyes and I made up my mind to intrust it to her.

She had met all my requirements up to the climax of the play. At this point came the situation, at once grisly, abject, and pitiful, in which the weakling, a victim of her own mendacity, and abandoned by the man who trusted her, seizes a pistol with the intention of killing herself, but lacks the courage and, with a shriek of terror, throws the weapon down. I had foreseen that this episode must be worked up to the highest possible pitch of frenzied hysteria.

I was at a loss for a long time how to make Miss Starr respond to the requirements of the scene. Then I saw it would be necessary to be harsh, to torment the little girl, and, by humiliating her before the company, to drive her to the point of hysterics. I was sure, if only once I could force her up to the pitch of frenzy which the scene demanded, that she would be able to master it and repeat it. We went over it again and again while the rest of the company looked on in silent anger. Miss Starr was trembling and as white as a ghost as, little by little, I drove her to desperation. At each attempt she still fell short. Then I remembered she often had told me how she idolized Sarah Bernhardt, so I resolved to taunt her.

"And you want to be as great as Bernhardt!" I sneered. "It makes me laugh!"

In a flash Miss Starr gave a terrific scream and dropped to the floor of the stage in a dead faint. As those nearest to her lifted her up, I clapped my hands and said:

"That's what I want! That's exactly what I've been working for these last three hours!"

Then I dismissed the rehearsal. The company walked out of the theatre without even bidding me good night. Every member was fairly exploding with resentment. Miss Starr's sister, who happened to be present, took charge of her and sent her home in a cab. I was glad when they had gone. I wanted to be alone, for I had accomplished a successful but most distasteful afternoon's work.

About two hours afterward the sister called me on the telephone, saying Miss Starr was more composed and wanted to see me. I lost no time in going to her apartment. The first words she said were:

"I think I made an awful fool of myself at the rehearsal. But I just couldn't do what you wanted."

She was still very much frightened and in doubt.

"On the contrary, you did exactly what I wanted you to do," I replied. "I knew it was in you, and I was sure you could do it."

Then I told her that when we rehearsed the scene again I would expect the same scream she had given that afternoon.

"I don't think I can ever do it again that way," she replied.

"All right," said I, "if you don't, then you will have to go through the whole thing again."

"No! No!" she cried. "I just couldn't!"

"Then scream," I said.

"Well," said Miss Starr, "I'll try."

When the next rehearsal was called I still had doubts as to what the result might be. But Miss Starr rose to the climax of the scene with perfect ease.

Two months later, when *The Easiest Way* was produced in my New York theatre, I watched the effect of Laura Murdock's frenzied scream upon the audience. The tense suspense, followed by the burst of applause, eased the pricking of my conscience for having tormented Miss Starr to the point of hysterics, for it became really the starting-point of her march to great success.

It was at the end of this play that Frances Starr caused a scandal with her curtain line, telling her maid: "Dress up my body and paint my face. I'm going back to Rector's to make a hit and to hell with the rest." Several women in the audience fainted upon hearing her decision, and clergymen found a new favorite to denounce in their sermons.

The Boys from Syracuse

The Shubert Brothers—Lee, Sam and Jacob—were Lithuanian immigrants to Syracuse, New York, from where they conquered the commercial theatre of their adopted country. After Sam's early death in 1905, the other brothers (they were known variously as Mr. Lee, Jake or J.J.—or together as the Messrs. Shubert) broke the power of the Theatrical Syndicate or Trust formed by A. L. Erlanger and Marc Klaw in an attempt to monopolize the show business throughout the United States. Even David Belasco was forced to use makeshift barns for his touring productions, but the brothers developed a chain of theatres from Broadway's Shubert Alley to the Shubert in Los Angeles, which still constitutes the largest theatrical empire in the world. With the Shuberts, real estate and money always preceded content and art. In sponsoring Sarah Bernhardt's tour in 1906, Lee Shubert met his match, as recounted by Jerry Stagg in his book The Brothers Shubert.

Mme. Bernhardt arrived in New York just before Thanksgiving, and Lee Shubert held a reception for her. The divine one was sixty-one years old, looked thirty-five, and was accompanied by a large entourage that included a young man to make her feel thirty-five. She spoke little English; Shubert spoke no French. Their conversation was conducted through Frank Connor, her manager and co-sponsor of the tour with the Shuberts. Lee had never heard of *Camille* and told his associates he was "worried about a play where the heroine dies coughing," but he went forward bravely with his plans. Each time he tried to explain the routing to Sarah Bernhardt, she volleyed in a barrage of French, which always seemed to translate into "How much?"

In later years Lee would imitate Mme. Bernhardt, his clumsy hands aping her expressive gestures, and his ridiculous pipsqueak voice trying to rrroll the dramatic octaves of the Bernhardt vocalization. Since he still didn't speak French, he would say, "Comment allez-vous? Il n'y a pas de quoi," over and over again in varying inflections as he sailed around his office. Then he would stop and, in his own little whisper, say admiringly, "English she couldn't talk; English she couldn't pronounce; but boy, could she count in English!"

Talent Search

In 1930, following the market crash, in which the brothers were reputed to have lost ten million dollars, the Shuberts still had their eyes on Europe, even if sometimes they had their eyes crossed.

Lee had been to Europe earlier that year and seen a French musical comedy that he liked a little for its plot and a lot for its male lead, Oskar Karlweiss. Through Shubert intermediaries, he advised Jake to see and buy the piece and the star. Jake made the trek to Vienna and liked the show. He too liked the male lead. There was a slight difference: Jake liked Walter Slezak. (Karlweiss had been granted a week off, and Slezak, his understudy, had taken over.) Jake bought the show and signed Slezak to play the lead in New York. Back in the States, through the Shubert communications system, he informed Lee that the piece and the star now belonged to the Shuberts.

Lee went to a rehearsal and saw king-sized Walter Slezak playing the role that slim Oskar Karlweiss had impressed Lee with. Lee shook his head in puzzlement. Finally, he returned to his office and sent for Jules Murray.

"My brother is a fool!" he told Murray. "He hired the wrong actor. You tell him to fire this big man and get the little man I saw."

"What was his name?" asked Murray.

"I don't know his name," said Shubert, "but he was a little fellow and very slim. This is not the same man."

Murray dutifully crossed the street to the Sardi Building, took the elevator to the sixth floor, and went in to see Jake. "Mr. J. J.," he began, "your brother thinks that there is some mistake in the casting of the male lead in *Meet My Sister.*

"Sure, there is," snarled Jake. "Sure there is. *He* thought of it." Then grudgingly he added, "I like Slezak."

Murray tried to explain that it wasn't Slezak; it was the other fellow. The more he explained, the more confused the conversation became. Jake finally dismissed him. "My brother made a suggestion; I accepted it. Now he wants to welsh on his suggestion, hey? Well, you go tell the son of a bitch across the street, I am holding him to his suggestion."

Murray delivered a censored version of Jake's reply, and Lee, determined to get to the bottom of this, came to see Slezak at the theatre. He introduced himself, and then asked, "You have gained weight?"

"A little," said Slezak. "Not very much."

"When I saw this play in Europe," Lee said slowly, "I could swear you were smaller."

Slezak did not understand.

Lee went on. "He—you—were much thinner."

Slezak was nimble-witted. "Oh, you must have seen my understudy!"

Shubert was satisfied. Slezak opened in *Meet My Sister* and went on to his successful American career.

Poetics

New Dramatists, the most established group of American playwrights, was hosting a luncheon for Broadway producers. Paul D'Andrea, one of the dramatists, found himself seated next to a vice-president of the Nederlander organization which, after the Shuberts, owns the largest chain of commercial theatres across the country. The playwright was interested in finding out what philosophy and criteria guided Nederlander in booking shows.

"Well, you know, Paul, there are two kinds of plays," said the producer chomping on his cigar; "there are your uppers and your downers."

Playing Doctor

Sometime in the 1940s producer Joseph Kipness was having problems with a highly literary play from England that bombed with New Haven audiences. Trying to fix the script, Kipness summoned the author to his hotel room where he was confronted with three play doctors, all of whom had bright ideas about how to cut, paste, and rewrite his play. The producer was visibly cheered by the suggestions, until the playwright reminded him that by contract only he could revise the script, and he would not change one line. Joe Kipness, a self-confessed mobster before becoming a legitimate producer, turned purple. "I'll be goddamned!" he pounded the table with all his fury. "This is the last time I ever do a play with authors!"

Expedience

George M. Cohan, along with half a dozen Hollywood moguls, is credited with the following. One day, his producing partner Sam Harris caught Cohan apoplectic over an actor he was in the process of firing. After the victim had cleared out, Cohan turned to Harris and said: "Remind me, Sam, never to hire that man again—unless we absolutely need him."

Competition

The Frohman Brothers (Gustave, Daniel, and Charles) were always known by their initials. George Blumenthal started working for them in the 1880s.

I remember wondering about the initials T.F. at the end of the ad copy I used to carry over every day to Brown and Pulverman's advertising agency at 31st Street and Broadway, where J. P. "Jake" Muller was then the office boy. I thought that a fourth Frohman was wandering around until I found out that T.F. meant "Till Forbid": run the ad until further notice.

George Blumenthal tells how the eldest of the brothers dealt with competition.

Once G.F. booked Calendar's Minstrels at the Grand Opera House at Eighth Avenue and 23rd Street. Haverly's Minstrels, with whom he had been identified some years before, opened that very day at the Cosmopolitan Theatre, at 41st Street and Broadway. G.F. was very bitter about their coming in to give him opposition, and competed with them in this manner. We took sheets of paper and by means of a hectograph machine that we had, turned them out like so many handwritten passes to the show, reading "Grand Opera House O.K. G.F.," and distributed them by the hundreds all around the town.

Tremendous lines formed in front of the box office of the Grand Opera House, which cut terrifically into the attendance of Haverly's Minstrels. Some time later G.F. said to me that he had made a great mistake: the O.K.s should have been printed on paper resembling greenbacks so that no one in line would have known that the other fellow had a pass.

He once said, "Put O.K. G.F. on my tombstone—and maybe I'll get into heaven."

The Producer's Closet

It is rarely that a producer is admired, especially by writers. But Charles Frohman (1860–1915) was, even by snobbish English gentlemen such as Cosmo Hamilton, whom he hired as an unproven talent in the theatre to write a show that somebody else abandoned. A few years after C.F. (as he was universally known) went down with the Lusitania, Hamilton remembered him.

An extraordinary man, Charles Frohman, a kind, simple, loyal, courageous, resilient, hard-working, honorable man, to work for whom it was a privilege and a pleasure. For one whose business it was to control theatres, collect plays and create stars on both sides of the Atlantic, who was the czar, the High Panjandrum, whose room was the Mecca of the dramatists, who loved Barrie as a brother, Sutro as a cousin, Pinero, Marshall, Guitry, Rostand, Haddon Chambers, Somerset Maugham, Granville Barker, Augustus Thomas, and an army of others, equally gifted, as his friends, but was scared to death by Bernard Shaw, Frohman knew more about the theatre but less about plays than any man I knew.

There was a closet in his sitting-room at the Savoy in which all the plays that were ever written were piled in a heap during his meteoric regime. And once, when I was waiting for him to come back from an early rehearsal of *Peter Pan*, at which he gazed with awe, amazement and many misgivings before it was produced, I opened the door of this black hole of Calcutta and gasped with horror at the sight.

There must have been hundreds of plays there, all in envelopes, each one being the brain child of a would-be dramatist, five feet deep. Hundreds of beseeching voices seemed to cry out to me as I stood there, appalled. "Help us, you who know this monarch, you who have been produced. Fish us out into the open, give us a friendly word. Remember that, but by the grace of God, you might be lying here too. We are better than your stuff, there is that in us to shake the world. We are the embryo Pineros, Maughams, Barries, Sutros. We have been written not in ink, but blood, and oh the joy, the effort and the heartbreak that went to the making of us."

And when Frohman came in, I turned upon him and demanded to know what right he had to treat these sleepless nights and strenuous days in such a cavalier way. This was Frohman's answer, with a twinkle of his eyes. "Every play that's got anything in it is alive," he said. "So every night I open this closet and take the first that comes to my hand because that's the one that's worked its way up to the top. The others are dead."

Yes Cigar

A cigar, under certain conditions, Sigmund Freud was supposed to have remarked once, may not be a phallic symbol, but simply a cigar. The makers of a popular brand in the late nineteenth century certainly hoped otherwise. When the Lillian Russell Cigar was at the height of its popularity, producer Daniel Frohman put her in a play, and said:

"If this play draws nearly as well as this cigar, we will all make money."

The Ex-Actor

Henry Miller (after whom the Broadway theatre is named) was starring in a barn of a place built after the great San Francisco earthquake. More accustomed to work in the intimate theatres of the nineteenth century, Miller had trouble filling the auditorium with his voice. When asked by the New York office to give an estimate of the anticipated box office, the manager wired from the West Coast that they would probably play to ten thousand a week, unless Miller could make his voice carry beyond the twentieth row, in which case they would take in twenty thousand.

Later Miller took the hint, and became a rich producer.

As producer, Henry Miller was known for his volatile temper. But because the first part of his career was spent on the stage, the ex-actor had great compassion for those who still trod the boards. After he had chewed out some unfortunate actor once, Miller commented to his stage manager:

"Thank God, he is no worse. But I'll make him play this part if I have to break his damned neck—and mine too!"

S.O.B.

Producer Gilbert Miller, son of Henry, inherited his father's temper and increased it. There was something mean-spirited about his way of dealing with people who worked for him. In a typical episode, Gilbert entrusted to an employee who had caused him dissatisfaction the task of handing out the Christmas bonuses. The man counted money into a pile of envelopes which had the names of everybody in the office. Everybody, that is, except him—as he found out when there were no more envelopes.

Gilbert was a master of the modern management technique of avoiding the firing of people he had hired in error; he mounted a campaign which made departure the much preferred alternative. The playwright Robert E. Sherwood once faced the not uncommon problem of telling a director he'd have to go. The gentle Sherwood told his intended victim in his slow, measured way:

"I haven't the temperament nor the experience to handle a situation like this, and when it arises I do not ask what Jesus would do, or what Abe Lincoln would do, but I ask what Gilbert Miller would do—and then I cannot do it."

Irresistible Offer

At one point, Gilbert Miller was trying to hire as his general manager
Frank P. Morse, a broker in Washington, who had strong theatrical interest (and later wrote the book about Gilbert's father, *Backstage with Henry
Miller*). The producer asked a mutual acquaintance to sound Morse out,
but the latter refused an attractive offer, because of Miller's legendary fits
of temper.

"But doesn't he realize," asked Miller semi-rhetorically, "that I would
be away in Europe six months of every year?"

You Can't Keep a Good Man Down

*Long before he made his reputation as a showman specializing in bawdy
humor and naked girls, Earl Carroll was singing in jazz clubs. Across the
country, in Los Angeles, Oliver Morosco was producing a musical revue,*
Your Neighbor's Wife, *which its author, Elmer Harris, was reluctant to revise. Morosco had heard of Carroll as a talented music man and he took
the risk of bringing him out from New York to the West Coast. This was
ten years before Carroll's famous editions of* Vanities *of the twenties, but
Morosco's portrait of the early Carroll clearly showed that he already possessed the necessary vision.*

Carroll threw himself into the work with all the verve of youth. Besides
writing the music he came forward with numerous suggestions for bits.
Some of them amazed me. For instance, he rushed up to me one day and
announced the birth of a new idea:

"First we'll have the girls shown in dressing rooms. They undress, get
stark naked, jump into pretty bathing suits quickly, and run into the surf
backstage for a swim."

I laughed at his seriousness. "I like everything about your idea, Earl,
with one exception."

"And what is that?" he asked eagerly.

"The idea of spending the rest of the winter in our city jail."

"But," he earnestly insisted, "we can have the lights fixed so the audience can't see too much. It's just the idea that they'll know they are
naked."

"Well, Earl," I agreed, "we'll compromise. We'll put them into strip
tights, and then your scene can go in."

Carroll pondered a moment, then decided the scene would register just
as well slightly cloaked.

Accordingly I wrote in the scene, putting the girls in back of a scrim drop, which merely meant the audience would have to look through an all but nonexistent transparent drop to see them. This gave a mellowed effect to the entire scene, and when the girls plunged into the water backstage, the scrim drop was lifted without the audience being aware of it. This proved to be one of the hit episodes of the show.

Penthouse

Earl Carroll, called for a while the Earl of Seventh Avenue, introduced the modern penthouse to New York. His was on the roof of 729 Seventh Avenue. It was at first known as a Starlight Bungalow. Carroll called it "Top o' the World."

The famous sign on his theatre read: "Through This Portal Pass the Most Beautiful Girls in the World." Carroll's friendship with W. R. Edrington, the man who designed his theatre, reached almost veneration. He had two pictures hanging in his office. The portrait of George Washington had the caption: "The Father of Our Country. Born February 22, 1732." Next to it hung a picture of Edrington, and the caption ran: "The Father of Our Theatre. Born February 22, 1872."

Columnist Sidney Skolsky described this office at the back of his theatre: "A rug, the color of pigeon blood, covers the floor. His desk is enclosed in a wall. The pressing of a button shoots it forward. He uses a sword for a paperweight. Has a statue of Buddha here. And a refrigerator with Chinese letters written on it. The letters spell—happiness. In the rear of the office there is a secret panel through which he can make a hasty exit."

Crying Producer

George White convinced himself that Broadway was being called the Great White Way because of him. The son of a Jewish garment manufacturer on Delancey Street, he was one of eleven children. As a kid, he blacked shoes, stole fruit and sold flowers and newspapers. He was Swifty, the messenger boy, when he was thrown out of a saloon by a singing waiter whose name was Irving Berlin.

Another time White was delivering a telegram to "Piggy" Donovan's saloon on the Bowery, when he asked the piano player to let him hoof. George picked up $12.30 which was tossed in his direction, and was hooked. He threw away all the other telegrams (including two marked "DEATH—RUSH") and developed a new vaudeville act, dancing on skiis.

Between 1919 and 1939, George White produced thirteen editions of his *Scandals*, revues with lots of girls, which made him a multimillionaire. White was so sensitive in the beginning that when Burns Mantle wrote of his first show that "the *Scandals of 1919* prove that a hoofer should stick to his dancing," the producer actually burst into tears.

This Man Needs Help

Even when he became a multimillionaire and drove a Rolls Royce, George White enjoyed selling tickets in his box office. Once, on the spur of the moment, he bought an entire building on Park Avenue, because he liked one apartment in it. Then he continued to live in his old apartment on Seventh Avenue, because he didn't want to pay to himself the Park Avenue rent he was charging others.

The Cowboy and the Showman

Will Rogers became a big Broadway star when he joined the famous *Follies* of Florenz Ziegfeld. The cowboy was with the *Follies* for most of the decade of 1914 to 1924 and remained close friends with the great Ziegfeld. After Rogers moved to the West Coast and had built his estate in Santa Monica Canyon, his physique was admired by a fellow player after a polo game.

"Boy, you've sure got a great pair of legs on you," he kidded as they were about to take a shower. Rogers' blue eyes twinkled as he grinned back:

"Why do you think Ziegfeld kept me in the *Follies* all those years?"

Ziegfeld was in the habit of sending telegrams to his stars when either he or they were out of town. At one point he had fired off about twenty of them to Will Rogers, who in his usual manner ignored them. Ziegfeld's telegrams grew longer and more colorful, until Rogers finally put an end to them. He wired back collect: "KEEP THIS UP. AM ON MY WAY TO BUY MORE WESTERN UNION STOCK."

Big Spenders

William Anthony McGuire was a favorite playwright of Florenz Ziegfeld. They shared a common love of extravagance, manifested in their passion for sending and receiving telegrams. McGuire's appeal became irresistible when in 1928 he sent the showman the commissioned scenario for *Rosalie* in forty-two rather lengthy cables.

In the following year, when a scene he had written for the pre-Crash hit *Whoopee* was criticized as old-fashioned, Bill McGuire protested: "Damn it, Flo and I are ahead of the times. Look at the way we both live on next year's income."

Delusion

Florenz Ziegfeld's *bête noire* was Arthur Hammerstein. One day, as he was standing in front of the New Amsterdam Theatre a man came along and hit Ziegfeld on the head with an umbrella. With no evidence whatsoever, Ziegfeld insisted for ever after that the man had mistaken him for Arthur Hammerstein.

Mere Money

Mike Todd was always in debt and always living beyond his means. "Money is only important if you don't have it," was a maxim he lived by. Todd was flat broke in 1946 when he charmed Joan Blondell away from Dick Powell. Todd complained to Lee Shubert that he did not have the money to get married, so Shubert called a friend and each put up a thousand. They each received a magnum of champagne and were invited to the wedding party on a chartered yacht. "He operated like he was a millionaire on just a couple of thousand we'd lent him," Shubert, a tight-fisted but real millionaire, observed in admiring envy.

Mike Todd had the greatest talent to fob off creditors and borrow money since the legendary Richard Brinsley Sheridan. He once approved and paid an employee's expense account for $27. Then he borrowed back $25, saying that he had to entertain some business clients at the Stork Club.

Another of his long-suffering employees who had been waiting for weeks to receive his pay timidly asked for his salary. "What are you trying to do," Todd turned on him, "make me lose confidence in myself?"

Billy Who?

Billy Rose was writing vaudeville sketches when he met Fanny Brice. Two years later they were married, and the same day the famous comedienne became Mrs. Rose, he became known as Mr. Brice. Billy Rose saw that the only people from the entertainment world around Fanny with clout were producers. So he became a producer. Soon he opened the Billy Rose Music Hall and had an electric sign eighteen stories long on Broadway spelling out his name. The first night after its installation, Billy Rose stood on Broadway to admire the sign.

"Billy Rose?" he heard a voice ask in the dark. "Who dat?"

"That's Fanny Brice's husband," came the reply.

Hamlet

George Grizzard created the role of Nick in *Who's Afraid of Virginia Woolf?*, which played for almost two years at the Billy Rose Theatre. The old producer, who had another couple of years on his meter, loved the play and even suggested writing ads aimed at secretaries, which said that they would understand it, even if their boss did not. Well into the run, Grizzard got an offer that few actors can refuse: the chance to play Hamlet. Just before leaving town, he ran into Billy Rose one night at Sardi's.

"How come you left my play?" he wanted to know.

"I'm going to Minneapolis to play Hamlet."

"You shouldn't leave the play, that's very dumb of you, it's the biggest hit on Broadway."

"I'm going to play Hamlet, Billy," said the actor.

"I was married to Fanny Brice," said the diminutive producer, "and Fanny never left a play until everybody who wanted to see her had seen her in it."

"Billy, I am going to play Hamlet," Grizzard repeated the old news.

"Oh, you actors. Hamlet—it's like Hedy Lamarr blowing hot in your ear. Right?"

A Great Unwashed

Billy Rose looked up to people whom he thought of as "real artists." He described himself as "just a saloon-keeper." During a preview of *Shaw's Heartbreak House* at the Billy Rose Theatre, he whispered to the director, Harold Clurman:

"This is a play for people who wash every day."

Wonder Boy

The enfant terrible of the American theatre, Jed Harris (1900–1979) was the producer and director whom everybody loved to hate. His heyday was in the 1920s, when he was known as the Wonder Boy of Broadway. Born as Jacob Horowitz, Harris adopted his first name from his favorite children's book, Jed the Poorhouse Boy. *Although he would end his long days in dire poverty again, by age twenty-eight he had four of the biggest hits running simultaneously on Broadway; a year later he lost five million dollars in the market crash. Working with him on* The Royal Family, *Edna Ferber found him a "strange, paradoxical creature, fated to destroy everything he loves, including himself. . . . He had a trick of turning on charm as you'd flick an electric light-switch." Hatred of Jed Harris inspired the profile of Walt Disney's Big Bad Wolf, Laurence Olivier's portrayal of Richard III, and the central character in Ben Hecht's satirical novel,* A Jew in Love. *Hecht, who collaborated with Charlie MacArthur on* The Front Page (1928), *developed a grudging admiration for Jed Harris, which he expounded with characteristic hyperbole in* Charlie, *his book about MacArthur.*

In the days when Jed was the town's head Earthshaker (a title given him by Dick Maney) MacArthur almost knocked his block off.

Charlie was sitting at his typewriter in Fortieth Street re-writing a speech in act three of *The Front Page.* Jed came in. He entered a room as noiselessly as smoke. Unaware of our visitor, Charlie kept on typing. Jed looked pensively over his shoulder at the words appearing.

"That's no good," said Jed, and yanked the copy paper out of the typewriter. It was the only time I ever heard Charlie roar with rage. Jed dashed for the door. I held Charlie's arm from behind. Carnage was averted.

We put the incident in the play. Hildy sits at a typewriter, trying to bat out a lead. Walter (Burns) says, "Wait a minute, Hildy." (The pentecostal fire upon him) "I got an inspiration. Now take this down, just as I say it." (He pulls the page out of Hildy's typewriter.) Hildy (Leaping): "Someday you're going to do that, Walter, and I'm gonna belt you on the jaw—you God damn know-it-all!" Walter (Chanting): "Here's your lead—the Chicago *Examiner* again rode to the rescue of the city in her darkest hour, etc. etc."

Thus the sorrows of life become the joys of art.

A year or so later Charlie received a letter from Jed. It was on quite another subject. It was in the Earthshaker's best scatological vein. "Disillusioned" with Charlie, Jed let go a furioso of "shits," "bastards," "stinkers" at his clay-footed playwright. Charlie sent the letter on to me in Hollywood. Across its top he wrote, "Shelley is loose again."

Jed took *The Front Page* to Atlantic City for a summer tryout. With him went his Court of Inferiors. This included not only the cast and two playwrights, but a flock of train-bearers—Woollcott, Connelly, Harpo, Kaufman, Tony Minor, Dick Maney, Harold Ross, Whittaker Ray and a small harem that was kept out of sight.

What a cast Jed had hired!

Watching them rehearse, Charlie said, "I give in. The sonofabitch is a genius."

What we had written came out of exactly the right faces and the right voices. You would have thought you were in Chicago, 1917, looking at the real beauties of the Criminal Courts pressroom. Lee Tracy was our friend Hildy Johnson (plus Charlie and me, who were also Hildy Johnsons) as if all three of us were on the stage together. There was never a better actor for a part than Lee Tracy for Hildy. For one thing, it was hard to believe he was an actor at all.

"Howey would give him a job on sight," said Charlie.

Osgood Perkins was a Jed victory. Charlie had bridled at his casting. So had I, to a lesser degree. It was Charlie who knew Walter Howey, his every gesture and intonation. Oggie had none of them. He was no more Howey than Tiny Tim.

Yet Howey appeared on the stage; not his gestures and intonations, but his soul. Even the original, sitting in the audience, swore the actor had copied every one of his mannerisms. There was no resemblance. Howey added that we had exposed his inner life for the laughter of the world, and he was going to have us shot. But he loved Charlie, and forgave us both.

We apologized to Jed about our stupidity in the Perkins debate, and thanked our director, George Kaufman. Dorothy Stickney, Frances Fuller, Claude Cooper, Frank Conlan and all the rest were equally perfect. It's a rare thing for a playwright to see his work intimately revealed. It is usually performed by in-laws.

While the actors prepared for the opening, we played games in the Marlborough-Blenheim Hotel. Harpo played the piano and I fiddled and Charlie blew the clarinet. The room emptied. Woollcott took on the field at cribbage and wiped everybody out. Charlie howled for his money back, contending that Woollcott had used marked cards.

We had a luncheon game. Each of the nine eaters took turns making up a dish named for its filthy ingredients. I'll offer no examples. Connelly was the loser. He took sick and had to leave the table, and pay the check.

It was a hot summer. Jed called Charlie, Kaufman and me to his suite for a conference. We arrived and found Jed sitting naked in a chair. His hairy and coleopterous nudity stuck in our eye for an hour. George was the most irked. We went on with the conference, however, as if our producer were vested in his usual royal purple.

As we were leaving, George, passing the naked Jed, said casually, "Your fly's open."

A Taste of Ashes

Moss Hart's first glimpse of Jed Harris was also in the buff, when Harris read *Once in a Lifetime* (1930), sent a telegram to the unknown playwright, summoning him to a meeting, and then kept Hart waiting for three days. In the end Sam Harris (an older producer, whose name Jed had adopted) optioned the first Moss Hart play and brought him together with George Kaufman as his director and collaborator.

By that time Harris and Kaufman were enemies. They fell out when the producer failed to distinguish between Kaufman, the director and playwright who worked for him, and Kaufman, the critic still in charge of the drama desk at the New York *Times*. In those days the *Times* used to report on the critical opinons a play received during tryout. *Serena Blandish* (1929) was so badly received in Philadelphia that Jed Harris called his good friend at the *Times* and asked him to kill a story about the play. Kaufman coldly refused, and allowed the story to run. Harris, who never understood the concept of professional ethics, was enraged. The two never worked together again, but the feud gave rise to one of Kaufman's most frequently imitated lines. "When I die," he instructed, "I want to be cremated, and have my ashes thrown in Jed Harris's face."

Hungarian Rhapsody

Jed Harris's first great success was *Broadway*, the play by Philip Dunning. It ran on its namesake for almost two years, and with six road companies. Harris became rich and famous. The producer was particularly proud when he received from his representative in Budapest, Alexander Incze, a telegram which said that the Hungarian production was so well received that *Broadway* would run at least until the Danube ran dry. Harris quoted this to all and sundry, even though there was no follow-up news from central Europe for several months. Finally, a long-awaited letter, stamped in Budapest, arrived. There had been such a buildup that Harris's entire office staff gathered around his palatial desk in the Sardi Building to witness its opening.

After the producer scanned the contents of the envelope, he simply said: "Incze is a son-of-a-bitch." There was silence, and then Harris looked at the enclosed money order and spoke again: "All Hungarians are sons-of-bitches."

According to the profit statement, the entire run of this runaway hit had netted Harris 500 pengős, or roughly eighty-five dollars. And as far as one could tell from the New York papers, the Danube was still flowing.

Whose Funeral Is It Anyway?

Great ideas and stunts only take you so far in the theatre. Someone has to do the day-to-day work. A great part of Mike Todd's success in the early days could be attributed to the quiet efficiency of Joe Glick, his general manager, who kept operations running smoothly, even after Todd had spent his money. Glick had gained his valuable expertise under Jed Harris in his heyday, but the self-centered producer drove most people he worked with to leave. After Glick went to work for Mike Todd in 1939, he had an announcement printed and sent to everyone he knew. The card, with a pleasant border of blue birds and other embellishments read: "Joseph Glick takes great pride and pleasure in announcing that he is no longer associated with Jed Harris."

Only a few years later, Glick died suddenly, and Mike Todd lost not only his right hand but also his boon companion at the turf. With his usual generosity he arranged a lavish funeral. The officiating rabbi was someone for whose synagogue he had just held a highly successful benefit at the Alvin Theatre only the week before. It was not surprising, therefore, that almost the entire eulogy was taken up by the rabbi's tribute not to the deceased but to the friend and employer he was fortunate enough to find in Mike Todd.

Jed Harris was too self-absorbed to hold grudges, so he also came to the Glick funeral. He sat patiently listening to the endless catalogue of Mike Todd's virtues. After about fifteen minutes, Harris, who was (or pretended to be) hard of hearing, turned to the person next to him and shouted in his most strident manner: "Who died?"

There was a momentary silence and then the funeral dissolved into laughter.

The Last Escape

At the funeral of Harry Houdini in 1926, producers Charles Dillingham and Florenz Ziegfeld were among the pall-bearers. As they carried the great escape artist's coffin, Dillingham whispered to Ziegfeld:

"I bet you, Ziggie, a hundred bucks that he ain't in here."

CHAPTER 9

There's No Business
in Show Business

Grand Opera

Oscar Hammerstein had sunk much more than all his money into building the Manhattan Opera House. Asked by a reporter, "What are you going to open with, Mr. Hammerstein?" the showman replied: "With debts."

After he opened, Hammerstein was pacing up and down in the lobby of the new Opera House, when a subscriber tried to engage him in conversation. "Grand opera is a great business, after all," he asserted, "isn't it, Mr. Hammerstein? "What?" Hammerstein corrected him, "Grand opera is not a business, it's a disease."

During this period a friend asked him: "Oscar, is there any money in grand opera?" "Yes," he retorted, "my money is in grand opera."

Snow Job

Among the many disasters that can befall a production are natural ones caused by the weather. Daniel Frohman recalled a famous event a hundred years ago which ended happily for the actor-manager involved.

Henry Irving played at the old Star Theatre at 13th Street and Broadway, formerly Wallack's, during the blizzard of 1888. No snowstorm in the city's history ever attained such prominence as that one. New Yorkers are proud of it. Press agents have been boosting it ever since. They toss stories of it about as though they are making open challenges to Alaska and Greenland. Even though I remember it well, I still don't believe that any snowstorm ever could live up to the reputation of that blizzard.

At that time, it seemed to me that its greatest defect was that it prevented people from getting to the theatre. At my old Lyceum we could not give a performance because the snowdrifts were so great our actors couldn't get through them. The old theatrical truism, "The show must go on," was crowded out by the elements who changed the wording to "The snow must go on." And it did with considerable enthusiasm. But Henry Irving was not in as bad a predicament as we were, for his company lived at a hotel close to the theatre. At the time he was playing to enormous business. He knew that if he gave no performance the box office would have to refund a great deal of money, or else exchange the tickets for some other night. So great was the business, that was practically impossible. Under these conditions, therefore, he gave the performance to an empty house, thus relieving himself from any obligation to the people who could not get there that night.

The Humorist as Producer

When a producer wants a play, he usually options it for a fixed amount of time and pays for the exclusive rights to exploit it. The following curious story appeared on May 31, 1886, in The Theatre Magazine.

Mark Twain is a humorist, as everybody knows. But everybody does not know what a clever, sagacious, hard-headed man of business he is. He will soon be one of the richest publishers in America, and he seldom makes a blunder in trade. It may be taken for granted, therefore, that when he gave Mr. Daniel Frohman $1,000 not to produce his new play, *The American Claimant* (written in collaboration with Mr. Howells), he displayed extraordinary forethought. He came to the conclusion that, since he could not stand his own play, the public would not be likely to stand it.

Mark Twain was a terrible businessman, and, like Sir Walter Scott, ruined himself by his various ventures. His way of dealing with Daniel Frohman is a small example of how he did it, as the producer explains.

The American Claimant was written for Mr. A. E. Burback, who was a humorous lecturer. He was desirous of adopting the stage as a profession. Twain and Howells organized a company to produce the play and they wished me to present it to the public, which I was quite willing to do. They entered into an agreement to reimburse me for any losses I might sustain. All profits were to be divided between us.

The play was about a scientist who had invented a machine that would instantly put out any fire, no matter how large it might be. He made his first appearance in the play through a second-story window of a house. He was carrying the machine on his back. As he entered he set fire to the place, and even though he had the machine with him, he couldn't put it out. This was the only funny scene in the entire play. It was a failure and it drew no audience. A week passed and I did not receive any money from the firm to indemnify me for my losses so I said to Mark Twain: "If your company does not pay me for my losses on this play I will keep it on."

Whereupon he instantly hustled around and made up with his colleagues the required sum and so the play was stopped.

Padding

William A. Brady, the well-known producer at the turn of the century, encouraged the managers of his road companies to pad their nightly reports of the box office receipts by always adding three hundred dollars. It served to boost morale at head office and to confuse his rival producers. However, people became suspicious when one of the managers wired: "No performance. Only theatre in town burned down. Receipts: $300."

Creative Accounting

It is common wisdom in the film business that promised net profit percentages are meaningless, since accountants at the studios have creative means of showing that the greatest of hits never made any profit. Like so many other practices in show business, this also came from the theatre. Oliver Morosco gives a fable of how he handled such an issue, which these days so often ends up in court.

One day [in 1916] Al Woods, a rival producer, called at my office to say he was staging a play called *Cheating Cheaters* and he wanted Marjorie Rambeau in the leading role. Although I had neither seen nor heard anything of Marjorie since her exodus from my regime, I held a contract for her ex-

clusive services for a period of three years. Woods offered me 25 percent of
the net profits on the production if I would release Miss Rambeau's contract to him.

Much to his surprise I readily consented. I had no desire to punish
Marjorie [Morosco was forced to close her previous show, *Sadie Love,* as
a result of intransigence over star billing by the actress and her mother],
and I was determined she would never play in one of my productions
again, so I drew up an agreement, and we signed it.

Cheating Cheaters opened to capacity business and continued to be a
rousing success.

For the first few weeks I received no percentages, but, crediting the fact
to the paying off of production expenses, I said nothing. But as time went
on, I began to look with suspicion on the no-profit statements that were
delivered to my office regularly every week. Al Woods continued to pack
them in, but he never seemed to take in any money. Knowing Al well
enough to be absolutely positive he wasn't working for art's sake, I sent
him word not to bother about sending me any more statements.

As soon as he got my message, he called up to declare his surprise at my
peculiar request.

"Al," I said, "*Cheating Cheaters* will run for a year or more, and since
it is such a tragic failure, I don't want to clutter my files with any more
no-profit statements."

"Why, Ollie," he demurred seriously, "I'm expecting any time now to
be able to show a profit, and—"

"Give it up, Al," I interrupted. "Try as hard as you may, you'll never be
able to play to more than capacity."

He laughed. "But sweetheart" (Al Woods would have applied that term
to Napoleon were he alive), "you know how high company and theatre
expenses are, and—"

Again I cut him short. I accepted it as a joke on me, and, aside from
letting him think he was really putting something over, I was ready to let
it go as such. Marjorie Rambeau was free of her contract to me, and Al
Woods was free of his. I never received a penny from *Cheating Cheaters,*
but my continued good friendship with Al Woods has been worth far
more to me than the money would have been.

The Lawsuit

Early in his career, the prolific librettist and lyricist Harry B. Smith (1860–
1936) was thinking of collaborating with his journalist friend Robert B.
Peattie on a farce. Then he ran across W. A. McConnell, a popular actor-

manager in Chicago, who was expressing to Smith his tremendous admiration for a young comedienne he had just discovered: she had not only talent but plenty of money to put into a production that would exploit her talents. So all they needed was a play. Smith immediately called on Peattie and the two of them went to pitch their idea for the farce. They laughed so much telling the synopsis of this unwritten play that Will McConnell needed no more convincing: he immediately gave them a contract.

In ten days Smith and Peattie completed their play which they called, a bit unwisely perhaps, *The Scarecrow*. After a tryout in smaller towns, McConnell brought the show to Chicago. It went so badly that after the curtain fell on opening night, McConnell found himself explaining to critics and anyone who would listen that through a bit of a mixup, the actors had played the last act first.

McConnell closed the play as soon as he could, at which point the authors had the audacity to sue him for royalties. McConnell responded to the lawyer who had filed the suit by pointing out that "these two men owe their lives to me for playing the piece only three weeks."

The litigants retained their sense of humor. Going into the courtroom, McConnell greeted Harry Smith:

"If my lawyer asks you your business and you say author, I'm going to have you jailed for perjury."

The question of authorship came up and McConnell testified that before the show opened Peattie told everyone he had written it, but after the first night, he always referred to it as "Smith's play."

Nevertheless, the two authors won their case and were awarded $365 by the court. Chronically insolvent, McConnell didn't pay. A few years later, Harry Smith ran into him at the Knickerbocker Cafe, where he was drinking with his set of cronies. He greeted Smith with a friendly laugh:

"Here's the man who holds a judgment against me for three hundred and sixty-five dollars. Imagine! A judgment against me! What good is it?"

Harry Smith offered to settle the whole thing, if anyone paid him ten cents—cash. McConnell handed him a dime. Then Smith wrote to his partner, asking whether he would accept fifty percent of anything he might be able to collect on the judgment. When Peattie replied that he would be happy to oblige, Smith sent him five pennies.

After the Crash

Eddie Cantor, who lost a fortune during the 1929 crash, wrote a book with which he was hoping to recoup. Its title was *Caught Short! A Story of Wailing Wall Street*, and the author inaugurated a new historical era with it—A.C., or After the Crash. A couple of years B.C., producer Gilbert Miller had wooed and married Kitty Bache, whose father owned the brokerage firm that later merged with Prudential. Although Miller was at the time one of the mightiest producers on Broadway and by most standards wealthy, Bache warned his daughter of the indisputable fact that theatre was a flimsy and undependable sort of business.

Then came the crash, and Jules Bache lost quite a bit of money, including some his son-in-law had given him to invest. "Don't feel too bad," said the broker to Miller, "at least you've got a good business, so you don't have to worry!"

Gilbert Miller was already a rich man when he married Kitty Bache. Commenting on their marriage, he said: "I didn't need her money, but I thought double is better."

The End of the Jig

Unlike Gilbert Miller, who was born into the theatre and riches, Max Gordon was born into poverty on the Lower East Side. His father was a pants-presser in a sweatshop, and the family boasted the name Salpeter, to which occasionally Max Gordon reverted under particularly stressful circumstances. A self-made man, Gordon lost a good deal of his money and his nervous system during the stock market crash and panic of 1929. Groucho Marx recalled the summer before the October crash, when stocks and optimism were flying towards the stratosphere:

"Max and I were playing golf in Great Neck—at least I was playing golf and Max was playing that kind of running hockey of his, hitting the ball and then running five yards to hit it again—and suddenly he said to me, strolling down the fairway and twirling his club, 'Marx, why should we work at all? Here we are playing golf and having a fine time, and I already made a profit of three thousand dollars on the market today. How long has this been going on?' "

Then a few months later, in late October, Groucho's phone rang and he answered it. "Marx?" said a barely recognizable voice at the other end. "This is Salpeter. The jig is up."

After the Crash, Before the Fall

Soon after the crash of 1929, lyricist Bert Kalmar was visiting publicist Richard Maney's office. He took off his pants and shirt, which he asked Maney to send to his broker, and then crawled out to the window ledge. "I'm just making a trial jump," he said.

Down but Not Out

Like Al Jolson, to whom she was frequently compared, Ethel Merman amassed millions through shrewd investments. She bought stocks cheap during the Depression and sold them at a huge profit. According to legend, two friends of Merman were talking about her various transactions, and at one point one of them said: "Poor Ethel—most of her money is tied up in cash!"

This brings to mind the time W.C. Fields was asked by a broke colleague for a loan. "I'd love to help you," said Fields, "but all my money is tied up in currency."

Rhapsody in Green

At the opening performance of *Porgy and Bess* (1935), the incorrigible Oscar Levant turned to critic John Weaver in the seat next to him and said: "It's a right step in the wrong direction." Since he claimed to worship the ground upon which George Gershwin walked, Oscar wrote that he felt a lifelong remorse for having made that comment—though this did not prevent him from retelling it several times in his books.

In another story, which even Oscar Levant called apocryphal (though, again, he retells it), George Gershwin once asked Maurice Ravel for composition lessons. Ravel asked how much money Gershwin made that year. "Two hundred thousand," said the Broadway composer. "You teach me," asked Ravel.

Gone to the Dogs

In the early 1930s, with the Depression and movies killing off vaudeville, Jack Benny felt his career was washed up. At one point, his agent Tom Fitzpatrick got a call from a New Jersey theatre manager offering twenty-five dollars for an animal act. Even though he had never used anything but his violin and a cigar in his act, Benny was desperate enough to agree. He borrowed a pair of Pekingese and went to New Jersey. When he came on stage, Benny tied the two dogs up to a piece of stage furniture, and proceeded to do his regular monologue and played a couple of tunes on his fiddle. The audience liked it, which meant everybody was happy. Afterwards, when the manager was paying him his fee, he said:

"That's the most peculiar animal act I've ever seen, mister. Don't your dogs do any tricks?"

"Not at these prices," Jack Benny said, pocketing the cash.

Make or Break

In 1935, still in the pits of the Depression, Billy Rose made his mark on show business by producing *Jumbo,* the musical circus extravaganza at the New York Hippodrome that involved every high-priced talent from Rodgers and Hart to Paul Whiteman and his orchestra, from Hecht and Mac-Arthur to George Abbott and Jimmy Durante, not to mention the eponymous hero of the show. *Jumbo* was financed by Jock and Joan Whitney, among the richest families in New York. So, as production costs mounted, the word on Broadway was: "This show will make Rose or break Whitney."

Tight

Tony Pastor ran the original dinner theatre in New York at the turn of the century. He was tightfisted, and never paid an actor more than forty dollars a week. Comic Ed Wynn used to tell the story of the rookie actor who was sitting in a bar writing to Pastor for a job. As he listed his qualifications and salary requirements, he called out: "How do you spell sixty?" A veteran actor standing nearby replied: "F-o-r-t-y."

The Question of Hamlet

At around the turn of the century, it was fashionable to debate different interpretations of Shakespeare. The question whether Hamlet was really mad, or simply "put on an antic disposition," was frequently discussed. Richard Mansfield was at a New York dinner party where the topic came up. After various views were stated, the great actor told a story.

One morning in the West I met a young friend of mine and asked him where he had been the night before.

"I went," my friend replied, "to see So-an-So's Hamlet."

"Aha, did you?" said I. "Now tell me—do you think Hamlet was mad?"

"I certainly do," said he. "There wasn't a hundred dollars in the house."

Rolling Stock

In the latter part of the nineteenth century, new communities were burgeoning all over the map, especially in the West. Many of them were not established or wealthy enough to book name attractions. Besides, there were not enough stars to feed the growing appetite for popular entertainment. This was provided by armies of nameless and transient infantry who

eked out a miserable existence on the exhausting circuits and were com-
pletely at the mercy of petty managers and exploiters. Among these foot-
soldiers was Ed Meade, who in 1916 published his miseries in a crudely
produced autobiography, Doubling Back. *Typical of his lifetime of bad*
experiences was this episode.

I came very near going to Juneau, Alaska, with a stock company. The
Klondike rush had just begun. My wife did not want to go. So I joined
"The Grovers" stock company direct from the Alcazar, San Francisco,
which was playing a stock engagement at the old Third Avenue theatre in
Seattle. They could not use my wife at the time, so she took a vacation
and I was to join her later at my sister's home.

"The Grovers" played short stock engagements at Seattle, Tacoma and
Portland. I remember that I went on for a specialty at a performance in
Portland and scored quite a hit as [the humorist] Bill Nye. *The Oregonian*
gave me about fifteen lines and the show nearly six. Old man Grover, "The
Governor," as every one called him, did not like this any too well, but
complimented me highly. At a social session of the Elks one evening (he
belonged to No. 1) where he presided as toastmaster, he called upon me
as Bill Nye to entertain for a few moments. Of course I responded and
retired to my corner amid great applause.

Instead of going south into California, the show went east to Walla
Walla, Boise, Salt Lake City, then north to Butte. My wife joined me
there and was engaged as musical director. Southern California did not
agree with her health.

The show did not do very well and it kept me busy trying to draw my
salary. I even tried to quit the show at Pocatello, Idaho, but Grover held
our trunks and would not give up the checks. They were doubling back
west to Walla Walla and intended going to Spokane, to the Auditorium
for summer stock. So I stayed, but after the second week "The Grovers,"
father and son, got into a fight with one of the actors, Guy Durrell, and
just about knocked Durrell out with a billy. He had them arrested. They
were fined seven and three hundred dollars—dad seven, son three hundred—and this was the means of breaking up the summer engagement.
We were obliged to take to the road. My wife was taken sick at Wardner
and I quit the show. Old man Grover gave me two dollars, which was the
largest sum of money that he ever gave to me at one time while I was with
him. They secured a three-day Fourth of July date at the Auditorium in
Spokane and being short of people they wired me to come for three days,
"salary sure." I answered: "Send round trip ticket and salary," which they
did. After the three days I returned to Wardner. "The Grovers," father and

son, went east and I have never seen them since. It was a case where the father did the gambling and the son took to drink.

Oversight

Successful as they were almost everywhere else, Alfred Lunt and Lynn Fontanne never seemed to do well in Pittsburgh. Lunt was puzzled about it, and shared his concern with the company manager, Larry Farrell, just before they were to open *The Taming of the Shrew.* "Would you like to take over the financial reins, while we are here?" the manager asked, and handed the star the books.

On Saturday night, when the show closed in Pittsburgh, Lunt showed Farrell the box office statement. "Look, Larry," he exulted, "we made $4000."

"Just one thing, Alfred," said the manager, "you forgot to pay the Lunts."

Profit Motive

Irving Berlin was once asked by Hal Eaton: "Do you write songs for posterity?" "No, for prosperity," replied the world's richest songwriter.

Farming

David Brooks was in the Irving Berlin musical Mr. President (1962).

That was the show that finally made me enough money to buy a farm in New Jersey across from Bucks County. Soon afterwards Mr. Berlin was celebrating his seventy-fifth birthday, and I wrote him a letter and thanked him for the fact that his musical enabled me to realize this dream. The old curmudgeon, who was never happy with the show and closed it down after eight months, replied by letter, "I wish I could have done the same."

I loved the farm but it got me into the worst trouble. I was standing by for José Ferrer in *The Girl Who Came for Supper* (1963) at the Broadway Theatre. All I had to do was actually to sit by the telephone within walking distance of the theatre until 8 p.m. and then I was free for the evening. One got paid a lot of money for that. Anyway, one weekend I was down at the farm, aiming to take an afternoon train back as usual with plenty of time for the evening performance, but there was a blizzard, and the train limped in at nine o'clock. I struggled to the theatre, where I found that the performance had been canceled. It turned out that Joe Ferrer, who was contractually forbidden from leaving the country, had gone to Puerto Rico, and they weren't allowing planes in to New York. I felt absolutely terrible, and things did not improve when the next morning the producer, Herman Levin—who also produced *My Fair Lady*, called me and said: "What did I ever do to you?"

Thank You for Not Smoking

Jules Leventhal, road manager for many a Broadway hit, was famous for his frugality. He had just sent out *The Male Animal* (1952) by Elliott Nugent and James Thurber. In one of the scenes a football coach has to hand a professor a cigar. When Leventhal saw the expense sheets after the first week, his eyebrows went up at the item, "Cigars—eighty cents." He immediately sent an order: "From now on, when the coach offers that cigar, have the professor answer, 'No thanks, I don't smoke.'"

Volume

Unlike most of the showmen, but like many working producers today, Lee Shubert was famous for his stinginess. But he was also in the volume business. Occasionally he would explain his philosophy by way of a parable. "A shoemaker makes one pair of blue suede shoes, and it may cost him five dollars. He sells them for ten dollars. So he made five dollars. But, if he makes a hundred pairs, he's in business."

And No Questions Asked

Arthur Hopkins was having trouble with Jules Bledsoe, in the folk operetta *Deep River*, which he produced in 1926. The baritone singer, whose main experience was on a concert stage, insisted on doing a solo act across the footlights instead of interacting with the other performers on stage. During opening night in New Haven, Hopkins was at the back of the auditorium, when the singer, in defiance of all his directions, strode downstage and began to render his dialogue into an aria. Hopkins could not help himself and muttered an oath or two which prompted a woman in front of him to turn:

"If you don't like the show, why don't you go to the box office and get your money back?"

Thinking of the $60,000 he had sunk into the production, the producer replied:

"Madam, I wish to God I could."

Percentage

In 1937 Margaret Webster had just directed Maurice Evans in Richard II on Broadway, when she encountered one of the great legends of the theatre.

When I made my contract I had not realized that American directors all got weekly royalties; and I had cut myself out of the acting job. I booked a sailing home.

One night Maurice and I were at a grand party, sitting close to Mrs. Patrick Campbell. She said wasn't it wonderful for me and wasn't I making lots and lots of money. I said yes, and no. Hadn't I got a percentage? Well, no. She proceeded to proclaim this fact to the world in her most Campbellian tones. "You poor child, you *ought* to have a percentage. Listen! this poor child hasn't got a percentage!" To Maurice: "*Why* hasn't she got a percentage? Have *you* got a percentage? But the poor child *must* have a percentage. *Why* haven't you given her one?" Maurice laughed amiably and said: "Because I'm too mean!" I stopped blushing and was delighted.

The *Mikado* Wars

The Hot Mikado was Mike Todd's first major hit on Broadway. He won his producing spurs fairly with this all-black, jazz version of the Gilbert and Sullivan classic, starring Bill Robinson. Todd was just preparing to open it in 1939 at the Broadhurst Theatre, when he found out that Bernard Ullrich, a Chicago producer, was booking something called *The Swing Mikado* into the 44th Street Theatre. This Mikado had been developed and subsidized by the Federal Theatre under the Works Project Administration, which enabled it to charge $2.20 for the top ticket against Todd's $3.30.

During the previous year, Todd had tried unsuccessfully to buy the rights to *The Swing Mikado*, which led him to develop his own version. Now he was completely outraged in seeing the same show booked across the street in direct competition with his Mikado. He dispatched a four-page telegram to the White House: "Is this the New Deal?" he wanted to know from FDR. "Is this why I, as a taxpayer, am supporting the Federal Theatre, so it can try to break me with cut-price competition on the same street?"

The White House did not reply (though in an unrelated move, Congress did abolish the Federal Theatre in the same year), but Todd's jungle survival instincts swung into action. Watching workmen putting up the letters on the marquee for the rival Mikado, the showman told his newly hired press agent, Bill Doll:

"I want a flag made. The biggest flag you can get, with an arrow pointing to our theatre. And when you've got it, hang it over there," and Todd pointed to a fourth floor window of the Sardi Building, next door.

That window belonged to the De Mirjian Studio of Photography. Doll went to see him at once.

"Mr. De Mirjian," he said to the tenant behind the window, "Mr. Todd is very much impressed with your work and would like to appoint you as the official production photographer." The man was overjoyed.

"By the way," Doll mentioned casually as he was leaving, "I don't suppose you'd mind if we hung a little banner out of your window?"

The flag went into place. It not only directed people effectively to the Broadhurst, but also totally blotted out *The Swing Mikado* marquee from traffic going east, precisely the way Mike Todd intended. He also scored an immense critical success.

"Multiplication is the enemy of novelty," wrote George Jean Nathan in *Newsweek*, "but Todd's *Mikado* is a decidedly better job in almost every respect than the Federal Theatre's version." *Time* echoed: "As a show *The Hot Mikado* wins hands down over *The Swing Mikado*." John Mason Brown raved about Bill Robinson's performance as Mikado, calling him "the most articulate man of our time . . . He is a titan, not of literature but with his feet, a superb master." When Bojangles, as the great tap-dancer was universally known, read this tribute, he said to Mike Todd:

"I ain't been so happy since I been colored."

Six years later, after the first atom bomb was dropped on Hiroshima, Mike Todd sent a telegram to General MacArthur: IF HIROHITO PROVES INTRACTABLE, PUT BILL ROBINSON ON THE THRONE OF JAPAN AND CALL HIM THE HOT MIKADO.

And That's the Way It Is

Because of Todd's extravagance—the show had sixty girls, a forty-foot waterfall of soap bubbles and a volcano that erupted—*The Hot Mikado* was a tremendous success while continuing to lose money. Remarking on the phenomenon, Sam Zolotow of the New York *Times* gave birth to a classic exchange about the nature of commercial theatre.

"Your auditor, Mike, says the show is losing money, and your publicity man says it is breaking records. How do you reconcile this discrepancy?"

"All I can say," the showman replied with complete seriousness, "is that both departments are functioning perfectly."

CHAPTER 10

Angels Rush In

Allah Wasn't Listening

Alfred Bloomingdale, scion of the department store family, was stagestruck from an early age. Having lost a bundle as an angel, he decided to shed his wings and become a full-fledged producer. He poured a vast deal of money into a musical called *Allah Be Praised!* The show was in difficulties and during its Boston tryout Bloomingdale called in his friend Cy Howard as a play doctor to see if he could work a miracle cure.

Howard sat through the comedy in silence. After the final curtain, the lights went on and he found himself looking at the producer's anxious face:

"Well, what do you think?"

"Al," Howard gave his considered advice, "close the show and keep the store open nights."

Pegasus *Manqué*

Billy Rose defined an angel as a "guy who likes to wear a black hat and meet blondes." Robert Dowling was a real-estate tycoon who occasionally put money into Broadway shows. He was so stiff in his manner that S. N. Behrman once remarked that "if you put a horse under him, he'd be a statue."

Self-criticism

During the brief run of *Let 'Em Eat Cake* (1933), a flop on which George Kaufman collaborated with George Gershwin, a disappointed backer mistook Kaufman for Gershwin.

"How could you let a thing like this happen, Mr. Gershwin?" he said to Kaufman during intermission.

"My score is perfect," Kaufman told the angel in good humor, "the whole trouble is with Kaufman's book!"

Recklessness

Like the stock exchange and the casinos, Broadway as a business has always attracted a small percentage of high-flying gamblers, who knew nothing about theatre—or business for that matter. In the late 1940s an Albany millionaire by the name of Anthony Brady Farrell went through $2.5 million in a year, part of which included buying for himself a Broadway house which he christened the Mark Hellinger Theatre, after the columnist who had died recently then. "I never knew Hellinger," said Farrell, "but I had read his stuff for years. He typified Broadway to me."

Farrell's model of recklessness may have been Edgar B. Davis, the heir to Texan oil money, who produced a play called The Ladder *(1926). Davis holds the Broadway record for the most efficient way of losing a vast quantity of money. Jack Gaver, in his book* Curtain Calls, *chronicles how he managed to do it.*

The story is that Davis became an angel purely by accident. Even had the play been a success he likely would not have stayed in the business. He is a native of Brockton, Massachusetts, who began to make his own way at an early age. Leather and shoes were his first interests, then he went to the Southwest and opened up oil fields that made him fabulously wealthy. He has been making and losing fortunes for almost fifty years.

One day Edgar Davis met on a San Antonio street an old schoolmate from Brockton, J. Frank Davis, no relation. The latter, a former New England newspaperman who had been permanently crippled in an ice accident while on assignment to meet explorer Commodore Robert Peary upon his return from the North Pole, had gone to Texas for his health. He was doing some freelance writing. Edgar Davis wanted to help him for old times' sake. Frank mentioned that he had been trying his hand at writing plays and Edgar offered to see that he got a New York production. *The Ladder* was the result.

Edgar Davis took the play to a friend, Brock Pemberton, then one of the rising younger producers, who agreed to present it. The original play was an elaborate affair, with scenes in four different centuries from the fourteenth to the twentieth. It dealt with a modern woman's indecision over which of two men to marry and the theory of reincarnation. The first of several rewrites of the script was done by Edward Knoblock, an important dramatist of the time, just before the New York premiere. When Knoblock expressed unhappiness over the result, Davis paid him off with a lump settlement. The late Antoinette Perry, who was to become Pemberton's production associate and director in a long and successful partnership, was the leading lady. Robert Edmond Jones, the leading stage designer of the day, created the four elaborate sets; laces costing $50 a yard were used in some of the costumes; a crystal chandelier from the old Delmonico restaurant was purchased for $6,000 for use in one brief scene.

But neither the splendor nor the play moved the critics. Nor did the public decide to make the reviewers look bad by perversely adopting *The Ladder*. It languished quickly and thoroughly, yet it did not close. Davis kept pouring money into it despite a weekly loss of around $10,000.

There were some who said that the oil millionaire was a firm believer in reincarnation. Others claimed that he merely was stubborn; that he had pulled victory out of defeat too many times in other fields to surrender so easily to Broadway. And there was the even simpler explanation that he had promised to help the author and wasn't going to let him down. Murdock Pemberton, brother of the producer, says that Davis has always had a deep religious sense and feels that any difficulty that has cropped up in his life is something that God expects him to overcome.

The public never heard a reason for his tenacity from Davis himself. He always has been a retiring sort of man, for all his spectacular exploits, and he wouldn't discuss himself or the play. He just kept it running. It stayed open through several revisions by Murdock Pemberton, each version getting a little farther away from the reincarnation theme. That would seem to explode the theory of Davis' occupation with the subject. In the end, the play was mainly a plea for a belief in the goodness of God and for tolerance toward sinners. Each time Murdock revised *The Ladder* he gave more lines to his friend, the late actor Edward J. McNamara, who had started out with one small role and wound up playing several. McNamara, who stayed with *The Ladder* throughout its life, liked the employment because the play freed him from the typecasting curse of his career—not once did he have to play a policeman. Producers, including Brock Pemberton, were to put him back in uniform in later years, but McNamara had had his fling.

Tickets went begging even at cut-rate prices, and many schemes were tried to attract customers. Prizes of several hundred dollars were offered weekly for the best articles about the play submitted by persons who had seen it. All of the Broadway rules were broken when the management guaranteed full money refunds to any dissatisfied patrons. Brock Pemberton withdrew as producer after five months on the grounds that he didn't want anyone to get the impression that he was simply taking advantage of an easy mark.

But Davis was the only one taking advantage of Davis. Actors recall that members of the cast who might mention that they should be making more money would receive salary increases from Davis. After several months he decided to admit the public free of charge. This policy lasted for eight months, during which the cast discovered that the audience had not followed the example of the dodo bird and become extinct. But after that period, sordid commercialism was re-embraced and the public became as ticket-shy as before.

Finally, after a little over two years, Davis cabled the closing order from abroad. He said only that he had reached the conclusion that it was poor economics for a play not to pay its way. There were fifty-four persons in the audience at the final performance—the 789th.

Miracle on 34th Street

In 1923 the producer Morris Gest brought Max Reinhardt's spectacular production of *The Miracle* to New York. Most of the money had been provided by the financier Otto Kahn, the most important angel and patron of the arts at the time. Kahn's protégé, the designer Norman Bel Geddes (of "edifice complex" fame), was hired to transform the Century Theatre into a medieval Gothic cathedral. Bel Geddes proceeded to rip out walls, proscenium arches, seats, transforming the entire house and driving up costs. Otto Kahn would not increase his $400,000 investment but he did help to recruit other Wall Street types. One of these brokers with wings came to a rehearsal to check up on his investment. This was the afternoon that Bel Geddes had come to the conclusion that the pit beneath the stage was not deep enough, so he ordered a drill, which was immediately put to work. One of the water mains on 34th Street was struck and a geyser shot through the stage up twenty feet into the air. Amidst all the confusion, the broker was allegedly overheard:

"Our fortunes are made: Bel Geddes has struck oil!"

Taken to the Cleaners

From the outside, show business combines glamor with seemingly easy money. The combination has always attracted some unscrupulous characters, including one profiled by John O'Connor in his book Broadway Racketeers *(1928).*

Stage rackets, if properly reviewed, would require a volume for themselves alone. In every branch of the profession one finds countless chiselers, all pecking away at the outer rim of a racket. Some have reached the inner circle on a rain check, but if they are ever submitted to a theatrical intelligence test, they'll bounce right back into the oblivion in which they belong. Schools in which amateurs are taught the various points of acting are perhaps the rawest of the racket species. This, of course, doesn't go for the legitimate institutions. But the big cities support a flock of phoney kindergartens that are nothing short of nickel snatchers. Now and then an exposé turns up one or two and investigations, starting with a blast and ending with a bubble, occasionally bring them to light, but as a rule they go along, grabbing a sucker here and there, promising much, but producing little.

The greatest of all racketeers in this division proved to be an ex-vaudevillian, Arthur Buckner, a former trick cyclist. Back in the days when big-time vaudeville was a reality, and not merely a page in theatrical history, Buckner was rated one of the best trick bike riders on the stage until he suffered a serious fall, bouncing right into several hoosegows, just as he was being universally recognized—and applauded, as one of the most daring racketeers on the big alley.

Arthur was a gifted conversationalist. And he knew the stage backwards and frontwards, for, it must be remembered, he was a finished showman. But he wearied of blowing up leaking bicycle tires and decided to employ his lung power in the more profitable and pleasant pastime of inflating equally leaky theatrical bladders, all dolled up in attractive corporation titles.

The chump who tosses his bankroll into any racket revolving around a theatrical enterprise is not referred to as a "Sucker." They dignify this particular brand of yokel with the label of "Angel." And if all the angels, whose financial wings have been seared by racketeers of the stage, head for the place where angels are supposed to go, there will be nothing left but standing room for those who qualify for entry on arrival.

The interior decorator who arranged Buckner's "Come-on Parlor" apparently was experienced in the construction of maze concessions for amusement parks. It would take a sheriff nine hours to reach the skipper, but a sap could find him in three seconds. He had a sheriff-proof entrance and a chump-proof exit.

And Buckner dressed his commercial stage somewhat like a musical comedy director would arrange a scene. "Secretaries" were distributed here and there; "dancing instructors" were properly planted, ready to go right into a hoofing spasm at the prearranged cue; vocal teachers idled in position, prepared to burst into song at the mere sight of a likely investor. And the minute a stranger ambled through the door, the balance of Arthur's supernumeraries began chattering about theatrical profits in figures that would better fit the national budget. A poor simp with only ten grand in his kick felt like a bum prowling around the U.S. Treasury on his initial bow into Buckner's studio.

Occupying the entire side of one large room was a miniature stage with regulation footlights and side hangings. A tubercular piano helped out the picture. Most of Arthur's investment went to a sign painter. His monicker was spread all over the glass front facing Broadway. A guy with weak lamps would go dizzy reading the list of corporations and enterprises Buckner was fathering. What a dish for an angel looking for a business opportunity!

They came, singly, doubly and in flocks. Arthur made a perfect first impression. A sucker was his pal five minutes after the initial meeting. How that boy could coo! Pig iron would melt in his mouth. Those who thought they would like to become actors banished the thought after a short confab with Buckner. He wouldn't allow them to waste time and money. Nice fellows like that should be allowed in on the ground floor. Buckner's enterprises would make them millionaires. And Arthur was so assuring, the applicants actually begged to be taken in.

The blow-off came when Buckner missed out on the count of his certificates. Somewhere a secretary had fallen asleep at the switch. He started off nicely selling quarter interests in the various propositions, with a few half interests distributed here and there. It was a silly error for a smart racketeer like Buckner to make, for he could just as easily have given birth to a few new corporations to take care of the overflow. However, he slipped upon his table of fractions.

One afternoon some of his angels happened to visit headquarters to check up on their particular corporations and became acquainted with each other. It developed that to a group of six investors there had been sold three half interests and as many quarter parts in one of the various companies.

Confronting the promoter they demanded an explanation or restitution. That was something even a financial wizard like Buckner couldn't explain, and his promotorial expenses had depleted his immediate cash account. The angels took a ride downtown to the District Attorney's office, and when Buckner's predicament became public, the prosecutor's office was besieged by a small regiment of tradesmen who were laboring under the delusion that they were headed for financial glory in the show business.

When he concluded singing his ballad of defense, Buckner was booked for a few short terms in stir and even convinced one jurist that he qualified for a rest cure in an insane asylum. He wound up his career on a train bound for his home in Canada, the Federal authorities finally ordering him deported.

Little Caesar Goes Legit

David Brooks, actor and director, saw the benign side of a mobster.

Soon after I started on the stage, I was in something called *Shootin' Star* (1946), a musical about Billy the Kid which didn't make it into New York. It was produced by a man named Joseph Kipness, who went on to become quite a well-known producer. You did not have to suspect Joe of being a gangster, because he was quite proud of his past in the Mob and would tell hilarious stories about dumping people in cement and depositing them into the East River during the time when he ran the trucking business for Louis Lepke. He was a short, stocky guy, with a broad-rimmed hat over his eyebrows, hands in pocket, dressed for the part of a typical movie gangster of the Edward G. Robinson type, except Joe was more quiet.

Rehearsals had been under way for a few days and I had not met him, when one afternoon after we broke for the day, I hear a voice from the house:

"Hey, kid, come here."

I said, "What? Me?"

And he said, "Yeah, you kid, come here."

So I climbed off the stage into the auditorium, and there he stands with his hands in his pockets, and he says:

"Kid, I like you." Then he introduced himself: "I'm Joe Kipness."

"Oh, Mr. Kipness," I said, "you're the producer . . ."

"Yeah, yeah . . ." he cut me off, "I'm producin' this thing here . . ."

I waited.

"Kid, I like you," he repeated. "Tonight's the big fight. You put your money on Joe Louis."

"Oh, gosh, Mr. Kipness," I said, "that's very, very thoughtful of you, but I don't bet on prize fights."

"Kid, I'm tellin' ya," he insisted, "you put your money on Joe Louis."

At this point I started walking away, when he grabs me by the lapels, just like mobsters do in the movies, and he repeated with much greater emphasis:

"Kid, I'm tellin' ya to put your money on Joe Louis, 'cause it's a fixed fight."

I tried to laugh while freeing my lapel and managed to get out of the theatre.

The next day Joe Kipness showed up about noon, and when we were breaking for lunch he says:

"Hey kid, come here."

"Yes, Mr. Kipness."

He pulls a large wad of bills out of his pocket, peels off a hundred dollar bill, and stuffs it in my shirt pocket.

"Here kid," he said, "you won this last night."

Word of Honor

David Brooks stayed in show business, which meant that he was bound to encounter the Mob again.

In the early 1960s I was involved with an off-Broadway company and we were looking for a theatre space. We finally found one in the Village and it was a lovely little theatre. The lease required $20,000. The owner of this property was a Mafia character known by everybody as Big Ben. He was the opposite of Joe Kipness: a huge guy, six feet seven, but he dressed exactly the same way as Joe—broad-rimmed hat over the eyes, hands in pocket, and dark glasses. Anyway, we made a verbal deal, and then we found out that Ted Mann, who was looking for another theatre for Circle in the Square, had heard about our find and he offered $40,000, exactly double, for the same lease. But Big Ben apparently told him, "Sorry, kid, I've got a deal." We didn't know about this the afternoon we went to see him about signing the lease. We didn't expect him to be there, especially after we had read in the morning paper that his brother had been just gunned down in a Brooklyn restaurant. But Big Ben was there, with his hat and dark glasses, towering above us, and he took his hand out from his pocket and signed the lease, true to his word.

Dear Angel

Not content with the success of their own plays, Howard Lindsay and Russel Crouse scored big as producers of Joseph Kesselring's Arsenic and Old Lace *(1941). They were an unusual type of producer; for one thing, they enjoyed writing checks, according to journalist Lincoln Barrett.*

As the profits poured in, Lindsay & Crouse dispersed them to *Arsenic's* financial backers—twenty-one in all—in monthly installments accompanied by facetious letters which soon became collectors' items on Broadway. Four weeks after the opening they wrote: "Dear Angel. Enclosed you will find our first statement. We think it is a charming document and we hope that others more charming will follow. If there is anything in this about which you wish to complain we shall be glad to hear from you. Just address us in care of the Dead Letter Office, Washington, D.C." A few months later *Arsenic's* angels received a letter signed by Crouse, beginning: "Dear Angry-Wangy. You may breathe easier! Open-hearted Crouse, the backers' boy friend, has managed to get hold of the checkbook again, and if I can keep Lindsay out of the office for a few minutes I'll see that you really get a check." In November Crouse wrote again: "Dear Lucky Stiff. We haven't the slightest idea where all this money is coming from. Hold your breath for the opening in Sweden this month. Of course we will be paid off in kronas, but remember the old saying, 'Prosperity is just around the krona.'" In February 1944, Lindsay sent out the checks saying: "Dear Limited Partner. You have been limited by Mr. Crouse long enough, and so I am sending along the enclosed check. This, I hope, will demonstrate to you that so far as the firm of Lindsay & Crouse goes, it is Lindsay who fights on the side of the angels." A few months later Lindsay wrote again: "Dear Friend. Enclosed is a check of a good round figure. Hoping yours is the same." In October 1944, the partners wrote jointly: "Dear Stockholders. There is no reason on earth why you should still be getting money from *Arsenic and Old Lace* except that you happened to fall in with the two most honest guys since Abraham Lincoln." A year later they wrote: "Sweetheart. Enclosed you will find a check for the amount of your original investment and 25% more. This is absurd."

Some of *Arsenic's* twenty-one backers were professional angels who regarded any Lindsay-Crouse enterprise as a gilt-edged investment. Others were friends whom the partners cut in after the show's success was assured. One of these was Boris Karloff. Dubious of the whole undertaking from the first, Karloff had rejected their offer of a chance to invest. Lindsay &

Crouse, nevertheless, set aside a block of shares in his name and kidded him for his parsimony throughout the run of the show. Once they handed him his weekly salary of more than $2,000 entirely in nickels. Another time they offered him a new contract setting his salary at $25 a week plus any money thrown up on the stage. In reprisal Karloff declared it an outrage that he had to pay for his own make-up and issued an ultimatum that he would resign from the cast unless he was granted an allowance for powder forthwith. A few nights later Lindsay & Crouse appeared in his dressing room with a big box tied up in ribbons. "Here's all your powder for the next five years," they said. "Now shut up." On opening the box Karloff found it crammed with bottles and tins of tooth powder, roach powder, foot powder, baking powder, louse powder, gunpowder, Seidlitz powders, and powdered eggs.

Finally a Reason

Howard Cullman, who with his wife was the best-known backer of plays in the 1930s and 1940s, liked to demonstrate how much he was on the ball, by calling his secretary at 8:30 a.m., dictating some letters, and by nine he would start calling his theatrical friends. When he roused Russel Crouse from his deepest slumber one morning, the producer-writer gave Cullman an earful: "Listen, you so-and-so: the only reason I got into show business is because I like to sleep late!"

Let Not the Left Hand Know

Herman Mankiewicz, the wit and assistant to George Kaufman at the New York *Times*, wanted to follow his boss to glory in the theatre. Since he couldn't write his own play, he thought he'd try his hand at producing. He found a play, *Love 'Em and Leave 'Em*, a comedy by John V. A. Weaver. During tryout at Asbury Park he ran out of money. The show ran to empty houses, and he did not know how he'd find the cash to pay the actors at the end of the week. His general manager was Dick Maney, who recklessly undertook to work for him without a contract. It was his painful duty to remind the neophyte producer that the show could be closed down any moment, since he had neglected to pay the mandatory advance of $500 to the author. The next day, Mankiewicz came to the theatre with a smile of triumph: he had just paid John Weaver his advance.

"Where did you get the money?" asked the incredulous Maney.

"I borrowed it," said Mankiewicz.

"But who'd lend you money?"

"My dear friend, Peggy Wood."

In private life the actress Peggy Wood was Mrs. John V. A. Weaver.

Fund-raiser

For some reason, angels inhabit mainly the commercial world of Broadway. Money for non-profit arts organizations is raised by development directors through connections the boards of directors have with the movers and shakers in business and high society. In her book The Beautiful People *(1967), Marylin Bender, then a fashion reporter for the New York* Times, *explained how it works.*

Mrs. Peabody is devoted to music, ballet and drama. She has been involved in theatre, first as a production assistant to Sidney Lumet, later as an off-Broadway producer of plays by Eugene Ionesco and other contemporary playwrights. In the fall of 1964, she was elected to the board of trustees of the New York Shakespeare Festival, which gives top-flight productions of the Bard's plays in Central Park without charging admission. Through the fiery zeal of its producer, Joseph Papp, a Brooklyn boy who reincarnates the rough charm of a John Garfield, the Festival had managed to stave off annual bankruptcy. In 1966, the Festival acquired a building for a permanent home and projected plans for experimental theatre, chamber music concerts and art exhibits.

Until this point, the Festival had been rescued from its crises by philanthropists like George T. Delacorte, the publisher, and Mrs. Louis K. Anspacher, a self-effacing dowager. Mrs. Peabody, who had backed up her verbal enthusiasm with important financial support, encouraged the other trustees to interest a younger segment of New York society through a fundraising supper dance. She recruited "two young, glamorous, marvelous, hard-working people, both so creative and involved in the life of New York," to be co-chairmen. They were Mrs. Burden and Susan Stein, one of the go-go girls of the new fashion society.

"I adore Judy, I adore Amanda, I adore Shakespeare," cried Miss Stein, the dark-eyed, raven-haired daughter of Jules C. Stein, chairman of the Music Corporation of America. Her father registered his approval by becoming a Festival donor (one who gives between $1,000 and $5,000). "I majored in drama and philosophy at Vassar. I love *Henry V* and *King Lear*. *The Tempest* I did at college. I wrote the music," said Miss Stein.

It was her idea to have designers create special dresses based on the new, nude look. "It seemed the newest thing," she said.

Donald Brooks, the first designer she approached, suggested tying the dresses in with Shakespearean characters. He and Miss Stein jointly decided to miscast the energetic, talkative and strong-minded co-chairman as Ophelia. Mr. Brooks provided her with what she described as "a cute dress that makes me look like I just came out of the water dripping flowers." And her bosom overflowed the neckline.

Miss Stein drew up a list of Shakespeare's feminine characters and let the designers and fashion socialites have their pick. She served as arbitrator. Most of the designers researched their assignments. Most of the models, with the exception of Miss Stein and Gloria Steinem, who knew that Lady Macbeth "was at least an intelligent, interesting woman even if she came to a bad end," had the vaguest notions about whom they were impersonating.

"I know Othello tried to kill her," said Minnie Cushing of Desdemona, whom she was impersonating. The tall brunette from Newport, R.I., was substituting for Anne Ford Uzielli, who was originally supposed to wear the dress of sheer net latticed with gold that Miss Cushing's employer, Oscar de la Renta, had concocted. Mrs. Uzielli had bowed out, pleading pregnancy as an excuse.

"Hermione's husband thought she was unfaithful but my husband and I don't like that interpretation," said Mrs. Montague H. Hackett, Jr., a spirited brunet lawyer's wife and *Social Register*-ite who had just taken up designing pants and hostess clothes for Saks Fifth Avenue. "I'm sticking to the fact that she turned into a white statue." For her character from *The Winter's Tale*, Emilio Pucci had designed a jumpsuit out of gossamer white jersey, with harem pants and a halter neckline that plummeted to the waist. He had arranged for Harry Winston to lend Mrs. Hackett $300,000 worth of diamonds to relieve the stark simplicity of the outfit. The jeweler sent a bodyguard who hovered doggedly at Mrs. Hackett's elbow.

Plans had called for the models to attend the performance of *All's Well That Ends Well* at the Delacorte Theatre and then proceed to the supper dance at the Plaza Hotel. The threat of inclement weather forced the cancellation of the performance in the open-air theatre and the gala event was reduced to just the party. It was enjoyed on two levels. The fashion socialites and their designers reveled in posing for the press photographers and marching in a procession around the dance floor.

Seated apart from the birds of brilliant plumage were the loyal Festival supporters. They quietly supped on chicken tetrazzini and rosé, danced and regretted that the play had been scratched. They observed the pretty show-offs politely but not avidly. Some of them looked a little puzzled. "This is the first time we've ever done anything like this and I think we'd better assess it," said an industrialist from the board of trustees.

"The real true Shakespeare lovers gave a hundred dollars and stayed home," a Festival employee said.

CHAPTER 11

Natural Enemies

A Noisy Bunch

Mel Brooks was once asked what he thought of critics. "They're very noisy at night," the comic replied at once: "You can't sleep in the country because of them." When the interviewer tried to explain that he was asking about critics, not crickets, Brooks went on: "Oh, *critics!* What good are they? They can't make music with their hind legs."

Self-Definitions

George Jean Nathan wrote that "there are two kinds of dramatic critics: destructive and constructive. I am a destructive. There are two kinds of guns: Krupp and pop."

And in the same vein, he also observed: "The dramatic critic who is without prejudice is on the plane with the general who does not believe in taking human life."

Percy Hammond called dramatic criticism "venom from contented rattlesnakes."

And in a more down-to-earth way, Walter Winchell defined the drama critic as "a newspaperman, whose sweetheart ran away with an actor."

Point of View

The subjectivity of critics comes from a multitude of sources, including their origins and environment. Stark Young, the famous drama critic for *The New Republic* in the 1930s and a thoroughly Southern gentleman from Mississippi, wrote a piece about a Group Theatre play in which he found fault with the depiction of some middle-class characters as not being sufficiently *soignée*. Ralph Steiner, the photographer, then wrote a letter to the magazine in defense of the production, mentioning that perhaps Young belonged "Way Down the *Soignée* River."

(It was Young who, after seeing Martha Graham's dance recital for the first time, said he would not go back to see her: "I'm so afraid," he explained, "she is going to give birth to a cube.")

Down the River

And speaking of the South and another river, Tallulah Bankhead got the worst reviews of her life in 1937, when she played Cleopatra in Shakespeare's tragedy. "Miss Bankhead seemed more a serpent of the Suwanee than of the Nile," wrote Richard Watts, Jr. in the New York *Tribune*." George Jean Nathan called her "Queen of the Nil," sending a note to the compositors that the misprint was intentional. The most descriptive line came from John Mason Brown, leaving the actress high and dry: "Tallulah Bankhead barged down the aisle as Cleopatra and sank."

Benign Critic

Walter Winchell tended to praise, no matter what, the first show he saw in any theatrical season. Asked about this predictable benignity, he responded: "Who am I to stone the first cast?"

The Unadmirable Crichton

In March 1931, producer George Tyler revived *The Admirable Crichton* by Sir James Barrie. On opening night, at the start of the third intermission and another long act to go, Walter Winchell staggered into the foyer of the New Amsterdam and exclaimed: "For Crichton out loud!"

Dorothy Parker was substituting that night for Robert Benchley at *The New Yorker*. She wrote that "the all-star cast, as is the manner of all-star casts, held hams' holiday, and did every line, every bit of business, for all it was worth and just that little touch more . . . I have, happily for me, never seen upon one stage so many discourteous, patronizing and exaggerated performances."

Miss Parker ended her review with a personal postscript: "Robert Benchley, please come home. A joke's a joke."

Reach Out and Touch Someone

Robert Benchley was watching a Broadway opening, when the telephone rang on a completely empty stage. Benchley, who was bored with the play, muttered "I think that's for me," and went for the exit.

The Critics' Corner

In the 1920s, nearly all critics attended opening nights in tuxedos. Indeed, Kelcey Allen, longtime reviewer for *Women's Wear Daily*, once remarked that you became a critic because you owned a dinner jacket. Brendan Gill of *The New Yorker* was the longest, and, after a while, the only upholder of this tradition.

Heywood Broun, who flaunted the general sloppiness of sportswriters, always carried a book into the theatre (he also reviewed books for his paper) just in case the play bored him.

Kelcey Allen developed the not uncommon critical habit of falling asleep during shows. One evening he began to snore, and Walter Winchell, sitting nearby, whispered to his companion: "I see that Kelcey's writing his review early."

One night before an opening, an actor saw Allen at Sardi's and kidded him:

"What's the matter, Kelcey? Aren't you asleep yet?"

"You are not on stage yet," the critic parried back.

Allen was one of the prime movers behind the founding of the New York Critics' Circle. He revealed his hidden agenda once by admitting, "It's the only way that I thought I might ever get to meet George Bernard Shaw in person."

Tales of Hoffman

Irving Hoffman, New York correspondent for the Hollywood *Reporter* in the 1940s, actively disliked the theatrical experience. When he got to his seat, he was often seen changing his dress shoes for more comfortable slippers, and then, soon after the lights went down, drifting off into sleep.

He sometimes asked the management to allow him to use an office, and proceeded to write his review in the first intermission. After that he left.

Hoffman ranked his dislikes by putting them on his "best-smeller lists." He wrote about a veteran comedy team that they "skunk up the show with immaterial material." Reviewing Billie Burke in *Mrs. January and Mr. Ex*, Hoffman explained: "We're sorry, but it's not our cup of teehee."

Since he was writing for the movie colony on the West Coast, Hoffman was indifferent whether the critics of the Eastern establishment liked a show or not. When in 1944 they heralded the Boston tryout of the musical comedy *Follow the Girls* (which went on to 882 performances on Broadway), Hoffman shrugged:

"Boston liked *Follow the Girls*. Boston also likes baked beans. It has one of those books found in library dens. When opened, they turn out to be a cigarette case."

Don't Bring on the Girls

Percy Hammond fiercely disliked lavish girlie shows, so popular in the 1920s: "The Messrs. Shubert seem to forget that the female knee is a joint and not an evening's entertainment."

About another vapid revue, Hammond observed, "I find that I have knocked everything but the chorus girls' knees, and there God anticipated me."

George Jean Nathan once summed up such a revue: "The girls are all eighteen years of age." On another occasion, Nathan commented that "the costumes looked as though they had been selected by Helen Keller." The most famous blind person in the world used to quote with delight this line to any reporter who had connections in the entertainment business.

Willela Waldorf, critic of the *New York Post* in the 1940s, was particularly bitchy in assessing the talents of other females. When the Hungarian bombshell Ilona Massey came from Hollywood to star in one of the *Ziegfeld Follies*, the acidulous critic wrote: "Miss Ilona Massey, the blonde film actress who is making her Broadway debut in this production, is doubtless very good in films." And when the popular Murtah Sisters appeared to sing in a review *Take a Bow*, Miss Waldorf remarked: "The Murtah Sisters murtahed several songs."

Carved Up

Alexander Woollcott did not like a performance given by Elsie Ferguson, a big star in the first three decades of our century. When George and Beatrice Kaufman were celebrating their fifth wedding anniversary, the incorrigible Woollcott dropped them a line: "I have been looking around for an appropriate wooden gift, and am pleased hereby to present you with Elsie Ferguson's performance in her new play."

Some years later one London critic described Harve Presnell's performance in the musical version of *Gone with the Wind* at Drury Lane as being "so wooden that they should have used him for kindling in the burning of Atlanta."

Capsules

Eugene Field, litterateur of a century ago and critic on the Denver *Post*, is considered the father of the so-called capsule criticism. The capsules are fast-acting poisoned pills compacted into one or two sentences. Field is responsible for such oft-quoted Shakespearean reviews as:

"So-and-so played Hamlet last night. He played it till one o'clock."

Or: "Mr. Creston Clarke played King Lear at the Tabor Grand last night. All through five acts of the Shakespearean tragedy he played the king as though under the premonition that someone was about to play the ace."

Famous examples in this genre include Kyle Crichton's capsule on a dramatization of *Tom Jones*: "Good Fielding. No hit."

Titles of bad plays are particularly vulnerable to attack. One critic who did not like *I Am a Camera*, the adaptation of Christopher Isherwood's Berlin stories, expressed his opinion in just two words: "No Leica."

And writing of *The Bishop Misbehaves*, Walter Winchell called it a "new high for misleading titles."

Robert Benchley took one look at the set of *Bitter Oleander* in 1935 and told his readers in *The New Yorker* that it had been "designed by Cleon

Throckmorton from sketches by Santiago Ontanon of an old Spanish intestinal tract."

Of the play itself, Gilbert W. Gabriel wrote in *The World:* "More like a Henderson Seed Co. catalogue than an honest-to-living drama."

George Jean Nathan demolished a play called *Tonight or Never* with a single sentence: "Very well, then: I say, Never."

And reviewing John Barrymore's clowning in *My Dear Children,* Nathan opened: "I always said that I'd like Barrymore's acting till the cows came home. Well, ladies and gentlemen, last night the cows came home."

Brooks Atkinson was the most mild-mannered of critics, at least until he encountered a handsome Valentino look-alike. "Guido Nadzo," Atkinson pronounced on his performance, "was Nadzo Guido."

Reviewing in 1934 a disaster at the Fulton Theatre, Brooks Atkinson wrote: "When Mr. Wilbur calls his play *Halfway to Hell* he underestimates the distance."

Robert Garland was famous for several zingers, including the one about *Victory Belles,* a show which he thought "must be seen to be depreciated."

Although there are other versions, where the lady in question was called April, it was Garland who wrote about the New York appearance of the English actress Lady June Inverclyde: "Oh, to be in England, now that June's here!"

Generic Reviews

Today's playgoer may want to substitute a more recent title for any of the following old reviews.

Writing about *Illya Darling* (1967), starring Melina Mercouri, Walter Kerr wrote: "I think they've made a slight mistake. They've left the show in Detroit, or wherever it was last warming up, and brought in the publicity stills."

Wolcott Gibbs said about one of the worst plays he had seen on Broadway: "This is a fine sample of what happens when somebody just goes out of his way to write a play."

George Jean Nathan wrote of *The Great Waltz:* "The mouse labored and brought forth a papier-mâché mountain."

Gilbert W. Gabriel told his readers that a play called *De Luxe* was "an ornamentally dull play about a lot of nearly dead people."

Brooks Atkinson recorded the fact that a play "opened last night." Then he added: "Why?"

John Chapman writing in the New York *Daily News* about a melodrama called *Last Stop:* "It is enough to make your flesh crawl—right out of the Ethel Barrymore Theatre."

Commenting on the fact that most of the excitement takes place off-stage, Chapman added, "The talk which does occur upon the stage must be heard to be disbelieved."

Willela Waldorf described her reaction to the plot of a play: "At first we thought the actors were making it up as they went along."

About another plot David Lardner wrote that it "was designed in a light vein that somehow became varicose."

Defense Mechanism

After Milton Berle was savaged in a production by Willela Waldorf, he made a solemn resolution never to eat any more of her salad. The critics seemed unanimous about that show:

"There was one, however, who was very nice to me," Berle admitted to Earl Wilson.

"In what way?" asked the columnist in the role of the straight man.

"He didn't see it," said Berle.

In Vino Veritas

In knowing just how far he could go within the libel laws, Leonard Lyons had an advantage over other Broadway columnists: he had studied law before becoming a journalist. An actor did sue him once, saying that Lyons had falsely accused him of being addicted to drink. The case had to be dropped when the plaintiff was found dead under the Third Avenue "L." The post mortem showed a very advanced stage of alcoholism.

Too Dumb to Be Bribed

During the Khrushchev era, Harold Clurman was part of a cultural delegation to Moscow, where he took part in a seminar about the differences between American and Soviet theatre. Somebody asked the question whether American critics were corrupt—if, for example, they took bribes.

"Oh, no," Clurman said casually, "our critics come by their stupidity quite honestly."

Cheaper by the Dozen

Not that bribing critics is unknown. At the turn of the century, William Winter was a powerful name in New York theatre, having been drama critic of the New York Tribune *for more than a third of a century. Major J. B. Pond, one of the important booking agents for the highly lucrative lecture circuit, recalled this story.*

Once a very prominent manager, knowing that Mr. Winter and I were friends, came into my office and asked for a confidential talk, which was granted. He began like this:

"You know William Winter well, do you not?"

"I have very little association with him. I know him well enough to understand that he is my friend and would go as far to serve me as he would any friend."

"Is he well fixed or is he poor?" asked the manager.

"He's not rich. How could he be, with only the resources of his pen as his income, and with a family of sons and a daughter to educate?"

"Major, would $2,500 be any inducement for him to visit the Union Square Theatre tomorrow evening, and give that girl, the greatest actress in the world, a send-off?"

I said: "It would be a waste of time and money. You would be as safe in offering $50,000 as any other amount. If Mr. Winter goes there he will write as he sees, and will do the subject justice."

The manager told me that he had made sure of every paper that he wanted but the *Tribune,* and he would give more for that paper than for all the others, because whatever Winter wrote the public believed. He had already secured the next best dramatic writer for less than half he offered me if I could secure Winter.

Futile Gesture

Percy Hammond became the influential critic of the *New York Herald Tribune.* He was chatting with humorist Don Marquis at an opening in the early thirties. A mutual acquaintance came up and said perhaps only half in jest:

"If you don't write a good review of this play, I'll slit your throat."

"Percy," observed Marquis, "has had his throat slit so many times that he has had a zipper attachment installed on it."

Offending the Critic

Occasionally a critic will venture into playwriting, leading to unhappy results for the producer. It happened in the 1880s to comedian and manager Nat Goodwin, who described the results.

A New York critic, A. C. Wheeler, submitted a manuscript entitled *Big Pony*, music by Woolson Morse, a very clever composer whose *Cinderella at School* I had previously produced at the Boston Museum. We accepted this play and gave it a magnificent production. On the reading I thought that the first and third acts were exceptionally fine and the title role, Big Pony, I fancied too. I suggested that the second act might be improved. The dialogue referred to political issues that were long since dead. Wheeler insisted that the play should be performed as he had written it and would not permit one change. He proved very obdurate and we were finally compelled to either accept it as written or give it up. We finally decided to produce it, and much to my dissatisfaction I was compelled to deliver supposedly funny lines which I knew were funereal.

The first act proved a sensational hit, my entrance receiving such a tumult of applause that it was fully a minute and a half before I was permitted to sing my first song. We had a very good third act, but the second act was so terrible that the play proved an unmitigated failure.

Wheeler, known by his byline as Nym Crinkle, one of the cleverest critics of his time, was a most unscrupulous fellow and he took his medicine as such fellows usually take it. Instead of accepting the inevitable as a true sportsman should, Wheeler attributed the play's failure to me and with my knowledge became my bitter foe. The papers were severe in their reviews of the play, but most gracious to all the players, particularly to me. This rankled in his diminutive heart. Having torn down so many houses, he could not stand having his own citadel stormed. While we often met in the private office and talked over the possibilities of resuscitation, he would smilingly, yet stubbornly, refuse to alter a line or allow anyone to suggest changes. The play evidently appealed to his vanity. He never missed a performance, occupying a box with a lady who owned a half interest in the piece, a Miss Estelle Clayton.

We all knew that the play was doomed, and, knowing that it was shortly to be taken off, many of us took liberties with the text and gagged whenever the opportunity presented itself. I remember a gambling scene that I had in the last act in which I threw dice with one of the characters, incidentally losing all my fortune and vast estates. One evening as my last dollar disappeared over the dice cloth I noticed Wheeler (as usual in the box) beaming at some of my sallies. I said to the opposite character, "Now, my friend, I will throw you for this play—manuscript, parts and all."

The players and the audience, knowing that the play was about to be withdrawn, screamed with laughter. Just as I was pondering over some other funny quip my heart came up into my throat as I saw the box party get up and file out, their backs expressing profound indignation. I said to myself, "My finish," and muddled through the rest of the performance. I had made an enemy for life of A. C. Wheeler and well he exercised his avenging powers. For years he assailed me from every angle, his vilifying articles never ceasing until his death. I was to blame, I presume, but I really intended no harm—only fun.

Closet Dramatists

In the days when H. L. Mencken and George Jean Nathan were editing and writing *Smart Set*, they also tried their hands at playwriting. Their first attempt was to adapt a German play by Ludwig Thoma called *Moral*, which was a bit ahead of its time. In a foreshadowing of *La Cage aux Folles*, the starring role was that of a president of the Anti-Vice Society who is exposed as the protector of a fashionable bordello. The part was declined by every leading man on Broadway and the play had to be abandoned. In 1920, the two critics collaborated on another piece they called *Heliogabalus*. The incorrigible Mencken recalled its genesis:

"One afternoon Nathan and I were sitting in his apartment at the Royalton, in Forty-fourth Street, New York, and fell into a discussion of playwriting. We came to the conclusion that writing a play was a much smaller job than writing a book, and decided to write one to prove it. I contended that a so-called plot was unnecessary. 'Very well,' said Nathan, 'but where is your character?' I had just been re-reading Edgar Saltus's *Imperial Purple*, and Heliogabalus came to mind. We then went to Rogers', on Sixth Avenue, for dinner. By the time we got it down Heliogabalus was planned, and six weeks later it was finished . . . Writing it turned out to be absurdly easy—in fact, a sort of holiday from criticism. I ceased to respect dramatists from that time. Their work, I am convinced, is child's play."

Although much admired when privately circulated in manuscript this drama too remained in the closet. To protect themselves against criticism, the critics safely announced that they would not "authorize an American production until the United States became civilized." And that is where the matter rests.

Savaging the Critics

William A. Brady tried his hand at a genre immensely popular in nineteenth-century America. The frontier drama often featured Indians as noble savages, sometimes as fierce scalp-hunters. Brady had produced at the Liberty Theatre one of these poetic concoctions called The Redskin *(1906). The critics savaged the play, and cast doubt on the bloodlines of the Sioux in the cast. In turn, Brady made nightly curtain speeches denouncing them: "If I had the nerve," he breathed heavily, "I'd send that band of Indians down to Newspaper Row to do a little real damage among the funny newspaper men." An anonymous eyewitness recorded a tense moment that followed one of these inflammatory speeches.*

There had been a first night in a neighboring theatre and after the performance a party of them gathered on the subway platform in Times Square, awaiting a train to take them downtown. Suddenly, with a rustle of wampum, a swish of feathers, and occasional grunts and guttural exclamations, Mr. Brady's band of real Sioux trooped into the station. It was a spectacle of truly barbaric awe. The Indians swung up to where the pale-faced critics were standing—among them the very man who had aroused the particular ire of Mr. Brady and his company by referring to them as cigar-store Indians.

For one brief moment there was a rising of hair on scalp-locks. Then the train rumbled in, and critics and redskins parted to board separate cars. The Sioux were on their way home after the evening's performance.

Persecution

Anne Nichols dashed off *Abie's Irish Rose* (1922) in three days while still in her twenties. This sentimental comedy promoting ethnic and religious tolerance broke Broadway's record for the longest-running show and held it for fourteen years. "It brought its author spectacular fame and fortune," Arthur Gelb wrote in a 1962 interview with her in the New York *Times*, "earning her more money than any single play has ever earned a writer."

The road to Broadway was rocky. It took three years of rejections before Oliver Morosco produced *Marriage in Triplicate* (as it was first called) at his Los Angeles theatre. The producer intended to take it to New York, but his preoccupation with a divorce and remarriage made the young playwright impatient. Anne Nichols used her house as a collateral to finance her own play at the Fulton Theatre. After a few indifferent and some downright nasty reviews, the play almost closed after the first two months. Nichols's resources were depleted, the actors took salary cuts to compensate for lowered ticket prices, when the show was rescued by an angel in the unlikely disguise of the gangster Arnold Rothstein: *Abie's Irise Rose* became what George Jean Nathan only half-facetiously called "the fourth biggest industry in the United States." During its record run of 2,327 performances one of the cast-members, Milton Wallace, handed out business cards which listed his permanent address at the Fulton Theatre, and Lorenz Hart wrote a lyric which included the lines: "Our future babies we'll take to *Abie's Irish Rose;* I hope they'll live to see it close—someday."

Even after this manifest triumph, critics continued to persecute the play. "In another two or three years, we'll have this play driven out of town," wrote Robert Benchley in an earlier magazine called *Life*, where he had to come up weekly with brief summaries of Broadway runs. "We understand that a performance of this play in modern dress is now under way," he wrote after a few years. At another time, he simply noted: "Hebrews 13:8." which sent mystified readers to the New Testament where they found the revelation: "Jesus Christ—the same yesterday, and today, and forever." *Abie's Irish Rose* exacerbated and finally exhausted Benchleys' ingenuity. He advertised a contest which offered a prize for the most apt comment on the play. Harpo Marx won with his faint praise: "No worse than a bad cold."

Nomination

A couple of years before *Abie's Irish Rose*, Robert Benchley actually came to the rescue of a play that had been savaged by other critics. George M. Cohan had bought the rights to a manuscript by Cora Dick Gantt on condition that he could adapt it any way he wished. After he had finished with it, only the setting, one character and a single line remained ("I am a fugitive from my own thoughts"). *The Tavern* (1920), as Cohan had retitled this semi-historical travesty, became known for a while for another line: "What's all the shootin' for?" The critics missed the fact that Cohan meant the whole play as a burlesque on melodrama; Cohan in his counterattack claimed that people came to see the play out of curiosity whether it could be really as bad as the critics claimed. With his customary perversity, Benchely swam against the tide. He wrote in *Life* that George M. Cohan was the greatest man in the world and, on the strength of *The*

Tavern, he nominated the song and dance man for president of the United States.

Man Proposeth

At the beginning of his career, when he was working for the Chicago *Evening Post*, Percy Hammond had a yearning for the stage. He managed to get a bit part with Richard Mansfield, a great star in the early years of the century. Mansfield was playing Peer Gynt at Hamlin's Grand Opera House, and Hammond was assigned the role of impersonating Bird Cries in Ibsen's poetic drama. After the first performance, Mansfield had the foresight to tell his stage manager: "This youth is at heart a critic, not an actor. Dispose of him as constructively as you can."

Sweeney Todd

Thomas Barry, manager of the Tremont Theatre in Boston in the middle of the nineteenth century, was often feuding with Colonel Greene, who edited the *Boston Post*. Despite the fact that Barry sometimes refused to give the usual first night tickets, the *Post* would still run a review the next day. The manager's pettiness resulted in a predictable loss of business, and after a particularly poorly attended performance of *The Barber of Seville*, Colonel Greene remarked in print that "the Barber appeared last night before a house not large enough to pay for the lather."

Those Who Ignore the Lessons of History

The Shuberts were famous for banning critics and offending reporters from their openings. They lost their celebrated feud with the New York *Times* when after barring Alec Woollcott for eighteen months in 1915–16, they were forced to re-admit him, because the newspaper refused to accept their money for advertising. But like the Bourbons, the Shubert brothers seemed to have learned nothing, and a few years later they barred Walter Winchell from all their theatres. They were angered by an anecdote that Winchell printed. He claimed to have overheard in the Astor Hotel lobby Lee Shubert say to his brother about a current flop:

"Why did we ever buy that lousy play?"

To which Jake Shubert supposedly replied:

"Every business has its flops. Look, for instance, at the Sesquicentennial Exhibition in Philadelphia . . ."

Not particularly strong stuff from Winchell, but the Shuberts were afraid of offending Philadelphians, so they let everyone know that the gossip columnist was persona non grata. It gave birth to Winchell's celebrated comment: "If I can't go to their openings, I'll wait three days and go to the closings."

Tempest

Like most theatre people, Joseph Papp is sensitive about criticism. Edith Oliver of The New Yorker *once received a letter in which she was "disinvited" to the Public Theatre.*

So I went and paid for my own ticket and was watching some Beckett plays sort of crouching in the back. Joe noticed, came up and said:
  "Why don't you sit down the front, where there are empty seats?"
  "Well, I thought you were furious at me, and . . ."
  "Furious?" said Joe. "But that was three days ago!"

The Revenger's Comedy

In their age-old animosity and feuds with critics, producers sometimes fantasize about revenge, but in Hamlet's words, usually their

native hue of resolution
Is sicklied o'er with the pale cast of thought.

David Merrick said during a preview of *Subways Are for Sleeping* about the two most powerful New York critics a generation ago: "I had a wonderful dream last night that Walter Kerr dropped dead on his way to Howard Taubman's funeral." After the show was panned by all the major papers, Merrick perpetrated what he called "a delicious gag." He searched through all the New York phone directories and found seven people with the same names as the critics. He paid them to give him glowing quotes which he published in full-page ads under their names. Walter Kerr's *Herald Tribune* was the first to discover the prank and to kill the ad. By that time the stunt was all over the city.

Another time David Merrick accused Walter Kerr of being influenced by his playwright-wife, Jean Kerr. If she nudged him, Merrick asserted, he would laugh and write a good review. Kerr was ready with his defense: "She likes me, that crazy girl. Surely, somewhere, sometime, someone must have liked you well enough, Mr. Merrick, to give you a dig with an elbow. No? Ah, well."

Simonized

Few critics have aroused as deep if negative passions as John Simon. According to friends Simon enjoys and cultivates his reputation for bitchiness. A good part of actress Sylvia Miles's legend in the theatre centers on her heroic stand against the critic. According to Ms. Miles in a recent issue of *TheaterWeek*, she met John Simon at a party after he had seen her in a play called *Nellie Toole and Co.* (1973). Instead of reviewing her performance, he characterized Sylvia Miles as "a Warhol actress and a gatecrasher." So the actress deliberately dumped a plate of food on the critic.

"I'll send you a bill for the suit," Simon said.

"Good," said Sylvia, "it'll be dry-cleaned probably for the first time."

Simon Says

What has made John Simon perhaps the most hated critic alive today is his technique of attacking *ad hominem*, and even more often and ungallantly *ad feminam*, as his notorious description of a naked and vulnerable Diana Rigg "built like a brick mausoleum with insufficient flying buttresses." He particularly likes to knock national treasures and icons, as in the following example of the Simon method.

Reviewing Shaw's *Mrs. Warren's Profession* a few years back at Lincoln Center, John Simon commented on Ruth Gordon being cast in the title role: "It is a generous role for womanly and impassioned actresses, and many performers have essayed it. I can think of four, however, who have not: Totie Fields, W. C. Fields, Tutankhamen's mummy, and a trained monkey. Not until now, that is; Miss Gordon's performance combines elements of all four."

Having killed Miss Gordon with that, Simon went on to praise extravagantly Lynn Redgrave's performance as Vivie. But, being John Simon, he could not leave the corpse of poor Ruth Gordon alone: "The actress [Redgrave] deserves every acting award we've got, and also—for performing with such unruffled calm opposite someone compared to whom a brick wall would be generous support—the Nobel Peace Prize."

Then came a final (and perhaps critically valid) dig at Joe Papp for casting Ruth Gordon: "Or was this just a piece of errant commercialism to pull in the crowds that grooved on the witch of *Rosemary's Baby?* Or, worse yet, sheer tastelessness and incomprehension of the work's meaning? *Mrs. Warren's Profession* may or may not be described as a problem play; Mr. Papp is certainly a problem producer."

A Choice of Weapons

Ladies and Gentlemen (1939) was one of the few flops co-authored by Ben Hecht and Charlie MacArthur, which starred Helen Hayes. A certain critic, well known for his sexual preferences, was not content with panning the play. He also attacked Mrs. MacArthur, saying that "the trouble with Miss Hayes is that she has been seeing too much of Charlie MacArthur." The next day when MacArthur joined his usual circle at "21," they wanted to know what he would do to avenge his wife's honor.

"I've already taken care of him," said the author. "I am sending him a poisoned choirboy."

CHAPTER 12

Type
and Hype

This Is Where We Came Out

*P. T. Barnum was so successful that he ran into an unusual problem,
which he solved in his own unique way.*

I received notice from some of the Irish population that they meant to
visit me in great numbers on "St. Patrick's day in the morning." "All
right," said I to my carpenter, "get your egress ready for March 17"; and
I added, to my assistant manager: "If there is much of a crowd, don't let
a single person pass out at the front, even if it were St. Patrick himself; put
every man out through the egress in the rear." The day came, and before
noon we were caught in the same dilemma as we were on the Fourth of
July; the Museum was jammed and the sale of tickets was stopped. I went
to the egress and asked the sentinel how many hundreds had passed out?

"Hundreds," he replied, "why only three persons have gone out by this
way and they came back, saying that it was a mistake and begging to be let
in again."

"What does this mean?" I inquired; "surely thousands of people have
been all over the Museum since they came in."

"Certainly," was the reply, "but after they have gone from one saloon to another and have been on every floor, even to the roof, they come down and travel the same route over again."

At this time I espied a tall Irish woman with two good-sized children whom I had happened to notice when they came in early in the morning.

"Step this way, madam," said I politely, "you will never be able to get into the street by the front door without crushing these dear children. We have opened a large egress here and you can pass by these rear stairs into Ann Street and thus avoid all danger."

"Sure," replied the woman, indignantly, "an' I'm not going out at all, at all, nor the children aither, for we've brought our dinners and we are going to stay all day."

Further investigation showed that pretty much all of my visitors had brought their dinners with the evident intention of literally "making a day of it." No one expected to go home till night; the building was over-crowded, and meanwhile hundreds were waiting at the front entrance to get in when they could. In despair I sauntered upon the stage behind the scenes, biting my lips with vexation, when I happened to see the scene-painter at work and a happy thought struck me: "Here," I exclaimed, "take a piece of canvas four feet square, and paint on it, as soon as you can, in large letters—

☞ TO THE EGRESS."

Seizing his brush he finished the sign in fifteen minutes, and I directed the carpenter to nail it over the door leading to the back stairs. He did so, and as the crowd, after making the entire tour of the establishment, came pouring down the main stairs from the third story, they stopped and looked at the new sign, while some of them read audibly: "To the Aigress."

"The Aigress," said others, "sure that's an animal we haven't seen," and the throng began to pour down the back stairs only to find that the "Aigress" was the elephant, and that the elephant was all out o'doors, or so much of it as began with Ann Street. Meanwhile I began to accommodate those who had long been waiting with their money at the Broadway entrance.

Your Name in This Space

One of the differences between Broadway and other theatrical cities is the tradition of naming theatre buildings after living personalities of the profession. The advantage of having your name on a building, whether you earned the honor or paid for it by purchasing the real estate, is that the marquee never changes.

One archetypical story of this phenomenon comes not from Broadway but from the Wild West of rugged individualism. In 1881, all Denver was agog with its new opera house, built by the mining magnate H. A. W. Tabor, who had struck it rich in the mountains of Colorado. An English company had been invited for the opening of the Tabor Grand. All of Denver society was there to pay homage to Mr. Tabor, who was strutting about grandly in the foyer, when he came upon a portrait, prominently exhibited, of some unfamiliar person.

"Who the hell is this?" he asked one of his hangers-on.

"That's Shakespeare, Mr. Tabor."

"Who?"

"Shakespeare."

"Who is Shakespeare?"

"He's the greatest playwright who ever lived."

By this time, Tabor's face was turning dangerous colors of purple and red.

"I don't care," the magnate exploded with the immortal line: "What the hell has he ever done for Colorado!?"

By next evening Shakespeare's portrait had been replaced with that of Mr. Tabor.

Promote Thyself

The competitive nature of show business makes self-promotion often a necessary part of gaining and keeping advantage. Robert Grau noted at the turn of the century the unconventional methods a couple of young comics used to attract bookings.

Fred Niblo was a born advertiser, and when, in his struggling days, he began writing to the agents and managers for bookings, he was determined to obtain a response. He would send, first, a postal card, then a letter, and then he would increase the size of his envelopes until they were so large as to attract widespread attention; still he did not seem to obtain the proper response. Finally, perhaps in desperation, he sent his application to managers and agents written on his collars with the postage inserted, and on these he had a P.S. as follows: "If this does not bring me time, I will write on my cuffs next." Still no bookings for Niblo, at least not the kind he wanted. After a few days every booking office in New York received an-

other application written on his cuffs, also containing a P.S.: "If this does
not get me the time I want, I'll write on my shirt next." It was not necessary for Fred to go to that extreme. The threat was enough; ever after he
was a leading figure in vaudeville and his rise has been constant.

Frank Bush also was wont to use extreme methods to impress the booking agents, and to keep their attention in his direction. Occasionally he
would return from a sojourn at the fisheries, a pastime for which he had
much inclination, and would make a visit to the principal booking offices
where he would relate his good fortune and the prodigious size and weight
of his catches. This would naturally be followed by a request from the
booking agent for a small portion of the comedian's captures. Bush would
then hie himself to a fish market and purchase the largest specimens of fish
obtainable and these he would send by messenger to the man whose influence he sought.

Turning Them Out

*Getting people out to see a show was a great deal easier in the nineteenth
century, before movies, radio, and television. But getting the public's attention for approaching attractions required constant ingenuity. Robert Grau
remembered in 1909 a couple of billboards that worked.*

Early in the year 1867, an avant courier swept into Louisville, Kentucky,
and secured a lease of the Mercantile Library Hall, then the only place of
amusement in that city, for a single evening. This agent at once placed, all
over the city and in the suburbs of Louisville, large posters, on which was
printed:

HE IS COMING!

Not another word of announcement was made, and after a few days, when
excitement began to run high, these bills were replaced by others, reading:

HE IS HERE!

Two days later the excitement was intense. However, on the afternoon
of the second day, the posters were again replaced by ones reading:

HE WILL BE AT LIBRARY
HALL TO-NIGHT!

About 7 p.m., on this particular evening, a young man took possession of
the box office in Library Hall, and soon a crowd began to gather, by seven-
thirty the streets were blockaded, and at a few minutes before eight, it was

impossible to squeeze another person into Library Hall. The paste boards sold for fifty cents each, and the audience contained an even division of the sexes and in an exceedingly anticipatory mood; at a quarter after eight the curtain rose. On the stage a beautifully painted canvas covered the entire breadth of the space inside the proscenium arch, this canvas was at least eight feet high and twenty feet wide, and the painting was in several colors, each letter being ornamented artistically. The sign read:

HE HAS GONE.

That consternation was the result of this display need not be here told. It was however found that no crime had been committed, no promise had been made.

The Golden Bicycle

After Oscar Hammerstein fell out with his brother-in-law Henry Rosen-berg, he put George Blumenthal in charge of the Harlem Opera House. This was a difficult challenge in the 1890s, because Harlem was perhaps even further then from the rest of the city than today. Young Blumenthal had to use all sorts of tricks to attract a public, as he recounts in My Sixty Years in Show Business.

Most of the theatre managers were still loath to take the gamble of sending their companies to Harlem. In order to get there from downtown, one had to take the Eighth Avenue horse-car, or walk 'way over from the Second or Third Avenue "L," or resort to carriages and horses. But in spite of every-thing a few great companies were already broken in and kept coming back every year. I immediately set to work to get others to do so.

One of the first attractions I secured was Lillian Russell to play a week in May 1896, in *The Little Duke*, under the management of Abbey, Schoeffel, and Grau. She had just announced that a golden bicycle had been presented to her—that she could be seen riding it in Central Park most any nice day.

I will confess that I was getting the press agent fever and wanted to try my hand at a few stories, true or untrue. The press agents were then hand-ing out such bunk as Anna Held's taking baths in milk and champagne, and about Mrs. Patrick Campbell insisting that tanbark be put over the street in front of the theatre where she was playing so that the noise from the vehicles would not disturb her on the stage.

I conceived the idea of springing a story that while Lillian Russell was riding in Central Park she fell off her golden wheel. When she arrived at the theatre the second night I told her of my plan. This included my greasing the apron of the stage so that when she came to the footlights she could slip, which would bear out the "truth." I then let out the story that she had had a bicycle accident to the Harlem representatives of the papers, who at that time included Frank McQuade of the *Herald*, Frank Shober of the *World*, and Jim Farrelly of the *American*. The "boys" came to the next performance to see what damage had been done, and Miss Russell followed out my instructions to a "T."

What hell there was to pay the next morning. Every paper had headlines of how Lillian Russell had fallen on the stage during her performance, probably as a result of her having fallen from her wheel that day.

Mr. Abbey called me up on the telephone and upbraided me unmercifully about the story, saying it would ruin the week's engagement. My answer was, "Come right up to the theatre and see the line at the box office buying tickets in advance."

It turned out to be a great week's engagement.

Truth in Advertising

William Collier (1866–1944), actor and wit, once opened *The Patriot*, one of his own plays, on December 30. On January 2 he advertised with some degree of truthfulness: "Second Year in New York."

Untruth in Advertising

The Greeks had a convention that kept slaughter, suicide, self-blinding, and other forms of violence offstage, leaving the audience to reconstruct such events in their imagination from lengthy messenger speeches. With progress, people went to the theatre (and later the movies) with the opposite hope: they wanted to see as much gore, sensation, and thrills as possible. The critic Walter Eaton recalled the stage version of Quo Vadis in 1896.

When the play was produced great posters depicted a naked damsel on the back of a bull, and a gigantic man grasping the bull's horns and breaking its neck. Rather a piquant situation, you thought, and hastened to the theatre. But you didn't see there any naked lady on a bull's back while a giant broke the creature's neck. You saw the spectators looking excitedly into the wings at the stage hands, and telling each other that the bull's neck was being broken. Of course, its neck had to be broken, and the audience had to know it was broken, or the story couldn't go on. But, since modern actors are not trained to break bull's necks, it had to happen offstage.

Poor old Pete Dailey, who was such a tower of humor in the Weber and Fields company, once put the prick of burlesque into this technical balloon. He was supposed to enter upon the stage from a dinner party in the next room, and his entrance was followed by the sound of applause from the invisible diners. Jerking his thumb back toward the wings, he remarked, "Jolly dogs, those stage hands!"

The Art of Promotion

In 1926 Richard Maney had his job cut out to publicize one of those really bad plays which make up the vast majority of any theatrical season. He excuses his success in his book of reminiscences, Fanfare.

The Squall was the sordid recital of the havoc wrought by a gypsy waif afflicted with pidgin English. Nubi—that was the name of the Jezebel—seduced every male in the household of her benefactor. Charged with malpractice, she sought a stay of execution. "Nubi good girl. Nubi stay?" she implored. This plea routed Robert Benchley, critic of the year-old *New Yorker*. Citing the deplorable events which had preceded it, Benchley fled the theatre. He explained to his readers, "Benchley bad boy. Benchley go."

Seeking to capitalize on this rebuke, I inserted "the Play that made a Street-Walker of Robert Benchley" in the daily ads. The New York *Times* rejected this flippancy. It relented when I changed "street walker" to "nocturnal nomad." To further inflame the community, I identified *The Squall* as "a passionate drama of the sexes." The implication that there were more than two sexes was a taunt the curious could not withstand. Appealing to the baser side of pedestrians, I plastered the front of the theatre with enlarged photographs of the play's sinful episodes. These bared Nubi's sultry charms to a degree not approximated in the three-act horror. *The Squall* prospered for eight months, thanks to Benchley and a relentless airing of its sexual heresies. Though I gained a shabby triumph, I did not exult. I had conspired in a swindle. I had some notable conspirators, among them Dorothy Stickney, Sylvia Sydney, Blanche Yurka, and Romney Brent. Actors must eat, too.

Not Necessarily the News

With a dozen newspapers churning out Broadway columns in the 1920s, the hunger for gossip and news, no matter how insubstantial or invented, was insatiable. The press agents, who most often were newspapermen themselves, were paid to think up daily absurdities for the jaded appetites of editors and readers. More often than not there was no news to report, especially with long-running shows. Emmanuel Seff, who worked for the Shuberts, owned up to it by sending out in 1926 a press release: "There is no news today about *A Night in Paris* at the Winter Garden Theatre."

A desperate James P. Davis scraped the bottom of the barrel when he wrote: "Helen Craig, star of *Johnny Belinda* at the Longacre, yesterday was elected a member of the Book of the Month Club. She will start receiving books almost immediately."

And an anonymous flak took flight into fantasy: "*Fielder's Choice*, the hit drama at the Ritz Theatre, played last week to 350 standees, has been sold to the movies for $500,000 and yesterday placed tickets on sale through the next five years." This archetypal Isuzu spokesman attached to each release a small sealed envelope on which he had typed: "Grain of Salt."

Lost at Sea

Publicity was Florenz Ziegfeld's lifeblood. He did not mind paying bills; however, he preferred to be taken to court, because it would get his name in the papers. Once he sailed for Europe during an international crisis which occupied the front pages of all the papers. The next day he used the ship's wireless to dispatch a query to his press agent: "Why did you sneak me out of America?"

Not Fatal

In 1925 Earl Carroll was mounting a production in Baltimore when he suffered what he described as a heart attack. He was taken to Johns Hopkins where Dr. W. R. Thayer, after examining the producer, gave his opinion:

"There's nothing wrong with Mr. Carroll except a terrible attack of publicity mania."

CHAPTER 13

Caught
in the Act

Owning Up

Maurice Barrymore was frequently charged with having too great an unacknowledged debt to French plays. Asked during a routine interview how his five-year-old son John was coming along, the proud father replied: "He is in the best of health—and I am very proud of him. He is in fact the only thing I ever owned that the newspapers have not accused me of taking from the French."

Led Astray

David Belasco was working in the frontier theatre of Virginia City. As a theatrical jack-of-all-trades he acted, stage-managed, adapted scripts. Once, while helping out Dion Boucicault, the most famous playwright of his day, he learned a lesson.

When Boucicault reached Virginia City, he was under contract to deliver a play to A. M. Palmer, of New York. *Led Astray* was its title. But his writing hand was so knotted with gout that he could scarcely hold a pen. Boucicault was noted for being a very secretive man. He would never have a secretary because he feared such a man might learn too much of his methods of work. He was in the habit of saying: "I can't write a line when I dictate. I think better when I have a pen in my hand."

But now he had to have assistance to finish *Led Astray*. At this time I had some slight reputation as a stage manager and author. In those days everything was cut and dried, and the actor's positions were as determined as those of the pawns on a chess-board. But whenever an opportunity offered itself, I would introduce something less rigorous in the way of action, much to the disgust of the older players. Boucicault must have heard of my revolutionary methods, for he sent me a message to come and see him and have a chat with him. With much perturbation, I went to his hotel and knocked on his door.

"They tell me you write plays," he began. Then followed question after question. He tested my handwriting, he commented on certain stage business he had heard me suggest the day before; then he said abruptly:

"I want you to take dictation for me,—I'm writing a play for the Union Square Theatre,—you have probably heard of the manager, A. M. Palmer,— at one time a librarian, but now giving Lester Wallack and Augustin Daly a race for their lives. I hope, young man, you can keep a secret; you strike me as being 'still water.' Whatever you see, I want you to forget."

So I sat at a table, took my coat off and began Act One of *Led Astray*. Boucicault lay propped up with pillows, before a blazing fire, a glass of hot whisky beside him. It was not long before I found out that he was the terror of the whole house. If there was the slightest noise below stairs or in the street, he would raise such a hubbub until it stopped that I had never heard the like of before.

Whenever he came to a part of the dialogue requiring Irish, I noticed how easily his dictation flowed. When he reached a dramatic situation, he acted it out as well as his crippled condition would allow. One thing I noticed particularly: he always held a newspaper in his hand and gave furtive glances at something behind it I was not supposed to see. I was determined, however, to know just what he was concealing from me.

The opportunity came one morning when he was called out of the room. Before he went, I noted how careful he was to place a newspaper so that it completely hid the thing under it. I went quickly to the table, and, turning over the pages, I found a French book, *La Tentation*, from which the entire plot of *Led Astray* was taken.

A Question of Copyright

William A. Brady (1863–1950) got his start in San Francisco. He made a deal with Walter Morosco to provide his huge dance hall operation with one play a week in return for 10 percent of the box office. Normally, of course, it was the author who received such royalties, but Morosco did not ask or want to know where Brady got his scripts. In reality, there is only one way for one man to come up each and every week with a new play that is guaranteed to work, and Brady was smart enough to figure it out. After all, there was a centuries-old tradition of borrowing others' work and adapting them—Shakespeare and Molière were both famous for it. Besides, San Francisco was a wild frontier town still, a very long way from New York and Europe where most of the true and tried scripts hailed from and where their authors lived.

Brady was doing very handsomely on his arrangement until he bought a fifteen-cent copy of Dion Boucicault's melodrama *After Dark*. Having made some of his customary cosmetic changes, Brady gave it to Walter Morosco, who produced it with great success. As luck would have it, the venerable Dion Boucicault showed up, pointed out his ownership of *After Dark*, and threatened to have the plagiarist thrown into jail.

Young Brady pointed out in vain that there was no copyright notice in the script he bought. He had not reckoned with Boucicault's decades of experience, especially in the field of copyright law, where he had led the fight to protect authors' rights before Brady had even been born. Boucicault explained that he never copyrighted his work, because infringement would leave him with recourse only to a civil suit to recover the royalties. On the other hand, the law looked on uncopyrighted work as personal property, and any trespass thereon constituted a criminal offense.

Thoroughly intimidated by Boucicault's forceful argument, Brady was forced to buy *After Dark* for $1500. Anxious to recover his investment, he mounted several productions, one of which he took to New York. There the punchline was waiting for him. He was immediately sued on the grounds that Boucicault's play was a crude but obvious plagiarization of Augustin Daly's melodrama, *Under the Gas Lights*.

Stealing a Scene

George Barrett (1794–1860) was one of the prominent actor-managers in New York and Boston in the early nineteenth century. Because of his elegant acting and appearance, he was sometimes called "Gentleman George." Walter M. Leman, in his Memories of an Old Actor, *recalled that the oc-*

cupation of managing a theatre was not always compatible with being a gentleman.

I remember an amusing incident which happened in those early days, when a young gentleman in a subordinate position completely turned the laugh on the stage manager, Mr. George Barrett. It was in Sheridan's farce of *The Critic*, which is, in point of fact, the Duke of Buckingham's Rehearsal, with another name.

Mr. Barrett was very fond of playing Puff, the author, and great license was admitted in the language and business of the play within the play, which forms the comic element of the piece, the ladies and gentlemen cast to the several parts in Mr. Puff's play having carte blanche to make any rejoinder or reply not violating the rules of propriety or good taste. The young actor was playing the Beefeater, and has to withdraw from the scene with—

> I never can endure a rival's bliss,
> But soft—I am observed!

He spoke his lines and went off, when Mr. Barrett called him back with—

"You mustn't make your exit that way; you mustn't bolt off, you must *steal* off. Please try it again."

Again it was tried, and again he was called back by Mr. Barrett.

"I told you not to bolt off; you mustn't go off so abruptly; you must *steal* off. Can't you do it thus? You look as if you knew how to steal."

There was a laugh here at the expense of the Beefeater, which he turned upon Barrett by retorting,

"I haven't had so much practice in stealing as you have, Mr. Barrett; I haven't been manager for twenty years."

Upstaging

Jimmy Durante almost got to be a singer, when the vaudeville act of Clayton, Jackson, and Durante appeared in Florenz Ziegfeld's Broadway revue *Show Girl* (1929). George Gershwin had written the song "Liza" for Ruby Keeler to tap to, and thought it might be funny to have Jimmy Durante to sing it. The Schnozz loved the idea of stretching himself, yet he was also nervous and spent all rehearsals practicing the song. During opening night of *Show Girl* in Boston, just as Jimmy Durante began to sing, Al Jolson, who was in the audience as Ruby Keeler's fiancé, stood up and sang "Liza" in a way that practically swept everybody, including Durante, off their feet.

The audience, of course, assumed that it had been a deliberate stunt and gave Jolson just the kind of ovation he had always craved. Gershwin then took the song away from poor Jimmy Durante, and Jolson sang it every night for the next several weeks both in Boston and later in New York.

A Den of Thieves

Walter Winchell once called Milton Berle "The Thief of Bad Gags." In his glory days in the thirties and forties, the comedian was also known for stealing the show from his colleagues. Sitting at the back of the nightclub, Berle would stand up and start telling jokes, while the regular entertainer tried to carry on from the podium. After a while, the whole thing became a gag, so he would be asked to interrupt. One night when Joey Adams was the featured comic at Leon & Eddie's, Milton Berle said it would be pointless to tell his jokes, when Adams would be borrowing them anyway.

"I wouldn't steal any of your jokes, Milt," Adams shouted back, "because I wouldn't want Bob Hope to sue me!"

Battle of the Wits

Frank Fay was a famous drunk on the nightclub circuit, even before he created the classic character of Elwood P. Dowd in *Harvey*. After a long stint in Hollywood, where he was married for a while to Barbara Stanwyck, Fay was back doing his monologues at the Copacabana. Milton Berle, the then-reigning king of insults, began to heckle Fay and throw barbs at him. As he saw his prey get confused and fluff his lines, Berle rubbed his hands in glee:

"This is really going to be a battle of the wits tonight."

There was a pause, then Fay rumpled up his still burnished hair, and said quietly:

"Well, if you insist, Milt. But I want you to know that it's against my principle to fight an unarmed man."

I Won't Thank You for Smoking

Milton Berle was appearing at a Banshee's luncheon in New York. It was part of his act to pick on a cigar smoker and then kid him about his cigar. It was his misfortune to pick this time a funny actor named Hugh Herbert. Trying to wave away the smoke, Berle asked him:

"Don't you ever inhale?"

"Not when you're in the room," Herbert topped him.

Teaching 'Em Manners

Earl Wilson attributed to comedian Lenny Kent the following definition of a nightclub: "It's a place where the tables are reserved but the customers aren't." Because of the informal atmosphere of clubs, and the higher level of inebriation than is common in theatres, performers have to deal with a great deal of obnoxious enthusiasm. Here are selected karate chops against troublesome hecklers from the golden age of the nightclubs, the thirties and forties.

Henny Youngman once told someone who was disrupting his nightclub act: "This is the first time I ever saw a pair of shoes with three heels."

Jack Waldron told a drunk: "Let's play horse: I'll be the front end and you just be yourself."

When a drunk came up to the stage and told Frank Fay that he stank, the egocentric comedian came back with one of his standard responses: "Remember, you are speaking of the man I love."

Jack White got fed up with interruptions from a female habituée of the club where he tried to perform. "Please, lady," he turned on her, "would you like it if I came over where you lived and turned off your red light?"

Once a customer threw a penny at Frank Tinney during his act. "There's only one animal," the comic told him in measured tones, "that throws a scent."

The Tedium Is the Message

Comedian George Jessel was a favorite toastmaster at the Friars' Club and at other banquets. At a dinner for Maurice Chevalier movie mogul Jesse Lasky kept losing his place in his speech which had obviously been written by some studio hack. Each time, Lasky would look confused and ask, "Now where was I?"

Jessel, a master speechmaker, could stand it no longer: "You're at the Hotel Astor," he instructed him, "and your name is Jesse Lasky."

George Jessel had a rule for after-dinner speeches: "It should be like a woman's skirt—just long enough and short enough to cover the subject." At a birthday banquet for Jimmy Walker, New York's colorful mayor,

Judge Mitchell May was in the middle of delivering an interminable eulogy. When the judge reached for his glass of water and paused to drink, Jessel jumped to his feet and saved the evening by proposing:

"As this is Mayor Walker's birthday, let's all hope that he lives as long as Mitchell May's speech."

A year after Jimmy Walker died, Jessel attended a memorial service for the disgraced mayor. Asked to comment why so few people had shown up, the comic remarked: "You don't live long after you die."

Apology

Gertrude Lawrence was asked to give an after-dinner speech. She felt she had talked a little too long, so she said:

"Pardon my long preamble. It's like a chorus girl's tights—it touches everything and covers nothing."

Cracking Up

The comedian who could reduce Jack Benny quickest into a quivering heap just by twirling a key ring was George Burns. Maurice Zolotow describes an instance in Hollywood in the late 1940s.

Burns was attending a soirée at Ronald Reagan's home. Jack entered. He said to Burns, "I just left the world's greatest comedian."

"Who," inquired Burns, in the rasping tone he affects for Jack's benefit, "is this great comedian?" He wondered if it was Ed Wynn or Jessel or Danny Kaye.

"Larry Adler," said Benny.

"Larry Adler?" screamed Burns. "That harmonica player? Now what in the world would make you think Larry Adler is the world's greatest comedian?"

Benny explained they had both been visiting a friend whose house had a flagstoned entrance and a gate, and as they pushed the gate to leave, Adler remarked, "Don't slam the door."

Burns gaped in bewilderment. "And that you think is funny," he said, shaking his head. "Now, Jack, I am going to prove to you what an idiot you are. I am going to prove you are an absolute jerk and moron and do not know anything about comedy. I am going to think of the unfunniest piece of business and I am even going to tell you in advance what I will do and I will guarantee to make you laugh."

"No," said Benny, "I refuse to laugh."

"Here goes," said Burns, as a crowd clustered around them. "I am going to take this cigar I am smoking and I am going to flick the ashes on the lapel of your suit."

"I am not going to laugh."

Burns slowly lifted his cigar and brought it close to Benny's chin. Then he briskly tapped some ashes on Benny's lapel. Burns watched Benny.

"Keep quiet everybody," Burns cried to the onlookers.

Benny's face was grim for a moment. He tried to choke down the spasms of laughter. He shut his eyes with the effort. But it was of no avail. The laughs broke. He began slapping his thigh and then he sank to his knees and was pounding the floor.

"Take him away," said Burns with a smug wave of his hand.

Enter Unsmiling

It was one of Jack Benny's longstanding ambitions to make George Burns laugh for a change. They both happened to be in Milwaukee one day, and Burns had called Benny's room to say that he was coming. "I thought I had him," Benny used to tell this story against himself: "I got undressed and stood naked on a table, posing like a statue holding a rose in my hand."

Benny left his door unlocked so that when the knock came, he would not break his pose. The door opened and in walked the maid, followed a few moments later by a triumphant and unsmiling George Burns.

Funny Man

After seeing Ray Bolger in *Where's Charley?* (the musical version of *Charley's Aunt*), Fred Allen said: "He's getting so thin that if he had an ulcer he'd have to carry it in his hand."

James Thurber once said that the funniest line he had ever heard was while watching Fred Allen in a vaudeville theatre. Allen noticed a gaunt and pale-looking cello player in the pit. The morose comedian leaned over the footlights and asked:

"How much would you charge to haunt a house?"

Another Thurber favorite from Fred Allen was about crows that had been "so frightened by a farmer's scarecrow that they brought back corn that they had stolen two years before."

In the early days of television, Fred Allen was worried about the way the small screen reduced everything in size: "It has small minds, small talents, and small budgets," he complained. "In fact, everything in television is so small that you can hide it in the navel of a flea and still have enough room beside it for Walter Winchell's heart."

Limited Hang-out

In the days before comics let everything hang out, Carol Channing was a pioneer in discussing personal problems with her nightclub audience.

"Do you remember, Miss Channing, the most embarrassing moment in your life?" she was asked one night.

"Yes, I do," she replied. "Next question?"

CHAPTER 14

Work
in Progress

It Needs Work

In 1845 Fashion *was one of the first comedy hits on Broadway by an American and by a woman. It was Mrs. Cora Mowatt's first play. From her autobiography we learn that tinkering with a playwright's work was already an established practice.*

The day after the performance of a new drama, it is customary to call a rehearsal, for the sake of "cutting" the play, if too long (and almost all plays *are* too long as originally written) and to make other necessary alterations. To this rehearsal I was formally invited by the managers. Accompanied by Mr. Mowatt, I gladly attended. On that day, for the first time, I crossed the stage of a theatre. I was conducted to a seat at the manager's table.

The theatre had undergone its transformation again. All was darkness and silence. The solitary gas-branch burned as blue and ghastly as ever, and the actors, in their everyday dresses, moved mysteriously about in its shadowy light. But on nearer view they looked like weary and care-laden human beings, instead of phantoms.

Again the rehearsal of *Fashion* commenced. Mr. Barry arranged the "cuts," requesting my approval in a manner which left me very little alternative. The principal actors were presented to me, and I made as many delicate hints concerning certain misinterpretations of the text as I dared venture upon. It was very evident that they singly and collectively entertained the opinion that an author never knew the true meaning of his own words. His suppositions to the contrary were mere hallucinations.

On Thin Ice

Around 1885 Nat Goodwin produced (with Frank Sanger) a farce called The Skating Rink. *The text had problems, and the actor-manager describes in his memoirs with some gusto how he fixed them.*

We opened in Buffalo to a packed house and when the curtain rang down I credited myself with another failure. I was amazed to ascertain the next morning that I had made another "artistic success." But this time the house sold out for that evening also. I was far from being satisfied, but I was convinced that if the public fancied the material offered at our opening I could improve the entertainment very much. I so informed Sanger, suggesting that he book us for four weeks at Hooley's. I guaranteed to give him an entirely new and better interpretation of *The Skating Rink* for Chicago. He acquiesced and started the next day for New York.

I called the company together the following evening after the play for a rehearsal. My idea was to ascertain if any of the company had a specialty that could be interjected into this porous play. It permitted all sorts of pioneering. The plot stopped at eight-thirty!

One gentleman proved capable of swallowing the butt of a lighted cigar during the rendering of the verse of a song, allowing it to reappear before finishing, and repeating the operation until his stomach rebelled. This appealed to me and was introduced the following evening with marked favor!

I resuscitated my imitations of famous actors which had been lying dormant for years.

Two or three of the young ladies interpolated some of the latest New York ditties, Fanny Rice and I cribbing the See-Saw duet. I also introduced an entire act of a play called *The Marionettes*, assisted by one of the skating trio, an Irish song written by a Jew, "Since Maggie Learned to Skate," and a burlesque on *Camille*. I appeared as the coughing heroine!

By the time we reached Chicago I had discarded all of the old manuscript. The plot stopped a few minutes earlier. But I kept my promise to Sanger!

I worked like a galley slave in this polyglot entertainment, making no less than fifteen changes. When not on the stage, which was but seldom, I was busy making my wardrobe shifts between scenes, my most trying effort being a very quick change from the ball gown (with all the female accessories, including corsets) of Camille to the apparel of an Irish hod-carrier. I made the latter change in less than a minute, disappearing as the dying lady on one side of the stage to return from the opposite as the Irishman in search of his daughter, Maggie. The company, I am pleased to say, made distinct successes and received great praise for their individual efforts.

Rough Diamond

Although William Brady's taste was far from highbrow, he developed a keen theatrical sense during his long years of producing. He came to know the niceties of acting, and his way of dealing with an inexperienced actress who could not keep still became for a while a byword. Good actors know when they are given nothing to do in a scene, the best thing to do is to keep still, whereas coarse amateurs think it necessary to invent all kinds of business which inevitably distracts attention from what is happening else-where on stage. Brady had asked the fidgeting actress several times to stop "acting"—all in vain. Finally, he lost his patience and yelled at her:

"Didn't I tell you to keep still? You're no diamond that has to sparkle all the time!"

The Seduction

Henry Miller scored one of his early successes as producer and director with *The Great Divide*, written by William Vaughn Moody. Up to that point this poet and former literature professor at the University of Chicago had composed verse dramas mainly for the closet. When he accepted, in May 1906, an invitation from the producer to travel from Chicago and meet him in New York, the play was still called *A Sabine Woman*. Over lunch, Miller professed to be enchanted with it. Indeed, he so charmed Moody that the once wary poet wrote with unrestrained enthusiasm to his fiancée, Miss Harriet Converse Brainard: "Henry Miller is not only a thorough gentleman with the unmistakable and indescribable hallmark of the species, but he is alert to the higher aspects of his profession to a degree for which I was totally unprepared."

Amid the flattery, Miller also managed to slip the point across that *A Sabine Woman* needed some revision: "His appreciation of the play is whole-souled," the innocent Moody rambled on to his beloved, "and his discussion of it exhibited an understanding both of its strong points and its weak, far beyond anything any one else has ever shown." Miller suggested to Moody that he would love to play the lead, but at the same time he earnestly declared "his first desire to have me make of it a thoroughly well-rounded and self-sufficing piece of dramatic art, without regard to his own particular role."

Now thoroughly seduced, the playwright went off to the wilds of New Hampshire to revise the play according to the producer's wishes. During his occasional returns to the city, Miller put him up in style at The Players and would casually introduce him to Ethel Barrymore and others who were household words, which made Moody even more desirous of pleasing the actor-manager. When the hopelessly stage-struck author returned with the revised script, he read it aloud to Miller until four in the morning. Miller was more or less happy with the changes, and he thought he could fix the rest during rehearsals.

He was wrong. The author, unaccustomed to the ways of the theatre and fairly in love with his own way of putting things, now fought even the smallest changes. Henry Miller was every inch a monarch of the stage; moreover, he was used to having his own way in his own theatre. He devised a simple stratagem of getting rid of the meddlesome author. Since the play required vast quantities of Indian blankets and Southwestern artefacts, Miller persuaded Moody that to achieve complete authenticity of effect, rather than the mere illusion of it, he should take a long train journey to pick up these props in New Mexico and Arizona. Moody was impressed by the director's devotion to realism and left town. After a couple of arduous weeks, tracking down his props, during which time Miller was enjoying peaceful rehearsals, the playwright returned, only to find that he had forgotten one of the essential objects needed for the play. Bertram Harrison, the stage manager, whom Miller had not made privy to his trick, immediately took Moody down the street to a shop specializing in Indian artefacts and where, of course, he realized at once that he could have bought all of his authentic props in half an hour.

After the usual *Sturm und Drang* and dress rehearsal blues that accompany most successful productions, *The Great Divide* opened at the Princess Theatre on October 3, 1906. On the following Saturday, William Vaughn Moody, who had fought Henry Miller on changing a single word, went to him and said that he saw a wonderful way to rewrite an entire act. "This was too much," wrote the actor-manager's biographer, Frank P. Morse:

"Miller literally exploded. He pointed out to the playwright his uncanny resemblance to a hopeless maniac with a definite nihilist complex. He dwelt in detail on the utter Moody lack of anything remotely resembling intestinal fortitude. He even touched on his pet theory about being completely surrounded by dolts and fools in the last stages of perdition. Before the star really reached an adequate finale, William Vaughn Moody had begun to suspect that his latest rewrite was somewhat lacking in definite, irresistible appeal to the Henry Miller judgment. Wherefore, he remembered an imperative engagement elsewhere and fled."

Play à la Carte

In 1920 Lynn Fontanne was rehearsing in *Chris*, which Eugene O'Neill later turned into *Anna Christie*. She objected to the many uncritical speeches in praise of mothers. Not only had Lynn run away from home because of her mother, she had just forced her young lover, Alfred Lunt, to choose between her or his mother. It was clear to her that Hattie Lunt did not think any girl would be good enough for her son.

Finally, Fontanne screwed up enough courage to talk to the playwright about the mother character. Tactfully, she tried to tell O'Neill that mothers did not necessarily symbolize all the beauty in the world, and that there were other, more interesting kinds of mothers. Those who were too possessive to allow their son to marry—who would rather destroy their son than give him to another woman—might be dramatically more interesting.

O'Neill agreed politely and said nothing more. Eight years passed, and Lynn Fontanne was cast in *Strange Interlude*. After one of the early readings, O'Neill asked her:

"Well, how do you like the play you suggested?"

She searched her memory but could not figure what he meant.

"Do you remember suggesting I write a play about possessive mothers?"

She nodded vaguely, and O'Neill said:

"Well, this is the play."

Dramaturgy from Beyond

Edward (Ned) Sheldon (1886–1946), an influential if second-rate playwright, became paralyzed in the prime of life. He turned to younger dramatists to collaborate with, including Charles MacArthur. In Charlie, *the biography he wrote of his friend, Ben Hecht describes how David Belasco took advice about scripts.*

MacArthur wrote his first successful play, *Lulu Belle*, with Sheldon. David Belasco produced it, and Charlie had another Sheldon assignment. It was to see that the "Guvnor" (Belasco) changed no line or plot turn of their joint work.

Charlie attended rehearsals and stymied Belasco, then lord of all Broadway, in his efforts to cut and rewrite. Despite the script-mugging that went on, Belasco delighted MacArthur. Belasco was the Land of the Theatre. He had a face borrowed from a thousand actors, mystic and foolish with sham importance that was not sham in the theatre. Charlie won most of the rehearsal debates. There were some he lost.

At one time Belasco cut a page of dialogue from Lenore Ulric's part. Miss Ulric was the star of *Lulu Belle*, and of the Guvnor's heart.

"I'm making the cut," said director Belasco in the metallic buzz produced by his antique dental plates, "so that you won't have to talk so fast on the stage, darling. It will enable you to get some sense and a little emotion into what you are trying to do, darling."

Miss Ulric screamed. Four other actors involved in the cut blanched. The Guvnor had cut out the best scene in the whole play, they cried out.

MacArthur protested vigorously.

"Quiet, you gray rat," Belasco responded in his dramatic gasp. "I am going to make you rich and famous with my genius."

"I'll tell you where you can stick your genius," the playwright retorted. And the stage, crowded with some forty white and Negro actors, exploded with mutiny.

The tumult bowed the Guvnor's silvered head. He listened in silence to the anger against him, and then raised a hand. Oddly, the stage quieted.

"Children," he spoke, "there will be a recess for ten minutes. I have an important decision to make. Please wait for my return."

"His pompous and mysterious remarks could always baffle any actress into silence," said MacArthur. "Lenore piped down and we all looked at him and wondered where the hell he had to go to all of a sudden. He had a weak bladder and used to make all kinds of impressive excuses to duck out to take a leak. But he didn't head for any can this time. He walked off the stage into the empty auditorium. Then he walked on to the back of the theatre.

"We watched him from the stage, pacing slowly and stopping, and nodding, and then he'd smack his forehead with his palm as if he'd discovered a new trade route. This silly performance went on for fifteen minutes, and he returned to the stage. 'I'm only sorry Ned isn't here to hear what I have to say,' he announced. 'Ned would understand it. He's a poet. I've just had a very interesting discussion about my proposed cut in the dialogue. I've been talking to Charles Frohman, the great producer who died so gallantly when the *Lusitania* went down. I told Mr. Frohman our problem, and how you and Ned feel about it, Charles, and you, Miss Ulric. He listened to both sides like a gentleman. And he told me I was right, and to go ahead and make the cut.' He glanced to the rear of the empty theatre and sort of moaned: 'I hope we don't disappoint Mr. Frohman. He's a very wise man and loves the theatre.'

"How," continued MacArthur, "could you argue with such a goddamn wonderful ham? I knew Ned would raise the roof, but I gave in."

Your Arms Are Too Short to Box with God

During the final dress rehearsal of the musical fantasy *Cabin in the Sky* (1940), Ethel Waters announced in the middle of a scene that she had just been warned by a message from God not to proceed because her role had become vulgarized. Producer Vinton Freedly followed the great black star into her dressing room and, knowing how religious she was, gently tried to tell her that God would not want all her fellow actors to be out of a job, or to ruin all the investors who put money in the show because of their faith in Miss Waters's talent. She said she had to have one more conversation with God, and then five minutes later she came back on stage and resumed the performance. The next day she scored a great hit with the audience and critics.

Marriage

Perhaps the best collaboration George Kaufman had was with the younger Moss Hart, who described their relationship in these terms:

"He shies at the slightest display of emotion, as most men flee from smallpox. At our first meeting I was wide-eyed with hero worship; Kaufman recoiled in horror. Later, however, everything turned out fine; we married and had several beautiful children."

An Odd Couple

Edna Ferber's happiest collaboration, shared by a number of others, was with George S. Kaufman. She recalled the experience of working on The Royal Family *in her memoirs.*

It seems unbelievable now, but day after day, for eight months, George and I worked on the writing of *The Royal Family. Every* morning at eleven George would appear at my apartment in Central Park West. When I say eleven I mean, not one minute before or two minutes after—

but eleven. We would start work. Lunch at one-thirty would be coffee and sandwiches or something equally portable, eaten on the march. My digestion is now a tottering wreck and George's is, I believe, not that of a hired man at threshing time. But for my part it's been worth it. I don't regret a single sweated hour. Better old age and soda-mint tablets than never to have written at all.

Considering that *The Royal Family*, is, after all, just a comedy, it is rather embarrassing to confess that eight months of work went into its writing. The wonder is that we weren't at each other's throats after that long grind. We actually emerged good friends. Gallons of coffee had been drunk, tons of sandwiches consumed, miles of floor had been walked, typewriter ribbons had been worn to rags, Jed Harris had come into the scene as producer—and still we two collaborators remained friends.

So many people have asked me what actual method of work we had used in our collaboration on *Minick*, *The Royal Family*, *Dinner at Eight* and *Stage Door*. I don't know, really, except in a sort of way. Not that the process is any twilight sleep. It just works itself out, finally, with the inevitability of a huge and intricate jigsaw puzzle.

Whatever the definition of the process, it never has varied. The work always is done at my apartment or house (with an occasional brief desperate leap into the fancied quiet of Brooklyn, Atlantic City or Long Island).

Shaved, brushed, pressed, shined, Mr. Kaufman appears at eleven sharp, wearing (among other things) one of his inexhaustible collection of quiet rich ties. I sit at the typewriter; George stalks. I mention the tie. He says it's really nothing. A few moments' light conversation about this and that—the newest bit of gossip, last night's party, if any, this morning's newspaper headlines, the play that opens tonight. One of us says, "Let's write the play!" Paper, carbon, we're off.

George jiggles the curtain cord; plays tunes with a pencil on his cheek which he maddeningly stretches taut into a drum by poking it out with his tongue; he does a few eccentric dance steps; wanders into the next room; ties and unties his shoestrings. He is a confirmed shoestring tier. In moments of irritation, puzzlement, embarrassment or special thoughtfulness he stoops, unties his carefully tied shoestrings and ties them again. He says they work loose.

No written word is safe from his gaze. A letter, telegram or note left lying about will sooner or later be read by the Paul Pry of playwrights. He can't help it. His curiosity is, seemingly, overpowering. I thought of a plan to punish him for this habit. Before he was due to arrive at eleven I typed a telegram on a Western Union blank and placed it face up on my desk almost completely covered by another sheet of paper. Only one corner of the telegram peeped out, folded and creased as though it had been read and reread. There wasn't enough of it exposed to make its reading possible, but one could see it was a telegram left open.

Immediately his gaze alighted on this. As we talked he stalked his prey. He would walk over to it and eye it hungrily. He would walk away from it, casting a longing glance over his shoulder. He bent his head and screwed it around to see if he couldn't thus make out a word or two. Finally, "Damn it, what's in this telegram!" he said. And picked it up.

I have heard that people's jaws drop with surprise. I never had hoped actually to see this. I saw it now.

This was the telegram I had typed:

GEORGIE KAUFMAN IS AN OLD SNOOPER.

Quick Study

When Clare Boothe's *The Women* became a great hit, some jealous tongues were quick to attribute its success to secret collaboration with or doctoring by George S. Kaufman, who had invested in the play. He was also there during the opening of its Philadelphia tryout, when he agreed with producer Max Gordon that the end of the third act was not working. They talked to Clare Boothe until two in the morning, and when a sleepy Kaufman bumped into her at noon the next day she had just delivered a totally revised third act to Max Gordon, while managing to look completely fresh and relaxed. So, after the play became a sensation, whenever anybody voiced the suspicion about its legitimate authorship, Kaufman would say: "Listen, if I had really written *The Women*, why would I want to sign it Clare Boothe?"

The dictum that writing is rewriting is particularly true in theatre, because what the playwright hears from actors is so different from what she might have imagined in her head. Clare Boothe possessed such facility for making quick revisions that she caused problems for actors trying to learn the old lines. After he produced *The Women* Max Gordon complained that when the play went into rehearsals, he should have liked to break the author's wrists. "You give her a suggestion about changing a line, and what does she do? She goes away for a little while and comes back with a whole new act."

Flying

Richard Rodgers had an amazing facility for writing music. His collaborator, Oscar Hammerstein II, once remarked: "I simply hand him a lyric and get out of the way." He composed one of his most famous songs, "Oh What a Beautiful Mornin' " for *Oklahoma!* literally as he first played it.

Days before rehearsals for *South Pacific* were about to begin, Rodgers was having dinner with a few friends at director Joshua Logan's home. Coffee was being served when Hammerstein arrived, waving the lyrics to "Bali Ha'i," the last missing song he had been laboring on. Rodgers quickly read the verses, took out a pencil, quickly drew a staff on the same paper that the lyricist had handed him, and began there and then jotting down musical notes. Within five minutes he was finished, and soon thereafter the song passed into Broadway history, without a note changed.

Rodgers seemed totally indifferent to his surroundings when it came to composing. On one occasion he was heading for a rehearsal when he received some newly written lyrics. He read them in the taxicab, he completed and played the melody in the orchestra pit while the actors were reading some dialogue on stage. A friend once asked Rodgers how long he took to compose the entire score of *Oklahoma!*.

"Do you mean flying time or elapsed time?" Rodgers asked. He explained the difference as follows:

"Counting everything—overture, ballet music, all the songs—the most I could make it come to was about five hours—flying time. But the total elapsed time covered months of discussion and planning."

Mannerism

During the rehearsal of one of his musicals, composer Jerome Kern was becoming increasingly irritated by a mannered actress who was constantly rolling her r's. She had once more interrupted the rehearsal to ask:

"You want me, Mr. Kern, to cr-r-ross the stage, but I'm behind the table her-r-e. How can I get acr-r-oss?"

"It's simple," Kern suggested, "just r-r-roll over on your r's."

Less Is More

There is a fundamental difference between the way Europeans and Americans look at work. In America to be considered hard-working you must be seen sweating and putting in long hours. In Europe, hard work must appear effortless and therefore performed in secret. That is why writers and artists spend so much of their time being seen at cafes and parties.

When Max Reinhardt fled from the Nazis to America, he arrived with the reputation as the greatest director in Europe, if not the world. He was also known, within the profession, for being the most prepared director, one who wrote lengthy analyses for every character and plotted their every move in production books which are still studied as models today. In 1938, producer Herman Shumlin engaged Reinhardt to direct Thornton Wilder's *Merchant of Yonkers* at the author's specific request. Since Wilder was loosely adapting an Austrian original by Johannes Nestroy, it made sense to have the great Austrian director stage it. (Later the play became *The Matchmaker* and then was further adapted into the musical, *Hello, Dolly!*). Shumlin was very surprised that Reinhardt, though allowed a full seven hours' rehearsal under union rules, usually called it quits two or three hours early. When asked to account for this, Reinhardt replied calmly:

"Four or five hours a day of good work are quite enough. Longer than that it becomes labor."

Quick Fix

The American visit of the Moscow Art Theatre in 1923 had a profound effect on the development of alternatives to the commercial theatre of Broadway. Theresa Helburn, executive director of the recently founded Theatre Guild, was vastly impressed by the discipline and ensemble spirit of the Russian company, and immediately inquired whether Stanislavski might try to direct a play for the Guild and achieve such results with American actors.

Stanislavski thought that it could be done.

"How long do you need to rehearse a play?" asked Hilburn.

"Two years," was the Master's response.

"Two years for one play. But that's impossible!" she exclaimed.

"Well, in that case," Stanislavski replied, "how about two weeks?"

She Who Gets Slapped

Jessica Tandy was acting the part of the scheming lady-in-waiting Abigail Hill in *Anne of England* (1941), a gorgeously costumed and forgettable flop about Queen Anne and the first Duke and Duchess of Marlborough. The latter was played by the formidable Flora Robson, who at one point slaps the lady-in-waiting when she tries to proffer a cup of brandy to the Queen. During one of the rehearsals Gilbert Miller, who was directing as well as producing the play, said to Miss Tandy:

"I don't understand why you go so quietly and put that cup down. Wouldn't you rather do something violent?"

"Well," replied the actress, "I could throw the brandy right in her face. How would you like to wash these expensive costumes eight times a week?"

"Oh, no!" said Miller, as the pragmatic producer won out over the realistic director. "What you've been doing is just fine."

Diagnosis

Moss Hart was much in demand not only as a playwright and a director, but producers would often ask him to give an expert diagnosis of a production during its out-of-town tryout. In an oft-told story, Hart went once to Baltimore on such a mission. The curtain went up on a matinee performance, revealing a series of green flats. Then suddenly, flying out of the wings on a rope came an actor dressed as a leprechaun, and sailed into the set, knocking over several flats. As the curtain was lowered again to repair the damage, Moss Hart turned to the producer next to him, and said:

"It's short, but I like it."

The Part That Ate the Play

The incorrigible Dorothy Parker once sent an opening night telegram to Uta Hagen: "A hand upon your opening and may your parts grow bigger." Most actors measure the importance of a role by counting the number of lines (or "sides" in the old days), and few would cooperate in the cutting of any words, unless they came out of somebody else's part.

Parts can grow in importance, sometimes to the detriment of the play. Walter Kerr put together a show about the history of folk music, *Sing Out, Sweet Land* (1944), which he felt might have succeeded had not a newcomer named Burl Ives overshadowed Alfred Drake, the central character. "In a sense Burl Ives cut the show in half," Walter Kerr remembered. "We found ourselves using Burl more and more, because he was so good. And the more we used him, "the more we reduced Alfred's function."

On a smaller scale, I* have seen the same phenomenon, while working at the Sundance Institute on *A Full-Length Portrait of America*, a marvelous play by Paul D'Andrea that had won the New American Play contest at the Louisville Actors Theatre. The smallest role was the villain's sidekick, a small-time hood played at Sundance by John Malkovich, just before his performance in *True West* at the Cherry Lane catapulted him to stardom. The actor endowed his few lines with such menace and humor that they assumed layers of significance perhaps never intended. Even though we were rehearsing in a field, with no lights or makeup, Malkovich's presence loomed larger by the day. Each morning Paul came down

* Peter Hay.

from the mountain with new lines for him, and all of us sat around rollicking with laughter while he tried them out, forgetting about the rest of the
scene, let alone the play.

Camp Eugene

In the old days a playwright had a director, a producer, and an occasional
play doctor in the night interfering in his play, which after some radical
surgery out of town, would either stand or fall before a Broadway audience. Today, there are readings, critiques, conferences, festivals, organizations, workshops, armies of actors, directors and dramaturgs in a whole
"developmental process," before a play is tried out off-off Broadway, in a
regional theatre, or at a university. It may take years before a non-profes-
sional audience gets to see and judge what this long collaboration had
wrought. Probably the best-known for developing plays is the Playwrights
Conference at the Eugene O'Neill Theatre Centre in Waterford, Connecticut, or "the O'Neill" for short. For a quarter-century, a few miles
from the O'Neill family's Monte Cristo cottage, theatre people have come
together every summer for a month to read, rework, and discuss a dozen
plays, many of which then go on to great success. Under the leadership
of George White and Lloyd Richards the Tony-award winning O'Neill-
Centre has exercised widespread influence over the American theatre. The
hundreds of people who have worked at Camp Eugene, including myself,
cherish memories of working together at a special place for a special cause.

Director Dennis Scott remembers the last performance at one conference,
when half a dozen people decided to wear name-tags with artistic director
Lloyd Richards's name. When Lloyd, who like a school principal always
seems to know what is going on, came to give his usual speech explaining
the nature of the work at the O'Neill, he simply called on all the other
Lloyds to take his place on stage and carry on.

Another veteran, the actor Bryan Clark, recalls watching *The Gazelle Boy*,
"a play of interminable camp," in which a high priestess was reading a
sermon lasting several pages. Toward the end, there was supposed to be
an attack of monster mosquitoes—a common occurrence at the O'Neill—
against which the acolytes surrounding the priestess defend themselves by
loudly slapping their bodies. Two of the acolytes, John Hurd and Ben
Masters, were busy thwacking themselves (no easy feat with scripts in
hand), when Hurd noticed that John Seitz, in the role of third acolyte,

stood motionless. In a whisper that reached only the front few rows of the outdoor amphitheatre, Hurd asked:

"Why aren't you slapping off those mosquitoes?"

And Seitz turned to him and improvised quite volubly:

"Funny, they don't bother me."

Bill Partlan was working as technical director in the Barn theatre one reading, when lightning struck the flagmast just outside. There was a blinding flash and a huge crash which practically threw the technicians with headsets across the booth. The script happened to have God as a character, and the actor who had to speak the next line made a perfect pause before delivering the line to God. The place went wild, both with relief and the knowledge that the ultimate dramaturg had just spoken.

Too Moved

Edith Oliver was the dramaturg on The Past Is the Past (1973), *a play by Richard Westley at the O'Neill.*

About a father and son who meet for the first time in a billiard hall in Harlem, it is probably the most moving play I have ever worked on. Throughout every rehearsal, the actors and all of us associated with the workshop were constantly in tears through every rehearsal: it turned out that Hal Scott, who was directing, and I were the only two who knew who our fathers were. Finally, I had to make an announcement:

"Gentlemen, this is our last wet run. Because if we don't stop crying, the audience never will."

(*Helen Hayes was once given the same note by Fanny Brice.*)

Tonight We Improvise

As a young dancer, Beverley Bozeman played a troll in the production of Peer Gynt *that Lee Strasberg directed at the ANTA Theatre in 1951.*

In the beginning we were all very excited. Instead of acting the text, Strasberg had everybody improvise the scenes. He refused to block. Karl Malden would bump into Eddie Beans; an actor turned around to address another actor and found somebody quite unfamiliar staring him in the face. Nobody could figure anything out. Our improvs improved, of course, but

Strasberg never saved anything so that all our beautiful inventions disappeared into thin air. I remember we spent two hours a day every day for five weeks on a big troll scene which involved all the actors and dancers. Strasberg said: "I want not just visual improvs—I want you all to be birds, parrots, insects, whatever." But he didn't assign any of these. "I want vocal improvs," he said, but he didn't assign any. So we all started glurping and gleeping and going wh-a-a-i-ee. I decided to be a wolf. We did it differently every day with no organization to it.

Finally, in the last week, Strasberg says to Nicky [Nehemiah] Persoff, who was playing the Troll King: "Nicky, why don't you come in on cue?" "Well," he says, "I don't have a cue to start the scene." Which was true, since some days our vocalization went for twenty seconds, at other times for twenty minutes. I raised my hand like a fool ready to rush in: "May I make a suggestion, Mr. Strasberg? Since I have a very high-pitched long sound, perhaps my howling could become his cue?" "Uh, okay," he said. We started up again—glurp, urp, eep—and in the middle of it I realize that *I* don't have a cue. The improv goes on for ever, and finally Strasberg says: "All right, where's the wolf?" I said I didn't have a cue. The company thought this was funny, there was so much tension built up, but Strasberg did not see the humor of it: "What do you mean?" he asked. "Perhaps, sir," I proposed, "if I counted as if this were a musical composition?" "What do you mean?" he repeated. "One two three four—one two three four—you decide whether it's four bars, six bars, or eight bars to the cut off." We get to eight bars and he says: "Now, wolf."

It worked. But it was the only thing that did with any consistency. Morale was down. During dress rehearsal everything went wrong. The central set did not turn. People were tripping over things. There was a stripper who had been hired, called Sherry Britton—well, her tit fell off. But worse was to come. After this disaster, Strasberg came in with a cloak and gave everybody the most cutting notes. He turned on John Garfield: "I don't know what you are doing. You are the worst actor. You are ruining my beautiful show. You stink." We all nearly died. I still do when I think of it. There was so much energy when we began, and if only we'd had a good traffic cop to give some pattern, some sense to what we were doing, we might have pulled through.

Method

Harold Clurman was once directing Luther Adler in a love scene, when the actor (and his brother-in-law) stopped and said:

"Harold, I just don't know what my action is supposed to be." Action, in the jargon of "method acting" is what Stanislavski meant by the actor's immediate will.

"Dammit, Luther, it should be perfectly clear," Clurman replied at once. "You want to fuck the girl."

Adler paused to think it through:

"Ah, now I understand," and he continued the scene.

Paying Attention

Rehearsing Arthur Miller's Death of a Salesman *(1949), Mildred Dunnock, who played Linda Loman, had problems during a long scene when the drama gives way to narrative. She remembers how Elia Kazan intervened.*

We were in Philadelphia just prior to the New York opening, and Kazan asked me to see him about the scene. When I came in I was told Mr. Kazan was at a concert across the street and had left a ticket for me at the backstage entrance. I arrived in the midst of a symphony, one of those symphonies that has five movements and that rises to an enormous crescendo. And as we left the hall, I said, "Gee, that symphony's like you, Gadge. That's the way you conduct, the big crescendo." And he said, "Well, I'm going to conduct tomorrow." The next day we rehearsed the "Attention must be paid" scene, and he took an old stick, I think it was the piece of an old broomstick, and he began to use it like a baton. And as I did the scene, he kept beating it and saying, " More! More! More! More! More!" Finally I was screaming at the top of my lungs, and I stopped and I burst into tears and I said, "I can't! I won't *do* it that way!" And he said, "That's *exactly* the way you will do it." And I said, "But where are all the nuances?" And he said, "Nuances? We'll come to those in a couple of months."

What's in a Title?

The producers of *Death of a Salesman* (1949), Kermit Bloomgarden and Walter Fried, were convinced that the title would not work. They conducted an informal poll on Broadway and found that 98 percent of the people they asked also said that it would not work.

There were last-minute pressures on changing the title of another famous play directed by Elia Kazan, Robert Anderson's *Tea and Sympathy* (1953). The playwright always remembered having jotted down the phrase after talking to a student of his first wife about what it was like for an actress to live in New York. "Well, it's not bad," she said; "I live in a rooming house where the woman has us down every once in a while for tea and sympathy." Years later, when the play was already a big Broadway hit, Anderson thanked the actress for having suggested the phrase. "I never said it in my life," she surprised him. "The landlady never had us down for tea, let alone sympathy."

Having finished the book of *Gypsy* (1959), Arthur Laurents showed the script to Gypsy Rose Lee on whose autobiography it was loosely based. He was quite apprehensive about her reaction, but the burlesque queen was only concerned that the musical be called *Gypsy*. Sensing that there was a story behind the name, Laurents probed about how she got that name. "Honey," she said, "I've given fourteen or fifteen versions. Yours will be as good as mine."

Fatal Critics

After the success of the movie *Fatal Attraction* in 1987, there was a rash of television dramas with the word "fatal" in the title. Producers and writers thought that the word guaranteed success. Interestingly, in 1932 Jed Harris produced a play called *Fatal Alibi*, starring Charles Laughton, after the critic George Jean Nathan had assured him that no play with the word "fatal" in its title had ever failed. It lasted three weeks.

Edward Albee found the title for *Who's Afraid of Virginia Woolf?* (1962) among the graffiti in a men's room of a bar in Greenwich Village. After finishing the play he sent it to Leonard Woolf in London, to get his permission to use his late wife's name in this context. He liked the play and graciously agreed. The woman who owned the song to "Who's Afraid of the Big Bad Wolf?" was less cooperative, so the tune was changed to that of the old nursery rhyme "Here We Go Round the Mulberry Bush."

Richard Barr, who co-produced the play, remembers standing on the curb after one of the early performances. He overheard, as two ladies were getting into their limousine, one of them remark: "Well, I loved it, but why did they call the wolf Virginia?"

Changes

Except for his early plays, Edward Albee has been directing his own work, claiming that he had studied with the best—watching the directors who had done his plays. The most important among these was the late Alan Schneider, who died tragically in London in 1984. In a panel discussion about the original production of *Who's Afraid of Virginia Woolf?* held at the Dramatists Guild, Schneider recalled discussing the script in minute detail with Albee until rehearsals began. When the actors were on their feet, he showed the first act to the playwright.

"That wasn't the way I had seen it at all," Albee said.

"What's wrong?" asked the director nervously, thinking that six months' work had just gone down the drain.

"I'm not sure," the playwright paced up and down, "but I think Nick and Honey sit down too soon."

"Well, that's a terrifically difficult problem," said the relieved director, "let me see if I can deal with it."

Alan Schneider made the actors sit down one line later. The next time Albee came to rehearsal, he observed:

"Oh, yes, you changed the whole thing, didn't you."

For the Record

One of the most persistent bits of contemporary theatre lore is that Edward Albee conceived *Who's Afraid of Virginia Woolf?* as a homosexual play. The playwright has always denied this and once tried to set the record straight: "If I wanted to write a play about two homosexual couples, I know how to write a play about two homosexual couples." A San Francisco group did not take heed and tried it with an all-male cast, until Albee and the original producers stopped their show after a single performance.

Actors and Elephants

Actors may occasionally have trouble with lines, but their memory can be elephantine about some other things. David Pressman recounts the time when he was directing The Disenchanted (1958), *in which Jason Robards played a character modeled after F. Scott Fitzgerald. There was a scene in which this character returns to his college and has a charming encounter with a couple of students.*

The show was too long by about twenty minutes, and Bill Darrid, the producer, agreed with me that as this scene did not add or subtract anything essential from the plot, we should cut it. It turned out that Jason was very fond of this episode, because it allowed him to do a drunk bit and it revealed an important aspect of his character. But he is also a pro, so that when I took the scene out, he let it go at that. The show had a moderately successful run of six months.

Fade out, and fade back in almost thirty years later. Quite recently, my wife Sasha and I went to see an off-Broadway production of an Alan Ayckbourn play. A friend of ours was appearing in it, and so was, coincidentally, Jason Robards's son. In the intermission, I ran into Jason, whom I had not seen for a few years, and during our chat, he suddenly said:

"By the way, David, you shouldn't have taken that scene out."

"What scene?" I asked somewhat alarmed.

"You know, the college scene in *The Disenchanted*."

"Oh, that . . ."

"Well, I resented it then and I still resent it."

I muttered my apologies and wondered what could be done about that thirty years later. As the second act began, I told my wife about the exchange, and we agreed that Jason was probably kidding. But afterwards, when we were backstage congratulating our friend, Jason was there with his son, and the last thing he said as we were leaving was:

"David, put that scene back!"

Guilt

A few years after The Disenchanted *David Pressman took over the direction of* A Cook for Mr. General (1961), *a play that was having trouble on the road.*

It was a charming, funny play by Steven Gethers about a Greek cook at an army rehabilitation center who wants to become an American but gets court-martialed. When I was asked to see it in Philadelphia, I literally couldn't tell what was going on, it was such a mess—not so much as a script, but because of the staging. So when I agreed to come in, there was no time to be lost. I called a ten o'clock rehearsal on Sunday morning to re-direct the first act. I began by telling the cast how much work we had to get done in a very brief time. I was about fifteen minutes into my talk, when one of the bit players, playing one of those screw-ups sent to this rehabilitation center, turned up. After I finished, I pulled this actor aside and asked why he had been late. He explained that his alarm had failed to go off, and I explained that I had to have everybody come to rehearsal on time, and asked him:

"This will not happen again, will it?"

"On no, sir, no sir," he hastened to reassure me. He looked really nothing, a pipsqueak of an actor. His name was Dustin Hoffman.

We worked hard, brought the play into New York, the Playhouse Theatre on 49th Street. We had a last technical run-through at 2:30 in the afternoon before the opening. The rehearsal started, and we come to the first scene at the rehab center, and I run up on stage to help the actors find their position, and suddenly I look around, "Where's Dustin?" He wasn't there. I look into the wings and right at that moment he shows up, but looking dishevelled—his shirt is torn, he is a complete mess.

"What happened, for God's sake?"

"I was in an accident," he said, "but I don't want to talk about it now."

"Are you all right? Are you hurt?" I was really concerned. But he said he'd be fine, and indeed he was for the rest of the rehearsal and the run of the play.

Five years later, Dustin Hoffman had become famous, following the movie *The Graduate*. We met at a New Year's party given by a mutual friend. After a few greetings, Dustin said with a troubled face:

"David, I've got to tell you something." He drew me aside and began:

"Do you remember the incident on the day we opened in New York?"

Actually, I had forgotten, but he reminded me about the accident.

"And do you remember," Dustin persisted, "that I was late on the first day of rehearsals in Philadelphia?"

I said something about having to keep discipline, but I could not remember that either.

"Well, you scared the hell out of me that day, and made me promise that nothing like that would ever happen again. I was completely petrified—this was my first Broadway job—so I promised. When we came to New York, I had a scooter to get to work from my room in the Bronx; it saved me the subway. So on the day of the opening, nice and early, I was scooting around Central Park and right in the middle of the park I ran out of gas, with only 25 cents in my pocket. By the time I got some gas, it was 2:15 and I knew I wouldn't make it. I was so petrified of your anger that I ripped my shirt, put dirt on my face and played the whole thing that I'd been knocked down in a real accident. But then you were so considerate and worried about me," said Dustin Hoffman, "that I've been feeling guilty ever since."

Leave It to the Pros

Designer David Hays recalls the flap during the opening night of Paddy Chayefsky's play Gideon *at the Plymouth Theatre (November 9, 1961). It was directed by the unflappable Tyrone Guthrie and starred Frederic March and Douglas Campbell.*

There had been a photo call in the afternoon, and we really had too many circuits for the lighting board, so that a couple of leftover circuits had to be replugged between acts. We finish the photo call and forget to replug. So, there comes this special moment at the end of a scene, where Freddie March just stands up, faces the audience, and delivers a monologue.

For this dramatic moment he was to be lit by a single light from directly overheard, which—we quickly realized—was not coming on. So Freddie stood in pitch darkness where his pool of light was supposed to be.

I was sitting with Marvin March, who was my assistant, and he was off like a flash through a tunnel that went from the lobby to the backstage area where the switchboards were. In those days you didn't have automatic boards or the little bits of board that operate from the front. By the time Marvin got backstage, Charlie Bugbee, the master electrician, and the best in the business, had already realized the error and was compensating for it the right way—rather gradually, bringing down another light to allow for the replugging before bringing up the right light. However, even before Marvin, Paddy Chayevsky had already arrived back there, and insensitive to the fact that this great craftsman who had made a mistake was trying to rectify it, began screaming: "That man is fired!" Then one of the producers, Fred Coe, got into the act and he got rather excited, and when Fred got excited, his Alligator, Mississippi, accent—that's where he was from—gained the upper hand. The audience couldn't hear any of this, and I was sitting out there among them; as the lighting designer, there was nothing I could do at that moment, except feel the sweat pouring down my back. Later on I met Paddy Chayevsky on 45th Street, and he took me by the lapels of my tuxedo, and lifted me right up into the air— he was shorter than me—and said:

"You've destroyed my play . . . three years of work." I said, "I haven't destroyed it all." "Well you've destroyed half of it." "Well," I said, "see you in a half . . ." He said, "God, how awful it is to write plays and have other people wreck 'em." I said, "Well, write novels." That was kinda mean . . . but he bought me a drink.

Anyway, there was somebody who reacted exactly the right way to this near-disaster. When the light failed, Tyrone Guthrie joined the stampede through the tunnel and rushed backstage, but as the great man said afterwards:

"Fortunately I didn't arrive in time to do any real damage."

The Reason Why

Tyrone Guthrie was absolutely direct with everybody, yet was so disarming that people generally could not take offense. During the rehearsals of *The Tenth Man*, its author kept interrupting and wanting explanations for the director's choices.

"Don't question what I am doing," Guthrie told Paddy Chayevsky, "I am a genius."

Getting to Real

Tyrone Guthrie was directing another play when an actresss stopped and said, "Mr. Guthrie, this scene just doesn't have any reality for me." "Young lady," replied Guthrie, "if you want reality, go out into the street and observe a fist fight. This is theatre and the theatre is not reality. Shall we press on?"

Life Class

Alan Jay Lerner first became involved with the musical adaptation of Shaw's Pygmalion *in 1952, four years before* My Fair Lady *reached the stage. While working on the film version of* Brigadoon, *he was approached by the maverick producer Gabriel Pascal ("a Rumanian who claimed to be a Hungarian and looked like a Himalayan"). Lerner was working on the lyrics with Frederick ("Fritz") Loewe in London, but it had not occurred to him that he might find inspiration from life.*

I ran into an old friend from Hollywood, Lewis Milestone (Millie, as he was called), the director of the immortal film *All Quiet on the Western Front*. I told him what Fritz and I were doing in London and he asked if I had ever been to Covent Garden when the market opened. "Never," said I. "Well," said Millie, "it seems to me if you are going to write about a flower girl from Covent Garden, you ought to go there." "What time of the day?" I asked. Millie replied, "When the day's activities usually begin, of course. At four in the morning." Ergo, one night I brought Fritz and Millie to Ben's house where we kept everyone up until it was time to depart for Covent Garden.

It was cold that early morning and I had forgotten from my childhood schooldays how cold English cold can be. The celebrated English humidity responsible for the celebrated English complexion may have added a dash of English pink to our cheeks, but from the neck down I was a large dash of blue. Millie, for some reason, was impervious to the weather. "Keep walking," he said "and you will be all right." We walked around Covent Garden for three hours. It was the first time I heard the Cockney rhyme language in action. It is a fascinating invention and for the uninitiated, worthy of a few lines of explanation.

Simply put, instead of a word they use its rhyme. "Wife" becomes "trouble and strife"; "man" becomes "pot and pan"; "stairs" are "apples and pears." So a typical sentence might be, "A pot and pan walked down the apples and pears with his trouble and strife." If that were not complicated enough, they then proceed to lop off the rhyming word. A "queer" is a "ginger beer," which becomes a "ginger." I had always wondered at the etymology of the expression "giving someone the raspberry," and I found the answer to it at Covent Garden that morning. The full rhyme is "raspberry tart." It takes little imagination to figure out what rhymes with "tart" and sounds like a "raspberry." They also insert words into the middle of words, as in "absobloodylutely." I made use of it in the lyric of "Wouldn't It Be Loverly?" but changed it to "absobloomin'lutely."

As we wandered around the market we saw a group of coster-mongers warming themselves around a smudgepot fire. It seemed to dramatize the climate perfectly and we used it in the play.

Dress Rehearsal

Getting into costume for the first time can mean unwelcome surprises for actors. Murray Gitlan remembers the time he was working on a revival of Noël Coward's *Blithe Spirit* and ran into Geraldine Page trying on the dinner-party costume: sequins, fringes, and peacock feathers in her hair.

"What do you think?" she asked the stage manager.

"Well, Gerry, I think . . ." Gitlan hemmed.

"Well, if you ask me," said Miss Page, "I think it's *Homage to Liberace*."

Blacklist

During the Washington tryout of *A Funny Thing Happened on the Way to the Forum*, Harold Prince felt that some of the songs needed to be restaged. Stephen Sondheim, whose first score it was, insisted on bringing in Jerome Robbins, with whom he had worked on *West Side Story*. Robbins was known to have cooperated with the House Un-American Committee during the McCarthyite hearings, and Prince felt that this choice may cause difficulties with the star of the show, Zero Mostel, who had been an unfriendly witness. But to Prince's surprise, Mostel agreed that if

Robbins could help the show, he should be asked to do so. "We of the left," he explained, "do not blacklist."

Below the Belt

There was a great deal of tension during rehearsals of the Broadway production of Neil Simon's *The Odd Couple* between director Mike Nichols and one of the stars, Walter Matthau. At one particular rehearsal, Nichols was ridiculing and belittling Matthau's efforts in a particularly abusive manner, so the actor stopped and said:

"Okay, Mike, can I have my balls back?"

"Certainly," said Nichols and snapped his fingers: "Props!"

CHAPTER 15

Life Among the Playwrights

Prophet Without Honor

One of the earliest, if minor, American-born playwrights was Mordecai Manuel Noah (1785–1851). He was also a journalist, politician, and visionary: almost a century before Theodor Herzl, he planned to set up a Jewish homeland (named Ararat) on an island in the Niagara River near Buffalo. American Jews responded indifferently to the idea, but at least without the venom that greeted his play *She Would Be a Soldier* (1819), when Samuel B. Judah called him a "pertinacious scribbler" and claimed that the "Muse had gained but a sorry jade and stumbling donkey." Judah expounded his criticism of Noah in Augustan (if not entirely grammatical) couplets:

> Thou bloated impudence; still turn thy pains
> To letters nature unknown, and art forgot,
> Without a character, a form or plot,
> New loads of words thou mayst together lay,
> And swear, though damned, it is a play.

Disaster Prone

Noah's dramatic career was plagued with misfortune. The premiere of The Siege of Tripoli at New York's Park Theatre on May 15, 1820, was supposed to be a benefit for the author. But the theatre burned down, and the playwright, "notwithstanding his own pecuniary wants," donated the entire box office to the performers "who had been stripped of their little all by the fire." Noah recounted a more amusing disaster in a letter to William Dunlap:

My next piece, I believe, was written for the benefit of a relative and friend, who wanted something to bring a house; and as the struggle for liberty in Greece was at that period the prevailing excitement, I finished the melodrama of the *Grecian Captive*, which was brought out with all the advantages of good scenery and music. As a "good house" was of more consequence to the actor than fame to the author, it was resolved that the hero of the piece should make his appearance on an elephant, and the heroine on a camel, which were procured from a neighboring menagerie, and the *tout ensemble* was sufficiently imposing, only it happened that the huge elephant, in shaking his skin, so rocked the castle on his back, that the Grecian general nearly lost his balance, and was in imminent danger of coming down from his "high estate," to the infinite merriment of the audience. On this occasion, to use another significant phrase, a "gag" was hit upon of a new character altogether. The play was printed, and each auditor was presented with a copy gratis, as he entered the house. Figure to yourself a thousand people in a theatre, each with a book of the play in hand—imagine the turning over a thousand leaves simultaneously, the buzz and fluttering it produced, and you will readily believe that the actors entirely forgot their parts, and even the equanimity of the elephant and camel were essentially disturbed.

Clairvoyant

Dion(ysus) Lardner Boucicault (1820?–90) was one of the dominant personalities of the nineteenth century, as a playwright, adaptor, and actor. He was perhaps the most prolific writer for the stage in English, and was particularly famous for his "sensation scenes," such as the rescue from a burning building in *The Poor of New York*. After its opening in 1857, Boucicault said: "I can spin out these rough-and-tumble dramas as a hen lays eggs. It's a degrading occupation, but more money has been made out of guano than out of poetry."

Daniel Frohman recalled that when Boucicault "was connected with Wallack's Theatre, he would stop at Brentano's Bookstore which was then at Broadway and Eighth Street, buy a special book and in a week he would have it dramatized. [Incidentally, he dramatized *Nicholas Nickleby* as far back as 1859.] He used to come to my theatre with his young wife, listen to the first act of a play, then he would retire to the smoking-room. He did not care to see any more of the play. He was able to tell from the first act what the entire play was about. In this respect he was almost clairvoyant for he seldom guessed wrong. He cared nothing for acting if it were good. If it were bad, he pondered over it, as a doctor might puzzle over an ailing patient."

Lifestyle of the Rich and Famous

Dion Boucicault fought some of the most important fights in the theatre for protection of the playwright's text against arbitrary changes by managers and stars. He became enormously rich from the benefits of the copyright law, which was passed in 1856. Robert Gaul, his manservant in the glory days of the Gilded Age, gives a portrait of the artist as anything but starving.

When Boucicault gave up his rooms at the St. James Hotel, he moved to Pinard's, the celebrated caterer, who had just built a new house on 15th Street. Boucicault occupied the entire second floor and furnished the rooms himself in luxurious manner. I believe he was one of the first persons in New York to have a tiled bathroom. The walls were imported Minton china and all the bathroom fixtures were of sterling silver. In the front room there was a log fireplace. On each side of the mantelpiece was a pedestal on which stood a bronze figure. One was Aphrodite, the other Diana, and each held a lamp. The windows were stained glass. As you entered the rooms there was a magnificent Bengal tiger rug on the floor over an antique Persian carpet. Facing the mantelpiece was a very long bookcase, above which was a panel picture of Balzac's *Comédie Humaine*. All Boucicault's manuscripts were in various compartments of the bookcase, the small panels of which were paintings on leather, scenes from Shakespeare.

The apartment consisted of two large rooms, bathroom and trunkroom. All meals were sent up by Pinard. Between the two main rooms were a series of cupboards, one of which was in the form of an ice-box, another was a wine cabinet, and the third was a place to keep logs. While no cooking was done in the apartment, he usually kept the ice-box well stocked with food in case he took anyone home with him after the play.

One morning Boucicault came to me and brought me a bag filled with letters. He said, "Now, Robert, you can tear those letters up and throw them in the waste-basket." I read many of the letters before destroying them. Had I known what I know today, I'd have kept them, for now they would be worth a great deal of money. There were letters from Tennyson, Longfellow, Charles Dickens, Disraeli, Charles Reade, Parnell, Victor Hugo, Ouida, and many celebrated people.

Boucicault entertained a good deal. He once gave a dinner to Gilbert and Sullivan at Pinard's. . . . On one occasion while he was putting on a stiff front shirt, which in those days had to be put on over the head, he became angry and said to me, "Get me a razor." I did so. Thereupon he slit the shirt down the front so that it could be put on like a coat. The next morning he sent me to Hutchinson, the haberdasher, who had a store on the present site of the Flatiron Building, to order three dozen shirts opening in front with buttons. This was the origin of the open-front shirt.

Plaza Suite

Like many Central European writers, Ferenc Molnár used the coffeehouse as an office: he read the newspapers and wrote for them, he received business associates, ate, and conducted his entire social life there. When the ultra luxurious Cafe New York opened in Budapest at the turn of the century, Molnár is reputed to have asked the proprietor for the key to the front doors. Having obtained it, the playwright threw it into the Danube, to make sure that the place would never close.

In 1921, following the international success of his bittersweet play *Liliom*, Molnár was besieged with offers to come to America. His agent assured him that he would travel first class on the Orient Express to Paris and then on a luxury liner across the Atlantic. Looking around at all the comforts provided by his favorite cafe, Molnár asked the agent: "But how will you get me from here to the railway station?"

Years later, when Molnár was forced to leave Europe because of the Nazi threat, he moved to the Plaza in New York where he had a permanent suite until his death in 1952. Molnár was a great celebrity in the theatrical world for his wit and talent, and he was greatly revered by the Hungarian émigré community for his fabulous wealth. In the beginning, he tried to recreate his Budapest existence by holding court at the Plaza coffee shop. Molnár knew, of course, that his compatriots expected him to pick up the tab. Once, when the discussion turned to which English phrase each of them mastered first, Molnár listened as one said "I love you," and another expatriate offered "Hello, goodbye," and another "Good morning," and so forth. Finally it was his turn. "The first English sentence I learned," the playwright said, "was 'separate checks!' "

God's Country

Moss Hart was born into a poor family in Harlem, and when his plays made him wealthy beyond his imagination, he could not resist buying all the things he had lacked in his poorer days. Hart himself referred to this as his "gold garter period"—and Edna Ferber said that he was "monogrammed in the most improbable places." Apart from his tailor, bootmaker, and butler, the successful dramatist was most proud of his country estate in Bucks County, Pennsylvania. It became the perfect sinkhole for his excess income, and he loved to show it off, swimming pool and all to weekend guests. "I've moved this oak tree so that it would shade my library," he explained to Wolcott Gibbs.

"It just goes to show," the critic reacted, "what God could do if He only had money."

Some, including Howard Teichmann, attribute this classic line to George Kaufman, who is also reported to have told Hart once: "I like to be near you, Moss. It comes under the heading of gelt by association."

Pastoral

Oscar Hammerstein II loved the country and had a farm near Doylestown, Pennsylvania. His estate included all the urban amenities, as well as a richly diverse vegetable garden, acres of corn and alfalfa, turkeys, chickens, and a herd of Black Angus cattle. The lyricist played the country squire to the hilt, eagerly pointing out to visitors from the city every cherished spot. Once he was trying to explain to George S. Kaufman just how much he loved to sit on his porch, staring out into the fields after sunset, and not think of anything.

"Anybody can sit and think of nothing," Kaufman replied; "the trick is to think of *something!*"

Department Story

After George S. Kaufman was married to his second wife, actress Leueen McGrath, he offered to accompany her on a shopping trip for redecorating their aparmtent. Getting visibly bored while his wife was trying to decide on some curtain fabric, the manager of the department store asked:

"Is there anything we can do for you, Mr. Kaufman?"

"Yes," said the playwright after a moment's thought. "Do you have any good second-act curtains?"

A Bridge Too Near

Abe Burrows recalled meeting George Kaufman, his future collaborator, during the war. Mike Todd was putting on a show at Camp Shanks and had sent a driver to take the two writers there. Kaufman was afraid of cars, and as the army chauffeur speeded along the sleety highway toward the George Washington Bridge, Kaufman put a hand on his arm:

"Sergeant," he warned, "don't cross that bridge till we come to it."

Vengeance Was His

Long after the Second World War, George Kaufman refused to allow his plays to be staged in Germany. Harold Clurman was visiting West Berlin and the dramaturg of one of the major theatres asked him to persuade Kaufman to change his mind. "Please tell Mr. Kaufman that we were never Nazis. We have Jews in our company as honored colleagues."

When Clurman relayed the message, Kaufman remained adamant:

"They can't have any of my plays. It actually gives me pleasure to refuse."

The Old Story

Writers are continually confused by mixed signals from the marketplace. They often read how producers are desperate for new material, but this is contradicted by the difficulties of even meeting a producer. Edward Peple, a now forgotten playwright whose play The Prince Chap (1905) *enjoyed some success on Broadway, tells a universal story.*

It may sound incredulous, but it really took me twelve years to get a hearing. Believe me, I have had a few experiences. I recollect the first visit I made to New York from my home in Richmond, Virginia. I had been reading that the managers were on their knees beseeching the dramatists to give forth librettos. I had been writing from my early boyhood, so I placed under my arm some things of a literary nature and started for New York. In four offices, bright Irish boys on the door told me irremediably that the manager was not in, and in the fifth I got a surprise. I was taken right into the sanctum sanctorum.

"Well," said the great manager, smiling, "you are a dramatist—a librettist, hey?"

"That is my allegation."

He led me to the front window and pointed to one of the large buildings across the street—fifteen stories high, I believe, and said:

"See all the windows in that building? It is a whole block long, too. Each one of those windows is filled with a young fellow like you. Go back home, my boy. Good day."

Desperately Seeking Plays

In the beginning days of the Theatre Guild, Harold Clurman was in charge of reading scripts. He found them dismal. One he treasured to the end of his days began: "Act One: Ten thousand years before the creation of man. Act Two: Two weeks later."

As for every new group seeking new directions, it was difficult to attract plays by people who had a proven track record. Established playwrights were not interested in an unknown group with radical views. So Clurman wrote letters to poets and novelists whose work he admired. One of the responses he got was from Ernest Hemingway. It read: "You ask me if I've written a play. Who the hell hasn't?"

Fame

Because of his early association with the sea, there have always been a number of sailor stories told about Eugene O'Neill. It was rumored that the only time he listened to advice was when a sailor buddy told him, after seeing *The Hairy Ape*: "For God's sake tell that Number Four stoker to stop leaning his prat against that red-hot furnace."

Another kind of story caught on after the opening of *Strange Interlude*, which made O'Neill a household word in America. The playwright bumped into one of his old seafaring mates on one of the avenues of New York. O'Neill asked him with genuine enthusiasm what he was doing. "Oh, I've married and settled down," said the former sea-dog. "Got a nice little business and doing pretty good. And you, Gene, are you still working the boats?"

Arthur Miller Meets a Salesman

Playwright Arthur Miller was once sitting in a bar, when a well-dressed and slightly tipsy man came up to him:

"Aren't you Arthur Miller?"

"Yes, I am."

"Don't you remember me?"

Miller couldn't quite place him.

"Art, it's me—Sam! I'm your old buddy from high school. We used to go out on double dates!"

Sam went on, filling Miller in on all that happened to him since those days and how well he had done working as a salesman at a department store. Finally he stopped and asked:

"And what do you do, Art?"

"Well, I write . . ."

"What, Art?"

"Plays mainly."

"Any of them produced?"

"Yeah . . ."

"Would I know any of them?"

"Perhaps you've heard of *Death of a Salesman?*"

Sam was finally speechless. He turned white as it sank in, and then he cried:

"Why, you're Arthur Miller!"

An Eccentric

S. N. Behrman, the playwright and biographer, was criticized as "the Boswell of the overprivileged" by producer Irving Drutman. Fanny Brice said that he was a "man who writes like silk herring." Most people would have agreed that he was charming and highly eccentric.

One evening Sam Behrman dropped by the Stork Club, where he saw George Jean Nathan, Tallulah Bankhead, Irene Dunne, and William Saroyan. He noted their presence, said goodbye to them, and later that night ended up at "21," where the first people he saw were George Jean Nathan, Tallulah Bankhead, Irene Dunne, and William Saroyan. "Good heavens," Behrman was astonished, since he was fairly sober, "there seem to be two sets of everybody!"

Behrman was nervous about making appointments, and as soon as he committed himself to an engagement, he either sought a way of breaking it or forgot about it. Once he announced to all his friends that he was going to sail up the fjords of Norway. After elaborate farewells and good wishes, he stayed in the city. A week later, his fellow playwright Elmer Rice saw him at his usual table at the Plaza. "Ah, Sam," Rice greeted him, "I see you're forgotten, but not gone."

This was the remark that Behrman later repeated to John F. Kennedy, who liked it so much he asked permission to use it. Behrman said that it was not his own. "Whosever it is," said the newly elected president, "it will be most handy in the White House."

The Hollywood Touch

Two of the best-known among the bestselling novelists in America began their careers in the theatre: Robert Ludlum and Sidney Sheldon. The latter tried his hand at adapting and writing plays and may have found that collaboration was not for him. David Pressman directed one of Sheldon's comedies, Roman Candle (1960).

Before rehearsals began, I had a conference with the writer. I had a lot of questions about the play and I was particularly puzzled that the leading character, called Mark, who was an inventor making rockets for the army, hardly had any lines. The character would listen to others on stage, many of whom had funny lines and then say nothing. The script simply noted, at least in a dozen places: "MARK (reacts)." When I asked Sidney about this, he said:

"O-oh, that. I know what this is. You see I used to write scripts in Hollywood for people like Cary Grant, and the humor came from the way he reacted. So all I had to put in the script was a note for Cary to react. That's what I must have been thinking about."

"But Sidney," I said, "this is the stage, and what we need in the theatre is literature."

Being a Hollywood type at the time, Sheldon also had quite a bit of control as a co-producer. He had veto over casting. The producer Ethel Reiner and I were trying to cast a really strong comedienne in one of the leads, while Sidney wanted a sexy blonde. At the time we were planning the production, Ethel and I had just opened *The Knock on the Door* by Sean O'Casey, and Tyrone Guthrie came to see it. When he came backstage, Ethel sought his advice about casting a strong comedienne like Anne Jackson versus the pretty Hollywood girl that Sidney Sheldon wanted. Guthrie interrupted with that booming voice of his: "Always get a good actress—the beautiful girl won't be noticed beyond the third row."

But Sidney wouldn't buy that. In any case, he had already gone to see some kind of fortune teller who assured him that his numbers looked good for a successful run. So with that Sidney took off to Florida and we didn't see him for the rest of the rehearsals.

(*Unfortunately,* Roman Candle *fizzled at the Cort Theatre after five nights.*)

Dream the Impossible Dream

Robert Ludlum started in the theatre as an actor. In his thirties he founded two theatres, one in a converted movie house in Fort Lee in New Jersey, and the more ambitious Playhouse-on-the-Mall in Paramus, N.J., which became an important stock theatre in the 1960s. Broadway and Hollywood stars appeared there, and Ludlum is fondly remembered by many in the profession. Richard Herd is one of them.

In those days you needed twenty weeks of work, before qualifying for unemployment insurance. Actors who were a few weeks short would call up Bob, and if he had something for them, they could make up their twenty weeks. Ludlum was always running around his Playhouse, which he operated almost as a family business, doing practically everything by himself, and running off to the city to to make ends meet with a few voice-over commercials. Bob was—still is—an awfully decent fellow, and he always had his ideas. One day, when he was pushing almost forty, he stopped running for a minute, and said with his usual, total enthusiasm: "I've got an idea for a novel . . ."

And some of us actors standing around scoffed: "Sure, Bob, everybody's got an idea for a book . . ."

Well, not too many years after that Robert Ludlum became one of the most famous authors on the planet.

Expert Witness

Plays are previewed before audiences, but even before previews there are rehearsals for a few invited experts. Al Hirschfeld, the show-business caricaturist, remembers a run-through of William Saroyan's *Hello Out There* (1942), which the author packed with his own friendly experts. One of them was a sidewalk artist called Bill Cody, who tried to dress the part. After the show, Saroyan asked him how he liked the play.

"It's the greatest goddamn show I ever saw," sobbed Buffalo Bill.

"How many plays have you seen?"

"This is the first show I ever saw," said Cody.

The great Hirschfeld recalls another occasion when the excited Saroyan, renowned for his ego, rushed through the stage door of the Lyceum Thea-

tre following the opening of his play *The Beautiful People*, and congratu-
lated the fireman posted just inside on his wonderful performance. "It all
seemed perfectly normal behavior for a man who not only wrote, directed,
and produced his own play but had the temerity to attend its opening."

Success Has Many Fathers

When she started writing plays, for inspiration Clare Boothe Luce kept a
photograph of George Bernard Shaw, the world's most famous dramatist, on
her dressing table. In 1939 she went to London for the British production of her play *The Women*, and sought and obtained an interview with
Shaw. Completely swept off her feet in the presence of her idol, the normally cool Mrs. Luce cooed girlishly:

"Oh, Mr. Shaw, if it weren't for you I wouldn't be here."

Knowing nothing about the part his photograph had played in helping
this beautiful woman's career, the 83-year-old dramatist simply nodded and
asked:

"Let me see—what was your dear mother's name?"

The South

Thomas Lanier Williams was born in Mississippi and adopted the name of
Tennessee as a gesture to some ancestors who had fought in the Indian
wars in that state. He made the change because he considered his early
writings which had appeared under his original name were not good enough
and somehow "compromised" it.

Although Williams does not deal in his plays with the race problems
which characterized the South during his childhood, he was scarred in
other ways. When he was very young, Thomas called Ozzie, the beloved
family mammy, a "nigger"—a term he had never heard used in his grandfather's house. Ozzie walked out, never to return. Weeks spent trying to
trace her were to no avail. The guilt from this episode stayed with the
playwright. Though no political activist, when he became successful in the
late 1940s, Williams inserted in his contract that his plays could not be
performed in a segregated theatre.

Happiness

Tennessee Williams was thirty-three when *The Glass Menagerie* finally
established him as a major new voice in the theatre. Following the failure
of his *Battle of Angels*, which the Theatre Guild dropped after a Boston

tryout at the end of 1940, the author struggled to revise it in New Orleans. Plagued by ill health, aggravated by severe hypochondria, Williams moved to New York on false hope of a production. Journalist Lincoln Barnett described his bohemian days for *Life* magazine a few years later:

"He was hired as a waiter in a Greenwich Village nightclub, primarily because he had just undergone another eye operation and the proprietor was enchanted by Williams' black patch on which a friend had drawn a fiercely libidinous eye in white chalk. In addition to serving drinks, Williams doubled as entertainer late at night by reciting bawdy verses of his own composition. When he lost this job following a dispute with his employer over tips, he was kept from starvation by a group of amiable alcoholics who liked his recitations. They wound up each evening at the home of an aging retired actress, and Williams found that if he stayed with them long enough somebody would eventually telephone for chicken sandwiches. For days he lived on nothing but highballs and chicken sandwiches and was wolfishly hungry for most of the time. There was never any food in the actress's icebox because she never ate—whenever she sensed that a collapse was imminent she went to a hospital and had a blood transfusion; next day she would show up at her favorite bar, her thirst and hemoglobin count back to normal."

The sensitive and sickly young writer might not have survived the disappointments and failures of these years of his obscurity without the faith and support provided by his agent, the legendary Audrey Wood. After the opening of *The Glass Menagerie* on December 26, 1944, the agent was watching her playwright during the cast party at "21" moving from one group to another, accepting their congratulations. Williams was visibly growing lighter and more extrovert, as the rave reviews began to come in from the early editions. Later, catching him alone and about to relapse into an introspective mood, Audrey Wood sneaked up to him:

"Tenn, are you really happy?"

"Of course I am," he replied, somewhat puzzled.

"Are you a completely fulfilled young man?" she asked inquisitorially.

"Completely," he said. "Why do you ask?"

"I just wanted to hear you say it."

Odd Man Out

Neil Simon went back to watch *Barefoot in the Park* after it opened. He saw that the audience was practically rolling in the aisles at every funny line. Then he noticed one man, who was sitting there stone-faced. Transfixed, from then on the playwright was unable to see anybody else. He

wanted to get through to that one person, and he couldn't. When his wife
later asked him how the show was going, Simon said:

"Terrible."

And he really meant it.

On Second Thought

Harold Clurman was introduced at a party to Neil Simon's business manager. Clurman told him that he had just written an article called "In Defense of Neil Simon."

"That's wonderful," said the manager, "I look forward to reading it."
They went their separate ways, but a little while later, the man came back
to ask Clurman:

"I don't quite understand why a man who earns forty thousand dollars
a week needs a defense."

Dallas Tragedy

When Preston Jones's *Texas Trilogy* came from Dallas to the Kennedy
Center (1976), it was considered the finest flower the regional theatre
movement had yet produced. It received rave reviews in the nation's capital,
and yet when it opened at the Broadhurst Theatre on Broadway, the critics
crucified the playwright. Walter Flannigan, who was in the cast, witnessed
a poignant moment in the lobby of the Algonquin Hotel a few days later
when Preston Jones, having just checked out, was about to call a cab to the
airport. A member of the company came up to him with a copy of *The
New Republic*, and urged him to read the review of his trilogy.

"No thank ye," said the playwright in his quiet drawl, "I've read enough
of these New York critics. All I want to do now is get to the airport and
then home to Texas."

The actor persisted, and finally managed to persuade Jones to read the
thoughtful and supportive minority report that Harold Clurman had
written.

Flannigan watched a tear trickle down the dramatist's face as he finished reading.

"Well," he said, "that's all I was trying to say . . ."

Yes, We Have No Bananas

The first show David Hays designed was The Innkeepers (1956), *a play
by Ted Apstein, directed by José Quintero.*

We were working on the show in Philadelphia—it was an interim booking, because all the theatres in New York were jammed; every day you prayed for somebody else's show to collapse and that somehow you'd get in. Meanwhile, the producer's checks began to bounce and the scenery went unpainted. Even though I was not supposed to be doing it, I was painting away at the scenery bit by bit. The producer, Gordon Pollock, was trying to send me home. Every day I found a note in my box telling me to go home, because he didn't want to pay me the $15 a day, which was the living allowance then. He was rather a flamboyant man who had started as a stagehand and was now trying to balance two or three shows. One day he flew in from Philly—in a little plane which took a good deal longer than by train, but that's what Gordon was all about—and he announced that we finally had a theatre in New York. But the next morning we read the paper and discovered that we had only an interim booking of a few days, a terrible situation which meant that if you opened you had to be a big hit, or there was no chance. In those days you could fight a play through more than you can now.

I remember the poor author, Ted Apstein, read this in the paper and got a splitting headache. After breakfast he stumbled out into the street and all he could think of while walking was that his wife had told him to get Mouseketeer hats for the children—they were out of them in New York. So Ted went up to Wanamakers' to the sixth floor and said to the salesgirl, "I need Mouseketeer hats age four and age six." And she looked at him and said, "We're out of Mouseketeer hats." At which point a giant tear rolled down the playwright's face, and she said, "Don't cry, sir, we have Daniel Boone hats."

(The play closed in New York after four performances.)

Experimental Formula

Sam Shepard is almost unique among American playwrights in staying away from New York. He was known on the West Coast a dozen years before winning the Pulitzer for *Buried Child* (1979), which finally gave him a national reputation. He achieved the distinction of becoming the most frequently produced American playwright without a single Broadway production, unless one counts the sketch he wrote for Kenneth Tynan's *Oh, Calcutta!*

In the mid-1970s, with ten years of playwriting behind him, Shepard received a phone call from Joseph Papp offering him a commission.

"Why don't you ever do any of my plays?" Shepard asked the czar of New York theatre.

"I'd like to do one of your plays," Papp replied. "Why don't you write one for me?"

"How much money will you give me?" asked Shepard who was habitually broke.

"Two hundred dollars."

"Two hundred dollars, sheeee!"

The playwright got the producer up to five hundred dollars and then asked what kind of play he liked.

"Oh," said Papp, who was fresh from his triumph with David Rabe's *Sticks and Bones*, "a family, two sons, one stays home, one goes off to Vietnam or anyway to war and gets fucked up."

(The commissioned play, Curse of the Starving Class, *was first done at the Royal Court in London and then at Joe Papp's Public Theatre in 1978.)*

Toilet Training

Sam Shepard never cared for the establishment and has used various means within his imagination *pour épater les bourgeois*. In 1975 he was teaching a playwriting course at the University of California at Davis. The class met in the scene shop of the theatre, and occasionally to relieve himself, the teacher went to a toilet in the corner. "But," as his biographer Don Shewey wrote, "since the prop toilet wasn't connected to any plumbing, it meant that some poor student would have to come along and empty out Mr. Shepard's piss."

Fleeting Fame

Bartley Campbell (1843–88), is sometimes called the first professional American playwright. He also tried his hand at management, and the combination drove him insane: he died in an asylum. Though now forgotton, Campbell's legend loomed large during his lifetime and in his own mind. His letterhead displayed dual portraits of himself and of Shakespeare with the motto: "A friendly rivalry."

CHAPTER 16

Palpable Hits
and Egregious Misses

What's Wrong with This Picture?

Despite his enormous success, Richard Rodgers retained a small-town, star-struck naïveté about show business, which perhaps only native New Yorkers share. While *South Pacific* was playing to sold-out houses, the composer was, in his own words, "walking down Broadway when I passed a billboard with a big picture of Mary Martin. And I thought to myself, 'Gosh, Mary's a swell girl. I'm so glad I know her. What's more, she's not only a swell girl, she's a big star. Just think, I know Mary Martin, and she's a big star in a Broadway show.' And then all of a sudden I stopped short and asked myself, 'Whose show? My show!' "

Another Cat Out of the Bag

For almost twenty years Ethel Merman had reigned supreme and unchallenged as the queen of musical theatre, when Mary Martin scored a sensation in *South Pacific*. Asked what she thought of the young star's performance, "Oh, she's all right," La Merman replied with a shrug, "if you like talent!"

Conventional Wisdom

Oklahoma! (1943), which gave new definition to success in Broadway's book, began inauspiciously under the title *Away We Go!* Conventional wisdom held that a show could not be a hit when there's a murder in it. And advance word confirmed that the firstborn of the newly formed Rodgers and Hammerstein team was in trouble. One of Walter Winchell's out-of-town informants witnessed the musical's premiere in New Haven and wired the columnist this famous forecast: "NO GIRLS, NO LEGS, NO JOKES, NO CHANCE."

Tunnel Vision

There is a famous story about the wardrobe mistress who had gone to see *Oklahoma!*, and when asked what she'd thought of it, she replied indignantly: "You call *those* seams?"

Remedy

When the critics panned Nunnally Johnson's Broadway show *The World Is Full of Girls*, the Hollywood screenwriter and wit sent a telegram to producer Jed Harris: "Change title immediately to *Oklahoma!*"

A Success by Any Other Name

Annie Get Your Gun was criticized for not following the new trend that had been started by *Oklahoma!* a few years earlier. When Irving Berlin heard that some people were calling his show old-fashioned, he retorted: "Yeah, it's an old-fashioned smash."

Dues

Stephen Sondheim began his career with a series of hit shows. Just before the opening of *A Funny Thing Happened on the Way to the Forum*, Burt Shevelove (who co-authored the book with Larry Gelbart) ran into Oscar Hammerstein. Both of those older, successful men had acted as mentors to Sondheim, and they started discussing their brilliant protégé. "You know," said Hammerstein to Shevelove, "Steve won't really be a member of the working theatre until he has a flop."

Triumphant Flop

It was Oscar Wilde who coined the bon mot that "the play was a great success but the audience was a total failure." Theatre people know the truth of this when they know they are working with great material and yet people are staying away in droves. This fairly common phenomenon has befallen a number of Stephen Sondheim's musicals. Lee Remick remembers the wonderful time she and Angela Lansbury had in *Anyone Can Whistle* (1964), which closed in the week after it opened. "During that week it became a cult piece. When the closing notice was posted on Wednesday, the remaining four performances were completely sold out. People were sitting in the aisles, and they are still talking about the emotional experience."

The Naked Genius

Gypsy Rose Lee turned from performing naked to co-authoring an autobiographical comedy called *The Naked Genius*. Her fully clothed co-author was no other than George Kaufman, who was also offering to direct the show. The only problem was that Gypsy's good friend and producer Mike Todd did not like the script, and the more the authors worked on it, the more he came to hate it. Even before it opened, Hollywood's top moguls were vying with huge sums to buy the rights; Todd did his utmost to persuade his friend Joe Schenck to change his mind. But he failed, and Schenck outbid MGM in buying a property that its producer considered "one of the worst plays he had ever seen."

By the time the production limped to Pittsburgh there was a strange turn-around. The audience clearly did not like any version of the play that Lee and Kaufman kept serving up. After innumerable rewrites, it was Kaufman who begged Todd not to take the show to Broadway, but by this time the producer was determined to face the challenge of pulling a rabbit out of his hat. He took the bad notices and countered with large advertisements that admitted to some truth in them: "Guaranteed not to win the Pulitzer Prize," read one. "It ain't Shakespeare, but it's laffs," said another in imitation of popular Elizabethan orthography.

After the second night of *The Naked Genius*, Kaufman phoned Todd and was horrified to learn that the play he considered beyond repair had sold out. The producer told him that there had actually been fourteen standees.

"I know you must be hysterical," Kaufman countered. "But, if you send me a verified statement, I'll quit show business."

Mike Todd blamed the success on the war. He told a press conference: "The public is so entertainment-hungry they'll look at anything. All you can do is hope your show somehow overcomes good notices."

Nothing Succeeds Like Success

Typically, when Howard Lindsay and Russel Crouse opened their first major hit, they did not know it. Journalist Lincoln Barnett chronicles the birth of a success.

Life with Father was tried out at Skowhegan, Maine, with Lindsay and his wife in the leading roles. Crouse prowled restlessly in the back of the house. At the end of Act I he went backstage and told his partner: "We've got something. I don't know what it is yet." After the final curtain he stood in the lobby and watched the audience emerge. Some people were laughing; others had tears in their eyes. That night Lindsay and Crouse took a long walk in the woods. "I'll settle for six months in New York," Lindsay said. "The most we can hope is it won't flop." On November 5, 1939, *Life with Father* opened in Manhattan's venerable rococo Empire Theater. The premiere was so fraught with missed cues and fluffed lines that Lindsay and his wife went straight home from the theater, eschewing supper parties and the 3:00 a.m. editions. But next morning the notices were good and there was a line at the box office. Although no one then forecast that *Father* would break all records for theatrical longevity, Lindsay and Crouse soon discovered from audience reactions that their play had the priceless asset of "universal appeal." It touched all people. A Polish expatriate told the playwrights: "You have written about my family in Poland." A French movie director said: "You must have known my father." Even Chinese found fragments of their own family memories in *Life with Father*.

The Lindsays, who had thought to indulge themselves for one season, found themselves trapped for five. They never grew bored, for each new audience, according to Lindsay, is "like a live fish at the end of your line—you have to land it." But their roles were arduous; their parts were long and Miss Stickney had to run up and down a staircase twenty-four times in each performance. Unlike many companies which become torn by jealous feuds in the course of a long run, the cast of *Life with Father* developed a kind of happy-family spirit. Domestic problems were shared. Birthdays, holidays, and anniversaries were celebrated together. The child actors grew up and sometimes were promoted to other parts. "We had twenty-eight children in five years, which is something of a record," Lindsay recalls. One night Crouse joined the cast. An actor who played the minor role of Dr. Somers had fallen ill. Crouse volunteered to understudy and proceeded to win press notices by making a "double entrance"—i.e., by coming on stage too soon, hastily withdrawing, then appearing a second time. Next day when friends asked him why he had bothered, he replied: "I just wanted to see if there was a doctor in the Crouse."

Overnight Success

The Fantasticks (1960) is by far the longest-playing show in the history of the New York stage, but some backers were urging producer Lore Noto to close it during the first week. It took more than three years for the musical to start selling out in an off-Broadway house with only 150 seats, and nobody believed they had a hit during the first five years. Tom Jones, who wrote the book and lyrics, was also in the cast on opening night (using Thomas Bruce as a stage name) and waiting to go on opening night when he heard a disturbance. Because the Sullivan Street Playhouse was too small to have any side exits, he saw one of the critics actually crossing the stage and leaving with his girlfriend who was loudly complaining, "What's this thing about?"

The early notices were so bad that Jones remembers "somebody crying, and I got into a cab and couldn't make it across Central Park, I just got out of the cab and vomited my way through Central Park."

That's Luv

Following the opening of Murray Schisgal's comedy *Luv* in November 1964, Eli Wallach was walking by the Booth Theatre with a friend when he witnessed one of those rare, heartwarming sights: a line around the block to the box office. "There's something about a crowd like that," commented Wallach, who co-starred in the show with Alan Arkin, "that brings a lump to my wallet."

Something in the Way She Moves

Dorothy Parker was attending the final dress rehearsal for *Close Harmony* (1924), a flop she had co-authored with Elmer Rice. At one point the producer suggested that the leading lady needed perhaps a tighter bodice to restrict her amply endowed charms from distracting from the performance. Miss Parker violently disagreed:

"You've got to have something in this show that moves," she said.

Moral Excuse

When E. H. Sothern was playing Hamlet at the Garden Theatre with
mediocre success, Maurice Barrymore was chided by a friend for not supporting a fellow actor by going to see his performance:

"Why don't you go and just sit through an act?" the friend encouraged.

"My boy," said Barrymore, "I never encourage vice."

Finally, a Reason to Go to the Show

Charles Hoyt (1860–1900), the newspaper columnist of the Boston Post
*who became a successful writer of Broadway farces, was noted for his
pungent humor. The comedian Nat Goodwin told the following story
against himself.*

The first night of my production of *Nathan Hale*, Hoyt had assured me of
his intention of being present with his wife. But when the time came she
refused to accompany him. Charley, having purchased two tickets and not
desiring to be alone, sought someone to go with him. He soon found a
friend and invited him to come along. Much to Hoyt's astonishment his
friend quietly but firmly refused the invitation.

"Why not?" asked Hoyt. His friend replied:

"I don't like Goodwin."

"Well," said Charley, "you like him as an artist, don't you?" His friend
replied:

"No, I don't like him, on or off the stage."

"Well," said Hoyt, "come along; you are sure to enjoy this play for they
hang Nat in the last act."

East Is East and West Is West

*Conquering Broadway is arduous under any circumstances, but there al-
ways seems to be that extra bit of difficulty when a show transfers from
Los Angeles to New York. Gordon Davidson, artistic director of the Mark
Taper Forum, has scored big successes with* The Shadow Box *and* Children
of a Lesser God. *But after ten years, he still smarts from the failure of
Luis Valdez's* The Zoot Suit, *one of the great hits in recent Los Angeles
theatre history, which did not find favor with the critics or audiences on
Broadway. Susan Dietz had bitter experiences with* Mail, *a successful revue
at the Pasadena Playhouse which exited after a few nights in New York,
pursued by some rather vicious critics. The rivalry between the two greatest*

American cities is easier to understand than the deep difference in taste between the two coasts.

If it is any comfort to Los Angeles producers, the problem is an old one and it can be licked. At the beginning of the century, Oliver Morosco became a pre-eminent producer in Los Angeles, and eventually he was dubbed as the Oracle of Broadway for his almost unerring commercial sense. But the Oracle failed with his first New York production, The Judge and the Jury *(1906), which he brought to the experienced Charles Frohman after a successful run in Los Angeles.*

For four weeks I rehearsed under the watchful eye of Mr. Frohman. Since he made no comments I went ahead diligently and put all the plot and action into my Western that I could. The play was scheduled to open at Wallacks' old theatre way down on Broadway, which in those days was a good location. Prior to the opening in New York we had the usual dress rehearsals, and Mr. Frohman sat in on the complete play for the first time. Up until then he had remained in the background. With the exception of Bill Desmond, my leading man from Los Angeles, who created his part, I had a New York company, including Ida Conquest, who played Marquita, and Julius Tannen, the Jewish comedian, who depicted a rough, tough cowboy and was wildly funny doing so. I would have liked to give Blanche Hall an opportunity to essay her original role; she had been so faithful and was such an exquisite genius, but Mr. Frohman wanted Ida Conquest to play the leading female part, so I refrained from suggesting my choice.

At that dress rehearsal I called the first act and had all the cowboys on hand. The curtain was raised on an eating-house scene in the roughest part of Arizona. I was intimately familiar with the West and Western ways, and I wanted to give Broadway a realistic view of the cowboy. The play went smoothly through the first act, and I thought it was great. When the curtain was lowered, I paused for a moment to see if Mr. Frohman had any comment. He apparently had none, so I called "Strike," which in backstage terminology, means to replace one set by another.

But before the stagehands could begin work Mr. Frohman said, "Just a moment, Mr. Morosco. I would like to see that act again."

The stagehands retired, and we started the first act again. The cowboys entered the railroad mess house with a whoop. Dinner was late, and they were irritated. Some of them began to shoot things up, not figuratively, either, but literally. I had never been so realistic before; I have never been so realistic since. Mr. Frohman objected. In fact, he started quietly to shred my first act to bits. My heart started down and kept going. He told the cowpunchers to eat quietly and refrain from shooting.

That was too much for me. "If I may suggest, Mr. Frohman," I remonstrated, "you are taking all the comedy out of my first act. You see, I come from the West, and I have actually seen such demonstrations. It may be unusual to an Easterner, but what I have done in this play is real."

"Remember this, Morosco, we don't want that which is real on the stage; we want that which appears to be real."

I instantly recognized that venerable bit of theatrical philosophy.

"But," I objected, "why can't the real be made to appear real? I know that if it were a choice between the two, we would choose that which appears real to the real, but I believe one of the big failings of the stage is that it doesn't make the real look real."

"Maybe you're right," conceded Mr. Frohman, then proceeded to go through the remaining three acts and take out all the punches which had endeared the play to my Los Angeles patrons.

When I objected again, he simply said, "This is not Los Angeles; you're in New York now."

The piece opened a rank failure. My heart was broken. I was not used to failures, and it hurt.

The papers treated the play terribly and me worse. That was my first experience with the New York deathwatch. The critics ranted, nursing their abused intelligence. "How could a youngster write such a play or even direct it?" they demanded of the reading public. I felt the eyes of New York upon me. I hadn't learned then that New York doesn't bother very much with either a success or a failure.

Why Can't a Woman Be More Like a Man?

Vesta Tilley was one of the most famous male impersonators in the British music halls at the turn of the century. Her visit to New York led to a vogue in this genre. But according to Miss Tilley (later Lady de Frece), the challenge proved too great for the greatest beauty of the age.

Lillian Russell had made her debut at Pastor's some time before I first appeared there, and was one of the biggest stars in America when I arrived. She was a very beautiful woman, and possessed a sweet voice. Her picture was in all the magazines, and she was a great favorite with all theatre-goers. When she appeared at Pastor's she was of very slight build, but in after years became what might be termed statuesque; but she still retained her beauty and her lovely voice, and was a great success at Weber and Fields' Theatre.

After I had made a hit in New York, there were many male impersonators, and, in a new revue at Weber and Fields', in which Miss Russell was to appear, the authors had written a scene for her in which she had to appear in male attire. I can quite understand that she undertook the task in fear and trembling, though pluckily. She waited in the wings for her entrance in a gentleman's full evening dress, but entirely covered with a silk dressing-gown, and remarked that she had never felt more uncomfortable in her life. And I must say that I have never seen anything less like a man in my life. She dreaded the time when she would have to discard her gown and step before the footlights in the garb.

As a matter of fact, the audience was delighted, and screamed with laughter at her evident discomfiture. When Pete Daly, the acknowledged wit and practical joker of the company, walked on and said to her: "Beg pardon, Sir, but Miss Russell has sent me to say that you have taken her corsets by mistake," she could stand it no longer, and rushed off the stage shrieking with laughter. Her next entrance was in a lovely evening costume, and she prefaced her number with the remark: "What a relief!" I do not know, but I venture to say that that was Miss Russell's first and last venture in a masculine role.

Turkey

Monologuist Frank Fay's career was littered with spectacular failures. A supreme egotist, even by the standards of his profession, he never seemed to learn from his previous mistakes. In 1924 he was producing a musical tellingly named *Frank Fay's Fables*. Fred Allen, who was in it, recalled how the opening was continually postponed, because Fay would not give the investors 51 percent control. Fay himself had no money in those days: he would feed the actors from canned food he claimed he got from a grocer friend who was about to invest in the show. *Fables* folded owing everybody, and for a while Fay was boycotted by Actors' Equity.

A few years later, Frank Fay was starring in *Harry Delmar's Revels*, a revue written by Billy Rose and Ballard McDonald. This time, Fay did not like the producers and after ousting them he refused to pay royalties. Rose took the matter to the Dramatists Guild, which threatened to close the show unless Rose was paid eleven hundred dollars. Fay was so put out by the author's unreasonable demand to get paid that in his fury he went to a bank and got 110,000 pennies which he dumped at Billy Rose's feet.

Even later in life, after he startled his creditors and friends with his comeback as a lovable drunk in *Harvey* (1944), Fay quickly demonstrated that he had learned nothing during the years. In November 1950 he spent $70,000 on a musical revue inappropriately named *If You Please. Variety's* stringer was less than kind: "Frank Fay had an unfortunate accident," he wrote. "He stumbled over his own ego and landed flat on his face in all the departments—composer and lyricist; writer of the sketches, scenes, and dialogue; director; producer and star . . ." The San Francisco critics were equally damning, and Fay did not make new friends by calling them "two-bit bums" in public. But after six nights Fay admitted defeat. He closed the show, and the day after Thanksgiving, as the stagehands moved the scenery out of the theatre, one of them overheard Frank Fay musing: "Looks like the turkey came a day late."

Gallows Humor

One of the memorable flops associated with David Merrick was a musical adaptation of Truman Capote's famous novella *Breakfast at Tiffany's* (1966) which closed in previews at the Majestic. The title role of Holly Golightly was played by Mary Tyler Moore; three heavyweight writers and rewriters—Nunnally Johnson, Abe Burrows, and Edward Albee—had tried their hand at the book. Out-of-town critics and preview audiences attacked the script; Truman Capote did not help matters by telling *Women's Wear Daily* that he disliked both the score and the leading lady. When the producer read this, he threatened to advertise the show as

DAVID MERRICK PRESENTS
IN COLD BLOOD
BREAKFAST AT TIFFANY'S!

Instead, Merrick announced to the press: "Rather than subject the drama critics and the theatre-going public—who invested one million dollars in advance ticket sales—to an excruciatingly boring evening, I decided to close the show. Since the idea of adapting *Breakfast at Tiffany's* for the musical stage was mine in the first place, the closing is entirely my fault and should not be attributed to the three top writers who had a go at it."

David Merrick was rare among producers in retaining his sense of humor while watching long-cherished dreams and large sums of money go down the drain. Less than a year after *Breakfast at Tiffany's* Merrick produced what Richard L. Coe of the *Washington Post* feared might become *Supper at Cartier's*. This was a musical based on the life of the World War I spy, Mata Hari, which marked Vincent Minnelli's first return to directing on Broadway since 1939. Inexplicably, the show starred an untried, unknown, and reportedly untalented Marisa Mell in the title role. During its first

Washington preview, which was a benefit for the Women's National Democratic Club with first lady Lady Bird Johnson, Merrick made a speech in which he expected the audience to be kind, since "Democrats are known for their tolerance."

The nightmare that followed would have strained the most partisan viewer's tolerance. Part of the set collapsed, several dancers stumbled and fell, and Miss Mell was accidentally caught by the lights half-nude while trying to change her costume during a blackout. Her own ineptitude, however, outshone anything that the lights might have concealed. When Mata Hari was supposed to be wheeled in for her execution on a moving wagon, which failed to move, and to be shot by a firing squad (the rifles failed to fire), the extinguished actress was observed wiping perspiration from her brows and looking up at the falling curtain to the great amusement of the Democratic ladies. "The night was so bad," *Variety* reported, "that there was no curtain call and the audience left." It was the season of Thanksgiving, and David Merrick stood up in the auditorium and shouted: "Anyone who wants this turkey for a buck can have it!"

Etymology

Producer John Golden (1874–1955), in the days before he had his own theatre named after himself, had put on a farce called the Three Wise Fools *at the Criterion, which opened to very slow business. On top of everything, Golden had to put up with constant recriminations from his fellow producer Winchell Smith, who hated the show.*

One Wednesday, when there was fifty-eight dollars in the box office, the two of us stood in front of the Criterion at the corner of 44th Street and Broadway, disconsolately watching a million people pass by.

My partner snarled at me: "You insisted on doing this farce, didn't you?"

"Yes," I replied miserably.

"Rotten cast," he fumed, "just nobodies!"

"I know it," I mumbled apologetically.

"And the Criterion Theatre!" he went on. "Hasn't had a decent show for two years. And you had to pick it."

I was almost on the verge of tears, but he continued relentlessly:

"Criterion! What a name for a theatre! Where did that word ever come from? What does it mean?"

"If you look in the dictionary," I said weakly, "you'll see that a criterion is 'a thing to go by.'"

"Well, just look at all these people," Smith cried. "They're going by all right—not a blasted one coming in!"

Deep Down He Was Shallow

Having written a string of hit comedies, Philip Barry tried his hand at serious, socially significant dramas. After one of these failed, Harold Clurman said to Brooks Atkinson: "We should encourage him to remain superficial."

Safe Haven

Since there never seems to be a rational explanation why some plays are successful and others fail, theatre people look for reasons according to their superstitions. A popular one is to blame failure on the building; for example, Edwin Booth's mismanagement of his theatre, which only lasted four years, was blamed on the house rather than on its management. Perhaps the unkindest cut was made by *Variety* in the days following Pearl Harbor, when New York was jittery with frequent air-raid sirens. The show business newspaper directed people to seek refuge at the Nora Bayes Theatre as a perfectly safe place, because it never had a hit.

Jinxed

Some shows are plagued by bad luck. Lee Remick was in Anyone Can Whistle, *the early Stephen Sondheim musical.*

We were rehearsing and one of the actors died of a heart attack. Then two weeks into the show in Philadelphia, there was some reblocking in the musical number at the end of act one; the positions were changed, but the markers on the floor were not. Tucker Smith, a tall and wonderful dancer— he looked like Tommy Tune—was at the center of this number, and as he gracefully ran forward and went for his mark, he flew head over heels into the orchestra pit and landed in the middle of a gaggle of musicians. Instruments were flying, and unfortunately, one man was so seriously injured he did not come back. It was the end of the act; while we were watching in frozen horror this nightmare in the pit below, the audience was largely unaware. They of course love this sort of thing, because they feel they are in on something. The show seemed jinxed and never really recovered after that. It was tainted for the rest of the run.

Freaked Out

Jean Arthur was trying to make a comeback in the title role of a comedy called *The Freaking Out of Stephanie Blake* (1967), when on the third day of previews she got down on her knees in the middle of the play and told the audience that she could not go on, and that her doctor advised against performing. The producer, Cheryl Crawford (one of the three founders of the Group Theatre in the thirties), knew that the actress had become suddenly ill after the Boston opening of Garson Kanin's *Born Yesterday* (1946) and was replaced by Judy Holliday. Before signing her on for the part of Stephanie Blake, she received reassurances from Miss Arthur that her days of sudden illness were over. So now Miss Crawford insisted that the Hollywood star keep her word and respect her contract. Before resuming, Miss Arthur addressed the audience once more: "I am told that that I must go on, and I'm going to because I believe in the show . . . but if something happens . . ."

The show closed that evening, and Cheryl Crawford informed Jean Arthur that it was her fault that the entire investment of a quarter-million dollars would be lost.

Sequel

Dore Schary owned the distinction of being the only playwright to have been a top executive in Hollywood (at RKO and MGM). That is where he may have acquired the instinct for sequels: in 1977 he followed up his highly successful Broadway play about Franklin Delano Roosevelt, *Sunrise at Campobello* (1958), with a short-lived one-man show called simply *F.D.R.* Linda Winer in the *Chicago Tribune* wrote that "you can't have a fireside chat without somebody lighting a fire," and *Variety* likened the monologue, which was performed by Robert Vaughn, to "listening to only one end of a telephone conversation."

The First Cry

Before Actors' Equity, the union representing stage actors, changed the rules, a performer could be summarily fired, without cause, during the first two weeks of rehearsals. Actors counted the days to the deadline with dread, and one of the grim jokes most often repeated in the profession features a telegram delivered just before the deadline. The actor opens it and says with enormous relief: "Only my mother (or other relative) died."

At the beginning of her career, Eva Marie Saint got the dreaded notice, when she was rehearsing in the part of the nurse in *Mr. Roberts* (1948). Director Josh Logan tried to explain that she simply looked too young and offered her the chance to stay on as an understudy. To avoid bursting into tears in front of the famous director, Miss Saint fled to her dressing room to have a good cry. As she sat sobbing, there was a rap on her door.

"Eva Marie, can we come in?" asked Henry Fonda and peeked into the room. "Then, one by one," the actress recalled almost forty years later, "all the guys in the show—thirty of them—came in. They told me they all had had their own disappointments and this could be one of the best things that happened to me, that I was young and this was my first cry in the theatre . . ."

Curtain Call

John Springer was at the opening night of Mr. Roberts *on Broadway.*

It was one of those magical evenings in the theatre. All the stars had turned out, dressed to the teeth; that's how openings were like in those days. Afterwards, the audience just clapped and clapped. They took curtain after curtain. I remember Marlene Dietrich standing up on her seat, screaming and clapping. Finally, after I don't know how many curtain calls, Henry Fonda stood there, and said:

"That's all that Josh Logan wrote for us, but if you really want us to, we'll do it all over again . . ."

Trying Tryout

Before its long run off-Broadway, Jules Feiffer's *Little Murders* closed on Broadway after only seven performances. The play was doing so well that during intermission friends were congratulating the author on what they expected to be a big hit. Feiffer later said that he learned during the Boston tryout an important lesson: "If the audience was happy at the first act, if the actors started playing the jokes and didn't play the characters, we were finished. When they played the characters there was a kind of tension."

George S. Kaufman took a different kind of opinion poll. "In Boston the test of a play is simple," he once observed. "If the play is bad, the pigeons snarl at you as you walk across the common."

Fear of Contagion

One of George S. Kaufman's few flops was *Someone in the House*, an adaptation of a French farce by Jacques Deval. The play opened during the influenza epidemic of 1918, when people were afraid to go into crowded places for fear of catching the disease. The show was so poorly attended that Kaufman had suggested to producer George Tyler that he advertise it with the slogan:

"Avoid crowds—see *Someone in the House* at the Knickerbocker Theatre."

Word of Mouth

The writer of a play that George S. Kaufman did not like was trying to persuade him that it was nevertheless a hit:

"When the box office opened this morning, they were lined up around the corner."

"Good," replied Kaufman mercilessly, "now all you have to do is stop the word of mouth."

CHAPTER 17

Surprises

Burning Ice Cream

Toward the end of his long life, producer Daniel Frohman (1851–1940)
recalled memories of New York theatre during his youth.

On September 1871, Sheridan Shook and Albert M. Palmer established
their famous Union Square Theatre on East 14th Street. Palmer's leading
man was Charles R. Thorne. The leading lady was Rose Eytinge. Thorne
was one of the greatest actors of his time. He played with dramatic force
and without the usual ranting which was common among many stars at
that time. The reason that ranting was so common in those days was because the gallery was the most important part of the theatre. Unless the
actors made a great noise on the stage, the people in the galleries held back
their approval. They believed that an actor should speak loudly. Now that
we have no galleries the method of the actors is more reserved. Thorne
was the first actor of his time to know that great effects could be reached
without too much physical and emotional upheaval.

Rose Eytinge, who afterwards became a star in Shakespearean roles, was
a splendid actress. She was a black-eyed, black-haired Jewess. One day

when she came to rehearsal Thorne said to her, "Miss Eytinge, the way you look at me, one would think that you were going to eat me." She replied, "Have no fear, Mr. Thorne, my religion forbids me from doing that."

I mentioned this story once to Clara Morris, greatest emotional actress of her time. She said, "Some years ago when I was starred in *Camille* I had a leading man who was very sensitive and temperamental. He was a good actor but he thought that nobody in the company liked him. That was not true. We had no reason to dislike him. It so happened that I had a great liking for celery while he detested the sight of it. One night in New York, when I came on as Camille and he was playing Armand Duval and making love to me, through some error on the part of my maid, I was not wearing a camellia on my breast, so I went to the supper table and picked up a piece of celery. I held it toward him and made the flower speech. When he saw the celery he thought it was a deliberate insult. Turning, he left the stage in anger and the curtain had to be rung down. Unfortunately it was the same night that the comedian set fire to the ice cream."

The Heart of Darkness

In 1889 Otis Skinner joined the company of Madame Helena Modjeska, a Polish countess, one of the famous Camilles of her day. In his Footlights and Spotlights, *Skinner recalled one of those occasions when neither of those functioned.*

An opulent production of *Henry VIII* opened the season at the Garden Theatre, New York. Madame's Katherine was conceived and acted with fine sympathy, though the character was less adapted to her Polish accent and personality than other things in her repertory. I was cast for the part of Henry VIII, that of Wolsey going to John Lane, a veteran actor whose elocution was unimpeachable.

Our stage manager was Beaumont Smith. He was something left over from another period. Like the thespians of the palmy days, he always acted whether in the theatre or out of it. His order to the waiter for his morning bacon and eggs sounded like blank verse. He combined the duties of stage management with those of a responsible player and he was the Duke of Buckingham of our production.

Buckingham has a splendid emotional opportunity in the episode of the farewell to the populace on his way to the scaffold. He meets his doom with fortitude and leaves his blessing on his country, his friends and his king. The people kneel sobbing, Buckingham turns to his guard saying,

"Lead on, o' God's name! . . . I have done." He clasps his hands reverently before the crucifix, held by the monk before his eyes, and the lights dim out on the effective picture to which the audience reacts with sympathy.

On the opening night of *Henry VIII*, Beaumont had lived quite up to the possibilities of this scene; he had the house with him, but just before the dramatic finish as he turned to the uplifted crucifix, he scarcely had his hands raised in prayer when the electrician, mistaking his cue, turned out the lights.

Then out of the darkness came the oratorical Beaumont Smith's voice booming in wrath, and the ears of the startled audience were assaulted with: "Lead on, o' God's name! Who the hell turned out those lights? Lead on, I have done. You blankety-blank idiot! O' God's name, lead—I'll show you who is running the stage. Lead on! Lead on!"

A Friend in Need

Lawrence Barrett, one of the great actor-managers of the second half of the nineteenth century, once had to replace at the last minute a fairly important character. He turned to an old friend who needed the work. Everything proceeded smoothly until opening night, when stage fright attacked his already shaky memory. The old actor was playing a king who sat royally in the middle of the stage and was supposed to bellow orders at Barrett as he came on stage. Barrett entered and waited. The old king just stared at him helplessly. Finally, he summoned presence of mind enough to say, "Come here."

Barrett approached the throne.

"I can't remember a damn thing you told me," whispered the royal one miserably. There was nothing for Lawrence Barrett to do but bow, and take his exit. Just as he was striding into the wings, he heard a majestic voice rumble after him:

"Forget nothing that I have told you."

It served well and the audience noticed nothing wrong.

Sangfroid

Near the beginning of his career, John Drew (the Younger, 1853–1927) was acting a young fop in Sheridan when in the middle of holding dialogue with a soldier, his memory failed him. He looked towards the prompter, whose lips he saw moving, but could not make out.

"Louder, prompter, louder," he muttered, but he only heard a murmur in return.

At such crisis many an actor crumples, but John Drew, already displaying the mastery of future years, simply waved his hand to the soldier, saying "I will return anon," and he stalked off into the wings to read up on his part.

What Was the Question?

Forgetting one's lines, or drying, is sometimes called "the actor's nightmare." In fact, it is everybody's nightmare and almost everybody has a story about it. This one is Virginia Bloomgarden's.

I remember a devastating thing that happened on the opening night of Lillian Hellman's *The Searching Wind,* during our first tryout in Wilmington. A marvelous elderly actor, Arnold Korff, had this one important scene with Dennis King and in the middle of it he dried completely. One could see that Dennis got terribly frightened: at first he tried to do some things, but then Arnold simply put his head down on the desk, and we didn't know whether he was ill or what, but I heard Dennis yelling almost to the stage manager, "Ben, bring down the curtain, bring down the curtain!"—which they did.

Herman Shumlin, the producer, ran backstage and saw that Arnold was probably going to be all right but could not pull himself together fast enough to continue. So Herman said to Dennis King: "Would you go out and tell the audience what transpires in this scene and we'll pick it up from there." "Yes, yes," Dennis agreed, and he went out in front. But after a few moments he came back. "Herman," he said in a weak voice, "I can only remember the answers."

Shakespeare Anthology

Katharine Cornell was acting in Clemence Dane's biographical play Will Shakespeare (1923), *in which Otto Kruger played the title role. In a love scene, young Will tells his sweetheart Mary that she was inspiring him to write a play about "two lovers who lived in Verona." At this point the curtain was supposed to be lowered, but, as Cornell wrote in* I Wanted to Be an Actress, *the young man in charge of performing this task had his mind on other things.*

He had just seen his own Dark Lady going up the alley and had stepped out. "Two lovers who lived in Verona . . ." I turned to stone while Otto carried on, "It will be called *Romeo and Juliet* . . ." ". . . a rose by any other name," etc., etc., etc. But even the balcony scene cannot be made to last forever. Still no curtain . . . "Then I shall write a play called *Hamlet*," declaimed Otto, getting his second wind, "and I shall have my hero say . . . 'To be or not to be,'" etc., etc., etc. "Then I shall have him say, 'Oh that this too too solid flesh would melt,'" I was so frozen, before the curtain boy was found and dragged back to the stark realities of theatre romance, that I had to be carried off stage and broken into pieces. But I always thought Otto rather regretted he hadn't had time for Lear's curse and perhaps for a few of Othello's more resounding periods.

Temperament

In the same year as the short-lived production of Will Shakespeare, *Katharine Cornell was in a play called* The Enchanted Cottage, *which lasted also only eight weeks. A lot more went wrong, she recalled, than a late curtain in this one.*

It was during that production that I had my first attack of temperament in the theatre—I've only had two of them. And they were both utter failures. *The Enchanted Cottage* was badly stage-managed; something went wrong every day. That was the first play I had been in in which there wasn't a star and two or three other people of high stage authority. In this Noel Tearle and I played the leads, and everyone said to me, "Really, you must do something about the stage manager."

I couldn't, and I couldn't. But finally one night the curtain didn't come down, the music cues were off, the lights went wrong—blinking on and off like a lighthouse—in the dream scene.

So, after the performance, I worked myself into a rage, walked up to him and said, "What on earth happened to the lights tonight?"

"Oh, a *million* things, Miss Cornell," he answered gravely.

I crumpled like a pricked balloon. You *can't* cope with a million things. The mathematics of the thing simply had me licked. Temperament, I thought sadly as I walked out to my dressing-room, must be a lot of fun if you can bring it off.

Nightmare

The actor's nightmare is drying; a teacher's nightmare is standing in front of a class with flies undone. In the recent musical Baby, *Martin Vidnovic experienced the latter.*

I was playing one-half of the infertile couple with Catherine Cox in the scene when the doctor (John Jellison) had given us the diagnosis that I was "just shooting blanks"—a line which usually got a big laugh. But one night, I noticed that the laughing did not stop, and we couldn't continue with the lines. So I figured that something had gone wrong. Just before this scene I had one of those terribly rushed quick changes, and now this dreaded thought hit me. I looked down, and lo and behold, my huge brass zipper was wide open. The spotlight had hit it perfectly, throwing a reflection of light right off into the audience. I crossed my legs immediately and there was a tumultous explosion of laughter. I looked at my wife with an imploring expression of "help me!" and then I crossed my legs the other way, and this got another burst of laughter. Meanwhile, the doctor was trying to continue with "Listen, Nick, what I would like you to do . . ." But I said, just as if it had been written in the text: "Wait a minute, doctor, there's something I've got to do first." So I stood up, turned my back to the audience and ham that I am, as I pulled up the zipper, I became airborne for a second. Then I returned to my seat, there was another tumultuous applause, and we resumed the scene. The next day, *The Daily News* reviewed my ad-lib, calling it a major gaffe from which I managed to extricate myself, while amusing the audience.

When Ya Gotta Go

Jimmy Durante was starring in *Jumbo*, the 1936 extravaganza produced by Billy Rose at the Hippodrome. One night Tuffy, the elephant, forgot that he had been housebroken. Durante got the greatest laugh of the evening when he ad-libbed:

"Hey, Tuffy, no ad-libbing!"

The Show Did Go On

Jimmy Durante was a master of improvisation when it came to unruly animals. The high point of *The New Yorkers* (1931) was a burlesque of a well-known magazine advertisement promoting the virtues of wood by the National Lumber Manufacturers' Association. In the middle of a long and complex monologue about wood, a small, trained donkey was supposed to come between Durante's legs, hoist him up and take him off stage while still expounding on the properties of wood.

One night the donkey rebelled and threw the comedian off his back, and trotting down the stage steps, decided to explore the auditorium. Durante refused to be thrown. While still on the floor, he addressed the audience:

"Folks, dat animal is sore. De management didn't pay him dis week. Dat's why he's quittin'."

Then, catching his breath while the audience laughed, Durante addressed his recalcitrant partner standing in one of the aisles:

"Listen, kid, don't walk out on me now. I'll pay you myself if you come back. I'll make the bosses give yuh a raise. I'll feed yuh. I'll do anyt'ing you want—but please come back. De show must go on."

The King of Ad-Libs

Bobby Clark was constantly cracking up the rest of the cast of *The Would-be Gentleman* (1946), especially the footmen who were supposed to face the audience stony-faced like the guards in front of Buckingham Palace. One night the great comic playing M. Jourdain would show up without a wig, on another, he would allow his hat sink so low over his eyes that he couldn't see, until the footmen actually had to turn upstage to compose themselves.

Al Henderson remembers the dinner scene one night during which one of the footmen began to ladle out the soup. A large ball of dust descended from the flies on to the middle of Bobby Clark's plate. The comic had not sat down to table yet, but was talking to his daughter on the other side of the stage, so the footman was trying unobtrusively to blow the dust from the table. After a couple of attempts, he heard the audience laughing where there was usually no laugh line. Clark was watching him with a pained expression and then he threw out an ad-lib, perfectly timed: "Marcel, I thank you to let me blow on my own soup."

Later in the run but in the same scene, a young soldier in his army uniform suddenly wandered on stage, apparently looking for the men's room. The footmen put down the tureen and plates and politely ushered the man offstage. Bobby Clark watched them patiently, and as they returned, he ad-libbed: "Everybody else keeps coming to my house, so why not the U.S. Army?"

Hayride

It was no secret during the run of *Mexican Hayride* (1944) that two of its stars, George Givot and Luba Malina, were feuding. During one of their entrances to a scene with Bobby Clark, George would pat Luba on her shoulder and say the line, "You want Dagmar, take her." One night that Al Henderson recalls, he must have decided that this was too tame, and he gave her a resounding whack on the backside, which propelled the visibly aghast Luba halfway across the stage. Bobby Clark was surprised at this new twist, but only for a moment. As Luba whirled about in a rage with both fists flailing the air, Bobby turned to the audience with a gleeful grin and quipped: "I didn't know they were married." This brought the house down, but Bobby still had to deal with the tearful Luba, whom George abandoned on stage with her mascara running while he contrived a hasty exit.

Happy Accident

Angel Street (1941) was an English thriller transported to Broadway in which a husband (Vincent Price) tries to drive his wife (Judith Evelyn) insane. The play seemed doomed when two days after its opening the Japanese bombed Pearl Harbor, yet it went on to be the longest running foreign play in Broadway history, with almost 1300 performances. It was made into a movie called *Gaslight*, starring Ingrid Bergman and Charles Boyer.

Perhaps the only memorable directorial feat connected with the production came about by accident. At one point a sympathetic detective visiting the wife has to hide from the returning husband. During one of the final rehearsals at the John Golden Theatre, Leo G. Carroll, who played the detective, left his derby hat on a table. Seeing the absolute panic this caused in the rest of the cast, the stagehands and assistants—they were all whispering and screaming, "Oh, my God, the hat!"—director Shepard Traube decided to leave the mistake in, and have Carroll retrieve the hat surreptitiously later in the scene. The play worked wonderfully, because almost every night the audience burst into shouting, "The hat! the hat!" People would actually go and see the show just for that moment. The director was considered a bit of a genius for having arranged this piece of suspense.

Gold

Neil Simon claims that the biggest laugh he got in the theatre happened
by accident. In *The Odd Couple*, Oscar tells Felix not to leave little notes
for him like 'We're all out of cornflakes—F.U.' Then he adds the punchline, "It took me three hours to figure out the F.U. was Felix Unger."

Simon says that he was writing one day, thinking up new gags for Felix
to get on Oscar's nerves. Leaving notes was one possibility. After he composed the note, the playwright wondered how the priggish Felix would
sign it. "And it just came by accident, that Felix Unger's initials were F.U.
I discovered it like a piece of gold lying there. I never thought that it
would get *that* big a response."

Photo Finish

Fred Voelpel designed the costumes for The Milk Train Doesn't Stop
Here Anymore *by Tennessee Williams.*

The play had been done at the Spoleto Festival in the summer of 1962,
and in the winter it was brought into the Morosco by Roger Stevens and
Lyn Austin, with Herbert Machiz directing. Some of the original cast
came with the show: the wonderful Hermione Baddeley as Flora Goforth,
and also Mildred Dunnock. The design had been done by an Englishman,
but Jo Mielziner and I were to redo them for Broadway.

One of the problems of the play is that there is no solid thread running
through it; each moment exists on its own and needs to be set up. For
instance, one needs to set up the leading character as an unpredictable and
bizarre woman, who had been indulged all her life, and she traipses around
her beautiful seaside home in a Japanese kimono, making giggly comments
about herself—and then out of nowhere she pulls out this Japanese wig.
It is supposed to create a big sensation as a wonderful, bizarre moment. I
am sure it went over big in Spoleto, but now we had a high-paying Broadway audience, used to some pretty spectacular stunts.

Every production has some problem that just could not be solved, and
this wig became it. Because it had to sit on stage for the first thirty or
forty-five minutes, without the audience knowing what it was, it could not
be the size of a traditional Japanese wig, which is more like the front section of a float at the Rose Parade. There were innumerable fittings—the
wig was too big, or too soft, too small and so on—with the end result that
we had to leave New Haven without it. We only had three days of the tryout left before the set was up, and not having the wig ready just made the

normal tension just that much more tense. Jane Greenwood (who was working as draper for Ray Diffen making the costumes) and I kept phoning New York, asking "Where is the wig?" "We're working on it."

The curtain went up that night with no wig onstage. It had been sent after us by bus from New Haven. We drove to the station, got the box and took it to the theatre and there was this ratty little thing that looked like it came from Dolly's Whoopee Shop on 48th Street, with a bun on top. I crawled on my belly out on stage with Jane holding my legs. We were behind a terrace, inching towards the alcove where Hermione was supposed to reach for the wig. Right up to that minute I was elbowing my way towards her, cradling this horrendous wig around my chest like a rifle. I did get it there, and when she put it on, it looked like something the cat brought in. I couldn't see or hear whether the moment made the required sensation. All I know that sometimes the drama that goes on behind the scenery can be more exciting than what was planned onstage.

The Seasons

A performance has different meaning for the performers than to the audience, as Ralph Williams found out early in his career.

I had already been playing in *She Loves Me* (1963) for a couple of months when my friend José Quintero came to see it. I opened the show riding a bicycle, which was big and awkward, so that I'd look younger. Carol Haney choreographed every turn I was supposed to make: pedal five beats, then apply the brake, then swing around to the orchestra. That evening the brakes failed, and as I tried to stop the bike, it swung into a flat. The snow and the leaves came down—meanwhile the orchestra kept playing, so I had to keep singing merrily along. When I came offstage, the company was waiting in the wings. They all knew that José was out there and they tried to reassure me: "You handled it beautifully—nobody could tell." After the show José came back:

"Oh, Ralph, it was wonderful," and then he asked: "Tell me . . . Were you drunk at the beginning?"

The snow and the leaves have a little story of their own. Harold Prince, who directed the show, decided after New Haven that when I said, "Look, autumn!" the leaves would fall, and when I said, "Look, winter!" the snow would come down. "Oh, Hal . . ." I began to protest, and he said, "You're too tasteful, but if you say it, I'll bet you five dollars that on opening night it will get a hand."

Though I hated to, I had to say those lines and I did get an applause. And you know who had to start that applause—Mr. Cheapskate himself— because afterward, when Hal was not in the house, it never got a hand again.

Strange Imaginings

Actors are much given to, in the words of Prince Theseus, "in the night to imagining some fear," when "how easy is a bush suppos'd a bear." Ralph Williams remembers one such evening.

I was in T. S. Eliot's *The Cocktail Party* at APA (with Nancy Walker and Brian Bedford), playing Peter Quilp, a ghastly part in a bad play. One night I came to the bit when Quilp has just heard the news that his be- loved Celia, whom he has not seen for ten years, has been crucified. After reacting to this extraordinary piece of news with some line like, "Well, that knocks the bottom out of it, doesn't it?" I turned upstage, to show that I was deeply moved. I heard a big thump behind me. There was stunned silence, and then from the audience a glissando of "oohs" and "ahs." I had no idea what had happened, and I couldn't turn back. My mind was racing: "Did one of the actors faint—or drop dead?"

Finally I heard my cue, and turning I could see Brian Bedford coming towards me—and he had no arm! I had met Brian many years before when he first came from England and I thought we knew each other pretty well. Could he have hidden the fact that he had a wooden arm? And why would it fall off? I couldn't figure it out, and Brian was already stretching his arm in sympathy, and it did not feel wooden at all.

When I went offstage, the stage manager told me that a rat had fallen from the fly above. It was stunned for a moment and then ran up the aisle, causing the audience to make that noise. I'm still not sure about Brian Bedford's arm.

An Eye for Detail

David Brooks was in the original production of Brigadoon (1947).

At the beginning of the musical, the chorus was supposed to come across the stage in front of the scrim, which was then to be removed to reveal the set. Opening night in New Haven the scrim got stuck and did not fly. In- stead it swung into the set, knocking over various pieces. The poor chorus was thrown into complete disarray. In the middle of this cacophonous disaster, Agnes de Mille, who had choreographed the show and was sitting out front with the audience, suddenly pointed at one of the chorus girls and exclaimed: "Oh, my God, Lillian has forgotten her stockings!"

Bumps and Grins

Beverley Bozeman had trouble with her dress in the 1952 revival of the Rodgers and Hart musical Pal Joey, *which starred Vivienne Segal and Harold Lang.*

I played the comedienne Gladys Bumps, and I had a sequin dress that was slit up to the crotch, though the designer secured it with a tiny sequin strap that went from zitch to zatch around the back of your neck. The costumes get cleaned a lot, and over time the threads rot. On the road one evening (at the Greek Theatre in Los Angeles) I finished my song "Red Hot Mama," and was into a five-minute dance number, when out of the corner of my eye I see something shoot through the air like a meteor. I also feel something happening to my front, so instinctively I grab the top of my dress to protect my boobs. The little strap that had anchored the dress finally snapped and blooooowing through the air fell onstage. The audience caught this before my partner or I did. He asked me if something was wrong. "All I know," I said, "something's not here." The audience was laughing because they could see right away what kind of trouble I was in. And it was something wonderful, which I had not encountered before: they saw what was happening first, I reacted to it, and they knew that they would have to react to me reacting to every decision that would have to be made during this complicated dance number, which involved all kinds of arms and lifts.

I hugged my partner so tight that when he lifted me my dress fled into his face. Three thousand people who saw it coming, began to scream. My poor partner was saying, "Oh, God, what do we do next?" He wasn't a strong partner, so I had to help and lift myself at the shoulder. We knew that we wouldn't be able to fake that, because I would be bare-breasted facing the audience, which was already in hysterics. So I said, "Let's do arms." So it was arm—boob, left arm—right boob, all the way off. The audience was screaming and we took several curtain calls. The stage manager told me to go out by myself and get this over with. The only thing I could think of was to bow very carefully over the top of my dress. That seemed to work, and we went on with the show.

More Sequin

In the musical *Two by Two*, Madeline Kahn wore a tiny costume with little plastic sequin spangles, which Fred Voelpel had designed. She came on late one night during a technical rehearsal and apologized: "I'm sorry, but a sequin has entered my system."

Reach Out and Kill Someone

During a production of *Julius Caesar*, two of the conspirators, played by Joseph Mahar and John Tillinger, were about to murder Caesar, daggers at the ready, when the stage manager's phone rang just offstage. It was heard throughout the house. So was Joe Mahar's low Elizabethan growl to Tillinger:

"What shall we do if it is for Caesar?"

The tragedy of the moment was drowned in mirth.

CHAPTER 18

We Do It All for You

Local Color

Although the best drama is universal, it still exercises a special fascination when seen in the local context where it is set or where it was written. There is something about seeing Sophocles in the theatre of Dionysus in Athens, or Shakespeare at Stratford-upon-Avon. Joseph Jefferson, who spent a large part of his career playing Rip Van Winkle, describes what it was like to visit the locale for Washington Irving's famous story.

In the village of Catskill there is a Rip Van Winkle Club. The society did me the honor to invite me to act the character in their town. I accepted, and when I arrived was met by the president and other members of the club, among whom was young Nicholas Vedder, who claimed to be a lineal descendant of the original "old Nick." I was taking a cup of tea at the table in the hotel, when I was attracted to the colored waiter, who was giving a vivid and detailed account of the legend of the Catskill Mountains to one of the boarders who sat nearly opposite me.

"Yes, sah," said the waiter, "Rip went up into de mountains, slep' for twenty years, and when he come back here in dis bery town his own folks didn't know him."

"Why," said his listener, "you don't believe the story's true?"

"True? Ob course it is! Why," pointing at me, "dat's de man."

When I got to the theatre, I scarcely could get in, the crowd was so great about the door. In the scene in the last act, when Rip enquires of the innkeeper, "Is this the village of Falling Water?" I altered the text and substituted the correct name, "Is this the village of Catskill?"

The name of the village seemed to bring home the scene to every man, woman and child that was looking at it. From that time on the interest was at its full tension. I never had seen an audience so struck with the play.

There was a reception held at the club after the play, and the president was so nervous that he introduced me as Washington Irving.

Straight Shooter

In 1865, Joseph Jefferson was about to try out in London the character of Rip Van Winkle, with which he came to be identified for the next forty years. Dion Boucicault, who had adapted the Washington Irving story, believed that it would fail. After seeing Jefferson's performance, he said to the comedian:

"You are shooting over their heads."

"I am not even shooting at their heads," said Jefferson. "I am aiming at their hearts."

Target Practice

Washington Irving attended the Park Theatre, the only one in New York in 1802. He found the audience providing the bulk of the action.

I can't say but I was a little irritated at being saluted aside of my head with a rotten pippin; and was going to shake my cane at them, but was prevented by a decent looking man behind me, who informed me that it was useless to threaten or expostulate. They are only amusing themselves a little at our expense, said he; sit down quietly and bend your back to it. My kind neighbor was interrupted by a hard green apple that hit him between the shoulders—he made a wry face, but knowing it was all a joke, bore the blow like a philosopher. I soon saw the wisdom of this determination; a stray thunderbolt happened to light on the head of a little sharp-faced Frenchman who seemed to be an irritable little animal. Monsieur was terribly exasperated; he jumped upon his seat, shook his fist at the gallery, and swore violently in bad English. This was all nuts to his merry persecutors; their attention was wholly turned on him, and he formed their target for the rest of the evening.

Interaction

The actress Olive Logan, in her informative book Before the Footlights and Behind the Scenes (1870), *tells several stories about how attentive and involved American audiences were later in the century.*

On one occasion the play of *Oliver Twist* was given in Lowell, Mass. When the curtain fell, the audience retained their seats for several minutes, but at length the stage manager appeared before the curtain and said: "Ladies and gentlemen, I wish to inform you that the play has terminated. As all the principal characters are dead, it cannot, of course, go on." The hall was soon cleared.

A California rustic, who was not accustomed to villainous saltpetre and cold iron, as used on the stage, went one night to see *The Robbers*. When the shooting commenced, he threw himself, at two movements, under a bench, and kept his place till the smoke cleared away. Quiet restored, he crept softly up to his place, and sat till the stabbing scene in the last act. As Charles de Moor stabbed poor Amelia, our rustic patron of the drama was wrought up to an agony which worked his countenance into horrible shape. He uttered one unearthly shriek, and made a break for the door— over the heads of everybody in his way—knocking down a doorkeeper, and vanished, howling, into the night.

The play of the *Long Strike* was being enacted at a theatre in Harrisburg, Pa., and, during the court scene, while the audience were deeply interested, and the Judge asked the question, Guilty or not guilty? a well-dressed, intelligent-looking man left his seat in the audience and pushed through the crowd to the front of the stage, and very calmly called out, "Stop!" The manager of the theatre, who was personating the part of Money-penny, thinking the man intoxicated, came to the footlights, and the following dialogue ensued: "Will you oblige me by taking your seat, sir?" said the manager. The man replied, "I want to give my evidence in this case. It was not that man" (pointing to the actor who represented the character of Jem Starkie) "who killed him. I saw who did it, I saw the man shoot him from behind the hedge." At this point a roar of laughter from the audience brought this unbiased witness suddenly to his senses, and he took his seat in confusion.

Why Couldn't They Just Lie?

On one of his tours, Nat Goodwin was standing outside the theatre in a mid-sized town, when he observed a small boy with an anxious, forlorn look on his face and a puppy in his arms. Asked what was the matter, the boy told Goodwin that he wanted to sell the dog in order to raise the price of admission into the gallery. The actor suspected at once a dodge to secure a pass on what was known as the "sympathy racket," but he allowed himself to be taken in and gave the boy a pass.

The dog was deposited in a safe place, and the boy was able to watch Goodwin as the Gilded Fool from a good seat in the gallery. Next day Goodwin saw the boy again near the theatre, so he asked:

"Well, sonny, how did you like the show?"

"I'm glad, sir, I didn't sell my dog," said the ingrate.

Comedian Henry E. Dixey (1859–1943) was strolling about the lobby of a Chicago theatre during intermission and overheard a conversation between the doorman and two young men seeking admission. Only one of the youths had a ticket stub, but he claimed:

"You remember him, he's with me."

"I remember him all right," said the ticket-taker, "but how do I know that he hasn't given his stub to somebody else?"

To which the young man solemnly declared:

"Why, he's a stranger here, and hasn't an enemy in the city."

How to Change Someone's Mind

Most performers are extremely sensitive to criticism, but few actually are prepared to do something about it. Chauncey M. Depew, who among his many accomplishments, also ran a railroad, recalled a story about Richard Mansfield that he had heard from a black porter in the Wagner Palace Car service.

He was acting as porter on Mansfield's car, when he was making a tour of the country. This porter was an exceedingly intelligent man. He appreciated Mansfield's achievements and played up to his humor in using him as a foil while always acting. When they were in a station William never left the car, but remained on guard for the protection of its valuable contents.

After a play at Kansas City Mansfield came into the car very late and said: "William, where is my manager?"

"Gone to bed, sir, and so have the other members of the company," answered William.

Then in his most impressive way Mansfield said: "William, they fear me. By the way, were you down at the depot to-night when the audience from the suburbs were returning to take their trains home?"

"Yes, sir," answered William, though he had not been out of the car.

"Did you hear any remarks made about my play?"

"Yes, sir."

"Can you give me an instance?"

"Certainly," replied William; "one gentleman remarked that he had been to the theatre all his life, but that your acting to-night was the most rotten thing he had ever heard or seen."

"William," shouted Mansfield, "get my Winchester and find that man."

So Mansfield and William went out among the crowds, and when William saw a big, aggressive-looking fellow whom he thought would stand up and fight, he said: "There he is."

Mansfield immediately walked up to the man, covered him with his rifle, and shouted: "Hold up your hands, you wretch, and take back immediately the insulting remark you made about my play and acting and apologize."

The man said: "Why, Mr. Mansfield, somebody has been lying to you about me. Your performance to-night was the best thing I ever saw in my life."

"Thank you," said Mansfield, shouldering his rifle, and added in the most tragic tone: "William, lead the way back to the car."

Count Me Out

When Arthur Hopkins was producing Tolstoy's *Redemption* with John Barrymore in the lead, he cast Alexander Moissi, the greatest German actor of his generation, in the important role of Fedya. Hopkins was pleased with the way the production was going, so just before opening in New York he invited Count Nikolai Tolstoy to the Plymouth Theatre as a tribute to his father and as a treat for the cast. It was a command performance, with only the Count in the audience. The director felt that Barrymore had never been better, and that Moissi did his superb if untraditional rendition of Fedya. After the curtain, Hopkins went over expectantly to hear what his guest had to say.

Count Tolstoy fixed a cold stare at him, and asked in an outraged tone: "Where is Fedya's beard?"

Encore, Barrymore

John Barrymore did not suffer unruly audiences passively. In the same production of *Redemption*, the actor was irritated by bronchial attacks from several quarters of the auditorium. During intermission, he despatched someone to buy a fairly large sea bass which he concealed under his coat when he went back for the second act. As soon as he heard a burst of coughing, he whipped out the fish and flung it at the audience in front. "There!" he yelled. "Busy yourselves with that, you damned walruses, while we proceed with the play!"

Once when he was playing Richard III, Barrymore's call for "A horse, a horse! My kingdom for a horse!" was greeted by a guffaw from the gallery. Barrymore painfully hobbled forward and pointed his sword in that general direction, while improvising a new line in Shakespeare's spirit, if not his text:

"Make haste and saddle yonder braying ass!"

Sometimes the Great Profile did not need provocation by the audience to improvise some text. Once he was playing an American newspaperman opposite Florence Reed as a Russian prostitute, who was forced to wear a yellow badge of shame. Hence the title of the piece, *The Yellow Ticket* (1914), which gave Barrymore the idea of bringing a long strip of yellow IRT subway tickets, and offering these to Miss Reed after a poignant and tearful monologue about her dreadful life.

"Here, my dear," he told her impulsively, "maybe business will pick up if you get around more, and in something faster than a droshky!"

Florence Reed was so thrown that she forgot her lines and signaled for the curtain to be brought down. Al Woods, the producer, came on stage to explain that Mr. Barrymore had succumbed to a sudden attack of gallstones. The next day, the producer received a small package with a pair of topaz cuff-links, and a note: "My gallstones, and thanks. Jack."

Hot Around the Collar

Billy Rose liked to tell the story of his fellow showman Henry Miller when he was on the road playing in *The Great Divide* (1906). The play had been panned originally during its tryout in Pittsburgh. Returning there, after a couple of successful seasons in New York, the play did well with both critics and audiences, but Miller was still sore at the city. So, when in the middle of his love scene with Margaret Anglin he heard some of the customers scurrying towards the exit, he stopped and came to the front of the stage.

"Get back to your seats," he yelled at them. "You had already insulted me once, the last time I played this oversized smudge pot, and I won't let you do it again!"

Some of the people did as they were told and returned to their seats, but a few moments later others rose and tried to leave. Henry Miller began screaming "Knaves and varlets!" when Margaret Anglin grabbed his sleeve:

"Stop acting like a jackass, Henry," she said. "The theatre is on fire."

What You See Is Not Always What You Get

Towards the end of 1934, a woman went up to the box office at the Henry Miller Theatre, interested in buying tickets for *Personal Appearance*, which was running there at the time. Being a conscientious consumer, she wanted to see and test the actual seats she and her companion would be occupying. It so happened that Ina Claire and Walter Slezak were on stage, rehearsing another play, *Ode to Liberty*. In a leisurely fashion, the potential customer made her inspection, and then reported her findings back at the box office: "The seats are all right," she said, "but the show is terrible."

Unkindest Cut

A story told by David Belasco concerns a handsome dramatist who had just lived through the first night of his play, which had failed miserably. As he sat dejected in the front row listening to the boos and hisses, a woman behind him leaned forward and tapped him on the shoulder.

"Excuse me, sir," she said, "but knowing you to be the author of this play, I took the liberty at the beginning of this performance of snipping off a lock of your hair. Allow me now to return it to you!"

Reproach

At the height of their success as playwrights, Howard Lindsay and Russel Crouse went into producing plays. Their first hit was with Joseph Kesselring's *Arsenic and Old Lace*. After changing the title from *Bodies in Our Cellar*, the playwright-producers also turned it from a serious thriller into a rollicking comedy. But they took all their duties seriously, and they never allowed the show to get stale. They frequently visited even road productions, using their finely tuned ears to fix spots where, because of an actor's carelessness or through a shift of emphasis, the laughs no longer worked.

During one such excursion to Pittsburgh, Russel Crouse was furiously scribbling notes at the back of the house. As the lights came up for intermission, a woman in the audience accosted him:

"What's the matter with you?" she said angrily. "You haven't laughed once tonight. You're one of the reasons Pittsburgh doesn't get more good productions."

Decline and Fall

Molly Picon, the great Yiddish actress, was starring in a musical comedy and packing them in on Second Avenue. Two ladies came to the box office but were turned away. "We came in all the way from Long Island," complained one lady. "I'm sorry," said the man at the box office, "but there's not a single seat left." "It's things like this," said the other woman, "that's killing the Jewish theatre."

Comic Relief

On numerous tours from the thirties to the fifties, Edward Everett Horton played Henry Dewlip in *Springtime for Henry* more than three thousand times. He thought he knew every trick in milking every laugh. During a benefit at the Brattle Theatre in Cambridge, none of his tricks seemed to be working, and the comedy was received by the descendants of the Pilgrims in hushed quiet. But after the show, a woman came backstage to congratulate him:

"You were so funny, Mr. Horton," she said with some embarrassment, "that we had difficulty to keep from laughing."

Even Cowboys Get the Blues

When he was headlining with the *Follies*, Will Rogers had problems with the topical jokes in his monologue on opening night. The average first-night audience on Broadway was not interested in current events, and as he tried out his gags on them, many of them fell flat. "They know about boots and shoes and automobiles," Rogers once remarked, "but they don't read the newspapers. Next season I won't appear on the first night. I'll open on the second night."

Plot Point

Revealing that Martha's child was imaginary and part of a game is central to the plot of *Who's Afraid of Virginia Woolf?*. Most of the reviews could not avoid spilling this "secret," so carefully developed throughout the play. Uta Hagen, however, remembers that Saul Bellow laid to rest any concern that foreknowledge would ruin the audience's enjoyment. The novelist was sitting behind a somewhat drunk couple who grew quiet as the performance progressed. At the end Bellow overheard one ask the other: "Whose kid was it?"

Intensity

Judith Anderson gave in Robinson's Jeffers's version of *Medea* (1947) one of the legendary performances of an era. But her intensity was controversial. Brooks Atkinson wrote that everyone realized that she had been destined for that role from the start. John Hemmerley, who picked an off-night, described her performance as "utter hysteria from her first word on. She made me feel that maybe Jason had been right to set up housekeeping elsewhere." Tom Ewell was in the production and remembers some extraordinary reactions from the audience. Arturo Toscanini was so much absorbed that he almost fell out of his box, while Thomas Mann crawled across the footlights and kissed Judith Anderson's gown when she took her bow.

Enemies

Following the suspicious death of her husband, tobacco-heir Smith Reynolds, singer Libby Holman tried to go back to the stage. She was often interrupted with hisses, boos and missiles, and audiences shouting "whore" and "murderess" at her. After a while, instead of asking the stage manager the usual question whether the house is full, Libby Holman would enquire: "How many enemies do I have out there tonight?"

It Hurts

Booing has gone out of fashion in our theatre which caters mainly to foreigners and middle-class audiences. It is so rare that it becomes noteworthy when it does happen, as it did in the case of "the Man Who Booed" during a performance of the famous *Hamlet* production at the Lunt-Fontanne Theatre, directed by John Gielgud and starring Richard Burton, Alfred Drake, Hume Cronyn, and a host of others. The late William Redfield, one of two members in the cast to write books about the production, recorded no fewer than six boos on May 6, 1964, interspersed between quiet soliloquies and Burton's curtain call, who stepped forward and said: "We have been playing this production in public for over eighty performances. Some have liked it, some have not. But I can assure you—we have never before been booed." This brought forth the booer's final boo.

The production coincided with the early days of Burton's first marriage with Elizabeth Taylor. Returning after the show to the Regency Hotel, where the Burtons occupied an entire floor, the wounded actor told his wife that he had been booed. Not having been a stage actor up to that point, Elizabeth Taylor did not see immediately what the fuss was about and continued to watch television. When, according to William Redfield's account, Burton failed to make his wife see the enormity of what had happened, he kicked in the television screen, shattering the picture tube and his foot with it. The next night he limped into the theatre, his foot stitched and bandaged, and unfolded his darker purpose to the players: "Some critics have said that I play Hamlet like Richard the Third anyway, so what the hell is the difference?"

Understudy

In a musical called *Minnie's Boys* Shelley Winters was starring as the mother of the Marx Brothers. The show was not doing much business and the previews had been largely papered, a theatrical term for giving away free tickets in order to get an audience. One night Winters was running a high fever and her understudy was prepared to go on. But the star insisted on doing the performance even against doctor's orders. The disappointed understudy commented: "I guess Miss Shelley is afraid that they'd have to give all that paper back."

Paper

The theatre has two needs which never change. One is to get a paying audience. And if it cannot be done, to get an audience at any price. Papering the house is an old solution to an old problem, as is apparent from this anonymous plaint published in 1909, when non-paying audience members were known as deadheads.

It is estimated on inside authority that in the thirty-odd "first-class" theatres in New York there might be counted at least six thousand deadheads on any Monday night this season, Monday night being the evening when paid attendance is always lightest. The various devices used by managers to secure deadhead audiences when they cannot induce the paying kind to come make an interesting phase of theatrical life.

A year ago I sat through Nazimova's performance of *The Master Builder*, and behind me sat two girls who chewed gum devotedly and endeavored to find out what the play was all about. From their conversation I gathered that they were parcel wrappers in a Herald Square department store. After the second act one of them remarked to the other in an injured tone: "And Mr. Hawkswell said this show was a comedy!" "A bug-house funeral, I call it," was the reply.

This autumn two girls of similar stripe sat behind a friend of mine in the orchestra of a leading Broadway theatre. But the play was not Ibsen. It was native, domestic melodrama, with a villain perfectly recognizable by his pearl-grey derby and his cigarette. As he made his exit at the end of the first act, laughing a prophetic and horrid laugh, one of the girls exclaimed with deep feeling: "Gosh! ain't it orful, this revenge!" And I have heard a girl of the same type inquire at a performance of *A Midsummer Night's Dream*, when Queen Titania and her train entered: "Are them things angels?"

It was at *Hamlet* that the pompadour beside me exclaimed, as the Prince plunged his sword through the arras: "He's killed old foxy Grandpa!"

To the initiated the presence of such girls in a Broadway theatre apparently crowded to the door indicates paper, it indicates that the theatre is being filled by artificial means, by the distribution of free seats in the big department stores.

The Emperor's New Clothes

Every theatregoer has had the experience of watching something incomprehensible or terrible on stage, and feeling obliged to like it, for fear of being exposed as a Philistine. The great Ben Hecht, in the days he still lived The Front Page, was in charge of the Chicago Literary Times, when the Moscow Art Theatre was visiting town in the 1920s. He recalled one of his proudest stunts in A Child of the Century.

I went to the Auditorium Theatre and sat through a performance of *The Brothers Karamazov* by Stanislavsky's actors. The theatre was packed. Along with three thousands others, I stared at the stage and watched a dozen men and women sit in chairs for three hours and talk in Russian. There was almost no walking or any other form of movement. A duller three hours could not be imagined, or more meaningless ones.

Yet at the end of the performance a fashionable first-night audience, 98 percent of them Americans, stood up and cheered, as loudly and rapturously as our twelve hundred Boy Scouts had cheered the incomprehensible Minister Sze.

Irritated by this exhibition of mass snobbery, I asked my friend Rose Caylor to write the review of this performance in Russian. Many of the art lovers who had cheered the Muscovites would be sure to be readers of my *Times*. I thought it would be a good joke to offer them a criticism as unintelligible to them as the play they pretended to adore.

Rose Caylor wrote a thousand-word essay in Russian. I had it set up in a Russian print shop. An accident happened as Renshaw, my printer, was sliding the pan of Russian type into the front-page form. Mr. Renshaw, in the grip of a hang-over, allowed the column of Russian type to slide out of the pan to the floor. We were going to press and there was no time to rush a linguist over from Chicago's West Side. We stuck the scattered type lines back into the pan. The lines were scrambled and the review would make no sense. But I was determined to print it anyway. I argued with Mr. Renshaw that if the audience could cheer Dostoevski played in Russian, they could "read" a pied review as well as an unpied one in a language foreign to them.

If the point of my joke was to expose the audience to themselves as fakes, I failed. Miss Caylor's Russian review appeared on our front page. It received more congratulatory letters from our readers than any other feature in the issue. Not one of the scores of reader communiqués mentioned the fact that the review was scrambled beyond all intelligibility.

Fantasy

George S. Kaufman hated latecomers. He once described his fantasy for his farewell night in the theatre: "I would produce Noah's Ark in modern dress. The curtain will not rise until the last straggler is in his seat. Then Noah will appear and announce: 'Now it's going to rain for forty days.'" At this point the ceiling in the theatre will open and drench the entire audience. If they try to escape, I will be standing by the exit with a hose to catch them."

He Knew What He Liked

Sir Cedric Hardwicke recalled in his entertaining memoirs that he had the most intense conversations about the theatre with New York cabbies. One time, he asked what one of them thought of John Gielgud's Hamlet which was then the talk of the town.

"I don't care for the name," said the cabbie.

"You mean Gielgud?" asked Hardwicke.

"No, Hamlet."

The Holy Theatre

Ruth Gordon, in one of her books, tells the story of Diana Wynyard arriving at the stage door of the Globe by taxi. She saw a line around the block to the box office, and said to the people nearest her:

"Oh you must be so cold."

"Oh we don't mind."

"But it's freezing."

"Oh, we don't mind."

"I suppose," the actress smiled charmingly, "you love the theatre."

"Oh, Miss Wynyard," said a woman with a troubled look, "we *dread* it."

Award

In 1964 Bert Lahr received the Tony Award for his role in *Foxy*. His son John tells the story in *Notes on a Cowardly Lion*, that when the great clown left the ceremonies, a wino emerged from an alley. As he came closer, Lahr shrank. The deadbeat stretched out his hand and held out a dollar.

"Here, Bert," he said. "And thanks."

CHAPTER 19

Forced to Tour

I Love New York

In the early 1880s, comedian Nat Goodwin was having to face one of his perennial tours, and he gave birth to the remark:

"When you leave New York you're camping out."

The playwright Howard Lindsay remarked that "the sole purpose of going out of town is to see if your tag lines play."

And George M. Cohan once observed: "If you're out of New York, you might as well be in Bridgeport."

Motion Sickness

Jimmy Durante hated travel by sea, so he refused all offers to tour in England. His manager Lou Clayton went ahead and secretly booked passage on the *Normandie*, packed his luggage and got it on board. There was still the problem of getting the Schnozzola to follow. On the day of sailing, Clayton mentioned that Ray Goetz, a Broadway producer, was aboard the

Normandie and had expressed the fond wish that Jimmy Durante would sing a few send-off songs before departure. The plan was that the performer would get carried away at the piano and not notice that the ship had left New York harbor. Things went well, until Jimmy Durante looked up from the keyboard and noticed the Manhattan skyline in motion.

"Lou, the ship's leaving," he cried.

"Don't worry, Jimmy," Clayton replied, "we'll get off at 125th Street."

Eldorado

In the more developed parts of America, the coming of the railroad made touring more comfortable and reliable. But the vagabond troupers continued to venture into wild and remote places, such as the gold country of California. Walter Leman recalls in his memoirs one tour with the legendary manager McKean Buchanan, who forced his actors to play poker for the wages they had already earned with their playing.

McKean Buchanan had organized a small company of what his bills called the "finest artists on the Pacific Coast," and we started from Sacramento for Folsom on the 13th day of May, 1856, to enlighten the central mining regions of the state with illustrations of the drama, as it had never been seen before and, as the bills declared, "would never be seen again." Mr. H. D. Palmer—the Harry Palmer of *Black Crook* fame, who subsequently in partnership with Henry C. Jarrett made a fortune by that spectacle— was Mr. Buchanan's advance agent, or rather avant courier, combining the position of agent with bill-sticker, and went ahead with a light and buggy and paste-pot to "bill" the camps. We had a four-horse team and carriage with capacity for ten passengers, were out six weeks, and played in some forty different towns and mining camps, traveling about seven hundred miles.

Among the euphonious names of the places in which "the drama as it had never been seen before" was exhibited, I recall the following: Tod's Valley, Yankee Jim's, Chips' Flat, Cherokee Flat, Smith's Flat, Woolsey's Flat, Rough and Ready, Rattlesnake, Mud Springs, Indian Diggings, Red Dog, Hangtown, Drytown and Fiddletown. In going from Smith's Flat to Woolsey's Flat, we had to climb the divide between two forks of the American River (I think it was), and the road being very precipitous, a team and span of mules were sent out ahead with the baggage; when they went off down the mountain in a "go as you please" style, scattering the baggage and wardrobe on the greasewood and manzanita bushes from the top to the bottom, a mile and a half of distance, with perfect impartiality;

Miss Vaux's skirts were dangling from one bush, Jimmy Griffith's russet
boots and doublet in one place, my scarfs and other articles of stage attire
in another, while Buck's trunk, being the largest and heaviest, had burst
and scattered all his regal finery in the dust of the road, from the top of
the hill to the bottom.

Any other man than Buchanan would have abandoned the idea of playing that night, for it was dark before we reached the hotel; but he was a
man that never lost a night, "rain or shine," and he sent men back on the
road to gather up what they could, got the curtain up—the curtain in that
particular "temple of the drama," I remember, was composed of four blue
blankets basted together—made a speech to the audience, which was a
good one, and all the better for the mishap which had befallen us, and
after the performance won enough at poker to repair damages.

The old hall in Placerville—better known as "Hangtown" by the early
Californians—had a supporting joist sustaining the roof, just in the front
center of the stage. When the room had been altered for theatrical uses, I
presume it had been found impossible to remove this square pillar without
endangering the safety of the roof. It was a very awkward obstruction for
the players, for we had to act round it, and it was a great eyesore to the
audience. With rare genius, Buchanan on one occasion utilized that ugly
pillar, in the last scene of *The Merchant of Venice*, when as Shylock he
exclaimed:

> Nay, take my life and all.
> You take my house, when you do take the *prop*
> That doth sustain my house.

He rushed to the center, and grabbing the ugly post, delivered the lines
with an energy all his own.

High Noon

The perils of touring in nineteenth-century America included malice with
aforethought by dissatisfied customers. There were places in the wild West
and in Texas, where some citizens claimed free passage to see a show, and
willingly drew their guns if a manager tried to resist their argument. Danger lurked also in the streets, as in the famous incident preserved in the
Barrymore family tradition.

Frederick Warde and Maurice Barrymore had bought the touring rights
for Sardou's play *Diplomacy*, and in 1880 their company, which included
John Drew, hit the road. The morning after their one and only performance in the Texan town of Marshall, some of the actors were having

breakfast at the station cafe and bar across from the Station Hotel where they had stayed. There a local desperado by the name of Jim Curry, who was already drunk, began to insult the visiting troupers in "extraordinary vile" language. Barrymore, a refined British gentleman by birth, asked Curry to stop. The drunk was eager to pick a fight:

"I can do anything I want to do with you," he glowered.

"Sure, with a gun," said the actor.

"I don't have a gun," lied the bad man.

Barrymore had started his career as a pugilist and he was getting into position to put his fists up, when Curry drew his gun and shot him in the shoulder. Ben Porter, another one of the actors, rushed to his aid, at which point Curry shot him dead. Finally, the sheriff came and arrested Curry, who actually turned out to be the deputy sheriff; after all, the town was small and the law was short-handed. There was a trial, and a jury of good ole boys acquitted Curry. They were, according to legend, literally his peers, because eleven of the twelve had themselves been cleared of similar murder charges.

Barrymore, whose eloquent testimony against Curry was not to the latter's liking, was strongly urged by his few well-wishers to leave town at once. There are several version of what happened next, but the story that circulated around the Lambs for years afterwards had Barrymore waiting at the tiny railroad station, when Curry caught up with him. The killer slouched up to the actor, and after a pregnant pause, smiled nastily:

"So, you are Mr. Barrymore?"

"I guess you know it," replied the player.

"Mis-ter Barrymore, eh?" Curry chewed upon the euphonious name. "Well, Mr. Barrymore—" and at that point he drew a rather large handgun. But before the actor could jump him, the murderer said:

"I thought you'd like to have the gun that killed your friend."

And leaving the weapon on the bench, he was gone.

Theatre Is Where You Make It

During the time that David Belasco was fighting the syndicate and couldn't find any theatres to book outside New York, he had to find alternative spaces. Blanche Bates, one of the Belasco stars, in later life recalled the following.

[We played] a fragile comedy under a tin roof in a convention hall in Chattanooga, shouting above the roar of a storm. We played in Memphis in a skating rink where they had forgotten to take the ice out; and in Paris,

Tennessee, over a grocer's shop. Ample southern mothers parked their babies with Tunis Dean, the Beau Brummel of company managers of that day. We played *The Darling of the Gods* in Tacoma in the dead of winter with no heat and no seats. We rented all we could from undertaking parlors, and then telephoned all the prominent citizens in town to bring chairs along with them. The people in the gallery stood. A good many queer things happened on stage, too, but nobody got pneumonia, and everybody had a good time.

The Mother of Necessity

Touring schedules were worked out months in advance and then promoted in each locality. Dependence on various means of transport to make it from one town to another, often separated by vast distances, required always faith, and sometimes extraordinary ingenuity. Owen Davis (1874–1956), who later became one of the most prolific playwrights in the annals of American theatre, began as a stage-manager for the impresario A. M. Palmer. To justify his salary, Davis usually played also four or five of the walk-on parts. He remembered one time managing a tour for Palmer starring the Czech actress Fanny Janauschek, who—so her legend went—had been one of the Kaiser's mistresses and had made off with some of the German crown jewels, which she had brought to America. She was supposed to play *The Great Diamond Robbery* in the nation's capital, but she missed her train and wired that she would be unable to give the first performance. The whole of Washington and all the critics had turned out to see the great actress, unaware that Owen Davis was tearing his hair out.

Finally, he hit upon an idea. There was a character actor in the company, Gus Frankel, who could mimic just about anyone. Madame Janauschek had a rather squat body, which did not become more feminine with the years. Gus Frankel, who was an artist with makeup, played her part to such perfection that nobody was wiser for it. Next day, the critics were particularly enthusiastic about the great actress's unique talent.

A Royal Tiff

Given the pressures of theatrical production, the strains of touring, and the volatile egotism of artistic temperament, frequent clashes are inevitable. The following is from the anonymous Diary of a Daly Debutante *about a tempest in a teapot in Augustin Daly's company touring a piece called* Royal Middy *a hundred years ago.*

On the train between Providence and Hartford, Wednesday, June 16.—A rather unpleasant incident occurred Monday night in the green-room; we came near having a free fight there. It was all on account of the music. During the week of the one-night stands Mr. Perry played the piano to accompany Mr. Mollenhauer and his son, until we got to Boston; and when we left that city Mr. Mollenhauer expected him to go on accompanying him in Providence and in other cities where we cannot have a full orchestra. But on Monday night Mr. Perry appeared in his courtier dress and went on the stage, instead of going into the orchestra seats, explaining that he had asked for an increase in salary for musical services and hadn't got it; consequently he was going to do only what he was engaged to do—that is, sing.

This put poor Mr. Mollenhauer in a terrible predicament, and the music sounded exceedingly thin with only two violins. Between the second and third acts he came up into the green-room and said to Mr. Perry, his big black eyes glowing like coals: "I have often thought it, Mr. Perry, and now I tell it to your face, before these ladies, that you are no gentleman, sir!" Then he shoved up his sleeves, saying, "Now, if you want to answer that, come on—I'm ready!" And he pranced up to the young man, and made brandishing motions with his clenched fists. Poor Perry looked frightened, but he was angry, too, and was about to say or do something when Mr. Brand interfered, speaking in a low, decided voice. Next old Papa Moore came trotting in and began to argue and plead with the two angry men, and the ladies all left the room. Somehow or other the fight was prevented, but Mr. Williams was indignant, and reported Mr. Perry's action to Mr. Daly, who telegraphed back to discharge the rebellious pianist and send for the first violin, who joined a summer orchestra in Long Branch when he left us in Brooklyn.

This was done, but the doughty first violin telegraphed a spicy reply to the effect that he had a good engagement, and didn't propose to leave it for any *Royal Middy*, Augustin Daly, or anything else! Then they *were* in a mess. Perry said he would go on playing if, when Mr. Daly joins us in Albany, his salary were raised. Mr. Williams promised to see to it, so Perry played last night, and all trouble is patched up for the present. Our audiences there were large and appreciative.

Peep Show

The same young actress in Augustin Daly's company mentions one of the indignities that resulted from makeshift facilities on tour.

Plankinton Hotel, Milwaukee, Wisconsin, Saturday Morning, July 3.—We had a pleasant journey to Grand Rapids, a beautifully situated town, with a good hotel and a bad theatre. The weather was very warm, and after supper we went up on the roof of the hotel and admired the fine view.

Something horrid happened at that theatre. I noticed in the daytime that the dressing-room where two other girls and I were to be had a single uncurtained window looking out on the low roofs of what appeared to be old-fashioned country horse-sheds, and no other buildings were anywhere near. At night, as it was terribly warm with the gas lighted, we just left the window as it was and proceeded to undress. While we were talking and laughing I thought I heard a strange murmuring sound and occasional laughs, but supposed the noise must be in some other dressing-room. Presently, however, I heard something that startled me. I went to the window and looked out, and those sheds were covered with men, gazing with all their eyes right up into our dressing-rooms! I screamed, and then the girls screamed; the horrid brutes on the roofs laughed and scrambled down, making off in a great hurry, for I suppose they knew we should report them and that someone would go out to investigate. Nice sort of men they have in Grand Rapids, I must say!

In my trunk I carry a shawl which dear, thoughtful mamma said I might need to throw over my shoulders—in midsummer!—so I fished it out and we pinned it over the window.

Cherchez la Femme

Actor Arnold Daly (1875–1927) was having trouble with his leading lady in a road show in Chicago, and he wired producer Charles Dillingham to send a replacement. She arrived, but Daly found her even less satisfactory, so he sent another cable:

WHY DID YOU SEND ME THIS TERRIBLE WOMAN?

The producer sent back the reply:

SHE HAD NEVER SEEN THE STOCKYARDS.

Noblesse Oblige

During a tour, Beatrice Lillie was playing Chicago long enough to have dresses made. She was trying on some of her new acquisitions when Mrs. Swift from Chicago's wealthy meat-packing family arrived for her appointment with the modiste. Unaccustomed to being kept waiting, she sent an assistant to "tell that actress that she was delaying Mrs. Swift." The actress, who in private life was married to Lord Peel of the British aristocracy, came out of the dressing room in her own good time. As she was leaving the premises, she said loud enough to be overheard: "And tell the butcher's wife that Lady Peel has finished now."

And speaking of butchers, on another occasion when Bea Lillie was shopping at a New York meat shop, a woman jumped ahead of her in the line and ordered fifty cents' worth of cat meat.

"I'm in an awful hurry," she then explained to the other patrons, "I hope you don't mind."

"Not at all," said Lady Peel, "if you're that hungry."

The Twenty-four-Hour Man

Richard Maney had his fire of baptism as a press agent on a national vaudeville tour headed by Anna Held, the Parisian music-hall singer, whom Florenz Ziegfeld married in 1895 and divorced in 1912 in a much publicized trial. It was to cash in on this notoriety that John Cort, who owned a number of theatres, decided to send the fading beauty out on the road. Maney, fresh out of college (his education itself was a rarity), had the job of being the so-called twenty-four-hour man. He was the last of three press agents who preceded the tour, and he traveled with them to tidy up any loose ends and solve last-minute crises involving publicity. He gives a vivid picture of touring in Fanfare, *his autobiography.*

That fifteen-week tour was a rich experience. When it ended I was a wiser young man. Through observations of performers at work and at play, I learned things listed in none of the almanacs. Their tribal customs, sexual practices and conduct under fire marked them as people apart. Travel doubled my knowledge of geography. We ranged as far north as Duluth, as far south as San Antonio. We played San Diego, near the Mexican border, and Vancouver, British Columbia. We played a matinee in Rome, Georgia, that night in Anniston, Alabama. In a day we confused Carolinians in Goldsboro and Wilmington. Together at the theatre and on the train at night, the players reinforced the adage "familiarity breeds contempt." Feuds were dime a dozen. Intramural romances flared up like brush fires in the Poconos. Most popular member of the company was the stagehand who iced the beer. The chorus men leaned to the epicene. Petulant and peevish, these types held midnight rituals "in drag." Garbed in women's clothes they'd invoke dark curses on fancied enemies. The company's musical headliner was a narcotics addict. When his snow ran low he'd forge a prescription.

Our train was made up of two standard Pullman cars, a drawing-room car, Miss Held's private car, a day coach and two baggage cars. We had the same porters and the same train crew throughout the safari. The day coach was for the bicycle act. Refusing to pay Pullman fares, the Charles Ahern pedalers sat up all night. Civil war raged between the sleepers and the drinkers. All had two problems in common—bathing and laundry. Some of us were a touch gamy detraining in New York. The pilgrimage lost $30,000. The company's last jump was from Youngstown, Ohio, to New York. Sometime during the night parties unknown invaded the drawing room of the orchestra leader. While he dreamed of Brahms and Beethoven, they sheared off the exposed half of his beard. His screams in the morning were tonic to the ears of performers whose tempos he had fouled up throughout the tour.

Bedroom Scene

Katharine Cornell toured the United States in the 1933–34 season with a repertory of plays. Two old ladies who were family friends in Buffalo went to see her in *Romeo and Juliet*. They had watched the succession of "bad woman" roles in her earlier successes with foreboding and reproach. When the curtain went up on the scene in Juliet's chamber, one of them whispered loudly to the other: "There! I told you Kit Cornell would act a play that had a bedroom in it!"

Notice to Thieves

During the same tour, Katharine Cornell played in a burlesque house in upstate New York. On the mirror of her dresser she found a note left for her by one of the burlesque queens who usually had that room:

"Dere Miss Cornele: Pleas do not steel this mirror. The last company of actors we had hear took my best mirror. Kindly let this one alone."

The Out-of-Towners

Virginia Kaye Bloomgarden was a young actress in her twenties, when her husband Kermit Bloomgarden worked as general manager for Herman Shumlin on Lillian Hellman's play The Searching Wind (1944).

The play was being tried out in Wilmington and then moved to Baltimore. In between, I was returning briefly to New York, so Lillian asked me to do her a favor: would I go by her house and ask her cook to make two roast ducks and some of her special potato salad, and also—to keep Herman happy—that lemon meringue which he adored. I was also to bring to Baltimore some salmon and salami. And her mail. Then Herman asked if I could please go by his office on 42nd Street and pick up his as well as Kermit's mail.

I remember it snowed in New York. It was the first day of April and everything was slush. I was carrying my little suitcase stuffed with everybody's mail, and I was heading to Penn Station carrying the ducks, the potato salad, the salami, the salmon, and of course the lemon meringue pie. The train was a mob scene, filled with soldiers—the war was on—and I had to stand from New York to Philadelphia, watching all my things very carefully. Then from Philadelphia to Baltimore I got a seat and somehow I got to the Belvedere Hotel through the slush and mud. Kermit helped to clean me up and then called Lillian's room. She was preparing for the evening's dinner party, and she said Herman was having one of his fits in her room. We didn't ask whether the fit was personal or professional, but when we went up, we found Herman in a heated argument with the hotel manager. A stick of salami had somehow fallen out the window and Herman wanted the manager to retrieve it from the parapet where it was lodged below. The man said he had discussed the matter with the hotel engineer who said it was unfeasible. So Herman gritted his teeth, even though Lillian presented him with the salami that I had just brought.

We had the dinner, and everything went fine until I was serving seconds. I was cutting a piece that broke loose from the leg of the duck and I hit the lemon meringue pie, which fell to the floor, face down. I let out a shriek, and saw my whole life pass in front of my eyes, especially the past twenty-four hours of gathering and transporting the ingredients for this wartime banquet. I saw Lillian lower her head on to the table in despair, but there was dead quiet in the room.

Herman said nothing, but his face went quite red. Without a word, this big-time producer got down on his knees and slowly, very methodically, he turned over the pie and began to scrape and assemble every last piece. Still nobody said a word. The mucky jelly that had been brought into the world to make Herman happy looked like an absolute disaster, but he put it back on the table and said very quietly: "You know, Lil, I think I picked this pie up better than anything I have done in my whole life." I looked at him to see if he was kidding, but he looked dead earnest, and apparently had meant every word.

Correction

Bug-infested lodgings have been a staple of theatrical lore and reality ever since actors have been touring. Bob Hope once joked that his hotel room was "so small that the rats are round-shouldered." The proprietor was not amused and threatened to sue the comedian. The next night, Hope issued a correction:

"I'm sorry I said that the rats in my hotel were round-shouldered. They are not."

Have Car Will Travel

Theatre people are frequently asked to stretch and improvise, which includes going out of town. Tony Giordano recounts one such occasion.

I was young and starting out when I got a call one day from Robert Ludlum who was running Playhouse-on-the-Mall in Paramus, New Jersey.

"We're opening Arthur Miller's *The Price* tonight—starring Luther Adler and James Broderick—our stage manager is ill—we know you're not a stage manager—but we called a stage manager friend of yours who can't do the show—he told us to call you because you have a car."

"Well," I said, "I don't know anything about stage managing—I've never done this before—is it a union house?"

"Yes, it is," said Ludlum patiently, "and believe me, we need you. Please come and just do this."

"All right," I said, "but don't ever treat me as a stage manager—you must understand that I'm a director."

(And to give Bob Ludlum his due, he rewarded me soon afterwards by giving me *Two for the Seesaw* to direct.)

I arrived at 2:30 in the afternoon and found Luther Adler in a frantic state: he didn't know his lines, didn't know his blocking, didn't know his business. They kept doing a scene with him instead of a runthrough, and I was watching, not knowing the play, and not knowing what I was supposed to be doing that night. Finally at around 4:30 Adler came up to me and said gruffly:

"What did you say your name was?"

"Tony . . ."

"Well, listen Tony," he growled, "any time tonight you hear a pause, you throw me a line. Really loud and clear."

He was already leaving, when I said:

"Excuse me . . . I've never seen the show . . ."

"What has that to do with anything?" he turned back to me.

"Well, how will I know when you're acting and when there's a pause?"

"I've just told you," he repeated emphatically, "any time you hear a pause, you throw me a line. I won't be acting."

I tried to read the play then, but everybody was very nervous, and they were all in Luther Adler's dressing room, giving him lines. We get to half hour, the tension is growing, then the show starts, and before Luther's entrance I notice him offstage with a flashlight, cutting his script up with a pair of scissors and taping bits and pieces of his speeches on the back of flats. He is sweating profusely, which works well for his role, because Solomon Gregory has to be out of breath for his entrance, having climbed several flights of steps. I watch him enter from my perch just a few feet away, and hear the audience give him an enormous hand. And Adler looks really fabulous; you'd never guess that just a few moments earlier he was a nervous wreck. He speaks the first few lines—brilliantly—and gets a big laugh.

Then there is total silence. The audience has stopped applauding and I hear nothing. So I shout out the next line as loudly as he told me to, he picks up, goes another four or five lines until the next laugh. Then the audience falls silent and so does Luther—I shout out the next line and he picks it up—until we develop a rhythm. He loved the audience reaction; they also threw him, so I'd always have to feed him the next line. By this time I was having a migraine headache from the tension, while Adler was growing more relaxed by the minute. In fact, when he has that piece of business of cracking the egg, he gets it all over his jacket, and both he and Jimmy Broderick are laughing hysterically, and meanwhile I'm developing a migraine.

The curtain came down on act one, and I saw the two stars standing on stage, still laughing and patting each other on the back, saying what a hit this show will be. Rather perturbed I went over and I said rather tensely:

"I want you to understand something: I've never stage managed before tonight."

"So?" said Luther.

"Well, I've never even seen this theatre before," I continued more lamely.

"So?" Luther asked.

"The point is that I am positive the audience heard every single line I threw you."

Finally Luther Adler noticed how nervous, upset, and very young I was. He looked at me calmly, put an arm around me, hugged me slightly, and said very kindly:

"Now, Tony, what do you think the audience prefers—to hear you, or to hear nothing?"

CHAPTER 20

Having Fun

Retaliation

The elder Sothern was notorious for his practical jokes, some of which verged on cruelty. His victims, members of his company, decided to band together to serve up their dish of revenge. They found out that Sothern had been pursuing one of Washington's literary celebrities, a woman famous for her strong mind and temper. Finally, he managed to get an invitation to call at her house.

The actor was met at the door with a volley of explosive epithets and abuse. But all that he could make out was the hostess furiously repeating the word: "Another!—Another!"

"Madam, I am Sothern the actor, who—"

But she cut him off angrily with "Another!" and slammed the door in his face.

Sothern was bewildered and crestfallen, but he also began to smell a plot. He shared his problem with three of his fellow actors whom he considered prime suspects. After listening to the story, the first one said sympathetically:

"I cannot understand it at all. When I called this morning, and represented myself as Sothern, she was most cordial, and listened to my praises of her writing with great delight."

"It seems very strange to me, also," the second chimed in. "I called on the lady with Sothern's card and she mentioned the preceding Sothern, but I praised her writing so much more aptly that she became convinced that you were an impostor. Her later temper is hard to understand."

Then the third actor remarked innocently:

"And she was amiable to me when I called and said that I was Sothern. She suggested that the other two were probably impudent rascals trying to impose upon her. Did she really slam the door?"

Sothern could see that he had been beaten.

"I was the fourth Sothern," he muttered gloomily. "She probably suspected that somebody had packed the jury."

Luck

Theatre folk are extremely superstitious, wearing exotic and sometimes bizarre amulets and charms. The list of prohibitions are endless—from whistling backstage to circumvention of any mention of the title of Shakespeare's accursed "Scottish" play. It was widely believed that the ghost of David Belasco haunted his theatre, at least until *Oh, Calcutta!* moved in there. Some other theatres are supposed to be jinxed, but there are also people who may bring luck. One such in the thirties was Sam Roseman, the propmaster at the Music Box Theatre. A tradition began with *Dinner at Eight* (1932) that for an actress to have success she must be photographed sitting on Mr. Roseman's lap. It was probably started as a joke, nobody quite knows by whom, but Richard Huggett, the English actor who wrote the book on theatrical superstitions, believes it might have been Sam Roseman.

Amateur Gaieties

The depression was still raging in early 1935, but people in the theatre are generally optimists and they wanted to usher it out. So a group of the brightest and the best got together to stage an all-star benefit called Post Depression Gaieties. *It consisted of a series of sketches and songs, spoofing Broadway shows then current. A chaotic concept and execution under the direction of the genial dramatist Marc Connelly, much of the fun was not taking place onstage, as* Stage Magazine *reported in its April 1935 issue:*

Backstage at the New Amsterdam it was like amateur night gone to

Heaven. Nothing notable happened, but it was all very homey, pleasant, almost naïve. The passage from the stage door to the wings was so choked with personalities that there wasn't room to cram in a flashlight bulb. The place rang with salvos of greeting, which stagehands tried, unsuccessfully, to hush. Judith Anderson didn't know her lines. Hope Williams had twice as many as Miss Anderson and didn't know hers. Nobody, it turned out, did. There was a good deal of giggling over it. A few were nervous. Noël Coward appeared to be having an excessive stage fright. Helen Hayes rushed in from Philadelphia; was sorry she hadn't put on an evening dress. Charles MacArthur, after he had hugged Jimmy Savo, reminded her to take out her chewing gum before she went onstage. John Weaver was upset because he hadn't been able to find a soft whistle anywhere in New York for Peggy Wood to squeeze as she walked up and down and wrung her hands. She was the grandmother in the *Children's Hour* sketch. Ethel Barrymore sat in the middle of the sound effects and told the electricians when to turn the spot on Charlie Winninger so that he could see to read his lines.

During the evening a table was set up offstage and bologna sandwiches, to which Tallulah Bankhead was particularly partial, celery, and beer laid out. That made things even jollier, but complicated. Several people nearly got onstage with supper in their mouths. Lily Pons, Gladys Swarthout, and Helen Jepson came in looking young and exciting, with ermine coats over their hillbilly dresses. All the people who were in the passageway sat on the piano in the wings, made faces at the people onstage when they could see them, told them how superb they had been when they got off. The fireman finally gave up trying to make people stop smoking. Nobody could find a dressing room or the right pair of tights and didn't care. The scene shifters were particularly anxious to find out which one was Lily Pons. Actors, they intimated, were an old story. The only serious thing that happened was that [critic] Percy Hammond couldn't get into the pants which went with his Daniel Boone costume. Even that didn't matter much. He played the scene wrapped up in a steamer rug.

No Sweat

Al Henderson remembers that Herbert Berghof managed to sweat profusely on cue every night during the run of *The Andersonville Trial* (1959). The rest of the cast wondered how he did it. The three best explanations they came up with:

1. He used a sponge hidden in his handkerchief.
2. He took "sweat pills."

3. He consulted with famed drama teacher Stella Adler, who advised him to go to a steambath and from then on—in line with Stanislavski's system—he used "sweat memory."

Bugged

An actor in *The Andersonville Trial*, Albert Decker, evidently believed that it was part of his character as the defense attorney to expose himself to one of the soldiers as he moved upstage to exit. The young actor, upon whom this was perpetrated, blushed beet red each time, and he had great difficulty in regaining his composure for the following scene. After a few nights of this, the extra planned his revenge on Decker. He bought some imitation bugs in a novelty joke store and secretly dropped a couple into Decker's glass. During the next performance, this had a boomerang effect that the actor did not anticipate. Decker did not pour any water from the pitcher; he waited until Berghof called for water during the court recess, then he filled his glass, causing the bugs to swirl about the bottom as he handed his glass to Berghof. The latter, with his quick eye for detail, immediately noticed the bugs and he injected a brand new line as he waved the glass: "They're poisoning me," he wailed, "they're poisoning me!"

She Wouldn't Be First—or Last

Earl Wilson was with Choo Choo Johnson in the Balinese Room of the Hotel Blackstone in Chicago when the actress remarked about the ongoing 1940 Democratic national convention. A great deal of speculation was going on as to who would be FDR's running mate. Choo Choo announced her candidacy there and then:

"If elected vice-president, I'll give them plenty of vice."

With Friends Like That

Max Gordon, who came from the slums of the Lower East Side and worked his way up vaudeville to become a producer of Noël Coward and other sophisticates, was also a frequent guest at the White House during the Roosevelt years. Just before the 1940 election, the "comparable Max" (as George Kaufman had dubbed him) was seated at Eleanor Roosevelt's left at a small dinner party. At one point, he asked her:

"Mrs. Roosevelt, have you heard the gag about the two actors outside the Palace Theatre? One of them asks the other, 'You gonna vote for

Roosevelt?' to which the other says, 'What's the matter with the guy that's in there?' "

According to Gordon this little gag "absolutely killed" Mrs. Roosevelt, who insisted that Franklin hear it. FDR roared when Max Gordon repeated it, keeping the punchline until a few weeks later. That's when Gordon voted for Willkie.

The Man Who Came to Dinner

Alexander Woollcott was a friend of the Roosevelts and liked to stay at 1600 Pennsylvania Avenue, which he called "the best boarding house in Washington." Just after the 1940 elections, when Woollcott campaigned actively (mainly on radio) for FDR, he came to the capital with the road company of The Man Who Came to Dinner. *In* Smart Aleck, *his biographer Howard Teichmann depicts how Woollcott played Sheridan Whiteside, the overreaching guest, both on and off the stage.*

When the Roosevelts learned that Aleck would be appearing in *The Man Who Came to Dinner* in Washington, a buff-colored card under the gold seal of the President arrived, inviting him to stay at the White House. Aleck accepted promptly.

The opening night in the capital brought enough important members of the government and Washington society to fill the orchestra floor. The second night brought the President and Mrs. Roosevelt. They occupied what Aleck termed the royal box. Following the performance, the entire company was invited to supper by the Roosevelts at the Executive Mansion. Janet Fox, Edna Ferber's niece, and an accomplished actress in her own right, played the role of the nurse, Miss Preen, in the East Coast company.

"Supper was served in the State Dining Room," Miss Fox recalled. "It was marvelous and we all enjoyed ourselves thoroughly. But Aleck continued the habit of midnight suppers at the White House, and word began to trickle back to us that the Roosevelts were getting a bit upset by these carryings-on. The White House chef gave his notice saying, 'I've served an awful lot of people, but at two in the morning . . . ?' "

As a guest of the First Family, Aleck had the finest quarters in the Executive Mansion. He told Beatrice Kaufman, "This time I have the big Pink Room that was occupied by Queen Elizabeth, so that the small and rather chilly bedroom adjoining gives Hennessey the status of lady-in-waiting which he seems to enjoy."

While appearing in Washington, Woollcott spent an evening after his performance with two friends, Thornton Wilder and the son of the man with whom Aleck had had such a difficult experience while he was broadcasting for Cream of Wheat, Paul C. Harper, Jr. Young Harper, now a lieutenant in the U.S. Marines, suddenly realized that they had talked so much he had missed the last train back to his barracks. Prewar Washington was so filled with defense personnel that hotel rooms were impossible to obtain.

"Don't worry about me," Harper said. "I'll spend the night in the Union Station waiting room."

"Ridiculous," Aleck snorted. "I have two rooms. You take one."

"Great," the Marine answered. "Where're you staying?"

"The White House."

Thornton Wilder heard Harper whistle softly and then begin to protest that he could not stay at the home of the Commander in Chief, but Aleck overrode his objections. Half an hour later, Lieutenant Harper was bedded down in the room recently occupied by Winston Churchill.

The next day Woollcott wrote Mrs. Roosevelt in Hyde Park, New York.

"I wish to deny in advance," his letter read, "the rumor that I quartered an entire regiment of Marines in the White House during your absence. It was only one Marine."

By return mail Mrs. Roosevelt answered.

"Any time there is an empty bed in the White House it could not be better filled than by a United States Marine."

Keeping It Topical

Political comedies are rare on Broadway. Howard Lindsay and Russel Crouse wrote *State of the Union* on a suggestion by Helen Hayes during the 1944 presidential campaign. The play opened its 765-performance run in late 1945 (winning the Pulitzer Prize for that year) and threatened to influence the 1948 elections. In fact, Crouse and Lindsay sold the film rights to Paramount much earlier than usual, and stipulated that the movie be finished and released by the fall of 1947, in order to influence the political conventions the following year. Audiences were so delighted by the topicality of some parts of the play that Lindsay and Crouse accepted it as a necessary part of its success. They got into changing and adding gags about rationing and inflation according to the morning headlines, wiring the daily changes to the various road companies. The Chicago *Daily News* suggested, only half in jest, that the two playwrights, if they did not both run for President, should at least write the platforms for both parties.

Often asked whether *State of the Union* was pro-Democratic or pro-

Republican, the authors invariably replied, "It's pro-American." And questioned whether the central character of Grant Matthews had been patterned, as rumored, on the candidacy of Wendell Willkie, Crouse usually denied it: "He's not Willkie. But he's certainly Crindsay—and maybe Louse."

Tea Party

One of producer Morton Gottlieb's fondest memories of his early career dates back to the time when he was general manager for Edward My Son *(1948), which had a number of English actors.*

Robert Morley occupied some kind of prop room close to the stage as his dressing room, to enable him to make all those costume changes. On matinees, every Wednesday and Saturday during the first intermission, he began inviting people to this dressing room for tea. I don't mean just Peggy Ashcroft and the other stars in the show, but everybody—stagehands, understudies, the wardrobe mistress, the dressers. We all had to take turns to bring cookies and other goodies, he provided the tea.

This became a wonderful routine. We began to invite people we knew in the audience backstage for tea. Then actors in other shows in the vicinity of the Martin Beck Theatre started to come over and have tea. Robert Morley's dressing room became the secret hot spot during Broadway matinees.

Nine years later I was company manager for *Time Remembered* (1957), which starred Helen Hayes, Richard Burton, and Susan Strasberg. I mentioned to Helen what we used to do, and she thought it'd be a splendid idea to revive it. The prop man got some fancy potted palms from underneath the stage, I think they were fake, and set up tables. We had four musicians in the show and they came backstage to play for us during our tea, so this was a more formal affair. Helen made and poured the tea, and again we rotated the bringing of cookies. People began to drop by again, and soon we had a fullblown revival.

We had a marvelous time.

Mr. Fixit

Morton Gottlieb later became one of Broadway's savviest producers. Robert Morley once confided to his New York Agent Milton Goldman that he planned to write a how-to book that would teach the reader how to be first at everything: how to be first off a plane, to recover one's luggage, to get a cab in Manhattan, or a table at the swankiest restaurant without a reservation.

"What are you going to use as title for the book?" asked Goldman.

"*Morton Gottlieb*," said Morley.

You're Entitled

One of the few remaining theatrical hangouts in this non-drinking age of dieting is the Drama Bookshop, which has been an institution since the 1920s. It used to be on the fabled strip of Swing Street (52nd), and it is still in the middle of the action, an oasis above the hurlyburly of Times Square. Arthur and Rozanne Seelen run the store as a family business: their family encompasses employees (including many an actor or production trainee) and customers, who come from all over the country and the world to stock up on new scripts and hard-to-find textbooks. Whenever I have visited the shop, I have been amazed how Arthur and Rozanne manage to conduct business, handle customers' questions, and answer the phone while chatting away a couple of hours with a single visitor in the back office, as if they were sitting in a cafe.

Arthur keeps a book in which he writes down what he calls "fractured titles" of books that customers ask for. A woman came in one time and wanted all the works of Anon. "Such as?" asked Arthur. "*The Second Shepherds' Play, Everyman,* and so on," she replied correctly. An actor (and tautologist) once asked: "Do you have any monologues I can do by myself?"

Here are some of the Seelens's favorite bloopers:

She Stops the Concorde

The Taming of the Screw

The Madwoman of Ohio

Tooth for the See-Saw

Andrew Cleves and the Lion

The Rhinoceros of Eldridge

Barefoot in the Dark

I Can't Bear You When the Water's Running

Lysistrata by Agamemnon

Canada by Shaw

The Caucasian Chalk Garden

A Pea in Her Ear

My Life in Art by Stradivarius

As a related hobby, Arthur Seelen likes to think up titles for shows that have yet to be written. He suggests:

For a stage adaptation of Hitler's *Mein Kampf: The Boys in the Bund.*

For a musical version of *Equus: Separate Stables.*

For a musical of *Lolita* (presumably in place of the disastrous *Lolita, My Love* (1971) which never made it to Broadway), Arthur prefers: *Take Her—She's Nine.*

Arthur referred to James Baldwin's *Blues for Mister Charlie* as *The Night on Baldwin's Mountain*, or *the Art of Impropaganda.*

And Arthur Miller's *After the Fall* was retitled *Miller's High Life*, which was later used by Anne Miller for her autobiography.

Miller Lite might also work.

Standing By

David Brooks was standing by (as an understudy) during the production of The Girl Who Came to Supper, *when he ran into his director.*

The show was directed by Noël Coward, and of all the theatre people I had ever worked with, he has made me feel most privileged to be a member of this profession. Anyway, because I was standing by for Joe Ferrer, I did not have to be on time. On opening night I was somewhat late and when I arrived into the great marble-floored lobby of the Broadway Theatre, it was completely deserted—except for Noël Coward. He was pacing up and down with his ubiquitous cigarette in its ubiquitous cigarette holder. Noël usually held one hand behind his back and he always strode very briskly, as if he was walking against a stiff wind. When I saw him, I said, "For God's sake, Noël, don't you have a seat?" and he replied instantly, "But of course I have, dear boy, and everybody's been wanting it for years!"

Confused Identities

Noël Coward once ran into Edna Ferber, who liked wearing tailored suits and remarked:

"You look almost like a man."

"So do you," said Miss Ferber.

Discussion

Wilson Mizner was in discussion with Lew Lipton, a playwright, about an actress they both knew. Lipton thought that she was a bit "mannish."

"Mannish!" exclaimed Mizner. "I understand it took her all winter to color her meerschaum pipe."

Role Playing

Actress Peggy Wood dropped by the Algonquin Round Table and found herself challenged by Aleck Woollcott.

"I don't think you'd make a good Lady Macbeth, Peggy. Do you?"

"No," Miss Wood replied unperturbed, "but you would."

That's No Gentleman

Frank Case, the famous proprietor of the Algonquin Hotel, once called Dorothy Parker's room and asked her whether she had violated one of the hotel's rules:

"Do you have a gentleman in your room?"

"Just a minute," said the incorrigible Miss Parker, "I'll ask him."

Gentlemen Prefer Ladies

Early in his career, Donald Sutherland had a startling introduction to Tallulah Bankhead, who knew an infinite variety of ways to startle people. The Canadian actor was making up when she entered his dressing room stark naked. Sutherland's jaw must have dropped. "What's the matter, darling," asked the aging actress, "haven't you ever seen a blonde before?"

The Female of the Species

A critic once described Harold J. Kennedy, the actor and director, as "a kind of masculine Tallulah Bankhead." Since they were friends, Kennedy reported this to Miss Bankhead, who replied: "A masculine Tallulah Bankhead? Darling, don't be redundant."

Journey's End

Actresses are prone to fall in love with authority or father figures, especially directors. Milton Goldman remembers Tallulah Bankhead once going up to Elliott Roosevelt at a restaurant and telling him: "There are only three men I have ever loved: my father, your father, and Winston."

Goldman also likes to tell the story about Maureen Stapleton, who after a couple of marriages fell in love with the director George Abbott, then still only in his eighties. A friend made a comment about the great disparity in their ages, to which the actress replied:

"Haven't you ever heard about May-December romances?"

"Come off it, Maureen," the friend persisted, "you are no kid for such a romance."

"How about August?" Maureen Stapleton asked hopefully.

Miss Stapleton's relationship with the legendary Mr. Abbott was for a while the talk of the town. Her friend Norma Crane was frankly incredulous that it could be a fulfilling romance.

"But, darling, he's only 82," said Ms. Stapleton, "and he is sensational in every way."

Finally convinced, Norma Crane asked: "Does he have an older brother?"

Walk Makes the Woman

Starting with Greta Garbo, many stars enjoy the relative anonymity of New York City. John Springer remembers walking down on Fifth Avenue with Marilyn Monroe and Eli Wallach.

She was fairly well disguised with dark glasses and a babushka scarf over her head. And as we were walking along, Eli said to her:

"If people knew who they were walking past . . . How do you do this?"

And Marilyn said:

"It's not the clothes. It's the walk." And she started to walk her famous M.M. walk. In no time at all, people began to turn their heads, stopped, pointed, and instantly recognized her.

Homework

Marilyn Monroe was a famous movie star when she started taking lessons at the Actors Studio. She applied herself to the classes and acting exercises with total seriousness. Late one evening, Eli Wallach's phone rang.

"Mr. Wallach," said a very small, girlish voice. "This is Marilyn . . ."

"Who?"

"Marilyn . . . you know . . . from school . . . ? Can you tell me what is our assignment for tomorrow's class?"

Havoc in Academe

A young professor from Columbia University became infatuated with June Havoc when she was starring in a musical comedy. He invited her to tea at the Faculty Club, filled with the usual assortment of staid and venerable academics. The actress (who was elder sister to Gypsy Rose Lee) took a look around and observed to her admirer:

"My! I've never been with such a lot of extinguished gentlemen before in the whole of my life!"

CHAPTER 21

Brief Encounters

One Character in Search of Another

George Handel Hill (1809–49) was widely known as "Yankee" Hill, on account of sketches he created based on New England characters. He made frequent field trips in search of material. On one such excursion he caught a real live one.

In the year 1835, Mr. Hill decided to visit Taunton for the purpose of meeting with such of his school-day companions as might still be living, and residents of that famous town, and also to pick up incidents and anecdote for the construction of a new drama, as an attraction for the future.

He was accompanied on this trip by a friend from Boston. The better to address themselves to such individuals as, from their peculiarities, might fill the pages of their notebooks, they started in a private carriage from their lodgings early in the morning, intending to reach Taunton by sundown.

They went on smoothly and without incident until the town of Quincy had been reached. Stopping at a farmhouse, having an air of comfort, neatness and "capacity without being ostentatious in any of its characteristics, Hill proposed to begin the real adventures of the day by asking some questions of an elderly looking gentleman who was standing at the door, apparently bidding adieu to some person with whom he had been conversing.

The old gentleman replied to Mr. Hill's salutation of "Good day, sir," in an easy and dignified manner, which convinced Hill that he had come in contact with a superior character. He was not one, however, easily embarrassed, and, pointing to a number of derricks, and other mechanical contrivances, used in quarrying the granite for which Quincy is so famous, asked what they were.

The old gentleman said: "In that locality abounded one of the staples of New England, granite, and those parts of machines, scattered around the lodge, were used in quarrying."

"You have lived long in this neighborhood?" said Hill.

"Yes, I have," was the reply; "I was born nearby."

"Then you must be some acquainted here," said Hill.

"Yes, I am acquainted some, with every part of the United States."

"Well, sir, I do not wish to detain you. I was about to ask you a few questions, as I am in search of Yankee character; but, perhaps, your time's valuable. I will call on some other occasion."

"Very well, sir, I shall be happy to give you any information in my power, whenever you feel disposed to ask it. Favor me, sir, with your address."

"Hill, sir, known as Yankee Hill, comedian."

"Ah, yes, I have heard of you, and, without meaning any offense, I should think you could act like a Yankee."

Hill said he hoped he had given no offense, and begged to know whom he had the honor of addressing?

"Young, sir," said the old gentleman; "in my life I have been called many names, but, for a period of nearly four-score years, one name has always been considered my legitimate property—the name my parents gave me, John Quincy Adams, at your service."

Hill replied, that he felt honored in taking so distinguished a man by the hand, made some apologies for his intrusion, and concluded by saying, "Good morning, sir."

"Good morning, sir," said the ex-President.

Hill made a short-cut to the carriage, and said he felt as if he should like to fall through his trousers. He often told this story of his meeting with the ex-President, and colored it with a great many variations, but the facts of the interview were as described. Some time after, Mr. Adams and the comedian met at Washington. The Sage of Quincy remembered well the incident. He was an admirer of Mr. Hill, as were many of the eminent men at Washington.

Lawyer to the Rescue

Joseph Jefferson (the Second) was an occasional scene painter who helped build one of the early theatres in Springfield, Illinois. The project ran into trouble, as his son recalled in his autobiography (1890).

The building of a theatre in those days did not require the amount of capital that it does now. Folding opera-chairs were unknown. Gas was an occult mystery, not yet acknowledged as a fact by the unscientific world in the West; a second-class quality of sperm-oil was the height of any manager's ambition. The footlights of the best theatres in the Western country were composed of lamps set in a "float" with the counter-weights. When a dark stage was required, or the lamps needed trimming or refilling, this mechanical contrivance was made to sink under the stage. I believe if the theatre, or "Devil's workshop," as it was sometimes called, had suddenly been illuminated with the same material now in use, its enemies would have declared that the light was furnished from the "Old Boy's" private gasometer.

The new theatre, when completed, was about ninety feet deep and forty feet wide. No attempt was made at ornamentation; and as it was unpainted, the simple lines of architecture upon which it was constructed gave it the appearance of a large dry-goods box with a roof. I do not think my father, or McKenzie, ever owned anything with a roof until now, so they were naturally proud of their possession.

In the midst of our rising fortunes a heavy blow fell upon us. A religious revival was in progress at the time, and the fathers of the church not only launched forth against us in their sermons, but by some political maneuver got the city to pass a new law enjoining a heavy license against our "unholy" calling; I forget the amount, but it was large enough to be prohibitory. Here was a terrible condition of affairs: all our available funds invested, the legislature in session, the town full of people, and we by a heavy license denied the privilege of opening the new theatre!

In the midst of their trouble a young lawyer called on the managers. He had heard of the injustice, and offered, if they would place the matter in his hands, to have the license taken off, declaring that he only desired to see fair play, and he would accept no fee whether he failed or succeeded. The case was brought up before the council. The young lawyer began his harangue. He handled the subject with tact, skill, and humor, tracing the history of the drama from the time when Thespis acted in a cart to the stage of today. He illustrated his speech with a number of anecdotes, and kept the council in a roar of laughter; his good humor prevailed, and the exorbitant tax was taken off.

This young lawyer was very popular in Springfield, and was honored and beloved by all who knew him, and after the time of which I write he held rather an important position in the government of the United States. He now lies buried near Springfield, under a monument commemorating his greatness and his virtues—and his name was Abraham Lincoln!

No Respect for Acting

Abraham Lincoln was very fond of Shakespeare. And though he enjoyed going to the theatre (one might say, to the bitter end), Lincoln followed the Romantic critics of the nineteenth century, who considered the Bard of Avon more of a philosopher. The President told a Frenchman, M. Laugel, who reprinted it in the *Revue des Deux Mondes:* "It matters not to me whether Shakespeare be well or ill acted; with him, the thought suffices."

Toil and Trouble

As is generally known, Lincoln's favorite Shakespeare was "The Scottish Play," so-called by superstitious theatre folk who for centuries associated Macbeth *with death and disaster. Mentioning its title or quoting from it may bring bad luck, something the Great Emancipator might not have known, but his assassin certainly did. Noah Brooks recalled his last visit to the Lincoln White House.*

At my last interview with Mr. Lincoln, a small dinner party at the Executive Mansion, the President seemed depressed and did not get warmed into his usual humor. The conversation turned mainly upon history and poetry. Mr. Lincoln had a fancy for the weird poems of Ossian, and recited snatches from one of the wars of Fingal. He quoted from *Macbeth*, which was a great favorite with him, from the lines commencing:

> If it were done when 'tis done, then 'twere well
> It were done quickly!

A Small Compromise

During one of his visits to Washington, Edwin Forrest wanted to meet Henry Clay, who with Daniel Webster was the most famous orator in Congress. His friend Colonel John W. Forney took the actor to Clay's office. This happened during the debates over the Compromise of 1850, the grand attempt to avert secession by the South and the consequent Civil War. Forney remarked favorably about a speech he had just heard Senator Soule deliver. This made Clay's eyes flash, and provoked him into a long harangue, which he ended by saying: "He is nothing but an actor, sir—a mere actor!" Then, suddenly realizing the presence of the great tragedian, Clay dropped his tone, and turning towards Forrest, said with a graceful gesture, "I mean, my dear sir, a mere French actor!"

After their visit, as they were descending the stairs, Forrest said to the Colonel:

"Mr. Clay has proved by the skill with which he can change his manner, and the grace with which he can make an apology, that he is a better actor than Soule."

I'll Never Forget What's His Name

Actors meet hundreds of people who come to see them. Even if they had been introduced once, in the afterglow of a performance, they may never meet again. Laurence Hutton noted down perhaps the most famous story about the difficulty of recalling "civilians"—people outside the profession— which concerned Joseph Jefferson and someone who turned out to be anything but a civilian.

He is fond of telling how, on one occasion, he had a little business to attend to on the top floor of one of the very tall buildings in the lower part of New York City. Entering the descending elevator he found a certain man who greeted him cordially, with whose face he was perfectly familiar but whose name he could not remember. He was peculiarly struck by the fact that the stranger was a stranger to no one else in the car; that everybody looked upon him with a certain respect; and that he was smoking a very strong and black cigar contrary to the printed rules before him. Mr. Jefferson noticed, also, that neither the stranger's hat nor his boots were brushed; that his clothes were not particularly well cut nor well made; and that at the bottom of his trousers hung certain tape strings with which his unmentionable underclothes should have been tied, but which had got loose and were dragging at his heels. He said:

"Mr. Jefferson, you don't remember me?"

"Oh, yes, I remember you perfectly. The last time I saw you was in the far West. We had some talk, but I—really—can't recollect your name."

The stranger said:

"I am General Grant!"

"And then," I asked Mr. Jefferson, when he told me the story, "what did you do then, sir?"

He replied, with the famous little twinkle of his eye:

"Why, I got out of the car at the next stop and walked down four flights of stairs for fear I'd ask him if he had ever been in the War!"

All the Way with LBJ

Susan Strasberg first encountered Lyndon Johnson at a 1963 White House dinner for André Malraux. A couple of months later she attended a fund-raiser in Madison Square Garden, the famous occasion when Marilyn Monroe breathlessly sang "Happy Birthday" to President Kennedy. Afterwards Strasberg went with a friend to a private party, where she met LBJ again, as she remembered in Bittersweet, *her aply named memoir.*

Guests jammed into the hallway to watch Jimmy Durante perform; people were standing and sitting on the staircase. I was precariously clinging to the banister when I felt a hand on my ankle. I looked down, then turned to Alan and whispered, "The Vice President's hand is on my ankle. Should I ask him to move it?" A few moments later, "It's on my calf now." Then the Vice President, Southern gentleman that he was, patted the space between his legs on the stairway and said, "Come sit here, little girl."

Second String

Dan Sullivan, now drama critic of the Los Angeles *Times*, was covering the re-opening of Ford's Theatre for the New York *Times* where he was second string to Clive Barnes at the time. It was a big social event, and President Lyndon Johnson sent his Vice President, Hubert Humphrey, to officiate. As a historic building, the theatre is administered by the Department of the Interior, and going down to take his seat, Dan Sullivan encountered coming up the aisle Stewart Udall, the Secretary of the Interior.

"Where's Lyndon Johnson for this?" asked the young reporter.

"Where's Clive Barnes?" came back Udall instantly.

Show Boat

The floating theatres on the Mississippi and other waterways are part of a great American tradition, which was already dying when Edna Ferber be-

gan to research and write her novel that would lead in 1927 to Show Boat,
the ever-popular musical by Jerome Kern and Oscar Hammerstein II. In A
Peculiar Treasure, *Miss Ferber describes the real thing.*

Next morning the James Adams Floating Palace Theatre came floating
majestically down the Pamlico and tied up alongside the rickety dock.
There began, for me, four of the most enchanting days I've ever known.

There, on the lower deck near the ticket window, stood Charles Hunter,
his eyeglasses glittering, his kind face beaming, and there stood Beulah
Adams Hunter, the Mary Pickford of the rivers, with her fresh gingham
dress and her tight little curls and her good and guileless face, for all the
world like a little girl in a clean pinafore. Show folks. My heart leaped toward them; like Tiny Tim I loved them every one, from Jo, the colored
cook, to the pilot of the tugboat.

Those four days comprised the only show-boat experience I ever had. In
those days I lived, played, worked, rehearsed, ate with the company. I sold
tickets at the little box-office window, I watched the Carolina countryside
straggle in, white and colored. I learned what Winthrop Ames had meant,
and why, in that dreary hour after the New London performance of Minick,
he had brought the show boat forth as a vague nostalgic memory.

Charles and Beulah Hunter gave me their own bedroom and found quarters elsewhere for themselves. I didn't know this at the time or I'd have
made a protest—but perhaps not a very wholehearted protest. It was such
a dear room. Maybe I only pretended not to know it was really theirs. A
large square bright room, with four windows looking out upon the placid
river and the green shores. Crisp dimity curtains flirted their pert ruffles.
There was a big square wooden bed, a washbowl and pitcher, a low rocking
chair, a little shining black iron wood stove. If wishing were transportation
I'd be back there now.

The playing company numbered ten, including the Hunters. Charles
Hunter and Beulah were, of course, the star leads. Then there was an in-
génue and a juvenile lead. In show-boat terms the juvenile lead was known
as a raver and his acting method was called spitting scenery. There was a
character team, and a general business team, a heavy and a general utility
man. Then there were, of course, certain members of the tugboat crew who
played in the band. It was the feminine half of the general business team
(a middle-aged married couple) who gave me the story of the snuffing at
childbirth which I used in *Show Boat* to describe Magnolia's labor when
Kim was born at floodtime on the river. It was this actress's lot to play
haughty dowagers, old Kentucky crones, widows, mothers and such rather
withered females. Her husband (bronchial, and the rivers didn't help by

any means) did bankers, Scrooges, old hunters and trappers, elderly comics and the like. It seemed to me a lovely life as we floated down the river. Sometimes, the Hunters said, they played a new town every night; sometimes, if the countryside was a populous one and the crops good, they stayed a week.

I was delighted with the dining-room entrance which turned out to be the little door under the orchestra pit. In my Ottumwa and Appleton days I had seen numberless orchestra players crouch through this little half-hidden opening and disappear into the world of enchantment backstage. And now I was doing it three times a day, delightedly. The dining room was just beneath the stage. The food on the James Adams Floating Palace Theatre was abundant, well cooked, clean. The female members of the troupe came to breakfast in kid curlers, wave combs, boudoir caps and spectacles, disillusioning but sensible. We all sat at one long table. The Negro cook and waiter, man and wife, placed the food, sizzling hot, on the table all at once. Hot biscuits in the morning, platters of ham and eggs, coffee, jam, pancakes. If you were punctual you got the best and got it hot. Late, you took it as it was, hot or cold. There was no mollycoddling.

The low dining-room ceiling formed the floor of the stage above. Leading off this, at the rear, were the dressing rooms which, after the show, formed the sleeping rooms of the troupe, as well—except the Hunters' room which I now was snugly occupying. Out front was the auditorium; and above this the balcony for the colored people of the South. There, at the entrance, was the little box office. Outside, the deck and the gangplank up which the audience streamed. New York was another planet.

They rehearsed in the daytime, they played at night. That first night's performance was a bastard resulting from the combination of *East Is West* and *The Shanghai Gesture*, pleasingly mated by Hunter. I sold tickets at the box office; I watched rehearsals and performances; I played a walk-on; I chatted with the audience. Sometimes, after the show, they pulled anchor and went down river that night; sometimes they waited until early morning. I slept in the cool airy bedroom, lulled by the purr of the water against the boat. There was a feud between show-boat troupe and tugboat crew. The actors kept the tugboat crew awake at night with their music, their talk and laughter in the relaxed hour following the performance; the tug crew with their early daylight activity disturbed the actors' morning sleep. After the show there was always a bit of supper to be prepared, each couple busy with their own saucepan or skillet over the spirit lamp; an egg, a bottle of milk; a cheese sandwich and a glass of beer. The heavy had a weak chest and his wife would heat liniment to be rubbed in and covered with a square of flannel. It was the Vincent Crummleses afloat.

The women made their own costumes. Beulah Adams' Chinese costume (Chu-Chu San, or approximately that) was cotton-back white satin, ordered by the yard from Sears, Roebuck, with silver braid complete and further enhanced with a sprinkling of diamants. It wasn't, perhaps, strictly Chinese, but the North Carolina audiences were enraptured.

The audiences were remote in type from anything that Chicago or New York had ever heard about. Their ancestors lay now in the little North Carolina churchyards, with beautiful English names engraved dimly on the tombstones and the vaults inside the crumbling churches. I had wandered through the churchyard at Bath. The old, old inscriptions were in Early English script with the letter s done with the flourish of the letter f. All the hardships and tears and hopes and fears of the struggling American Colonies could be pieced together from the reading of those weather-worn annals. It was here that I got the idea for the dashing Gaylord Ravenal's background. . . .

It was early on the morning of my fourth day that Charles Hunter and I settled down in the quiet sunny corner bedroom, he with a pack of cigarettes, I with a chunk of yellow copy paper and a pencil. He began to talk. It was a stream of pure gold. I sat with my eyes on him and my pencil racing across the paper, and wrote and wrote and wrote. Incidents, characters, absurdities, drama, tragedies, river lore, theatrical wisdom poured forth in that quite flexible voice. He looked, really, more like a small-town college professor lecturing to a backward student than like a showboat actor.

Sheet after sheet of yellow copy paper, crudely numbered in the upper right-hand corner, littered the floor around my chair. Noonday came and went, it was three, it was four and time for the early dinner, but still he talked, and dinner was put off.

By the time he had finished I had a treasure-trove of show-boat material, human, touching, true. I was (and am) in his everlasting debt.

When I asked him what I could do to show my appreciation he said, "Send me a So Big with your name in it." When (perhaps not very tactfully) I accompanied this little gift with a check he pasted the check in the flyleaf of the book and wrote me: "If I ever need it I'll write and ask if it's all right to cash it. Who knows?"

Years later the James Adams Floating Palace Theatre sank in mid-river, with every scrap of scenery, costumes, papers, furnishings. It was then that Charles Hunter cashed the check and I wish it had been double its size.

Poor Baby

During World War II, John Springer was touring in a big variety show that had been produced by Joshua Logan. They toured the various theatres of war and army bases throughout the United States.

We had played a week at the Stage Door Canteen in New York, when Bette Davis and Jack Garfield had asked us to do the show at the Hollywood Canteen. En route we stopped, among many other places, in Chicago to do a national radio show with Kate Smith. We were quite well known by this time, celebrities in our own right, and a big party was thrown for us. All the theatre people turned out for us—Alfred Lunt and Lynn Fontanne, Cornelia Otis Skinner, and there was this young actor who latched on to me. We chatted, and finally he said:

"There's a show in Chicago, which is supposed to be going to New York, but it's simply dying at the box office. Claudia Cassidy, a critic here, is desperately trying to keep it alive, and all of us working in the theatre are doing everything we can to get people excited about it. Will you come and see it tomorrow?"

I agreed to meet Montgomery Clift—for that was the young man's name—at the play, which was *The Glass Menagerie*. God knows how many times Monty had seen it, but throughout he was giggling, crying and grabbing my arm, whispering, "Isn't it marvelous—just marvelous!"

Afterwards we went back to Laurette Taylor's dressing room. I have yet to see anyone—including all the great ladies whom I love—to come even close to that performance. And Monty, who was always very demonstrative, fell on his knees before Miss Taylor and started kissing the hem of her dressing gown, while she tried to shoo him off:

"Montgomery, you silly boy, just stop that this minute!"

And Monty poured it on even more. He would always do things like this. I remember listening once to Ella Fitzgerald, when Monty went up to her between songs, knelt before her, saying, "You Goddess!" Poor baby . . .

Auditions

Auditions are the necessary evil and the terror of most working actors' lives. Actress Kathleen Hoyt captured the experience in Stage Magazine *(October 1938).*

The night was sopping with rain and heat. A hundred of us actresses were crammed on the bare stage of the Music Box waiting for the final, decisive interview with the authors of *The Fabulous Invalid*, Messrs. Kaufman and Hart. We all were trying to appear casual and at ease, and we all were sick with nervous stomach-ache. We did want those jobs—and we didn't want to show it. The week before a certain amount of winnowing had taken place in preliminary interviews with John Kennedy and Myra Streger, the official Harris casting team, and now the decision rested with the high priests themselves.

Finding people for *The Fabulous Invalid* is a touch difficult. It's the history of a local playhouse and includes a cavalcade of the more luminous personalities in the American Theatre who presumably have trod its boards. And the trick is to find actors who resemble these people sufficiently to make the audience's collective heart crumble with nostalgia as each once-famous face appears. Not at all simple.

. . . But to return to the rainy night of the final test—sitting on those awful folding chairs trying to preserve verve, style, and "personality." Just try it for two hours. There is something about numb buttocks which does appear to take that bright lustre from a young actress. My postcard had said nine. It was now almost eleven. From the back of the shadowy auditorium Mrs. Streger would appear from time to time, cross the gangplank that bridged the orchestra pit, and, standing in the harsh blaze of the work-light, read the names of the next group to be inspected. Then these eight or ten, stirring and fluttering like anxious pigeons, would vanish into the shadows with her. The intervals between her appearances were endless. We looked around, gauging our rivals. Someone with furious red ringlets and a silver-fox cape. Eva Tanguay? A tall flaxen girl reminiscent of Ann Harding. But I couldn't find a better bet for Madge Kennedy than myself. Really.

Then three girls were called at once, leaving only a most exotic creature and myself to rattle lonesomely about in the hall—which permitted a discovery. All evening the stage had been inundated by a strangling perfume—and shifting one's chair didn't help. That odor was everywhere. Even on the trek to the upper hall it remained. After all but the black-haired lady with the amazing eyelashes (they were a full inch long, uncut and virgin, fresh from the manufacturer) had gone in—and the asphyxiating quantities of musk, civet and attar of roses had abated not one jot—it became apparent by the sheer process of elimination that one of us was the dispenser. And I, alas, was provided with no more seductive an employment-lure than a little of Macy's own eau de Cologne, lilac. We fell into conversation. I asked her if she knew whom she was supposed to resemble. "Jane Cowl," she said. The eyes—large, very dark, those heavy sorrowing lids. . . .

"Well," I exclaimed in admiration. "You're a natural. There can't be any question, you'll get the job." She acknowledged this appraisal with a slight smile. She was inclined to be of the same opinion.

The door opened. They called in my sweetly scented friend. I was abandoned to the questionable amusement afforded by the drinking fountain, the ladies' room, and the telephone booth. By that time I had concluded I was really pretty good for Madge Kennedy. Research at the library had revealed that she was a comedienne, demure, bright, and engaging. I endeavored to direct my mind to pleasant things—to feel demure, bright, and engaging. I recalled a smiling photograph of Miss Kennedy. I went to the mirror in the ladies' room, adjusted the angle of my chin and smiled. Not bad, I thought. Not a dead ringer, of course, but not bad.

I returned to the fascinations of the drinking fountain when suddenly my own name shattered the air. Somehow I arrived inside. I was in the same room with George Kaufman and Moss Hart. Gods of the theatre. Arbiters of the fate of all the little people. They were enormous. God Hart sat in awful quietness behind a desk, his celestial knees crossed. God Kaufman ranged up and down. Dazzling. Terrifying. From his Olympic height God Kaufman took notice of my crackling red rain cape, asking, "Is it Cellophane?" I replied that it was the same as our shower curtain, which the salesgirl in Bloomingdale's basement had assured me was oiled silk. There didn't seem to be anything further to say on that subject.

At this point Mr. Kennedy saw fit to call the meeting to order and to announce the actress for whom they had considered me. I adjusted my chin to the Madge Kennedy angle and attempted to smile. "This young lady," he told them, "is another possibility for Jane Cowl."

Destruction! The heavenly glance was cast upon me. Diagnosis was rapid but politeness reigned: "Let her read that speech from *Within the Law*."

I tried to salvage the appropriate fury, bitterness, and revenge from the remains of the demure, engaging brightness. I read, but it was more like Snow White crying in the woods. There was a pause and then God Kaufman said in that stubbornly cheerful tone one associates with the medical profession in desperate cases, "Al-l-l right! We'll let you know."

Well, it would at least be good to get back into the air. There are always compensations in these circumstances. God Hart looked at his watch and remarked from across his desk, "Eleven forty-five: we can begin on the men." I glanced into the auditorium as I ran out the front door. There were a hundred men sitting on the stage—sitting on the hard little folding chairs, trying to preserve their verve, style, and personality.

Wonder Why?

It has been said that auditions and job interviews are often decided in the first fifteen seconds. Actor Richard Herd was at the beginning of his career when he wished he had been given that long.

It was one of my very first auditions—for a Broadway musical at that. I had prepared two numbers. One was upbeat—"Nothing Like a Dame," from *South Pacific*, and the other was "Wonder Why?"—a melodic strain from a movie score. They usually only ask for one of them, but you never know which mood will fit. Over-rehearsed, I was waiting in the wings with 20–30 guys, until the stage manager came over, took my music and told me to wait until he called my name. Finally, he called and I walked out into the vast stage, illuminated by a single powerful naked lightbulb.

"Richard Herd will be singing 'Wonder Why,' " the stage manager formally announced and he went over to give the music to the accompanist, sitting miles away on stage right at her piano.

I had not reached even the center of the stage, when I heard a voice boom out from the house:

"Thank you, Mr. Herd."

I was stunned and tried to squint into the blackness of the auditorium, when I heard again:

"Thank you, that is all."

Somehow I managed to get off stage center stage and stumbled towards the pianist to pick up my music. And as she handed back the score, she sang *sotto voce* and very sweetly the opening words of my song: "Wonder why . . . ?"

On Not Being Typecast

Richard Herd did not become a musical star, but years later when his acting career was well established, he happened one day to be at his agent's office. Bernard Rubinstein was on the phone making notes on the casting needed for a commercial. The party at the other end mentioned that for one of the parts they needed a Richard Herd-type.

"Well, Richard is standing right here," the agent suggested, "why don't I ask him."

"I said we need a Richard Herd-type," the casting director replied, "not Richard Herd."

The Importance of Staying

Professionals rarely go to see a play without a reason, and once in the theatre, sometimes the slightest excuse to leave is welcome. David Hays just missed designing The Rope Dancers (1957), *but wanted to see how it turned out.*

I went with my wife, Leonora, and we sat in the balcony. When the audience was in, came the announcement over the speaker that Art Carney would not be performing. This was his New York debut. So Leonora and I looked at each other: "Well, let's get our tickets refunded"—we wanted to see the regular show. And then we said: "How could we? We're theatre people. This is an event. Let's watch it." So, when the curtain goes up and there, as Art Carney's replacement, is somebody we know: Joe Julian. He performed very well. The play was exciting. We went backstage afterwards to Joe's dressing room and he literally fell on his knees:

"David, Leonora, it happened so fast I couldn't call anybody. Thank God, you were here. Somebody I know from the theatre has seen me."

People in the theatre mean a great deal to each other in that way. We had known Joe, but after that we became really good friends.

Backstage Romance

Going backstage after a show to congratulate friends, whether they were good or bad, is an imperative. To see strangers is an option, and carries its own rewards and risks. Actor Max Showalter explains.

I had never met Barbara Cook until I saw her in *She Loves Me*. I adored her from afar. I had just come in from Hollywood, and I thought that didn't make any difference to me, and I've got to go back and tell her. So I went and knocked on her door, she opened it and I looked at her and said, "I love you." And she said, "I love you, too," and threw her arms around me. From that moment on we have always been so close.

I had another encounter after *A Little Night Music*. I had never met Len Cariou, but I wanted to tell him how wonderful I thought he was. I knew that theatre, and the doorman told me to go up. I went and knocked on his door, and he said, "Come in." He's sitting there taking off his makeup. And I said, "My name is Max Showalter and I just wanted to tell you how brilliant I thought you were tonight. Every nuance was impeccable and you did an absolutely marvelous job." And he, without ever turning round, continued to take off his makeup, and still looking in the mirror, said, "Yes, I know." So I just turned and walked down the stairs and that's the last I've seen of Len Cariou.

Old Friends

Marlene Dietrich once went backstage to congratulate an old friend who was in a show. "I heard a woman sitting just behind me declare: 'This is the most exciting night of my life' . . ."

"Oh, thank you, Marlene . . ." the actress glowed.

". . . seeing me!" Dietrich concluded the sentence.

The Actress and the Self-Made Man

Actor West Dobson tells an old story about Gladys Cooper, the beautiful English actress whose sweet nature was sorely tried on a transatlantic flight. Miss Cooper was trying to work on a script, while a prominent American businessman in the first-class seat next to her kept talking in a vain attempt to kindle her interest in him. "I own several lumber mills in the Midwest, I own two houses in Palm Beach, my wife has some of the most beautiful jewelry on earth which I have given her. And you know, I started out with absolutely nothing—I am a self-made man." Finally, Gladys Cooper closed her script, looked the self-made man straight in the eye and pronounced in her most ladylike manner:

"Which all goes to prove the perils of unskilled labor."

Top Seed

Mr. Burpee, founder of the seed and flower empire, once sat down at a Washington theatre next to Clare Boothe Luce, the playwright and glamorous wife of *Time* magazine founder, Henry Luce. The magnate rose, offered his hand and introduced himself:

"I am Burpee."

"I quite understand," the lady replied. "I am often troubled that way myself."

CHAPTER 22

Pathos

Somebody

The funniest American comic at the beginning of the century was a sad black man known by the song "Nobody." Bert Williams, born in the West Indies, was part of a blackface minstrel show, and after his partner George Walker died, he joined the *Ziegfeld Follies* and became its greatest star. One of his colleagues there, W. C. Fields, called him "the funniest man I ever saw, and the saddest man I ever knew." The sadness came from the racial discrimination and bigotry he encountered everywhere except on-stage.

Eddie Cantor, who claimed to have learned his comic timing from Bert Williams, recalled one New Year's Eve, when they were staying in a New York luxury hotel. They had gone out after the show to pick up some food and parted before entering the hotel, where Williams was allowed to stay only on condition that he would use the service elevator. "It wouldn't be so bad, Eddie," he observed to Cantor, "if I didn't still hear the applause ringing in my ears."

De Lawd Is Dead

One of the most memorable plays of the 1930s was Marc Connelly's *Green Pastures,* which recreated the medieval concept of the mystery cycles in a Southern black church's Sunday school class. Heywood Broun wrote that he found it "more stirring than anything I have seen in the theatre"; while Robert Littell in the *World* called it "simply and briefly one of the finest things that the theatre of our generation has seen."

This unlikely candidate for Broadway, with its enormous black cast, ran at the Mansfield Theatre for 640 performances. A huge part of its success was due to Richard B. Harrison, who played the central part of De Lawd more than two thousand times. When, after months of fruitless search for somebody to play the role, Marc Connelly found him, this son of fugitive slaves had never appeared in a professional production, though he had done almost everything else in his long life—worked in hotels, on the railroad, had been a Pullman porter on the Santa Fe and lectured on the Chautauqua circuit. He was already sixty-five when he began playing De Lawd and died five years later still doing it.

"I was backstage," Broadway columnist Ward Morehouse recalled a few years later, "during the performance given on the evening of the day of De Lawd's death. With this performance seventy-seven Harlem negroes met the supreme test; this was the show that was the hardest to give. They wept openly—the Angel Gabriel, Noah, Moses, the Stout Angel, the Thin Angel, and the children of the Fish Fry. De Lawd was dead. They knew that they'd never again see him at his rolltop desk in his celestial cubicle, frowning and fumbling over his papers; would never again behold him, as he stood aboard the Ark saying, 'Dis thing's turned into quite a proposition,' or see him, eyes shining and face brightening, as he discovered 'dat even God must suffer.' "

Real Hams

Toward the end of his life, in 1947, the influential director Arthur Hopkins gave a series of summer seminars to drama teachers and students at Fordham University. His reminiscence about a great vaudeville team goes to the heart of the art of theatre.

The most perfectly coordinated acting team I have ever seen was McIntyre and Heath. For over fifty years they played their blackface sketches, *The Georgia Minstrels, The Man from Wyoming, On Guard,* and other classics of their own creation.

None of these sketches had been written. They were improvised in the way of old afterpieces, the commedia dell'arte of vaudeville and burlesque.

The young McIntyre would suggest, "Now you say this—and I'll say that," and Heath might say, "Or, maybe it'll be better this way," and so through years of saying this and saying that, they had built up gems of character study, which had become firmly fixed long before the time I was to see them.

Despite thousands of repetitions, the last performance had that ultimate of stage magic, the sense that everything was being said and heard by them for the first time.

In those days of two-men teams, there was usually a straight man and a comedian, the comedian having all the answers and the laughs. With McIntyre and Heath it was impossible to designate the straight man. Both were comedians, and by their quality of earnestness both were straight men.

In the portrayal of the stranded, foot-sore, hungry Georgia Minstrels, Heath painted maddening pictures of a magic land to which he was leading his starved companion, a land where hams grew on trees, and where flowed the peaceful beer river. Here were perfect pictures of the defeated and the undaunted.

Here, in miniature, was a magnificent portrayal of the age-old vicissitudes and hopes of man in the muck seeking the high ground. Here was mythology and man.

For over fifty years these men held their twice-daily ceremonials, in spite of the fact that in their later years they never spoke to each other except on the stage. Some unknown misunderstanding had erected a barrier of bitterness between them, but never a sign of this bitterness appeared in their performance. Here again, they were one. Perhaps that was why they would not give up playing.

When Tom Heath was dying he asked them to send for Jim. Jim came. They were left alone together, these two young dreamers from Texas, who carried their dreams through honky-tonks and beer halls to the highest peak of stage artistry.

Now they are both gone, perhaps still searching for that magic land where the ham tree grows.

Cain and Abel

The great tragedy of Edwin Booth's life was played out at Ford's Theatre, and he was not even in it. Toward the end of his life (1915), the critic

William Winter recalled two brothers who were both actors, one famous, and the other infamous.

John Wilkes was (so Edwin told me) his father's favorite child, but the father depended more on Edwin than on any other member of the family. As an actor John—whose acting I saw and carefully observed, at Wood's Broadway Theatre—was raw and crude, and much given to boisterous declamation and violent demeanor, but he was talented, and if he had lived longer and carefully studied his art he might have attained to a high position. He was handsome and dashing, he gained some measure of public admiration, and with members of the dramatic profession he was a favorite. His brother Edwin loved him and pitied him, and to the last he kept a framed picture of him in his bedroom. Everybody was horrified by his terrible crime,—no person more horrified or afflicted than Edwin, who immediately withdrew from the stage, and would never have returned to it if he had not been compelled to do so by the heavy financial responsibilities resting on him at that time, as manager of theatres in Philadelphia and New York.

The stage associates of John Wilkes Booth at first utterly disbelieved and scoffed at the statement that he had shot the President,—declaring it incredible that such a man could do such a deed. But so it was, and the wretched fugitive outlaw was shot and his body brought to Washington and buried beneath the granite basement floor of the old Capitol Prison: some years afterward the remains were disinterred and given to Edwin, who conveyed them to Baltimore, for interment near the grave of the elder Booth, in Fairmount Cemetery. A ridiculous story went the rounds of the newspaper press, not many years ago, to the effect that John Wilkes Booth escaped and went into the Southwest and was there recognized by several persons who had known him in early life, one of them being the comedian Jefferson. Another idle tale that was circulated told of Edwin's malediction on the memory of his brother,—the fact being that he carefully avoided the subject, seldom mentioned John's name, was haunted and unspeakably distressed by remembrance of his monstrous deed and tragic fate, and deplored it, and mourned for the wretched doer of it, all the days of his life. One strange scene in that afflicting tragedy was the destruction of the stage-wardrobe of John Wilkes. This occurred at night, in the basement of Booth's Theatre, where, under Edwin's direction, only one other person being present, every garment that had been owned by his brother was cast into a blazing furnace and totally consumed.

When Edwin reappeared on the stage, about nine months after the murder of Lincoln, a cruel attempt was made in the press of New York,—

not in all the papers, but in one, particularly, of great influence,—to incite hostility toward him, because of his brother's crime, but that malignancy, unjust and cruel, utterly failed. I rejoice to remember that, as a journalist, speaking through several mediums, I used every means in my power to defend Booth and defeat that dastardly attack on him. His re-entrance was made, January 3, 1866, at the Winter Garden, as *Hamlet*, and the welcome extended to him surpassed in its enthusiasm anything of the kind that old playgoers had ever seen, and it left no shadow of doubt that the community had no intention of permitting an innocent man to be ruined for the offense of a crazy relative. The theatre was densely crowded, and as Booth came on the stage the audience rose and cheered him again and again, making every possible demonstration of sympathy and friendship. As I looked around on that tumultuous assemblage I saw not even one person who had remained seated. The excitement was prodigious, and Booth was so much affected that he could hardly control himself sufficiently to begin his performance. He never acted better than he did on that memorable night.

Ironies

Edwin Booth voted for the first time in 1864 for the re-election of Abraham Lincoln. Upon hearing this, his brother John Wilkes became upset and predicted that he would live to see Lincoln crowned as king of America.

A couple of months before Lincoln's assassination, Edwin Booth was at the railroad station in Jersey City on his way to Philadelphia. The war was still on and there were great crowds on the platform. As the train began to move, the actor noticed a tall young man lose his footing and fall off the platform. Booth dropped his suitcases, got hold of the man's coat by the collar, and pulled him back to safety.

Robert Lincoln, the president's son, recognized the most famous actor of the day and muttered his gratitude.

"That was a narrow escape, Mr. Booth," he said.

Mother's Boy

Mrs. Gilbert (1821–1904), one of the mainstays of Daly's company, had something good to say in her Reminiscences *about John Wilkes Booth, whom she thought the most perfect Romeo she had ever seen.*

He was very handsome, most lovable and lovely. He was eccentric in some ways, and he had the family failings, but he also had a simple, direct, and charming nature. The love and sympathy between him and his mother were very close, very strong. No matter how far apart they were, she seemed to know, in some mysterious way, if anything was wrong with him. If he were ill, or unfit to play, he would often receive a letter of sympathy, counsel, and warning, written when she could not possibly have received any news of him. He has told me of this himself.

No, I never felt that it was madness that carried him into the plot to assassinate the President. I know from my own limited experience how high feeling could run in those days. A man lived so wholly with people who thought as he did that anyone on the other side was hateful to him. Whatever drew Wilkes Booth into the plot, it was not quite dare-deviltry. And if the lot fell to him to do the thing, I feel sure that he went through with it without a backward thought. He had that kind of loyalty, that kind of courage. Perhaps the devotion of a high-strung Nihilist, who believes in his cause, comes nearest to expressing it. I ought to say that this is just my fancy from having known the man.

Latin

The essayist Christopher Morley noted that when news of Lincoln's assassination reached the ears of Matthew Arnold, the one detail that seemed to interest the professor of poetry at Oxford was the fact that John Wilkes Booth had shouted *Sic semper tyrannis!* in Latin as he shot the President and leapt on to the stage. This convinced Matthew that there was still hope for America.

Passing Strange

Edward H. Sothern recalls in his Remembrances (1916) *the passing of two great spirits of the theatre.*

It has been my fortune to encounter two rather startling coincidences in connection with the death of Mr. Booth and John McCullough. The night that Edwin Booth died, I was taking supper in the dining-room of The Players with three friends. There were no other men in the club. It was about two o'clock in the morning. We, of course, knew that Mr. Booth was ill, but his death was not expected immediately. While we were talking over our meal, suddenly every light in the club went out. My companions began to call for the waiter and to protest loudly. From the darkness right at our elbows, a voice, that of Mr. McGonegal, the manager of the club, said: "Hush! Mr. Booth is dead."

The day Mr. McCullough died I happened to be studying the play of *Cymbeline*. I was reading the song in Act II:

> Fear no more the heat o' the sun,
> Nor the furious winter's rages;
> Thou thy worldly task hast done,
> Home art gone and ta'en thy wages;
> Golden lads and girls all must,
> As chimney-sweepers, come to dust—

when a friend of mine opened the door of my room in the Sturtevant House Hotel and said: "McCullough's dead."

That Way Madness Lies

More than twenty years after the death of the tragedian John McCullough (1832–85), who had ended his days insane, his friend Laurence Hutton found the dead actor being exploited (no doubt without residuals being paid) in a newfangled medium at the local nickelodeon.

I put a nickel in the slot the other day, on the leading thoroughfare of a civilized city, to hear in a phonograph "The Ravings of John McCullough," so advertised in large letters under an old lithograph of the dead tragedian. It was his voice, or a clever imitation of it, from *Virginius*, *Spartacus*, and *Brutus*, and ending each with that dreadful laugh, half insane, half idiotic, which was so distressing to those of us who knew him when his mental infirmities were beginning to make themselves evident.

It was a brutal exhibition. But, startling as it was, it brought up memories of an unusually attractive personality; and it has made me think very often since, pleasantly rather than painfully, of a man of whom I saw not a little in a social way at one time and whom I greatly liked.

I had no knowledge of McCullough's failing physical and mental powers until I met him by chance one Sunday evening in Mr. Millet's studio in New York. McCullough had come in to discuss a costume for *Virginius* which Mr. Millet was designing for him and he talked like his own self until we all walked out together, about ten o'clock. We started toward Sixth Avenue, and when he stopped his car, I said "Goodnight, John," and turned to go up the street with Mr. Millet who had come to exercise his collie dog. John—poor John,—who knew that it was not my way home, thought that I wanted to get rid of him and burst into a torrent of tears. I went with him to his hotel, he holding my hand in the street car! I stopped with him for a while in his room; finally I put him to bed as if he had been a baby and held his hand until forgetfulness came.

There were no ravings on that occasion. He spoke of his past life, professional and personal; of what it had been and of what it might have been; he told me something of his mother, of childish trials and troubles, and he asked affectionately after my mother, forgetting that she was gone. And I think he breathed a little prayer before he went to sleep.

Some time before that I found him sitting with Florence* at a small table in Delmonico's cafe. I joined them, when Florence said to him: "John, this boy is going to be married. His engagement is just announced." McCullough replied that he was glad, very glad of it. He knew that I would select none but a good woman. And then he spoke as a bishop might have spoken of the ennobling influence upon any man of a good woman's love. Florence coincided with him in every point; and rarely has woman received a more touching tribute than was paid her by those two play-actors in a public restaurant.

Unfinished Actress

Margaret Webster met a lot of interesting theatre people through her stellar parents, Benjamin Webster and Dame May Whitty. She was eighteen and in Venice when she met one of the lost great hopes of the American stage.

One night there was a gondola festival on the lagoon, and the distribution of personnel among the available gondolas was difficult. I found myself a probably unwanted third with two people I hardly knew, except that Sydney Howard was a playwright of fame, currently on a reporting tour of Central Europe, and his not-long-married wife was an actress, Clare Eames. I had seen her at a couple of dinner parties; she was lean, elegant, with a sharply cut profile like a silver coin. She wore fluted dresses by Fortuni. She would be by turns fastidious and remote; generously partisan; mocking, scornful, raffishly amusing; never anything by halves, never less than passionate.

I was always exceedingly shy in the presence of the nobility of my parents' world, and these two very evidently bore its patients. I felt young and ignorant and heavy and aware of my defective eye. But Clare and Sydney did not appear to see me like that. They lured me on to talk and pretty soon I began to feel that I really could do what I wanted to do, be what I set my mind to be. Amid the Chinese lanterns and the guitar music

* William James Florence, the well-known actor.

and the water lapping against the sides of the gondola, attainable mountains became visible. Sydney and Clare, like Robert Edmond Jones, were life enhancers; this still seems to me the most important thing of all to be.

The record of Clare Eames's work in the theatre is not very large; her whole professional career lasted little more than ten years. Yet a well-known actress who was her friend said to me recently: "I remember Clare more clearly than anything that happened yesterday." She could have had a great influence on the theatre. She did on me. At a time when acting tended to vary from the florid to the slipshod and "damn-natural," hers showed me another road.

I have been told that her acting during her first onslaughts on Broadway was harsh, extravagant, fearless to the point of being ridiculous. She had burning convictions but no trained or tempered instrument. But she learned fast. During the three or four years after I met her in Venice, she played in many of the Theatre Guild's most famous productions, including the plays Sydney Howard wrote for her, *Ned McCobb's Daughter* and *Lucky Sam McCarver*. She played Lady Macbeth (she would still be my choice, among all the actresses I have ever seen, living or dead) to James Hackett's Macbeth, which must have been a ludicrous juxtaposition of styles. Her capacity for satire made her an incomparable Prossy to Katharine Cornell's Candida. Her Hedda Gabler, according to Eva Le Gallienne, who probably knows more about Hedda than any other living actress, was "still unfinished, but potentially the greatest Hedda of our time."

The New York critics were apt to apply to her work the word "cold." A sillier adjective it would be hard to imagine. It was probably due to her bone structure—she looked irretrievably intellectual—and partly because she was never sentimental or mushy; she was stripped of unnecessary flesh. But if she was cold, it was the coldness of the metal which burns your hand.

In 1926 she came to London to play in Sydney's *The Silver Cord*, and returned a year or so later to live and work there. By this time she had acquired an extraordinary economy and a concentrated discipline. She "did" almost nothing; without raising her voice she could sear an audience with irony or hatred or compassion. "Do you read?" says the mother-in-law in *The Silver Cord*. "I can," answered Clare with a raised eyebrow, quietly destroying all mothers-in-law forever.

In 1929, while she was playing in Maugham's *The Sacred Flame*, she came to see a matinee of the *Medea*, in which I was playing. That night she asked me to supper. I was at a very low point of frustration and self-doubt, and she gave me an injection of faith and courage to which I still return. She said: "You have much to give; you must give it. Never stop

believing that. Never stop doing it." After a little pause she added, in a
rather odd voice, as if she were surprised, "Please don't forget that I said
this to you." A year later she died, quite shockingly and unnecessarily, as
the result of two successive operations for an internal injury. Having taught
me some of my earliest lessons about life, she taught me the first about
death. I wish, even now, that she had lived. So few people ever saw her,
and she was a great actress.

Turn Out the Light and
Then Turn Out the Light

The last appearance of Vivien Leigh in America was after her divorce from
Laurence Olivier, when she was dying from tuberculosis. So she was playing a deserted, tubercular wife in John Gielgud's production of *Ivanov*
(1966). When she heard that many of her fans were bitterly disappointed
that her character died after the first act, Vivien Leigh tried to make light
of it:

"That's better than the whole show should die."

An Unhappy Man

*Alan Jay Lerner remembers with gratitude the encouragement he received
from Lorenz Hart in the sad days after the breakup with Richard Rodgers.*

I deserted "the old familiar places" and faces of my youth and moved from
the East Seventies to West Forty-fourth Street. First to the Lambs' Club,
the famous old theatrical establishment, now extinct, where I met the first
man who ever encouraged me to believe that I might have a future as a
lyric writer. He also happened to be one of the great lyric writers of our
time—Lorenz (Larry) Hart of Rodgers and. During the three years before
he died we became good friends, not because he found me particularly
fascinating but because he was so terrifyingly lonely, and I worshipped
him so that I made myself available to join him at any hour of the day or
night, usually for gin rummy which I played badly because I was not
interested, and he played badly because he was usually drunk. I do not
know his actual height, but I imagine he was about four feet and ten
inches. It is inconceivable that his stature was not a major contributor to
his perpetual torment. His education was vast; he spoke German fluently
and was a blood descendant of Heinrich Heine. I believe he was also a
literary descendant. There is a bittersweet quality in so many of Larry's
lyrics that seem redolent of Heine. Because of his size the opposite sex

was denied him and he was forced to find relief in the only other sex left. But all this I only heard about from others and never saw a sign of myself. He was kind, endearing, sad, infuriating, and funny, but, at the time that I knew him, in a devastating state of emotional disarray.

When Dick Rodgers turned to Oscar Hammerstein as a collaborator and their first effort became the greatest success Dick had ever had, namely *Oklahoma!*, Larry's pain must have been unbearable. One of the saddest moments I can remember happened a few months after the musical opened. We were in Fritz Loewe's living room. There was a blackout and the room was pitch dark. The only light came from Larry's cigar. Fritz turned on the radio and an orchestra was playing something from *Oklahoma!*. The end of the cigar flashed brighter and brighter with accelerated puffs. Fritz immediately switched to another station. Again someone was playing a song from *Oklahoma!*. And Larry's cigar grew brighter and the puffs became faster. It happened three times and then Fritz turned off the radio. The glow from the cigar subsided and the breathing so slow the cigar almost went out. The whole incident probably took less than two minutes and during it not a word was said, but I wept for him in the dark. The moment the lights came on Larry continued the conversation that had been interrupted by the blackout without a trace of what had happened in his voice or on his face.

He died the following year at the age of forty-seven and I believe Fritz was the last one to see him alive. Larry had a cousin who was a close friend of Fritz and late one night he called Fritz, worried because he could not find Larry. It was about three in the morning and raining heavily. Fritz went out looking for him. He found him sitting in the gutter outside a bar on Eighth Avenue, drunk and drenched to the skin. He put him in a cab and took him to Delmonico's where Larry was staying at the time. He made Larry promise he would go upstairs and go to bed and stayed in the cab until he saw him enter the hotel. Then he went home. Larry, true to his promise, went up to his room and got into bed. When he fell asleep he never awakened. He had contracted pneumonia and was gone by noon the next day. Life had ended for him much earlier and death was but a formality.

This Is Only Intermission

Charles Frohman was on the fateful voyage of the Lusitania in May 1915, when the German torpedo sank her, killing twelve hundred people. According to a survivor, the producer stood next to the actress Rita Jolivet, holding on to the ship's rail and, as the vast ocean liner began to sink, he said to her: "Don't be afraid of death. It's the most wonderful experience in life."

The Last Reviews

Henry W. Savage (1859–1927), a colorful producer who preferred to be called the Colonel, was fond of telling a story about Maurice Barrymore, as an example of how a real trouper takes life's heavier blows. After Barrymore's wife Georgie died, the Colonel went to present his condolences. He found the actor sitting in bed, surrounded by newspapers, his eyes rubbed red with crying. "It's a cruel loss, Hank," he told Savage, "and I shall never get over it. But I must say they've given the old girl some damn good notices."

It's His Funeral

The burial of Maurice Barrymore in 1905 was attended by many of the greatest actors of the day, including members of his own large family. As the coffin was being lowered, one of the straps holding it got twisted, and the casket had to be raised again. As it reappeared, Lionel nudged his brother John:

"How like father—a curtain call!"

CHAPTER 23

Family Ties

It's a Small World

When Max Gordon was doing vaudeville, as part of the Lewis and Gordon team, they scored a hit on the Keith circuit with a one-act, *In the Zone*, by a promising young writer, Eugene O'Neill. The playwright needed an advance of fifty dollars in order to get married. The payment was authorized by the president of the Keith circuit, who happened to be E. F. Albee, whose adopted grandson turned out to be the playwright Edward Albee.

Clare Boothe, the playwright, Congresswoman and socialite, was distantly related through her father to the famous acting Booths. After John Wilkes Booth assassinated Abraham Lincoln, the Maryland Booths added an "e" to distance themselves even further. Clare Boothe, whose second marriage was to Henry Luce, had a witty if wicked tongue. On one occasion in the forties, when she heard from a third party that a happily married friend was having her fifth child, she referred to her marriage as an *enceinte cordiale*. When this got back to the expectant mother, she simply said:
"Ah yes, Clare *Wilkes* Boothe."

341

All God's Chillun Have Wings

*The idea that actors, or indeed artists, are like other human beings with
the same social needs and rights is comparatively recent. Throughout
European history, they have been treated like vagrants and beggars, often
whipped out of town. In the second decade of this century, the tiny God-
fearing suburb of Los Angeles known as Hollywood tried to defend itself
from the early onslaught of movie people by putting up signs which read:
"NO ACTORS, OR DOGS, OR JEWS." Laurence Hutton told a typical
story about the profound prejudice against even the most admired actors
in a conversation recorded in 1909.*

When Frederick Warde, the English tragedian, young, promising, with
his undoubted American success not yet fully established, brought his wife
and children from London to make their home with him in the new world,
he was after various vicissitudes of fortune—most of them discouraging—
engaged by Mr. Booth to play leading parts during the coming season.
They were to open in Baltimore on a certain Monday evening and Warde
was to be Othello to the Iago of the star. The company, long associated
with Mr. Booth with this single exception, was not assembled and there
could be but one or two rehearsals before the initial performance. Warde
had never even seen the play of *Othello*, and had no idea how to dress
it—a very important item to a man who had little money to devote to
costumes. There were, of course, professional persons who could have
fitted him out from wig to sandal, but to these he could not afford to go.
He read the tragedy many times, studied his part till he was what is called
"letter perfect," and at the Astor Library he copied many drawings, colored by his own hand, of the dresses he had to wear. These garments and
effects were made out of the cheapest material from his own patterns, cut
and sewed by his wife, and for six weeks nothing in that house was thought
or talked but Othello. The young man, realising what it all meant to him,
was exceedingly anxious about results, as was his wife. They lived in a
poor, humble little apartment and he was to take a midnight train to the
scene of his great effort only a day or two before he was to make his début
in one of the most important and trying parts of the English-speaking
drama.

I went with him to the train, and just as we were starting Mrs. Warde
came down with her eyes swimming, and said:

"I've just put the children to bed and I must tell you what Arthur
prayed"; Arthur was then a lad not out of his frocks. It seems that the
child, kneeling by his little cot, had gone through the regular formula,

"Our Father," "Now I lay me," "Please, God, remember papa and mamma and little sister and dear grandmother in England," and had then added, as an impromptu, "and O God, do please help papa through with Othello."

On the Tuesday morning there came to me a telegram from Warde saying, simply, "I think God has heard Arthur's prayer."

I told this story at a dinner one night, as I am trying to tell it now, and was startled by an inquiry from the wife of a well-known New York clergyman who, with wonder and doubt in her voice, demanded,

"Do you mean to tell me that actors' children say their prayers!"

Like Father, Like Fun

In 1912 Eugene O'Neill made his last voyage as able seaman and got his discharge papers. He was unemployed and his father—who was rich and mean—refused to give him money. Instead, James O'Neill took his two boys, Jamie and Eugene, on tour with his perennial production of *The Count of Monte Cristo*. One of the actors in the company had succumbed to the temptations of New Orleans, and decamped there. James offered Eugene the chance to replace him in two minor roles of a gendarme and a jailor. The ex-sailor learned both parts on the train west. He hated acting, and particularly hated the creaking vehicle that had served his father for three decades. It must have showed, because after a performance in Ogden, Utah, O'Neill *père* told his son: "Sir, I'm not satisfied with your performance."

"Sir," the future playwright responded, "I am not satisfied with your play."

Following this tour the O'Neill family was reunited in their New London, Connecticut, house, and Eugene chose an August day that summer for the setting of *Long Day's Journey into Night*. The bad experience with *The Count* started him reading and writing plays. Dr. Joseph M. Ganey remembered in the fall of 1912 how Eugene reeled into the city room of the local newspaper, where the managing editor reproached him:

"If you weren't James O'Neill's son, you'd be down in the gutter with all the rest of the bums."

The young playwright was not too drunk or shy to make an accurate prediction:

"The day will come," he retorted, "when James O'Neill will be remembered only as the father of Eugene O'Neill."

Life with Father

Being from an acting family has clear advantages for pursuing a theatrical career, and the theatre has been enriched by some of the great dynasties that ruled the stage. But following a famous parent into the profession, and carving out a separate identity for oneself, can be quite painful and difficult. Joseph Schildkraut (1895–1964), the son of the great Viennese and Yiddish actor Rudolf Schildkraut, came to America in 1920 and went on to create such memorable roles as Liliom and Anne Frank's father. But he never quite stepped out from the shadow of his father: even his 1959 autobiography was titled *My Father and I*.

When the Moscow Art Theatre was visiting New York in 1923, its founder, Konstantin Stanislavski, went to see the Theatre Guild's ambitious production of *Peer Gynt*, in which Joseph Schildkraut played the title role. Congratulating each member of the company backstage, Stanislavski paused when he was introduced to the young Schildkraut. Then he offered his hand with the unkind cut: "Ah, your father was a great actor."

Minnie's Boys

Behind many a success in show business stands a stage mother. Sophie Tucker remembers the mother who stood behind the Marx Brothers.

It was while I was playing a long run in Chicago that I got to know the Four Marx Brothers and their redheaded driver of a mother, Minnie Palmer. Everybody called her Minnie. She was hell-bent her boys should be a success. She put on their act and rehearsed them; one minute she was out in front of the house, watching, the next she was backstage ready to wallop the kids for doing something wrong; arguing with them, protesting that if only they would listen to her they could be headliners. When the kids did well, Minnie would laugh louder than even Milton Berle's mother laughed at his act. The few times the boys played on the same bill with me I would sit out in front with Minnie and she'd ask me to watch them so she could go back and remind them of something they missed doing. After a show I would listen to what the audience said about the boys and report it to Minnie: "Can Harpo talk at all?" "Is he really dumb?" "Chico, he's an Italian." "Groucho, what is he supposed to be?" "Zeppo, that's the baby." "They can't be brothers; they all look different." She would think over such comments as these and sometimes get ideas from them. Minnie lived to enjoy the boys' success for a long time, and nobody enjoyed it more than she, who had put her whole heart and soul into creating it. They were four wonderful boys to her, and four grand friends to me to this very day.

They Really Do Exist

Fanny Brice had an authentic Jewish mother. Watching her daughter perform, she would nudge the people sitting next to her: "That's my daughter. She's good, isn't she?" And whenever Fanny visited her, she was sure to hear the two lines: "Oh, did I cook a good soup yesterday. It was like gold." And: "Fanny, save your money."

My Daughter the Playwright

Virginia Kaye Bloomgarden remembers the opening night of Another Part of the Forest (1946), *which her husband had produced.*

I could see Lillian Hellman's father in the audience, sitting far down towards the stage. When some discussion was going on in the play about money, I saw Mr. Hellman take out a big wad of bills, as if he was going to offer it to one of the characters, but I was relieved when he finally put it back in his pocket. There was a big applause when the act was over, and he stood up facing the audience: "Ladies and gentlemen," Mr. Hellman announced, "that's my daughter!" Fortunately, Lillian wasn't around the theatre or I think she would have killed him.

What Rhymes with Tallulah?

Tallulah Bankhead came from an old political family; her father was Speaker of the House of Representatives. George M. Cohan once sang the following song:

> My messages to Congress
> Are a lot of boola-boola.
> I'm not so fond of Bankhead,
> But I'd love to meet Tallulah.

Meet My Parents

After her brushes with the fringes of off-off-Broadway, Joan Rivers began to think of herself as a comic. An essential step in her career was to get a

manager, whom she wanted to introduce, like a new boyfriend, to her
parents, who had the normal parental reaction.

When I told my parents about Harry Brent, they glanced quickly at each
other and I could see a new set of worry messages whizzing back and forth.
My father breathed deeply, exhaled, and described for the twentieth time
his visits as a young doctor to the Magistrates Court and how prostitutes
arraigned before the judge always said, "I'm in show business." He went
on, "The whole business doesn't smell good to me. I've heard about auditioning in front of so-called managers—everybody's a manager these days—
and you're auditioning in this man's apartment. And we hear things on
radio and television, how one out of hundreds makes a go of it in show
business and the rest are terribly disappointed and very often go astray
altogether because of certain pressures by so-called producers."

Right away I was defensive, shouting my litany: "Why do you always
assume the worst! Why?"

"Because look what you hang out with. Look what you bring home.
Scum. Look at your sister. She's a lawyer."

"Harry Brent is a professional and he thinks I'm good."

"He's either out to take your money or he's a pimp," he said, my mother
nodding in agreement.

"Just meet him. That's all I ask. Just meet him."

"Okay," said my father, "let's see this big deal who can make you a
star."

A dinner with Harry was arranged at Lindy's on Broadway and we met
on the sidewalk—Harry in his slightly frayed camel's hair coat bought at
Klein's on the Square shrugged over his shoulders, the collar up, a white
silk aviator's scarf around his neck. As though I was introducing my fiancé,
I was very nervous, hoping they would like him, hoping he would not eat
too much because I knew my father would have to pick up the check.

At dinner Harry had a wonderful time, chatting away between bites:
". . . when I was a kid . . . always loved the business . . . best brisket
in town and, waiter, I'll have a bottle of beer, make sure it's imported . . .
used to tell Frankie, known him since he was making twenty-five dollars
a week in Newark . . . I prefer to work with unknowns . . . pass the
pickles . . . this little lady here . . . waiter, another order of brisket . . .
Deano said to me . . ."

My mother sat expressionless, frozen by culture shock, none of the food
ever reaching her lips. My father, hardly touching his dinner, his eyes filled
with confusion, was trying to be jolly but was paralyzed by the knowledge
that he was paying. For them, it was dinner with an alien being, an extra-

terrestrial—this man with the pinkie ring saying hello to waiters who did not know who the hell he was. He waved to anybody famous—to a Jan Murray—calling out, "Hi, Jan. Best to Danny," and then turned back to my mother to say confidentially, "I remember like it was yesterday the first time I saw Danny. He was just a kid but killed 'em. Jesus, he destroyed 'em. I swear to God—if you'll pardon me—I pissed in my pants."

My mother's hand *flew* to her pearls.

Finally, after finishing his second piece of cheesecake, wiping his mouth with the napkin, Harry pushed back his third cup of coffee and said, "Let's talk about your little girl here. I know it's crazy, I know you're not going to believe me, but I think she's got something." My mother and father stared in disbelief. Harry continued, "I want to manage her. No fooling around—I'm not that kind, believe me."

At last my mother spoke her first words. She said enigmatically, "Well, we'll see. We'll all see."

On the drive home I could tell that my parents, against their better judgment, were impressed. They were thinking in terms of instant fame— like making instant cocoa—and Harry Brent was the first person who had ever said, "She's not crazy," and he was just professional enough for them to think, *Well, maybe this will do it for her.* In the car my mother asked, "So what do you think, Meyer? Do you think he's a good manager?"

"I don't know if he's a good manager or not," my father said. "But I'll tell you one thing, he's a damn good eater."

Mom Is the Word

George Ade, the well-known humorist, had scored a success on Broadway with his comedy *The College Widow* (1904). His mother came to see it one night and asked:

"George, do you really get more than $500 a week for doing that?"

"Yes, I do, mother," Ade replied.

"George," she advised, "you keep right on fooling them."

With Family Like This, Who Needs Critics?

Most artists remember every encouragement, and also each critical barb aimed at them during their career. Playright Robert Anderson keeps the latter in the family album.

My practice has been never to discuss a play in progress. Not with anyone. In 1952 I was working on what was to become *Tea and Sympathy* and my wife Phyllis begged and begged me to reveal the subject of the play. Hers was more than a casual interest, as she was at the time head of the literary department at the Theatre Guild. Finally, I gave in. "All right. But all I will tell you is that it's a play about a boys' school." To which she groaned: "Not another play about a boys' school!"

My mother had not read *Tea and Sympathy*. Along with not discussing my plays while I was writing them, I didn't show them to my parents, thinking that they would rather see them than read them. When it was announced that Deborah Kerr had signed for the leading part, Mother said: "It must be a much better play than I thought it was."

When my play *Silent Night, Lonely Night*, starring Henry Fonda and Barbara Bel Geddes, opened in 1959, my mother had died. My father, now rather deaf, sat in the fourth row with my wife-to-be, Teresa Wright. Shortly before the curtain went up, he turned to Teresa and said in a very loud voice: "No matter how bad this is, I'm going to tell the poor boy I like it."

Dagger in the Heart

Soon after Beth Henley won a Pulitzer prize for *Crimes of the Heart* (1981), her sister C.C. was going into the local dress shop in the Mississippi town where the sisters were born to get some alterations done. "C.C.," said the seamstress, "I know you're just as smart as your sister, why don't you go out and get one of those Pulitzer prizes?" As Beth Henley remarked in an interview: "C.C. said she felt like Billy Carter."

Talk That's Not Cheap

Eddie Cantor, the father of five girls, tended towards monologizing onstage and off. Visiting Borah Minnewitch, an American entertainer living in retirement outside Paris, Cantor went on in his unstoppable way, until his wife Ida ordered him to shut up. "If I shut up," the comedian retorted, "you and the kids would starve to death."

The Androgynous King

When Jacob Adler died in 1926, fifty thousand New Yorkers turned out for his funeral. Harold Clurman, who later married Jacob's daughter Stella, described this king of the Yiddish stage as possessed of a magnetism that combined "devastating charm with strong physical appeal . . . He 'seduced' not only his audiences, but his servants, his colleagues, his community, and most of all his family." Jacob also seduced numberless women and was patriarch of a large brood, both legitimate and otherwise. Clurman, observing how Adler had attracted not just women but also men ("There was something maternal in his fatherliness, an enormous tenderness") repeated a story he had heard from Jacob's third wife Sarah.

Jacob Adler was preparing to act in one of Jacob Gordin's plays, and his feelings of frustration about his adequacy to do the role justice made him frequently break into tears. On one of these hysterical occasions, Sarah slapped him hard on both cheeks: "Of course you can do it, get up and begin." She later explained: "He had to be treated like a woman."

The Name in the Title

The Group Theatre was closely knit in more ways than one. When Robert Lewis heard that Harold Clurman, who was married to Stella Adler, planned to write a history of the Group, he suggested—in waggish deference to Stanislavski's autobiography, *My Life in Art*—that he call it *My Wife in Art*. Clurman finally published the book under the title *The Fervent Years*.

Domestic Violence

Zero Mostel first turned down the part of Pseudolus in *A Funny Thing Happened on the Way to the Forum* (1962), which became one of the high points in his career. He told Craig Zadan:

"Then Hal Prince went to my wife and asked why I wouldn't do it, and she came to me and said: 'I heard you turned down *Forum*.' And I said, 'Oh yes, I forgot to tell you.' And she said, 'If you don't take it, I'm going to stab you in the balls.' So I said, 'All right, but this is the last time I'm gonna do something for money for you!' "

Married Life

When designer Boris Aronson first met Marilyn Monroe, he said he immediately knew why Arthur Miller found her desirable. But as for marrying her, Aronson added with a Yiddish lilt—"that's a *wife?*"

Elia Kazan, who recalls this in his recent autobiography, adds a story about the time Aronson's wife surprised him in bed with another woman. Boris leaped out of bed screaming and protesting: "It's not me! It's not me!"

Pastime

Marilyn Monroe was notorious for always being late. She once told *Look* magazine: "I've been on a calendar but never on time." When in May 1962, she was scheduled to sing "Happy Birthday, Mr. President" for JFK, she kept 22,000 people waiting at Madison Square Garden so long that Peter Lawford introduced her as "the late Marilyn Monroe." (She died three months later.)

Gossip columnist Radie Harris once asked Arthur Miller how he could stand having to wait around for Marilyn all the time.

"It really doesn't bother me," said the playwright. "I can always use the extra time to write."

French with Tears

Alan Jay Lerner said after divorcing his French wife: "That's the most expensive French lesson I've had."

Compliment

Dorothy Stickney was once making up to play the role of a 75-year-old woman, while her husband, playwright Howard Lindsay, watched her. "Darling," he complimented her, "I can hardly wait."

Art Imitates Life

After her husband, Richard Halliday, had died, Mary Martin went into semi-retirement, but she had lost none of her vitality. As she told columnist Radie Harris, who was visiting her in Palm Springs, one of the actress's grandsons had once introduced her to his playmate: "I want you to meet my grandmother—Peter Pan!"

The King

John Springer, press agent for Richard Burton, remembers taking his son Gary, then six years old, to see Camelot.

We went backstage afterwards and Richard took Gary out on the empty stage and did the whole bit dubbing the little page with his sword. Then he said:

"Let me just get out of these clothes and meet you over at Sardi's." So Gary and I walked over to Sardi's, where Jimmy, who I'm sorry to say has recently passed away, greeted my son:

"Well, Gary, and what are you doing here?"

"I'm here to meet the king."

"The king? Who's the king?"

And Gary, very disgusted at his ignorance, said:

"Katie Burton's daddy."

The Facts of Life

My friend, actress Didi Conn, told me this story of the opening night of the musical *Baby*. During the show, her husband David Shire (who composed the music) was nervously pacing up and down at the back of the orchestra seats. His eight-year-old son Matthew was sitting with Didi on the aisle nearby, watching the scene in the doctor's office where an infertile couple are being given the rules they must follow in order to conceive. The doctor tells them it is very important for them to avoid foreplay. Suddenly Shire heard his son's voice directed at him from the dark:

"Dad, what is foreplay?"

It was the last place and time for a father to think about how to answer his son's first question about sex. He wanted to brush it off with a clever riposte but already the boy was repeating the question with greater urgency:

"Dad, what is foreplay?"

At this point, Didi and David decided to yank Matthew out into the lobby.

David was still thinking of getting by with something like "Son, it's like between three play and five play," when Didi interposed:

"Honey, foreplay is like a lot of hugging and kissing. Just another kind of play."

"Oh, I see," said Matthew and went back to enjoy the show, which his father originally conceived around the time his son was born.

Present After the Creation

Alexander Woollcott was a lifelong bachelor (some said "old maid"), but he was frequently asked to be godfather to the children born to his large circle of friends. Invited by Helen Hayes and Charles MacArthur to perform his regular role at the baptism of their daughter Mary, Woollcott was overheard sighing: "Always a godfather, never a god!"

CHAPTER 24

Ah, The Theatre!

Fall Guy

William Collier once ran into Al Wilson, another comedian, at a railroad station, about to leave with a road show. Asking why Wilson was at one end of the platform while the rest of his company at the other, he received the answer:

"I never speak to my company."

"I saw your show," Collier came back, "and I don't blame you."

To Be Perfectly Candida

When Cornelia Otis Skinner scored a great success in the 1935 revival of Shaw's *Candida*, the author sent her a cable:

"Excellent—Greatest!"

"Undeserving such praise," she wired back.

Shaw sent another telegram: "Meant the play."

"So did I," Skinner cabled back.

Frankness

Tallulah Bankhead could be depended upon to speak her mind at all times. After she saw the film version of *Orpheus Descending*, she told Tennessee Williams: "Darling, they've absolutely ruined your perfectly dreadful play."

Parting Shots

One of Wilson's Mizner's friends tried to argue that a well-known Broadway producer "must have a head" or he would not be so successful.

"They put better heads on umbrellas," Mizner observed.

Alexander Woollcott was eating at a resturant when he noticed Arthur Hopkins at a nearby table.

"You wouldn't want to read a play, would you?"

Sensing a setup, Hopkins said nothing.

"I forgot. You're a producer," said Woollcott, "you don't read."

Noël Coward had heard that one of his unfavorite producers, who had the reputation of being somewhat dim-witted, had blown his brains out.

"Must have been rather a good shot," Coward marveled.

Over the Rainbow

Before a matinee performance of *The Voice of the Turtle*, Margaret Sullavan got so angry that she broke a mirror over the head of the company manager, Sam Schwartz. During intermission she sent her dresser to enquire whether he was going to take her to dinner as usual.

Foot-in-Mouth Disease

During Miriam Hopkins's debut in 1921 in the chorus of the *First Music Box Revue,* an aging soprano was being tried out of town for a leading role. Desperate to impress, she confided to the young actress:

"You know, my dear, I insured my voice for fifty thousand dollars."

"That's wonderful," said Miss Hopkins in all sweet innocence. "And what did you do with the money?"

Color

Dorothy McGuire was playing the title role in Rose Franken's comedy *Claudia* (1941), in which Frances Starr played the dying mother. The older actress, a legendary star of David Belasco's stable, was now sixty with beautiful natural hair which Dorothy McGuire very much admired. Much to her horror, Miss Starr remarked one day that she intended to have "a bit of color put into it."

"But why," said McGuire, "it is so beautiful as it is?"

"It looks better on the pillow," said Frances Starr, thinking only of her death scene.

Danger: Comic at Work

George Jessel was listening to an actor acquaintance telling of his latest triumphs:

"Last night I was a sensation at the Roxy. I had the audience glued to their seats."

"How clever of you to think of it," Jessel remarked.

During World War II when his friend Larry Adler, the harmonica player, came back from a tour of Palestine, he boasted to Jessel:

"Georgie, I actually got to pray at the Wailing Wall in Jerusalem."

"What for?" Jessel asked. "Better billing?"

Performance Artist

Spalding Gray, the monologuist and performance artist, sometimes gets depressed by the small audiences that avant-garde theatre attracts in America. He was forcibly reminded of this situation when he went to see his pal John Malkovich in the recent revival of *Death of a Salesman*, which was S.R.O. on Broadway. They decided after the show to go for a drink. "I don't know how people recognized him," Gray told interviewer Don Shewey, "he had a beret on—but these autograph hounds and people with flash cameras started chasing him across the street. And John, in his inimitable way, turned to me and said, 'Don't you wonder why performance artists don't get followed like this, Spalding?'"

The Avant-garde

As a long-time chronicler of the off-Broadway scene for the New Yorker, *Edith Oliver has seen much—sometimes too much.*

Went to see the Living Theatre at the Brooklyn Academy doing some damn fool play [probably *Paradise Now*] in which everybody stripped naked and they were walking up and down the aisle in their natural state—unbathed [here Miss Oliver held her nose]. Somebody then sat on my feet, and Clive Barnes, who was sitting across the aisle, yelled, "Get off Edith's feet!" And an enormous fat woman, a member of the cast, sat on Henry Hewes's lap—and Henry is a living skeleton, as you know—and sitting behind them, I said, "Tell her to fuck off, Henry," and Henry said, "Fuck off," and she did.

The Brooklyn Academy once flew a group of critics over to the Edinburgh Festival. We were sitting at the Cafe Royal, it was one a.m., when a director of the Fringe Festival, quite well known, came up and said:

"I have a new show at my theatre at 2:30 a.m.—come!"

So like a bunch of sheep we trooped over to his theatre. The minute we arrived, we were told to hang our coats—somehow they always ask you to do that at avant-garde events—and sure enough there was one of those ubiquitous Polish theatre companies in residence.

"Let's get out of here," I said. "Go back to Poland," I said. "It's rotten for you there, I know, but it's rotten for us here." And I left.

Louis Jouvet, the great French director and actor has said it long ago: "The one thing constant in a changing world is the avant-garde."

Pain

Actors are mostly creatures of the night; for one thing, performing winds them up and they need hours afterwards to wind down. Harvey Fierstein remembers that after four hours of tour de force performance in his award-winning *Torch Song Trilogy*, "I would get home at one-thirty in the morning . . . and cry for three or four hours, because there was no place at the end of that play to dump all that pain and emotion."

The pain was such that Fierstein would take eight to ten aspirins a performance. His peculiar voice had been ruined earlier, during the off-off-Broadway run of a play called *Xircus, the Private Life of Jesus Christ*: "I had to deliver a five-page monologue over a recording of Kate Smith singing 'God Bless America' at full blast. The director refused to turn the volume down, and I wanted every word heard."

The Eternal Question

Actress Helen Menken, at one time president of the American Theatre Wing that gives out the Tony Awards (and also Humphrey Bogart's first wife when she was the more famous of the two), was performing during

World War II in a very moving sketch by Moss Hart about a nurse reading a letter to a blind soldier. Menken spied the playwright during final dress rehearsal and greeted him with tears in her eyes and a choking voice:

"It's so beautiful and touching, I don't think I can do it justice without breaking down." Then after the slightest pause, she gathered herself and asked:

"Tell me, Moss, must the blind soldier interrupt me so much?"

The Price Is Right

Sarah Bernhardt suffered an accident in 1915 while playing the title role of Sardou's play *La Tosca* and had to have one of her legs amputated. The convalescent star received a cable from the director of Pan-American Exposition in San Francisco, offering her a hundred thousand dollars if she permitted her leg to be exhibited. The actress wired back, asking, "Which leg?"

Doubles, Anyone?

Milton Goldman recalls having lunch with his client John Gielgud at the Four Seasons in 1967. That morning's paper carried the story that producer Alexander Cohen had bought the rights to *Madame Sarah*, Cornelia Otis Skinner's biography of Sarah Bernhardt, and was planning to make a musical from it.

"I suppose," said Sir John with a glint in his eyes, "Barbra Streisand will play the first two acts, and Dame Judith Anderson take over in the third with a wooden leg."

Epitaph

As a cub reporter, Ben Hecht was assigned to go to a press conference with Bernhardt, who was performing for the last time in Chicago.

"Go see what you can get out of the Divine Sarah," editor Henry Smith said, and I bounced off to the Congress Hotel in Chicago where Bernhardt had agreed to meet the press. I found a wrinkled old lady sitting in a wheelchair. Her face was lavender, her hair was orange and a white tulle scarf billowed around her neck. She had a wooden leg. She had just finished a matinee at the Majestic Theatre playing the seventeen-year-old boy L'Aiglon.

My fellow reporters asked innumerable questions and I hung back. I knew nothing of Bernhardt except one fact. I had read it a few weeks ago in Vance Thompson's delightful book, *Parisian Portraits*. One of the portraits had been of Jean Richepin, the French playwright and African big game hunter—a powerful heller of a man.

My silence finally attracted Bernhardt. She pointed a finger at me and inquired of the interpreter in French if that young dummy had any questions.

I answered in English that I had one, and asked it.

"Is it true," I asked, "that Jean Richepin playing opposite Miss Bernhardt in the play he had written for her, *Miarka, the Bear*, tried to lay her during their love scene at the end of Act Two so that they had to ring the curtain down?"

The one-legged old lady in the wheelchair listened to the translation of my question and then stared at me. Tears filled her eyes. She reached her arms up and embraced my neck. And a voice shaking with tears and chuckles spoke in my ear. "Yes, yes, it is true! It is true! I loved the big Richepin. I loved many people, many things. But all I can remember now is that I loved the stage. Write of me only that—please, young reporter, that I loved the stage."

Cause of Death

At the 1986 Kennedy Center salute to Jessica Tandy and Hume Cronyn, actress Glenn Close mentioned an incident which captures the spirit and tradition of old troupers down the centuries. During the run of *The Gin Game* (1977), Hume Cronyn had caught the 'flu, but he insisted on going on for several nights, during which time he grew more and more sick. Despite his temperature running at 101°, and Jessica Tandy's overwhelming anxiety for her husband, the starring couple played with the same precise perfection as the public had grown to expect from them. Finally, director Mike Nichols had to insist on closing down the show, as he said, "to save my stars from death by professionalism."

Going Pro

After the Lunts had fallen out with the Theatre Guild, they hinted to a friend that under the right conditions they wouldn't mind being asked to come back and act at the Guild again. Referring to the unprofessional chaos that often reigned in the company, their friend said: "You can't. It's like the Olympics: you've lost your amateur standing."

The Dead Gull

The Theatre Guild was producing *The Sea Gull* with Lunt and Fontanne (1938), and the set was almost finished except for the stuffed seagull that is supposed to be mounted on a bookcase, according to Chekhov's stage directions. The Russian playwright of course could not know that after his death the United States Congress would pass a law—the Federal Migratory Bird Treaty of 1915—making it a serious offense to shoot and stuff a seagull. The company tried borrowing one from a museum, and when that failed, to dress up a duck with goose feathers. But the results were too comic. When things were growing desperate, Marty Fantana, the props master, actually found a dead gull down in Southampton, on Long Island. He took it to a taxidermist, who at first refused to stuff it, and only agreed after papers were drawn up and signed by witnesses who testified that the bird was found dead.

As soon as Alfred Lunt walked on to the set and noticed the stuffed bird, he could not resist quoting his friend Noël Coward, who disliked Chekhov in general and *The Sea Gull* in particular. "I *hate* plays," Coward had said, "that have a stuffed bird sitting on the bookcase screaming, 'I'm the title, I'm the title, I'm the title!' "

Chekhovian Moments

In 1950 Joshua Logan wrote and directed a complete adaptation of *The Cherry Orchard*. He set it in the South and called it *The Wisteria Trees*. But the profession was not fooled by these changes and the play became known as "Southern fried Chekhov."

Margaret Webster's production of *The Cherry Orchard* in 1944 contained a moving performance by Joseph Schildkraut. It was somewhat ruined one night when the actor's recently divorced wife invaded the theatre. She hissed her ex-husband on his first entrance, then saluted his first speech with a Bronx cheer. She was thumbing her nose at him as ushers guided her towards an exit.

Working with Lillian Hellman on her Chekhovian play *The Autumn Garden*, Harold Clurman wanted to encourage her to make her characters more lovable like Chekhov does. "But Harold," she disarmingly told the director, "I'm not as good as Chekhov."

She Wasn't a Methodist

After the establishment of the Actors Studio (1947), "method acting" became a dominant style in American theatre. It was also a hot topic for the
press. Geraldine Page was in the cast of Lillian Hellman's last play, *Toys
in the Attic* (1960), and overheard a reporter ask the formidable English
actress Wendy Hiller what her method of acting was. "Well, I have a bash
at it," said Miss Hiller, "and if it doesn't go, I have another bash at it."

The Rest Is Silence

Lee Strasberg alienated many of the people with whom he started the
Group Theatre and the Actors Studio. Stella Adler fell out with him over
interpretation of the Stanislavski System: he emphasized emotional recall
from the actor's memory, she stresses the needs of the character in a particular set of circumstances.

Miss Adler insists that the differences with Strasberg were philosophical
and never personal. The day after his death in 1982, she asked her acting
class to stand for a moment of silence.

"A man of the theatre died last night," she started solemnly. Then when
the class sat down again, she continued: "It will take a hundred years before the harm that man has done to the art of acting can be corrected."

Process

*The Group Theatre reached its peak with the production of Clifford Odets'
Golden Boy (1937), directed by Harold Clurman. Margaret Brenman-
Gibson, in her 1981 biography of Odets, captures a moment that seems
quintessential of the theatre.*

A few days before dress rehearsal Odets made a proposal to Clurman for
last-minute revisions of the central meaning of the play. In a scene where
the gangster Fuseli is berating Lorna for leading Joe on "like Gertie's
whoore" ("You turned down the sweetest boy who ever walked in shoes
. . . the golden boy, that king among the juven-niles! He gave you his
hand—you spit in his face!") Odets, in a misogynous burst, decided, as
Clurman recalled, that "Fuseli brings out his gun with the intention of
shooting Lorna." When Clurman heard this idea, he became enraged.
Purple and choking, he began to scream, "That's all wrong! You can't
change it now! That's not what you meant at all!" Finally, as in an epileptic
convulsion, he fell upon the floor, rocking, rolling, screaming, and, in his

misery, pounding the floor with fists and feet. The cast, thinking their director was truly in a fit of epilepsy, or psychotic, looked on aghast. No one moved until Odets said quietly. "All right, we'll do it the way it is." Clurman arose with dignity and continued the rehearsal. Group actor Sanford Meisner, impassively smoking a cigarette in his long holder, smiled and remarked coolly, "I wouldn't be in any other business."

Bibliography

Books Cited and Consulted

Abbott, George. *"Mister Abbott."* New York: Random House, 1963.

Adams, A. K. *The Home Book of Humorous Quotations.* New York: Dodd, Mead, 1969.

Adams, Cindy. *Lee Strasberg: The Imperfect Genius of the Actors Studio.* Garden City: Doubleday, 1980.

Adams, Joey. *From Gags to Riches.* New York: Frederick Fell, 1946.

Aldrich, Richard Stoddard. *Gertrude Lawrence as Mrs. A.* New York: Greystone Press, 1954.

Alexander, Diane. *Playhouse.* Los Angeles: Dorleac-MacLeish, 1984.

Alger, William Rounseville. *Life of Edwin Forrest, the American Tragedian.* Philadelphia, 1877.

Allen, John. *Great Moments in the Theatre.* New York: Roy Publishers, 1958.

Allen, Mearl. *Welcome to the Stork Club.* San Diego: A. S. Barnes, 1980.

Allen, Steve. *Funny People.* New York: Stein & Day, 1981.

Arden, Eve. *Three Phases of Eve.* New York: St. Martin's, 1985.

Arliss, George. *Up the Years from Bloomsbury.* New York: Blue Ribbon Books, 1927.

Asbury, Herbert. *All Around the Town.* New York: Knopf, 1934.

Ashley, Elizabeth (with Ross Firestone). *Actress—Postcards from the Road.* New York: M. Evans, 1978.

Atkinson, Brooks. *Broadway.* New York: Macmillan, 1970.

————. *Broadway Scrapbook*. New York: Theatre Arts, 1947.

Atkinson, Brooks, and Albert Hirschfeld. *The Lively Years (1920–1973)*. New York: Association Press, 1973.

Ayres, Alfred. *Acting and Actors, Elocution and Elocutionists*. New York: D. Appleton, 1894.

Bailey, Pearl. *Talking to Myself*. New York: Harcourt Brace Jovanovich, 1971.

John Bainbridge. *The Wonderful World of Toots Shor*. Boston: Houghton Mifflin, 1951.

Bárdi, Ödön. *Thália Mosolya*. Budapest: Bibliotheca Kiadó, 1957.

Barker, Barbara M. (ed.). *Bolossy Kiralfy, Creator of Great Musical Spectacles—An Autobiography*. Ann Arbor, Michigan: UMI Research Press, 1988.

Barnett, Lincoln. *Writing on Life—Sixteen Close-ups*. New York: William Sloane Associates, 1951.

Barnum, Phineas T. *Struggles and Triumphs: Or, Forty Years' Recollections of P. T. Barnum. Written by Himself*. Buffalo, N.Y.: 1872.

Barrett, Raina. *First Your Money Then Your Clothes—My Life and Oh! Calcutta!* New York: William Morrow, 1973.

Barrymore, Ethel. *Memories—An Autobiography*. New York: Harper & Bros., 1955.

Barrymore, John. *Confessions of an Actor*. Indianapolis: Bobbs-Merrill, 1926.

Barrymore, Lionel (told to Cameron Shipp). *We Barrymores*. New York: Appleton-Century-Crofts, 1950.

Barton, Peter. *Staying Power—Performing Artists Talk About Their Lives*. New York: Dial Press, 1980.

Beaufort, John. *505 Theatre Questions Your Friends Can't Answer*. New York: Walker & Co., 1983.

Behan, Brendan. *Brendan Behan's New York*. New York: Bernard Geis Associates, 1964.

Bel Geddes, Norman. *Miracle in the Evening*. Garden City: Doubleday, 1960.

Belasco, David. *The Theatre Through Its Stage Door*. New York: Harper & Bros., 1919.

Bender, Marylin. *The Beautiful People*. New York: Coward-McCann, 1967.

Bennett, Joan, & Lois Kibbee. *The Bennett Playbill*. New York: Holt, Rinehart & Winston, 1970.

Berger, Phil. *The Last Laugh—The World of Stand-Up Comics*. New York: William Morrow, 1975.

Berkowitz, Gerald M. *New Broadways: Theatre Across America (1950–1980)*. Totowa, N.J.: Rowman & Littlefield, 1982.

Betsko, Kathleen, & Rachel Koenig. *Interviews with Contemporary Playwrights*. New York: William Morrow, 1987.

Billington, Michael. *Guinness Book of Theatre Facts and Feats*. Enfield, Eng.: Guinness Superlatives, 1982.

Bishop, Jim. *The Mark Hellinger Story—A Biography of Broadway and Hollywood*. New York: Appleton-Century-Crofts, 1952.

Blum, Daniel, and John Willis. *A Pictorial History of the American Theatre 1860–1976*. New York: Crown, 1977.

Blumenthal, George (told to Arthur H. Menkin). *My Sixty Years in Show*

Business—A Chronicle of the American Theatre (1874–1934). New York: Olympia Publishing, 1936.

Bonanno, Wander. *Angela Lansbury: A Biography.* New York: St. Martin's Press, 1987.

Bordman, Gerald. *American Musical Comedy—From Adonis to Dreamgirls.* New York: Oxford University Press, 1982.

———. *American Musical Revue—From the Passing Show to Sugar Babies.* New York: Oxford University Press, 1985.

———. *American Musical Theatre—A Chronicle.* New York: Oxford University Press, 1978.

———. *American Operetta from H.M.S. Pinafore to Sweeney Todd.* New York: Oxford University Press, 1981.

———. *Jerome Kern—His Life and His Music.* New York: Oxford University Press, 1980.

———. *The Oxford Companion to American Theatre.* New York: Oxford University Press, 1984.

Borns, Betsy. *Comic Lives—Inside the World of American Stand-up Comedy.* New York: Simon & Schuster, 1987.

Bowen, Croswell (with Shane O'Neill). *Curse of the Misbegotten.* New York: McGraw-Hill, 1959.

Bradshaw, Jon. *Dreams That Money Can Buy—The Tragic Life of Libby Holman.* New York: William Morrow, 1985.

Braude, Jacob M. *Braude's Treasury of Wit and Humor.* Englewood Cliffs, N.J.: Prentice-Hall, 1964.

Brenman-Gibson, Margaret: *Clifford Odets, American Playwright.* New York: Atheneum, 1981.

Brough, James. *The Prince and the Lily.* New York: Coward, McCann & Geoghegan, 1975.

Broun, Heywood Hale. *A Studied Madness.* Garden City: Doubleday, 1965.

Brown, John Mason. *Dramatis Personae.* New York: Viking, 1963.

Bruce, Lenny. *How To Talk Dirty and Influence People.* Chicago: Playboy Press, 1965.

Burrows, Abe. *Honest Abe—Is There Really No Business Like Show Business?* Boston: Atlantic Monthly Press, 1980.

Campbell, Patricia J. *Passing the Hat: Street Performers in America.* New York: Delacorte Press, 1981.

Case, Frank. *Tales of a Wayward Inn.* New York: Frederick A. Stokes, 1938.

Cavett, Dick & Christopher Porterfield. *Cavett.* New York: Harcourt Brace Jovanovich, 1974.

Celebrity Research Group. *The Bedside Book of Celebrity Gossip.* New York: Crown, 1984.

Cerf, Bennett. *Anything for a Laugh.* New York: Grosset & Dunlap, 1946.

———. *Laugh Day.* Garden City: Doubleday, 1965.

———. *Laughter Incorporated.* Garden City: Garden City Books, 1950.

———. *The Laugh's on Me.* Garden City: Doubleday, 1959.

———. *The Sound of Laughter.* Garden City: Doubleday, 1970.

Chinoy, Helen Krich, and Linda Walsh Jenkins. *Women in the American Theatre—Careers, Images, Movements.* New York: Crown, 1981.

Churchill, Allen. *The Great White Way: A Re-creation of Broadway's Golden Era of Theatrical Entertainment.* New York: E. P. Dutton, 1962.

Clurman, Harold. *The Fervent Years.* New York: Knopf, 1945.

———. *All People Are Famous.* New York: Harcourt Brace Jovanovich, 1974.

Cocroft, Thoda. *Great Names and How They Are Made.* Chicago: Dartnell Press, 1941.

Cohn, Art. *The Joker Is Wild—The Story of Joe E. Lewis.* New York: Random House, 1955.

———. *The Nine Lives of Michael Todd.* New York: Random House, 1958.

Connelly, Marc. *Voices Offstage—A Book of Memoirs.* New York: Holt, Rinehart & Winston, 1968.

Cornell, Katharine. *I Wanted To Be an Actress.* New York: Random House, 1939.

Crawford, Mary Caroline. *The Romance of the American Theatre.* New York: Halcyon House, 1940.

Cullman, Marguerite. *Occupation: Angel.* New York: W. W. Norton, 1963.

Davis, Christopher. *The Producer.* New York Harper & Row, 1972.

Davis, Owen, *I'd Like To Do It Again.* New York: Farrar & Rinehart, 1931.

———. *My First Fifty Years in the Theatre.* Boston: Walter H. Baker, 1950.

De Angelis, Jefferson, and Alvin F. Harlow. *A Vagabond Trouper.* New York: Harcourt, Brace, 1931.

Depew, Chauncey M. *My Memories of Eighty Years.* New York: Scribner's 1922.

Diary of a Daly Debutante. New York: Duffield & Co., 1910.

Downer, Alan S. (ed.). *The Memoir of John Durang.* Pittsburgh: University of Pittsburgh Press, 1966.

Drew, John. *My Years on the Stage.* New York: E. P. Dutton, 1922.

Drew, Mrs. John. *Autobiographical Sketch.* New York: Scribner's, 1899.

Drutman, Irving. *Good Company—A Memoir, Mostly Theatrical.* Boston: Little, Brown, 1976.

Dunlap, William. *History of the American Theatre and Anecdotes of the Principal Actors.* New York: Burt Franklin, 1963 (reprint of the 1797 edition).

Eaton, Walter Prichard. *Plays and Players: Leaves from a Critic's Scrapbook.* Cincinnati: Stewart and Kidd, 1916.

———. *The Actor's Heritage—Scenes from the Theatre of Yesterday and the Day Before.* Freeport, N.Y.: Books for Libraries Press, 1970 (reprint of 1924 edition).

Eells, George. *Ginger, Loretta and Irene Who?* New York: G. P. Putnam's Sons, 1976.

Elsom, John. *Erotic Theatre.* New York: Taplinger, 1974.

Engelbach, Arthur H. *Anecdotes of the Theatre.* London: Grant Richards, 1914.

Enters, Angna. *First Person Plural.* New York: Stackpole, 1937.

Eustis, Morton. *B'way, Inc!—The Theatre as a Business.* New York: Dodd, Mead, 1934.

Fred Fehl, William Stott with Jane Stott. *On Broadway.* Austin: University of Texas Press, 1978.

Fellows, Dexter W., & Andrew A. Freeman. *This Way to the Big Show—The Life of Dexter Fellows*. New York: Halcyon House. 1936.

Ferber, Edna. *A Peculiar Treasure*. Garden City: Doubleday, 1939.

Fields, Ronald J. *W. C. Fields by Himself—His Intended Biography*. Englewood Cliffs, N.J.: Prentice-Hall, 1973.

Fisher, Charles. *The Columnists: A Surgical Survey*. New York: Howell, Soskin, 1944.

Foley, Doris. *The Divine Eccentric—Lola Montez and the Newspapers*. Los Angeles: Westernlore Press, 1969.

Forbes-Robertson, Diana. *My Aunt Maxine—The Story of Maxine Elliott*. New York: Viking, 1964.

Fordin, Hugh. *Getting To Know Him—A Biography of Oscar Hammerstein II*. New York: Random House, 1977.

Fowler, Gene. *Good Night, Sweet Prince*. New York: Viking, 1944.

Franklin, Joe: *Encyclopaedia of Comedians*. New York: Bell Publishing, 1985.

Frece, Lady de. *Recollections of Vesta Tilley*. London: Hutchinson, 1934.

Freedland, Michael. *The Secret Life of Danny Kaye*. New York: St. Martin's Press, 1985.

Friede, Donald. *The Mechanical Angel*. New York: Knopf, 1948.

Friedman, Lee M. *Pilgrims in a New Land*. Philadelphia: Jewish Publication Society of America, 1948.

Frohman, Daniel. *Memoirs of a Manager*. Garden City: Doubleday, Page, 1911.

———. *Encore*. New York: Lee Furman, 1937.

Garfield, David. *A Player's Place*. New York: Macmillan, 1980.

Gaige, Crosby. *Footlights and Highlights*. New York: E. P. Dutton, 1948.

Gargan, William. *Why Me?* Garden City: Doubleday, 1969.

Gaver, Jack. *Curtain Calls*. New York: Dodd, Mead, 1949.

Gilbert, Douglas. *American Vaudeville—Its Life and Times*. New York: McGraw-Hill, 1940.

Gill, Brendan. *Here at the New Yorker*. New York: Random House, 1975.

Goldberg, Isaac. *The Man Mencken—A Biographical and Critical Survey*. New York: Simon and Schuster, 1925.

Goldman, William. *The Season—A Candid Look at Broadway*. New York: Harcourt, Brace & World, 1969.

Gordon, Ruth. *Myself Among Others*. New York: Atheneum, 1971.

———. *My Side*. New York: Harper & Row, 1976.

Gottfried, Martin. *Jed Harris: The Curse of Genius*. Boston: Little, Brown, 1984.

Gottlieb, Polly Rose. *The Nine Lives of Billy Rose*. New York: Crown, 1968.

Graham, Philip. *Showboats—The History of an American Institution*. Austin: University of Texas Press, 1951.

Granlund, Nils Thor (with Sid Feder and Ralph Hancock). *Blondes, Brunettes, and Bullets*. New York: David McKay, 1957.

Grau, Robert. *Forty Years Observation of Music and the Drama*. New York: Broadway Publishing Company, 1909.

Green, Abel, and Joe Laurie, Jr. *Show Biz—From Vaude to Video as Seen by Variety*. New York: Henry Holt, 1951.

Green, Stanley. *Broadway Musicals: Show by Show.* Milwaukee: H. Leonard
    Books, 1985.
———. *The Great Clowns of Broadway.* New York: Oxford University Press,
    1984.
———. *Ring Bells! Sing Songs!—Broadway Musicals of the 1930s.* New
    Rochelle, N.Y.: Arlington House, 1971.
———. *The Rodgers and Hammerstein Story.* New York: John Day, 1963.
———. *The World of Musical Comedy.* South Brunswick, N.J.: A. S. Barnes,
    1974.
Guernsey, Otis L. Jr. (ed.). *Broadway Song and Story—Playwrights Lyricists/
    Composers Discuss Their Hits.* New York: Dodd, Mead, 1985.
Guernsey, Otis L. *Curtain Times: The New York Theatre (1965–1985).* New
    York: Applause Theatre Books, 1987.
———. *Playwrights, Lyricists, Composers on Theatre.* New York: Dodd,
    Mead, 1974.
Guthrie, Sir Tyrone. *A Life in the Theatre.* New York: McGraw-Hill, 1959.
Hagen, Uta. *Sources—A Memoir.* New York: PAJ Publications, 1983.
Hamburger, Philip. *Curious World—A New Yorker at Large.* San Francisco:
    North Point Press, 1987.
Hamilton, Cosmo. *Unwritten History.* Boston: Little, Brown, 1924.
Hapgood, Norman. *The Stage in America 1897–1900.* New York: Macmillan,
    1901.
Harding, Alfred. *The Revolt of the Actors.* New York: William Morrow, 1929.
Hardwicke, Sir Cedric (as told to James Brough). *A Victorian in Orbit.*
    Garden City: Doubleday, 1961.
Harriman, Margaret Case. *Blessed Are the Debonair.* New York: Rinehart,
    1956.
———. *Take Them Up Tenderly: A Collection of Profiles.* New York: Knopf,
    1944.
Harris, Jed. *A Dance on the High Wire.* New York: Crown, 1979.
Harris, Radie. *Radie's World.* New York: G. P. Putnam's Sons, 1975.
Hart, Moss. *Act One.* New York: Random House, 1959.
Hartnoll, Phyllis. *The Oxford Companion to the Theatre.* New York: Oxford
    University Press, 1983.
Hatton, Joseph. *Henry Irving's Impressions of America.* London: Sampson
    Low, Marston, Searle & Rivington, 1884.
Hay, Peter. *Theatrical Anecdotes.* New York: Oxford University Press, 1987.
Hayes, Helen (with Sanford Doby). *On Reflection.* New York: M. Evans,
    1968.
Hayes, Helen, and Anita Loos. *Twice Over Lightly—New York Then and
    Now.* New York: Harcourt Brace Jovanovich, 1972.
Hays, David. *Light on the Subject.* Calcutta, India: Seagull Books, 1988.
Hecht, Ben. *Charlie: The Improbable Life and Times of Charles MacArthur.*
    New York: Harper & Bros., 1957.
———. *A Child of the Century.* New York: Simon & Schuster, 1954.
Helburn, Theresa. *A Wayward Quest.* Boston: Little, Brown, 1960.
Hellman, Lillian. *Pentimento.* Boston: Little, Brown, 1973.
———. *Scoundrel Time.* Boston: Little, Brown, 1976.

Henderson, Kathy: *First Stage—Profiles of the New American Actors.* New York: Wililam Morrow, 1985.

Hennessey, Joseph (ed.). *The Portable Woollcott.* New York: Viking, 1946.

Heston, Charlton (with Hollis Alpert). *The Actor's Life—Journals 1956–1976.* New York: E. P. Dutton, 1978.

Hewitt, Barnard. *Theatre U.S.A. 1668 to 1957.* New York: McGraw-Hill, 1973.

Hill, George Handel. *Scenes from the Life of an Actor.* New York: 1853.

Hirsch, Foster. *A Method to Their Madness—The History of the Actors Studio.* New York: W. W. Norton, 1984.

Hirschfeld, Al. *Show Business Is No Business.* New York: Simon & Schuster, 1951.

Hopkins, Arthur. *Reference Point.* New York: Samuel French, 1948.

Hopper, DeWolf (with Wesley Winans Stout). *Reminiscences—Once a Clown, Always a Clown.* Garden City: Garden City Publishing, 1927.

Houghton, Norris. *But Not Forgotten.* New York: William Sloane Associates, 1951.

Houseman, John. *Run-through.* New York: Simon & Schuster, 1972.

———. *Front & Center.* New York: Simon & Schuster, 1979.

Hoyt, Edwin. P. *A Gentleman of Broadway—The Story of Damon Runyon.* Boston: Little, Brown, 1964.

Huggett, Richard. *The Curse of Macbeth—With Other Theatrical Superstitions and Ghosts.* Chippenham, Eng.: Picton Publishing, 1981.

Hughes, Glenn. *A History of the American Theatre 1750–1950.* New York: Samuel French, 1951.

Humes, James C. *Speaker's Treasury of Anecdotes About the Famous.* New York: Harper & Row, 1978.

Hurblut, Gladys. *Next Week—East Lynne!* New York: E. P. Dutton, 1950.

Hutton, Laurence. *Curiosities of the American Stage.* New York: Harper & Bros., 1891.

———. *Plays and Players.* New York: Hurd and Houghton, 1875.

Hyde, Henry M. *Through the Stage Door.* Cairo, Ill.: Commercial Distributing Company, 1903.

Jablonski, Edward. *Gershwin—A Biography.* Garden City: Doubleday, 1987.

Jefferson, Joseph. *The Autobiography of Joseph Jefferson.* New York: Century, 1890.

Jenkins, Stephen. *The Greatest Street in the World—The Story of Broadway, Old and New, from the Bowling Green to Albany.* New York: G. P. Putnam's Sons, 1911.

Jessel, George. *So Help Me.* New York: Random House, 1943.

Jones, Robert Edmond. *The Dramatic Imagination.* New York: Theatre Arts, 1941.

Kalter, Joanmarie. *Actors on Acting: Performing in Theatre & Film Today.* New York: Sterling Publishing, 1979.

Kaminska, Ida. *My Life, My Theater.* New York: Macmillan, 1973.

Kanin, Garson. *Cast of Characters—Stories of Broadway and Hollywood.* New York: Atheneum, 1969.

Kaplan, Mike. Variety's *Who's Who in Show Business*. New York: Garland
    Publishing, 1985.

Kasha, Al, & Joel Hirschhorn, *Notes on Broadway—Intimate Conversations
    with the Great Songwriters*. Chicago: Contemporary Books, 1985.

Katcher, Leo. *The Big Bankroll—The Life and Times of Arnold Rothstein*.
    New York: Harper & Bros., 1959.

Kazan, Elia. *A Life*. New York: Knopf, 1988.

Keese, William L. *A Group of Comedians*. New York: Burt Franklin, 1970
    (reprint of 1901 edition).

Kelly, Fred C. *George Ade—Warmhearted Satirist*. Indianapolis: Bobbs-
    Merrill, 1947.

Kennedy, Harold J. *"No Pickle, No Performance"—An Irreverent Theatrical
    Excursion from Tallulah to Travolta*. Garden City: Doubleday, 1977.

Kerr, Walter. *The Theater in Spite of Itself*. New York: Simon & Schuster,
    1963.

Ketchum, Richard M. (ed.). *Will Rogers—His Life and Times*. New York:
    American Heritage Publishing, 1973.

Kotsilibas-Davis, James. *Great Times Good Times—The Odyssey of Maurice
    Barrymore*. Garden City: Doubleday, 1977.

Kraft, Hy. *On My Way to the Theater*. New York: Macmillan, 1971.

Lahr, John. *Notes on a Cowardly Lion*. New York: Knopf, 1969.

Lait, Jack, and Lee Mortimer. *New York: Confidential!* Chicago: Ziff-Davis,
    1948.

Langner, Lawrence. *The Magic Curtain*. New York: E. P. Dutton, 1951.

Lawrence, Jerome. *Actor—The Life and Times of Paul Muni*. New York:
    Samuel French, 1974.

Leman, Walter M. *Memories of an Old Actor*. San Francisco: A. Roman,
    1886.

Leonard, William Torbert. *Broadway Bound: A Guide to Shows That Died
    Aborning*. Metuchen, N.J.: Scarecrow Press, 1983.

Lerner, Alan Jay. *The Street Where I Live*. New York: W. W. Norton, 1978.

Leslie, Peter. *A Hard Act To Follow—A Music Hall Review*. London: Pad-
    dington Press, 1978.

Levant, Oscar. *The Memoirs of an Amnesiac*. New York: G. P. Putnam's Sons,
    1965.

———. *The Unimportance of Being Oscar*. New York: G. P. Putnam's Sons,
    1968.

Lewis, Philip C. *Trouping—How the Show Came to Town*. New York:
    Harper & Row, 1973.

Lewis, Robert. *Slings and Arrows: Theater in My Life*. New York: Stein &
    Day, 1981.

Lieberman, Gerald F. *The Greatest Laughs of All Time*. Garden City: Double-
    day, 1961.

Lillie, Beatrice (with James Brough). *Every Other Inch a Lady*. Garden City:
    Doubleday, 1972.

Lipsky, Louis. *Tales of the Yiddish Rialto*. New York: Thomas Yoseloff, 1962.

Little, Stuart W. *Off-Broadway: The Prophetic Theater*. New York: Coward,
    McCann & Geoghegan, 1972.

————. *Enter Joseph Papp—In Search of a New American Theater.* New York: Coward, McCann & Geoghegan, 1974.

Little, Stuart W., and Arthur Cantor. *The Playmakers.* New York: W. W. Norton, 1970.

Logan, Joshua. *Josh—My Up and Down, In and Out Life.* New York: Delacorte Press, 1976.

Lombardo, Guy (with Jack Altshul). *Auld Acquaintance.* Garden City: Doubleday, 1975.

Lynes, Russell. *The Lively Audience: A Social History of the Visual and Performing Arts in America (1890–1950).* New York: Harper & Row, 1986.

Lyons, Jimmy. *The Mirth of a Nation.* New York: Vantage Press, 1953.

Machlin, Milt. *The Gossip Wars—An Exposé of the Scandal Era.* Self-published, 1981.

Mahony, Patrick. *Barbed Wit & Malicious Humor.* New York: Citadel Press, 1956.

Malina, Judith. *The Diaries of Judith Malina 1947–1957.* New York: Grove Press, 1984.

Mallen, Frank. *Sauce for the Gander.* White Plains, N.Y.: Baldwin Books, 1954.

Maney, Richard. *Fanfare—The Confessions of a Press Agent.* New York: Harper & Bros., 1957.

Marks, Edward B. *They All Had Glamor—From the Swedish Nightingale to the Naked Lady.* New York: Julian Messner, 1944.

———— (as told to A. J. Liebling). *They All Sang—From Tony Pastor to Rudy Vallee.* New York: Viking, 1934.

Martin, Charlotte M. (ed.). *The Stage Reminiscences of Mrs. Gilbert.* New York: Scribner's, 1901.

Mason, R. Osgood (ed.). *Goodwin's Sketches and Impressions—Musical, Theatrical, and Social (1799–1885).* New York: G. P. Putnam's Sons, 1887.

Massey, Raymond. *When I Was Young.* Boston: Little, Brown, 1976.

Mates, Julian. *The American Musical Stage Before 1800.* New Brunswick, N.J.: Rutgers University Press, 1962.

Mathews, Brander, and Laurence Hutton. *Kean and Booth and Their Contemporaries.* Boston: L. C. Page, 1900.

May, Robin. *The Wit of the Theatre.* London: Leslie Frewin Publishers, 1969.

McArthur, Benjamin. *Actors and American Culture, 1880–1920.* Philadelphia: Temple University Press, 1984.

McCabe, Jr., James D. *Great Fortunes, and How They Were Made.* Philadelphia: George Maclean, 1871.

McCarthy, Joe. *Days and Nights at Costello's.* Boston: Little, Brown, 1980.

McCrindle, Joseph F. (ed.), *Behind the Scenes: Theatre and Film Interviews from the Transatlantic Review.* London: Pitman Publishing, 1971.

Meade, Edwards Hoag. *Doubling Back: Autobiography of an Actor—Serio-Comical.* Chicago: Self-Published, 1916.

Meisner, Sanford, & Dennis Longwell. *On Acting.* New York: Random House, 1987.

Merman, Ethel (with George Eells). *Merman—An Autobiography*. New York: Simon & Schuster, 1978.

Miller, Arthur. *Timebends—A Life*. New York: Grove Press, 1987.

Millner, Cork. *Santa Barbara Celebrities—Conversations from the American Riviera*. Santa Barbara, Calif.: Santa Barbara Press, 1986.

Moody, Richard. *The Astor Place Riot*. Bloomington: Indiana University Press, 1958.

Moore, Isabel. *Talks in a Library with Laurence Hutton*. New York: G. P. Putnam's Sons, 1909.

Mordden, Ethan. *The American Theatre*. New York: Oxford University Press, 1981.

———. *Broadway Babies—The People Who Made the American Musical*. New York: Oxford University Press, 1983.

Morehouse Ward. *Forty-five Minutes Past Eight*. New York: Dial Press, 1939.

———. *George M. Cohan—Prince of the American Theatre*. Philadelphia: J. B. Lippincott, 1943.

———. *Just the Other Day—From Yellow Pines to Broadway*. New York: McGraw-Hill, 1953.

Morell, Parker. *Lillian Russell—The Era of Plush*. New York: Random House, 1940.

Morley, Sheridan. *The Great Stage Stars—Distinguished Theatrical Careers of the Past & Present*. New York: Facts on File, 1986.

Morosco, Helen M., & Leonard Paul Dugger. *The Oracle of Broadway*. Caldwell, Idaho: Caxton Printers, 1944.

Morris, Clara. *Life on the Stage*. New York: McClure, Phillips, 1901.

Morris, Lloyd. *Curtain Time*. New York: Random House, 1953.

———. *Incredible New York*. New York: Random House, 1951.

Morse, Frank P. *Backstage with Henry Miller*. New York: E. P. Dutton, 1938.

Mosedale, John. *The Men Who Invented Broadway—Damon Runyon, Walter Winchell & Their World*. New York: Richard Marek Publishers, 1981.

Moses, Montrose J. *Famous Actor-Families in America*. New York: Benjamin Blom, 1968 (reprint of 1906 edition).

Mostel, Kate, & Madeline Gilford (with Jack Gilford and Zero Mostel). *170 Years of Show Business*. New York: Random House, 1978.

Mowatt, Anna Cora. *Autobiography of an Actress, or, Eight Years on the Stage*. Boston: Ticknor, Reed and Fields, 1854.

Muir, Frank. *An Irreverent and Thoroughly Incomplete Social History of Almost Everything*. New York: Stein and Day, 1976.

Murray Kathryn. *Family Laugh Lines*. Englewood Cliffs, N.J.: Prentice-Hall, 1966.

Nathan, George Jean. *Art of the Night*. New York: Knopf, 1968.

———. *Materia Critica*. New York: Knopf, 1924.

———. *The Popular Theatre*. New York: Knopf, 1918.

———. *The Theatre of the Moment*. New York: Knopf, 1936.

———. *Theatre Book of the Year 1950–1*. New York: Knopf, 1951.

Neff, Renfreu. *The Living Theatre/USA*. Indianapolis: Bobbs-Merrill, 1970.

Nelson, C. M. *The Fortunate Years*. New York: Vantage Press, 1983.

Nobles, Milton. *"Shop Talk."* Milwaukee: Self-published, n.d.

Novick, Julius. *Beyond Broadway—The Quest for Permanent Theatres.* New York: Hill & Wang, 1968.

Nugent, Elliott. *Events Leading Up to the Comedy.* New York: Trident Press, 1965.

Oblak, John B. *Bringing Broadway to Maine.* Terre Haute, Ind.: Self-published, 1971.

O'Brien, P. J. *Will Rogers—Ambassador of Good Will; Prince of Wit and Wisdom.* Chicago: John C. Winston Co., 1935.

O'Connor, John. *Broadway Racketeers.* New York: Liveright, 1928.

Odell, George C. D. *Annals of the New York Stage—From the Beginnings to 1894.* New York: Columbia University Press, 1927–49.

Oppenheimer, George (ed.). *The Passionate Playgoer—A Personal Scrapbook.* New York: Viking, 1962.

Phelps, William Lyon. *Autobiography with Letters.* New York: Oxford University Press, 1939.

Pilat, Oliver, & Jo Ranson. *Sodom by the Sea—An Affectionate History of Coney Island.* Garden City: Doubleday, Doran, 1941.

Poitier, Sidney. *This Life.* New York: Knopf, 1980.

Poland, Albert, & Bruce Mailman (eds.). *The Off-Off Broadway Book—The Plays, People, Theatre.* Indianapolis: Bobbs-Merrill, 1972.

Poore, Benjamin Perley. *Perley's Reminiscences of Sixty Years in the National Metropolis.* Philadelphia: Hubbard Brothers, 1886.

Prince, Hal. *Contradictions—Notes on Twenty-six Years in the Theatre.* New York: Dodd, Mead, 1974.

Quinn, Jim. *Word of Mouth—A Completely New Kind of Guide to New York City Restaurants.* New York: Mixed Media, 1972.

Quintero, José. *If You Don't Dance They Beat You.* Boston: Little, Brown, 1974.

Reader's Digest Treasury of Wit & Humor. Pleasantville, N.Y.: Reader's Digest Association, 1958.

Redfield, William. *Letters from an Actor.* New York: Viking, 1967.

Reed, Joseph Verner. *The Curtain Falls.* New York: Harcourt, Brace, 1935.

Rees, James. *Life of Edwin Forrest.* Philadelphia: Peterson & Brothers, 1874.

Richards, Dick. *The Curtain Rises . . . An Anthology of the International Theatre.* London: Leslie Frewin Publishers, 1966.

Rigdon, Walter (ed.). *The Biographical Encyclopaedia & Who's Who of the American Theatre.* New York: James H. Heineman, 1966.

Rigg, Diana. *No Turn Unstoned—The Worst Ever Theatrical Reviews.* London: Hamish Hamilton, 1982.

Rivers, Joan. *Enter Talking.* New York: Delacorte Press, 1986.

Rose, Billy. *Wine, Women and Words.* New York: Simon & Schuster, 1948.

Rosenfeld, Lulla. *Bright Star of Exile—Jacob Adler and the Yiddish Theatre.* New York: Thomas Y. Crowell, 1977.

Ross, Lillian, and Helen Ross. *The Player—A Profile of an Art.* New York: Simon & Schuster, 1961.

Rovere, Richard H. *Howe & Hummel—Their True and Scandalous History.* New York: Farrar, Straus, 1947.

Rubin, Benny. *Come Backstage with Me* . . . Bowling Green, Ohio: Bowling Green University Popular Press, n.d.

Ruggles, Eleanor. *Prince of Players: Edwin Booth.* New York: W. W. Norton, 1953.

Runyon, Damon. *Short Takes.* New York: McGraw-Hill, 1946.

Russell, Ray. *The Little Lexicon of Love.* Los Angeles: Sherbourne Press, 1966.

Ryan, Kate. *Old Boston Museum Days.* Boston: Little, Brown, 1915.

Samuels, Charles & Louise. *Once Upon a Stage—The Merry World of Vaudeville.* New York: Dodd, Mead, 1974.

Sann, Paul. *The Lawless Decade.* New York: Crown, 1957.

Sardi, Vincent, & Richard Gehman. *Sardi's: The Story of a Great Restaurant.* New York: Henry Holt, 1953.

Schildkraut, Joseph (as told to Leo Lania). *My Father and I.* New York: Viking, 1959.

Schneider, Alan. *Entrances—An American Director's Journey.* New York: Viking, 1986.

Scott, John Anthony. *Fanny Kemble's America.* New York: Thomas Y. Crowell, 1973.

Sharaff, Irene. *Broadway and Hollywood.* New York: Van Nostrand Reinhold Company, 1976.

Shaw, Arnold. *The Street That Never Slept—New York's Fabled 52nd Street.* New York: Coward, McCann and Geoghegan, 1971.

Seilhamer, George O., *History of the American Theatre Before the Revolution.* New York: Benjamin Blom 1968 (reprint of 1889–91 edition).

Seldes, Marian. *The Bright Lights—A Theatre Life.* Boston: Houghton Mifflin, 1978.

Selznick, Irene Mayer. *A Private View.* New York: Knopf, 1983.

Shaw, Dale. *Titans of the American Stage—Edwin Forrest, the Booths, the O'Neills.* Philadelphia: Westminster Press, 1971.

Shewey, Don. *Sam Shepard.* New York: Dell, 1985.

Shewey, Don, and Susan Shacter. *Caught in the Act: New York Actors Face to Face.* New York: NAL Books, 1986.

Sillman, Leonard. *Here Lies Leonard Sillman—Straightened Out at Last.* New York: Citadel Press, 1959.

Silvers, Phil (with Robert Saffron). *This Laugh Is on Me—The Phil Silvers Story.* Englewood Cliffs, N.J.: Prentice-Hall, 1973.

Simon, Kate. *Fifth Avenue—A Very Social History.* New York: Harcourt Brace Jovanovich, 1978.

Sinden, Donald. *The Everyman Book of Theatrical Anecdotes.* London: J. M. Dent, 1987.

Skinner, Cornelia Otis. *Family Circle.* Boston: Houghton Mifflin, 1948.

Skinner, Otis. *Footlights and Spotlights.* New York: Blue Ribbon Books, 1924.

Skolsky, Sidney. *Times Square Tintypes.* New York: Ives Washburn, 1930.

Smith, H. Allen. *The Compleat Practical Joker.* New York: William Morrow, 1980.

Smith, Cecil. *Musical Comedy in America.* New York: Theatre Arts Books, 1950.

Smith, Harry B. *First Nights and First Editions.* Boston: Little, Brown, 1931.

Sobel, Bernard. *Broadway Heartbeat: Memoirs of a Press Agent.* New York: Hermitage House, 1953.

——. *A Pictorial History of Vaudeville.* New York: Citadel Press, 1961.

Sobol, Louis. *The Longest Street.* New York: Crown, 1968.

Sothern, Edward H. *The Melancholy Tale of "Me."* New York: Scribner's, 1916.

Spitzer, Marian. *The Palace.* New York: Atheneum, 1969.

Stagg, Jerry. *The Brothers Shubert.* New York: Random House, 1968.

Stasio, Marilyn. *Broadway's Beautiful Losers—The Strange History of Five Neglected Plays.* New York: Delacorte, 1972.

Stein, Charles W. (ed.). *American Vaudeville As Seen by Its Contemporaries.* New York: Knopf, 1984.

Sterne, Richard L. *John Gielgud Directs Richard Burton in* Hamlet. New York: Random House, 1967.

Stevens, Ashton. *Actorviews.* Chicago: Covici-McGee, 1923.

Stevens, David H. (ed.). *Ten Talents in the American Theatre.* Norman: University of Oklahoma Press, 1957.

Stevenson, Isabelle (ed.). *The Tony Award: A Complete Listing of Winners & Nominees with a History of the American Theatre Wing.* New York: Crown, 1985.

Stewart, George Woodbridge (ed.). *The Players—After 75 Years.* New York: The Players, 1963.

Stickney, Dorothy. *Openings and Closings.* Garden City: Doubleday, 1979.

Stoddart, Dayton. *Lord Broadway: Variety's Sime.* New York: Wilfred Funk, 1941.

Stoddart, James H. *Recollections of a Player.* New York: Century, 1902.

Strasberg, Susan. *Bittersweet.* New York: G. P. Putnam's Sons, 1981.

Sullivan, Edward Dean. *The Fabulous Wilson Mizner.* New York: Henkle Company, 1935.

Sweet, Jeffrey (ed.). *Something Wonderful Right Away.* New York: Avon Books, 1978.

Sylvester, Robert. *No Cover Charge.* New York: Dial Press, 1956.

Talese, Gay. *The Overreachers.* New York: Harper & Row, 1965.

Teichmann, Howard. *George S. Kaufman: An Intimate Portrait.* New York: Atheneum, 1972.

——. *Smart Aleck—The Wit, World and Life of Alexander Woollcott.* New York: William Morrow, 1976.

The Truth About the Theater—By One of the Best Known Theatrical Men in New York. Cincinnati: Stewart & Kidd, 1916.

Thomas, Augustus. *The Print of My Remembrance.* New York: Scribner's, 1922.

Thomas, Bob. *Marlon: Portrait of the Rebel as an Artist.* New York: Random House, 1973.

Thomas, Lately. *Delmonico's: A Century of Splendor.* Boston: Houghton Mifflin, 1967.

Toll, Robert C. *Blacking Up—The Minstrel Show in Nineteenth-Century America.* New York: Oxford University Press, 1974.

————. *On with the Show: The First Century of Show Business in America.* New York: Oxford University Press, 1976.

————. *The Entertainment Machine—American Show Business in the Twentieth Century.* New York: Oxford University Press, 1982.

Traubner, Richard. *Operetta: Theatrical History.* Garden City: Doubleday, 1983.

Tucker, Sophie (with Dorothy Giles). *Some of These Days.* Self-published, 1945.

Turner, David Steele. *Actors About Acting, Loving, Living, Life.* New York: Random House, 1972.

Tyler, George C. (with J. C. Furnas). *Whatever Goes Up—The Hazardous Fortunes of a Natural Born Gambler.* Indianapolis: Bobbs-Merrill, 1934.

Tynan, Kathleen. *The Life of Kenneth Tynan.* New York: William Morrow, 1987.

Tynan, Kenneth. *Show People—Profiles in Entertainment.* New York: Simon & Schuster, 1979.

Ujváry, Sándor von. *Ferenc Molnár, der Lachende Magier.* Vaduz: Verlag Interbook, 1965.

Vandenhoff, George. *Dramatic Reminiscences; or, Actors and Actresses in England and America.* London, 1860.

Walker, Stanley. *The Night Club Era.* New York: Frederick A. Stokes, 1933.

————. *Mrs. Astor's Horse.* New York: Frederick A. Stokes, 1935.

Warde, Frederick. *Fifty Years of Make Believe.* New York: International Press Syndicate, 1920.

Weatherly, Tom. *Main Stem Stuff—The Brighter Side of Broadway and Manhattan.* New York: Library Publishers, 1954.

Webster, Margaret. *The Same Only Different.* New York: Knopf, 1969.

West, Mae. *Goodness Had Nothing To Do with It.* Englewood Cliffs, N.J.: Prentice-Hall, 1959.

Wilder, Marshall P. *The Sunny Side of the Street.* New York: Funk & Wagnalls, 1908.

Wilk, Max. *Every Day's a Matinee—Memoirs Scribbled on a Dressing Room Door.* New York: W. W. Norton, 1975.

Wilson, Earl. *Earl Wilson's New York.* New York: Simon & Schuster, 1964.

————. *I Am Gazing into My 8-Ball.* Garden City: Doubleday, Doran & Co., 1945.

————. *Hot Times—True Tales of Hollywood and Broadway.* Chicago: Contemporary Books, 1984.

————. *Let 'Em Eat Cheesecake.* Garden City: Doubleday, 1949.

————. *Show Business Laid Bare.* New York: G. P. Putnam's Sons, 1974.

————. *The Show Business Nobody Knows.* New York: Cowles Book Company, 1971.

Winter, William. *The Life of David Belasco.* New York: Moffat, Yard and Co., 1918.

————. *Vagrant Memories—Being Further Recollections of Other Days.* New York: George H. Doran, 1915.

Wit and Humor of the Stage. Philadelphia: George W. Jacobs, 1909.

Wittke, Carl. *Tambo and Bones—A History of the American Minstrel Stage.* Durham, N.C.: Duke University Press, 1930.

Wodehouse, P. G., & Guy Bolton. *Bring on the Girls!* New York: Simon & Schuster, 1953.

Wood, Audrey, and Max Wilk. *Represented by Audrey Wood.* Garden City: Doubleday, 1981.

Woolcott, Alexander. *Mrs. Fiske—Her Views on Actors, Acting, and the Problems of Production.* New York: Century, 1917.

———. *Enchanted Aisles.* New York: G. P. Putnam's Sons, 1924.

Zadan, Craig. *Sondheim & Co.—The Authorized, Behind-the-Scenes Story of the Making of Stephen Sondheim's Musicals.* New York: Harper & Row, 1986.

Zeidman, Irving. *The American Burlesque Show.* New York: Hawthorn Books, 1967.

Zolotow, Maurice. *No People Like Show People.* New York: Random House, 1951.

———. *Stagestruck.* New York: Harcourt, Brace & World, 1965.

Newspapers and magazines

American Theatre, Billboard, The Bookman, The Dramatists Guild Quarterly, Educational Theatre Journal, Life, The Los Angeles Times, Newsweek, New York Dramatic Mirror, The New York Times, The New Yorker, Performing Arts Journal, Playbill, Players Magazine, Stage Magazine, The Theatre, The Theatre Annual, Theatre Arts, Theater Week, Variety.

377

INDEX OF NAMES, PLAYS,
AND THEATRES